Place, time and tide—these were the problems, though not necessarily in that order . . . The bigger landing ships needed twenty-nine feet of water to get in, and there would be that much only on September 15, October 11 and November 3. But the tides would stay at this height only twice each day, for about an hour at a time . . . That meant two separate landings some twelve hours apart, each to be accomplished with incredible speed. . . .

Time? MacArthur wanted the earliest possible date, not only to relieve the perimeter as soon as possible, but for political reasons . . . By the time Inchon was definitely decided upon, that left a bare thirty days in which to get ready for it; no major amphibious landing in history . . . had been planned in less than six months.

General Douglas MacArthur's plan to land at Inchon in the fall of 1950 was carried out in a race against the clock and against the greatest natural odds that had ever faced an attacking force from the sea. Yet it succeeded. And it was the master-stroke that turned the tide of the Korean War.

HELL OR HIGH WATER

MacArthur's Landing at Inchon

Walt Sheldon

BALLANTINE BOOKS • NEW YORK

Acknowledgments

Greatest thanks goes to the scores of persons interviewed in the United States, Japan and Korea, who supplied either eyewitness accounts or important corollary data. Their names, with the exception of a few who wished to remain anonymous, are in the text and notes.

I was greatly helped by the personnel of the Department of Defense Magazine and Book Branch, Pentagon, Washington, D.C., and was given particular and cheerful assistance by Major Barbara Smith (Army) and Lieutenant Commander Dan Dagle (Navy). In Korea, the staff of Colonel Stacy Capers, Eighth Army Information Officer, were most gracious and obliging. Dr. Vernon Tate of the U. S. Naval Academy Library at Annapolis, Maryland, was generous with time and facilities. Karl Schuon, editor of *Leatherneck* Magazine, gave much smiling support. Mr. Rowland P. Gill at the Historical Section, Headquarters, U. S. Marine Corps, went out of his way to assist me. Finally, I wish to express appreciation for the encouragement and professional advice given by fellow author John Toland.

Library of Congress Catalog Card Number: 68-13208

SBN 345-03361-2-150

This edition published by arrangement with The Macmillan Company

First Printing: July, 1973

Printed in the United States of America

Cover photograph: U.S. Army photograph

BALLANTINE BOOKS, INC.
201 E. 50th Street, New York, N. Y. 10022

Contents

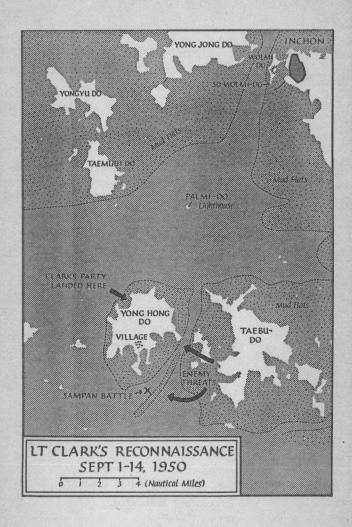

LT CLARK'S RECONNAISSANCE
SEPT 1-14, 1950

0 1 2 3 4 (Nautical Miles)

Chronology

NOTE: Events in this chronology were selected primarily to make the narrative clear and not necessarily for their historical or military significance. All dates are given in Japan–Korea time (14 hours later than Eastern Standard Time), which usually puts them one day behind the equivalent U. S. date.

—1950—

June 25. North Korean Army begins invasion of South Korea across the 38th parallel.

June 27. Ambassador Muccio and his staff leave Seoul.

June 28. Han River Bridge at Seoul is blown up at 2:15 A.M.

June 29. General MacArthur arrives by plane at Suwon, drives thirty miles north to observe Han River and enemy in Seoul.

June 30. President Truman authorizes MacArthur to send U. S. military strength to Korea.

July 1. Task Force Smith (about 500 strong) flies from Japan to Korea as vanguard of U. S. troops.

July 5. Task Force Smith meets enemy between Suwon and Osan in first major land engagement of the war, fails to stop enemy advance.

July 13. General Walker arrives at Taegu to assume personal control of Eighth Army operations.

July 23. General MacArthur informs Department

of the Army that an amphibious landing is scheduled for mid-September, but does not finally name Inchon as target site.

July 26. U. S. troops, pushed back, assume positions approximately along the lines that will become the Pusan Perimeter.

July 27. General MacArthur visits General Walker's headquarters in Taegu, says withdrawals must cease.

July 29. General Walker issues his "stand-or-die" order.

August 3. First elements of 1st Provisional Marine Brigade arrive in Pusan and go ashore.

August 4. U. S., R. O. K. and some attached U. N. forces establish the relatively stationary lines of the Pusan Perimeter.

August 6. Eighth Army begins counterattack from Perimeter with Task Force Kean (Army's 25th Infantry Division and 5th Regimental Combat Team plus 1st Provisional Marine Brigade—primarily 5th Marine Regiment).

August 12. General MacArthur in dispatches to Washington specifically names Inchon as his amphibious invasion target.

August 14. Task Force Kean, after bitter struggles, including the First Battle of the Naktong, is relegated approximately to its original starting line. The Perimeter remains.

August 15. General MacArthur establishes Special Planning Staff, nucleus for X-Corps.

August 16. Far East Air Forces "carpet bomb" near Naktong River.

August 17. Obing-ni, in Naktong Bulge area, is taken by U. S. forces after battle with heavy Marine losses.

August 18–21. U. S. tanks help stop enemy armor attack in "Bowling Alley," 13 miles north-west of Taegu.

August 19. R. O. K. Marines land at Tong Yong on southern tip of Korea in "rehearsal" for Inchon.

August 23. General MacArthur holds Tokyo conference with U. S. Chiefs of Staff from Washington, wins them over to Inchon plan.

August 26. General MacArthur establishes X-Corps as overall unit for the Inchon landing, assigns General Almond to command.

September 1. Lieutenant Clark is sent to island near Inchon for reconnaissance, begins his two-week stay. On the western line of the Pusan Perimeter, the North Koreans begin the second Naktong offensive, breaking through at Haman and routing the 24th Infantry Regiment.

September 3. Typhoon Jane hits Kobe, where elements of the 1st Marine Division are loading for departure to Inchon.

September 6. Lieutenant Colonel Murray's 5th Marine Regiment is withdrawn from Perimeter line to Pusan for embarkation to Inchon landing operation.

September 10–12. Colonel Puller's 1st Marine Regiment sails from Kobe; Murray's 5th Marine Regiment sails from Pusan; General Barr's Army 7th Infantry Division sails from Yokohama. Destination: Inchon.

September 13. Typhoon Kezia passes between seaborne elements of the invasion fleet. MacArthur departs from Sasebo, Japan, for Inchon, aboard U. S. S. *Mt. McKinley.* Meanwhile, at Inchon, Rear Admiral Higgins' gunfire support group of four cruisers and six destroyers moves up Flying Fish Channel and begins its close bombardment of Inchon and Wolmi-do.

September 15. First elements of invasion force (3rd Battalion, 5th Marines) land on Wolmi-do at 0633 hours. On second high tide, that evening, other 5th Marine units land on Red Beach, across from Wolmi-do, while 1st Marine units assault Blue Beach, just south of the city proper.

September 16. 1st and 5th Marine Regiments advance rapidly inland, closely followed by R. O. K. Marines. Marine air and armor bombardment destroys North Korean tanks a few miles inland.

September 17. 5th Marines take Ascom City. Six enemy tanks destroyed on Inchon-Seoul highway. General MacArthur comes ashore at Inchon. Two enemy YAK planes bomb Admiral Struble's 7th Fleet flagship U. S. S. *Rochester* in Inchon harbor; one is shot down.

September 18. 5th Marines secure Kimpo Airfield. First elements of Army 7th Division go ashore at Inchon.

September 19. The battleship U. S. S. *Missouri* arrives near Inchon harbor and bombards inland targets. A small reconnaissance company swims across the Han River near Kimpo at night and is driven back.

September 20. The 5th Marines make a successful assault crossing of the Han River, landing on the north bank and west of Seoul.

September 21. Captain Barrow's penetration of the town enables Puller's 1st Marines to take Yong Dong Po just across the river from Seoul. The 7th Marine Regiment unloads at Inchon, completing the three-regiment make-up of the 1st Marine Division. The Army's 7th Division meanwhile advances inland far south of Seoul and Lieutenant Van Sant's forward-probing tank platoon enters the city of Suwon.

September 22. Heavy fighting begins between 5th Marines and defenders in rugged hills just west of Seoul.

September 24. Puller's 1st Marines cross the Han from Yong Dong Po, enters southwestern outskirts of Seoul.

September 25. The Army's 32nd Infantry Regiment crosses the Han, outflanking Seoul from the southeast and taking South Mountain.

September 26. X-Corps now holds approximaely half of Seoul but bitter street fighting continues and the advance is slow.

September 27. Government House, symbolic head of both Seoul and the Republic of Korea, is taken by the Marines.

September 28. The last of the enemy defenders flee Seoul to the north.

September 29. MacArthur holds victory ceremony in Seoul Government House, formally returning South Korea to President Rhee.

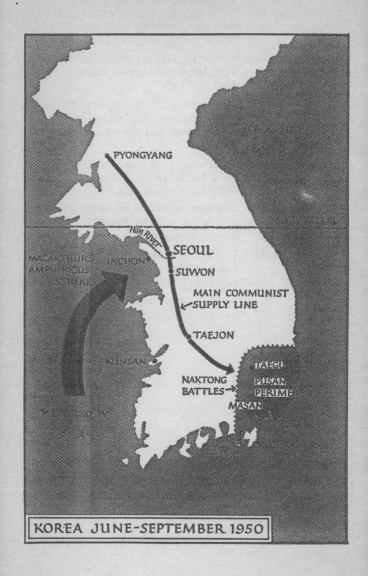

KOREA JUNE—SEPTEMBER 1950

Hell or
High Water

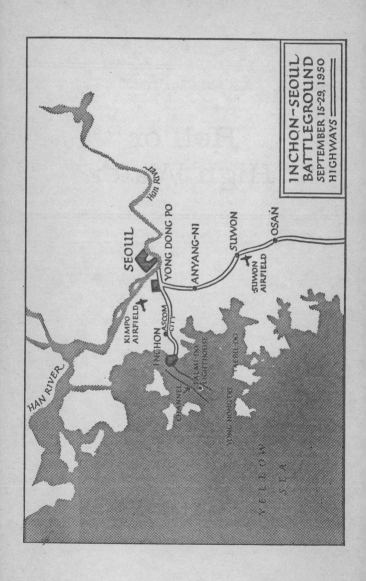

INCHON-SEOUL
BATTLEGROUND
SEPTEMBER 15-29, 1950
HIGHWAYS

Han River

SEOUL
YONG DONG PO
ANYANG-NI
SUWON
OSAN

KIMPO AIRFIELD
SUWON AIRFIELD

HAN RIVER

ASCOM CITY
INCHON
PALMI DO LIGHTHOUSE
CHANNEL
YONG HONG TO PENINSULA

YELLOW SEA

Prologue: "All this for me?"

LIEUTENANT EUGENE F. CLARK, UNITED STATES NAVY, STOOD on the deck of a surplus World War II patrol boat and eyed the rolling swells between himself and the island of Yong Hong Do, three quarters of a mile away. The patrol boat's young Korean skipper, Commander Lee He Chung, Republic of Korea Navy, was bellowing through a bullhorn and demanding that sampans be sent out to fetch the lieutenant and his gear.

Clark was not in love with the idea of making a landing on that rocky beach in a rickety, unpainted fishing craft smaller than an ordinary lifeboat, but that might be the least of the hazards he'd be facing in the next two weks. He'd been ordered to set up an observation post on the island, only a few miles off the shoreline of the west coast of Korea, an area firmly held by the Communists. As a matter of fact, the Communists held most of the rest of Korea this Sunday morning, the second of September, 1950. At the moment, they were hemming in a whole United States army and its attached units in a small perimeter near the tip of the peninsula some two hundred miles southeast of Clark's lonely position. The outlook wasn't very bright, there at the perimeter. And in such places as Tokyo and Washington, observers, commentators, reporters,—along with a few generals and admirals—were beginning to mutter uneasily about an "American Dunkerque," a shameful and bloody defeat should this army be pushed into the sea.

Lieutenant Clark this Sunday morning was weighted with the rather awesome knowledge that the reports he would send back from the island in the next two weeks—if he managed to stay there—would be part of a daring strategic plan to turn that imminent defeat into a brilliant victory. He was not a strategist; he was a mustang junior officer from the ranks doing a bizarre job for the moment, but even from his relatively lowly viewpoint he could see that this plan was something of a wild gamble. As one of the comparatively few men who now knew about the scheme, he fervently hoped it would work not only for his country's sake, but for the preservation of his own neck which would be rather well exposed between now and the date of the next exceptionally high tide, September 15.

As he watched from the deck of the former American sub-chaser designated PC-703 by the Republic of Korea Navy, he saw that the smattering of people who had appeared on the rocky beach of the island were not responding too quickly to Commander Lee's loudspeakered demands. Yong Hong Do was about six miles long and three wide, dotted with several low hills. There was a small village, barely visible, near the northeast corner of the island, facing the mainland. Between the island and the mainland was a larger island, Taebu-do, on which there was a North Korean Communist garrison, and at certain low tides the mud flats between the two islands would be exposed and offer a land bridge for any force that might decide to attack him once he was set up on Yong Hong Do.

He gazed to the northeast, into the gray distance on this cloudy, half drizzly day. Some eleven miles away was the port city of Inchon, which for centuries had been the sea gateway to the capital of Seoul, eighteen miles inland. That was the target. He'd been told that probably two thousand North Korean troops were there, but it was likely that huge reinforcements would be poured in once the Communists realized a major amphibious landing was planned, and with newsmen in Tokyo sardonically calling the Inchon plan "Operation Common Knowledge," he felt it wouldn't be long before this formidable opposition began arriving.

Clark was beginning to wonder whether it might not have been more prudent on his part to decline this mission, since he had been given a choice. He had been working at a comfortable desk job as one of the attached naval personnel to General MacArthur's GHQ staff in Tokyo when he was mysteriously called to a secret conference only one week ago, and he still wasn't sure why he in particular had been picked, unless it was because he'd served many years in the Orient and would have a way of getting along with the Korean natives on whom the success of his mission would largely depend. Clark was a tall men, trimly built, with rather sharp features that gave him the look of an amiable hawk. He did not regard himself as a swashbuckling or heroic type, and sometimes stewed a little in disappointment that by his mid-thirties he hadn't advanced beyond the rank of lieutenant. His rating as an enlisted man had been yeoman, a specialty calling primarily for clerical duties. He'd risen to chief petty officer and had finally attained a commission. In World War II he'd seen action in the Pacific, and afterward did sea duty along the China coast, where he'd gained small-boat experience, and on Okinawa where he'd worked with the Army for a while. Anyway, he'd been called, and when the importance of his reconnaissance to the landing plan—and the importance of the landing itself—were explained to him, he was unable to turn the assignment down.

It was a good half hour, which made it around 11:30 A.M., before three sampans finally came out from the shore and putt-putted toward the waiting patrol craft. Clark signaled for the two Korean interpreters who would accompany him to get ready. He called them Joe and Sam. Like many Orientals, they seemed younger than their actual years, and the one he'd dubbed Sam was actually an ex-Japanese Army colonel named Kae, one of the many Koreans who had fought for Japan; Joe's real name was Yen, and he had formerly been a naval officer. Both had worked as interpreters in the intelligence section of MacArthur's GHQ in Tokyo. Kae, the older of the two, spoke better English, but Clark found both men remarkably energetic, cheerful and self-effacing. He was also to be accompanied by young Ensign Che of the South Korean Navy, a tiny round-faced lad who seemed no more than a schoolboy, and by two Korean radio operators.[1]

The sampans finally came alongside and Clark's equipment, which ranged from presents of dried fish and rice for the islanders to machine guns and TNT for Clark, was loaded aboard. Clark shook hands with Commander Lee and, with some difficulty in the rough waters, transferred himself and his crew into one of the small boats. It headed for the rocky beach.

At the moment of Clark's transfer to the shore, a second South Korean patrol boat—PC-701—was rounding the western tip of the Korean peninsula to sail up to the waters off Inchon and stand by for possible assistance to Clark during the next two weeks. Its skipper was another young commander of the fingerling R. O. K. Navy, Hahm Myong Soo. He was a stubby, energetic youth with a deep voice just made for bawling orders from a bridge, and he was proud of his American nickname, "Spike." He'd received it from the U. S. Navy advisors who had helped train the R. O. K. Navy as it began to expand in the first two months of the Korean War. Spike Hahm delighted in the plan to put a reconnaissance party on Yong Hong Do and suspected that it might have sprung from a previous recommendation he'd submitted to his own headquarters to establish an intelligence post on one of the islands off the coast near Inchon. He also felt rather honored to realize that he, as intelligence chief of the R. O. K. Navy, was one of the few Koreans who knew about the proposed landing on September 15.

Spike Hahm was something of a hero in the still tiny circle of regular R. O. K. naval officers. Early in August he had made a daring sortie to a small port just north of the 38th Parallel, rowed into the harbor of Mong Gum Po by rubber boat late at night, and jumped on a minesweeper the North Koreans had captured when they'd taken Inchon in their drive southward the previous month. Killing two guards with a hand grenade, he rushed forward, put a pistol to the North Korean skipper's head and forced him and his crew to sail the boat back to South Korea.

The R. O. K. Navy desperately needed any boats it could get its hands on. Before the war broke in late June of 1950, its seagoing strength consisted of only a little over thirty boats: fifteen old wooden surplus YMS's (minesweepers) left over from the United States efforts in World War II, and fifteen steel-hulled minesweepers from the Japanese side, as well as an ancient LST, one small freighter, a yard oiler and two tugs. The heaviest armaments on any of its boats were machine guns. To man eight naval bases around the coast and naval headquarters in Seoul, there were only about two thousand men.

Its strength in ships wasn't much greater now, and its handiest boats were perhaps the three former sub-chasers, PC's 701, 702 and 703, that Admiral Sohn Won Yil, head of the Korean Navy, had had the foresight to purchase in the spring of that year. He had heard that they were available, possibly through a mysterious American who called himself Dr. Staggers and headed a Seoul firm that procured surplus military equipment for the Koreans, often despite the disapproval of United States diplomats and advisors. On one occasion, he was said to have procured for the Korean Army a number of Smith & Wesson .38-caliber revolvers, without spare parts or ammunition, when they were supposed to have been equipped with standard U. S. Army Colt .45's and he was thought to have had a part in arranging for several AT-6 trainer planes deemed inappropriate for the Koreans by United States advisors.[2]

At any rate, Admiral Sohn heard that four patrol craft were available and went to Washington to buy them, while transfer crews stood by in San Francisco to sail them back to Korea. One broke down on the way across the Pacific. The remaining three arrived at Chinhae, the main naval base on the tip of the peninsula near Pusan, on June 18, 1950, only a week before the war started. The Korean government had been hesitant about parting with funds for these ships, but they proved to be a wise purchase. On the night of June 26 —the day after the war started—a North Korean transport with an invading force of one thousand men had steamed toward Pusan and might well have taken the key port city if PC-701, on routine night patrol, hadn't spotted it and attacked, sinking it after an all night running gun battle.[3]

Spike Hahm, aboard PC-701 this morning in early September, was anxious to take part in an operation as significant as the projected amphibious landing at Inchon. Now that PC-703 had landed Clark, it would be his job, on PC-701, to stand by near the island and help Clark if called upon, then evacuate him just before the landing assault began. There was a good chance that Clark might be captured between now and then, or Spike Hahm himself might fall into enemy hands if he attempted a rescue. But oddly enough, he was less apprehensive about this than about the plan for the landing itself, for he knew the Korean coast well and realized that the vast tide spread and swift currents at Inchon, among the greatest in the world, would be a fantastic handicap to any force trying to take a narrow beachhead in a well-populated and easily defended city. It would be a show that, for better or worse, he didn't want to miss.

By late Sunday afternoon, Lieutenant Clark had pitched his eight-man tent outside the village on the north side of the island, about a hundred yards from the high-water mark on the shore, and was proceeding to make things livable. The rice and fish he had brought opened the way to friendly relations with the island's mayor and its approximately four hundred inhabitants, and he had already recruited a small army of over a hundred boys who promised enthusiastically to act as lookouts. He'd been told that about three hundred enemy soldiers were on Taebu-do, the larger island just across the mud flats. Facing Taebu-do, therefore, he set up two of his .50-caliber machine guns and told his lookouts that if they should see any North Koreans starting to cross, they should merely "watch and run."

He was greatly relieved to find that the islanders were not only friendly but anti-communist, as Spike Hahm had pointed out in his original recommendation for an intelligence outpost. The mayor had supplied him with two girls to cook, do laundry and keep the tent clean. One of them, Lim, a Christian whose father was the village schoolmaster, spoke some English. Although she was twenty-one Clark thought she looked no older than his own twelve-year-old daughter, Genine.

Clark accomplished his basic digging-in before the day was out and put his mind to his mission objectives. The Navy back in Tokyo had set up a special study group to gather data on the site of the projected landings, but they'd found the information available through charts and documents not only incomplete, but sometimes of questionable accuracy. There were, for example, the standard tide tables published for all areas of the world. Both Korean and Japanese sailors who had been consulted felt that these might be slightly in error for Inchon, and even a slight error was not to be tolerated; the planners wanted a first-hand check on the exact times of high and low tides, the currents, and slack water conditions. Exact measurements of the sea walls to be scaled during the landing at Inchon were unavailable. Another item was the quality of the mud that would be exposed for nearly two miles out when the racing tide ebbed. How much would it support? The weight of a tank perhaps? Walking men? In addition they wanted a more accurate report on the fortifications and number of gun emplacements than that provided by aerial photo reconnaissance. All this information was to be radioed back by Clark—if the enemy didn't get to him first.

Clark's two-week reconnaissance would be divided into three principal operations. First, he would send islanders out to gather information, which they could do without arousing suspicion because it was normal for them to make inter-island or mainland trips. At night he himself would attempt to make close observations of items like the sea walls at Inchon, and in the daytime he would arm a sampan, cruise the waters around the islands, and try to capture prisoners for interrogation.

On Monday morning, therefore, he went to arrange for a sampan. The mayor of the island told him that of some twenty-four sampans on the island, only one had an engine. Clark inspected the boat, which was about twenty-five feet long, powered by an old Japanese type of one-cylinder diesel he'd seen on fishing boats in Okinawa, where it was called a "pompom." It was rusty and full of dubious repairs. The skipper of the boat was an ancient fisherman with no teeth and a leathery skin, but wiry and full of knowledge about the local waters. He considered it an honor to be selected and was as eager as Clark to sally out for a raid and take some prisoners.

Clark mustered his crew aboard. There was, besides himself, the old fisherman, Sam, Joe and two of the many youths he'd enlisted. Each man was issued a Thompson submachine gun, a revolver and a carbine. Clark had had the foresight to bring a supply of cigars to the island and he stuck one into his mouth as the sampan got under way. With his unshaven cheeks, Navy hat and Marine fatigues, he felt quite a proper pirate as he stood in the bow of the sampan and stared toward the gray shore where, if all went well, the tide of the entire war would be violently reversed less than two weeks from this moment. . . .

Lieutenant Clark managed to capture—if that was the word—three other sampans that morning. None offered any resistance and all the "prisoners" he took back to Yong Hong Do turned out to be simple fisherman, either loyal to South Korea or disinterested in the political situation. But they did give him valuable information about the local area and positions of the enemy on the mainland and among some of the other scattered islands nearby.

As the next few days passed, Clark found himself somewhat the master of the local seas in his motor sampan. All the other fishing boats he met had sails, and whenever Clark's strange crew would point their machine guns, the fisherman would sigh, drop their mainsails, and raise their hands. Then they'd be thrown a line and towed back to Clark's island.

Each day he would radio back the information he had gathered. Meanwhile, some of the island boys he'd recruited blithely and cheerfully made their ways by boat to Inchon itself, measured the sea walls and counted gun emplacements quite unmolested by the garrison there, and brought their intelligence back to Clark.

The enemy outpost on the neighboring island of Taebu-do was by now well aware of Clark's presence on Yong Hong Do. In the dark, at low tide each night, they would send probing parties across the mud flats to find out what was going on. Clark and his companions blasted at them with machine guns several times and believed, on occasion, that they'd killed or wounded a few. One or two North Korean soldiers got as far as the village, thinking Clark might be bivouacked there. The villagers captured them. Clark was puzzled to learn that they carried only hand grenades as weapons. He wondered why, with at least three hundred troops on hand, the North Koreans would send out only small, lightly armed patrols, when one good attack could take the whole island.

On the morning of September 7—about a week after he landed—there was thundering to the north. As part of the softening-up process for the invasion, British warships were shelling Inchon from the sea. Colonel Kae frowned and said there'd be trouble at the island that evening. Clark wondered why he thought so. Kae said that Koreans had a peculiar psychology; that ordinarily they didn't like to pick fights, but now that Inchon, close by, was being bombarded. Clark's little detachment on Yong Hong Do could expect some sort of retaliation. This also explained why there had been no attack in force up until this time.

Clark thought it nonsense until, a little before midnight, a boy came running from the village to report four sampans filled with troops heading for the south side of the island. He immediately sent Commander Yen to that part of the shore with one of the .50-caliber machine guns and a crew to man it. Then he rushed down to his own commandeered motor sampan, which he had dubbed "the Flagship," mounted another .50-caliber machine gun in its bow, packed some sandbags around the gun, and told the leathery-faced old skipper to shove off.

By the light of the moon, Clark could see from the sampan the outlines of his own island and the dim, threatening shape of enemy-held Taebu-do. Its primary mass was about three miles off, but a connecting island, Sanjae-do, virtually formed a bridge across the mud flats from Taebu-do to within half a mile or less of Yong Hong Do. According to the official charts, the strait between the two islands was anywhere from two to five fathoms—twelve to thirty feet—deep, plenty of clearance for a sampan or even a patrol boat, but the nature of the eldritch tides around Inchon rendered the conventional charts less than fully reliable. There were rocks everywhere, some charted, some not. In one moment the presumed channel between the islands could be a dry, Red Sea passage, but a few hours later, it might boil like the rapids of the Colorado. These, Clark reflected with some uneasiness, were the waters where MacArthur planned to send over two hundred ships and 70,000 men in a major amphibious assault.

Suddenly there was an echoing blast and a spurt of water half a mile ahead of the sampan. Clark raised his binoculars. The enemy, he discovered, had also been doing some improvising. Five sampans were approaching, all carrying enemy soldiers, and in the bow of the lead sampan was the big 37-mm. antitank gun that had just been fired at him.

It fired again and again, and none of the geysers came even close to Clark's boat. The parchment-faced skipper of the little sampan began to jabber in terror, but Clark urged him to keep steering toward the enemy fleet, and hoped that their marksmanship would continue to be bad. He could sense that the big antitank gun, weighing down the bow and throwing the entire boat out of trim, couldn't be properly laid.

Clark's sampan captain now began shouting that they'd be grounded any minute in the shallow water. Clark went aft and jabbed a long bamboo pole into the water several times to prove they had clearance. The skipper, lacking a further excuse to turn back, kept the boat headed toward the enemy flotilla.

Clark took his place in the bow again. They were now, he judged, about a hundred yards from the boat with the antitank gun. He fired his .50-caliber machine gun from its nest of sandbags, listening to its leopard cough in the night, and watching the tracers—at first orange, then greenish as their fires cooled—sail across the water. His bursts rained upon the enemy sampan and its crew. The boat sank. Men swam from it. Some cried out, a few in pain, others calling directions to their companions. Clark turned his fire on another of the sailing sampans and destroyed that, too. The remaining craft headed back for Taebu-do.

Two hours after he'd come out to meet the enemy, Clark was back on his own island sending an urgent radio message for the patrol boat to return and give him some help. There was no sleep for anyone that night as they sat up and waited for a counterattack.

But by morning, nothing had happened. That afternoon an American destroyer, the U. S. S. *Hansen*, appeared off-shore, lowered a whaleboat, and sent it to the island. A Navy commander was in it and said he'd come to get Clark out, but Clark wasn't ready to leave yet, and asked instead that Taebu-do be bombarded.

The Navy responded immediately and it was quite a show. The *Hansen* lay white phosphorus and high explosives on the island, and four Corsair fighter planes from a carrier swept down on it with strafing runs. Clark watched, rolled a cigar back and forth in his mouth, and thought: "All this for me?"

It was indeed. Taebu-do, for the time being completely neutralized, was no longer a threat and Clark continued his reconnaissance without interference.

In the next few nights, Clark took the little diesel sampan up to Inchon harbor itself at low tide and tested the long, mud-flat approach to the shore. At places he sank nearly to his waist. His message when he returned from this sortie confirmed that neither troops nor vehicles would be able to cross the mud.

On September 10, he made a night voyage to a point some five miles north—about halfway to Inchon harbor—where a lighthouse stood on a tiny rock in the narrow shipping channel that led to the port. The islet was called Palmi-do; the lighthouse was 232 feet high and its group-flashing light, when lit, was visible for twenty miles on a clear night. In the nest of the lighthouse Clark found that the North Koreans hadn't destroyed its light but had merely disconnected the batteries that gave the power to turn is reflector. The light itself burned kerosene and bore a metal tag saying, "Made in France." Clark radioed back that night that he would be able to light the beacon for the invasion so that it might guide the warships up the dangerous channel. The next morning, he received orders to be prepared to do so—at midnight on September 14.

The next several days passed routinely. Clark's young spies continued their casual trips to the mainland and brought back additional information on the height of the sea walls at Inchon, the places where they'd observed troops, the locations of gun emplacements. All day on September 14, Clark heard the steady rumble of bombs and gunfire as Inchon was pounded from the air and the sea. By late afternoon, as he was preparing to go to Palmi-do and the lighthouse, half a dozen enemy sampans approached his island. After dusk fell, his lookouts peered across the narrow strait to Taebu-do and saw moving lights; it appeared that some North Korean troops, at the fall of an extra-low tide this evening, were attempting to wade across the rocks and mud to Yong Hong Do to attack in addition to the ampans. This time Clark decided that lighting the beacon was more important than fighting. He shoved off, after saying goodbye to the villagers and leaving them nearly all his equipment including his guns and ammunition.

He reached Palmi-do, climbed the lighthouse, lit the lamp at midnight, then sat there, chilly in a blanket, waiting for dawn and the great invasion.

While Clark sat in the lighthouse, some four hundred enemy soldiers were swarming over his former base at Yong Hong Do. All night they slaughtered villagers, including the mayor who had helped Clark, while about sixty hastily organized defenders under the boyish Ensign Che held them off and made a slow withdrawal from the town. Somehow the enemy had managed to connect Commander Spike Hahm with Clark's reconnaissance, and they now brought his picture to the island, asking the villagers if he'd been there. At 5:00 A.M. on the morning of September 15—at the moment the landing at Inchon, some twelve miles to the north, was about to begin—refugees on Yong Hong Do were streaming toward the beach and trying to scramble into the fishing boats there. Sporadic gunfire sounded all over the island.

By dawn Spike Hahm was offshore in PC-701. With much apprehension, he watched through his binoculars as Ensign Che, one of the last to withdraw, came toward the beach, firing at his pursuers with a pistol. Hahm feared for Che's life in a personal way, of course, but even more important was the fact that Che knew many of the Inchon landing plans and, if caught, would surely be tortured and forced to give information. True, it was a little late in the game for the enemy to derive any benefit from this information—the invasion ships were already standing offshore at Inchon and the first landing wave was scheduled for high tide at 0630 hours —but they still might be able to squeeze enough from Che to offer a bloodier resistance to the entire operation, which included not only the taking of Inchon, but the push inland to Seoul, the main objective.

At the beach, only yards from a fishing boat that could take him out to PC-701, Ensign Che saw that he would not make it without being captured. As Spike Hahm watched through the binoculars in horror, young Che pulled the pin on a grenade, thrust it into his stomach, and waited until it blew him backward, gutted and dead.

In fury, Spike Hahm began firing at the North Koreans from the patrol boat and at the same time bellowing curses at them through his loudspeaker.

Lieutenant Eugene Clark's island reconnaissance in those first two weeks of September 1950 was only one of dozens of widely scattered but strategically interlocked maneuvers and operations that were planned and executed with one ultimate result in mind—the landing of a decisive military force at the port of Inchon, Korea, on September 15. In this period, invasion plans were made final—althought relatively minor revisions took place up until the last minute—and the entire complicated scheme, involving tens of thousands of men, hundreds of thousands of tons of matériel, and operations over an area extending from the Yellow Sea to Tokyo, was drawn together into a cohesive pattern with the assault on Inchon as its focal point.

The stage was set for the last act on September 1, the day Clark landed on Yong Hong Do. The following week was the period of greatest apprehension in the Pusan Perimeter, the relatively small arena on the top of the Korean peninsula that was the center of the war, and where the alarming situation that called for the Inchon landing had developed.

For well over a month, a desperate, stalemated clash of armies had been taking place in this area. It was a rectangle of land, about ninety miles long north to south, and about fifty miles wide and its nearest corner was a little over a hundred miles southeast of Inchon. Its eastern and southern borders were the sea. It contained two cities, the big port of Pusan in the south, and the agricultural center of Taegu near its northwestern corner, with an air distance of about sixty miles between them.

The defense of this Pusan Perimeter was being conducted by the Eighth United States Army—plus its South Korean and other United Nations allies—commanded by Lieutenant General Walton H. Walker. Walker kept his headquarters in

Taegu, near the northwestern corner of the Perimeter, and in this first week of September he could hear the sound of North Korean artillery as his own nearest units fought to hold the line. He knew perhaps better than anyone else that the trend of this particular war must be reversed soon or the United States of America would be badly hurt, and he himself would be finished as a soldier—if not dead or captured like a good many senior officers so far in the violent, heartbreaking two months since the conflict had begun.

Walker's Eighth Army headquarters was in one of several school buildings that had been commandeered as military centers, and he had several times considered moving south to Pusan on the seacoast, not out of personal fear, for "Johnny" Walker's courage under fire was as legendary as MacArthur's, but simply because it seemed more sensible to conduct operations from a place where movement, communications and supply were not practically under the enemy's eyes, or likely to be overrun any minute. With this in mind, he had telephoned Tokyo in late August and told MacArthur's Chief of Staff, Major General Edward M. Almond, that it was urgent for him to speak to the Supreme Commander.[4]

The upshot of the call was that MacArthur, who opposed the move, visited Walker at Taegu near the first of September. In the course of his visit somehow the subject of moving Eighth Army headquarters was shoved into the background, and MacArthur spent most of the time complimenting Walker on the fine job he was doing in holding the line. This was the MacArthur technique. Virtually without mentioning the idea of moving headquarters to Pusan, he managed to make Walker feel that it was unwise from a political and public relations standpoint, and Walker decided to stay put. Walker was learning what others who differed with MacArthur had learned. After a conference with the Supreme Commander you felt, in one way, that you had been taken and manipulated like the victim of an exceptionally skillful confidence man, but like many such victims you were also pleasantly dazed and ready to come back for more.

So Johnny Walker, that first week of September 1950, was still in Taegu within the sound of enemy guns, bustling about his headquarters, flying and jeeping to various parts of the front like a fire chief, too busy to worry about anything but holding the Perimeter, and even too busy to speculate very deeply on the chances for success of the end run he knew was scheduled for September 15 at Inchon, far to the north and west, astride his enemy's supply line.

Walker was a scrappy, bantam cock of an armored cavalry-man, who in World War II had been a protégé of the famed George Patton,[5] and here in the Perimeter he commanded a total force of about 140,000 men. In his own Eighth United States Army were four divisions and a provisional Marine Brigade of about 4,700 men. They were augmented by the Republic of Korea Army of 82,500 men. A few token units from some of the United Nations countries were attached. Mathematically, Walker's force outnumbered by about 20,-000 the enemy that was holding it in the Perimeter. But this was a deceptive statistic. Most of the South Korean troops, though often wildly courageous and spirited, were either ill-trained and equipped, or not trained or equipped at all. As for matériel, only so much could be funneled through Pusan, the one port available, or delivered by air to the strips at Pusan and Taegu, and most of this was needed by the U. S. troops.

The American officer primarily concerned with Walker's South Korean allies was Brigadier General Francis W. Farrell. He was chief of the Korean Military Assistance Group, or KMAG (pronounced Kay-mag), that had originally been set up to train the South Korean Army under peacetime con-ditions. He was conferring frequently with Walker in this first dark week of September 1950. Farrell, a quiet, unruffled man from St. Louis, tall, trim and ruggedly handsome, spent most of his time flying back and forth among the various Korean Army Command Posts where his American advisors were stationed, finding that light-plane travel even over enemy lines was fairly safe, because the North Koreans re-garded all small planes as artillery spotters and had no desire to fire upon them and reveal their positions.

One night Walker sent for Farrell and said, "Frank, I need troops. Bad. Have you got anything? I mean *anything*." Far-rell said he had only a cadre of South Koreans acting pri-marily as instructors in a replacement training center, an outfit perhaps the size of a small battalion. "I'll take them!" said Walker. They were assigned to the First Cavalry Division where, in ensuing days, they fought so well that the First Cavalry commander didn't want to let them go—even though, as veterans of the early war, they'd had more than their fair share of the bitterest kind of combat.[6]

As a favorite GI expression of the day had it, things were

rough all over. Along the big inverted L that marked the border of the Perimeter, many units fought hard and well, and there were, as in any campaign, countless individual acts of heroism. Unfortunately, however, there were also scattered throughout Walker's Eighth Army too many outfits softened by occupation duty in the island-paradise-with-all-modern-comforts that was Japan; they had been thrown into the Korean War shortly after its outbreak, unprepared, largely untrained and often not adequately supplied. There was, for example, the last all-Negro regiment ever maintained by the United States Army, the Twenty-fourth Infantry, and it wasn't doing too well. On the first of September, two of its battalions broke and ran before the enemy in the southwestern part of the Perimeter, near a town called Haman, and nearly permitted a major breakthrough. The 24th was commanded by Colonel Arthur S. Champney, an officer who had no particular prejudices, but who recognized the low morale and lackadaisical attitude of his regiment from the first, and had said to Ned Almond, "If I hadn't had so much service, I just wouldn't take this command."

The inadequacy of the 24th Regiment sprang from causes that were difficult to analyze at the time. Ned Almond, a Southerner, had reminded Champney that he'd commanded a Negro regiment in World War II and that they had fought magnificently.[7] But somehow an infection of low morale had crept into the 24th and they were bad, indeed, in this campaign, so bad that a popular chant throughout the Eighth Army went:

> *When the mortars begin to thud,*
> *The old Deuce-Four begins to bug . . .*[8]

The Perimeter was almost lost when the 24th bugged out of its place in the line that first week in September. The entire sector in that southwest corner was commanded by Major General William B. Kean who, just after daylight on September 1, put in an urgent telephone call to Walker, said the line was ruptured and requested immediate reinforcements. Walker released one battalion of another regiment—the 27th—which was being held in reserve on the seacoast a little to the south. This 1st Battalion, commanded by Lieutenant Colonel Gilbert J. Cheek, arrived at Champney's 24th Regiment Command Post, near Haman, at about ten in the morning.

Check found Colonel Champney desperately trying to stave off a complete rout almost single-handedly. The demoralized soldiers of the 24th were choking the roads in their efforts to flee on foot or in trucks; they would not listen to officers or, if they did, would merely snarl obscenities at them; they were wild-eyed as Communist mortar rounds fell all around the road, doing little physical damage but increasing the terror and the traffic jam. South Korean troops were scattered among them, caught up in their panic. None of the troops could be assembled as units; many had thrown away their weapons, most had discarded their helmets, and some even ran without shoes. It was possibly the worst headlong rout of an American force of this size since First Bull Run.

General Kean had ordered Colonel Check and his battalion of reinforcements to make an immediate counterattack upon arriving at Haman, but the one road through the countryside and the surrounding fields and hillsides were so clogged with retreating troops that he couldn't get through. It was late afternoon before he could launch the counterattack. U. S. Air Force planes, most of them F-80 jets from Japan across the straits, were called in to bomb, strafe, rocket and baste with flaming napalm the enemy-held ridges facing Haman. An old-fashioned artillery barrage followed. By 4:30 P.M., the reinforcements were able to move forward at last, and at about this time the harried Champney managed to collect some 150 men out of his 2nd Battalion and assemble them in the rear.

That night, as Check's relief battalion dug in a few miles westward, unable to advance against what was later discovered to be four North Korean battalions in well-fortified positions, the Communists rubbed salt into poor Champney's wounds by dropping flares and mortar fire on his now withdrawn Command Post and forcing him to take it still further to the rear. But an all-out effort, bolstered by air attack, managed to plug the hole as the Air Force flew 135 sorties the next day and was joined by Navy and Marine pilots from the carriers *Valley Forge* and *Philippine Sea,* two hundred miles away but coincidentally steaming toward Korea at twenty-seven knots to be on hand for the projected landing at Inchon.[9]

The 24th had been a problem ever since it had arrived in Korea in July. Its composition as an all-Negro unit was precisely its problem. The world had changed, even since World War II, and Negroes simply didn't want to be regarded as a people apart and went into a sullen, resentful apathy when they were. General Kean hit upon the right solution when on September 9, shortly after the near breakthrough, he strongly recommended to Walker that the 24th Infantry Regiment be disbanded and its troops scattered throughout other units in Korea. In the heavy way of the military with administrative matters, it was a year before this was done, but when it finally was, Negro performance came right up to white performance in general throughout the Eighth Army and, indeed, throughout all the United States armies which never again activated an all-Negro unit.

The rout of the 24th at Haman was one dramatic example of the weakness of the hastily thrown together defensive force in Korea. The Perimeter line, in fact, was painfully tender in other areas, too. Only a few weeks before, MacArthur had enjoined Johnny Walker to hold at all costs in his fifty-by-ninety-mile enclave, and carrying out that order had been hard enough; now the word from Tokyo was that Walker should not only hold but get ready to mount his own offensive by the 15th of September to counteract any pressure the enemy might apply at Inchon. It was a little like telling a fighter who has just staggered up from several knockdowns to go out and finish things in the next round.

Even as the hole was being plugged at Haman, the enemy was starting to break through twenty miles to the north where the Naktong River ran for some distance along the western border of the Perimeter. The only relief General Walker could send handily to this weakened spot was the Provisional Marine Brigade, a force of about 4,700 built around the 5th Marine Regiment. At this moment the Marine Brigade was already near the coast and making ready to board ships at Pusan for the invasion at Inchon, around the western edge of Korea and far to the north. Walker knew the Marines were earmarked for MacArthur's precious amphibious landing and he had to call all the way to Tokyo to ask for permission to use them now, in this emergency. It turned out that he could, but he'd only have them a few days, so he'd better use them well in that time.

By the 3rd of September, the 5th Marine Regiment was in place near the Naktong again, launching an attack at 9:00 A.M., shortly after its arrival. The regimental commander, Lieutenant Colonel Raymond L. Murray, set up his tent Command Post on the side of an unnamed hill, watched his battalions and their companies go forward through what looked to him like a model landscape on a sand table, each unit clearly distinguishable, and reflected that it must have been like this in some of the battle of the Civil War when generals sat on horses at the crests of ridges to watch their neatly formed units maneuver.

Murray, in his late thirties, was a tall, deep-voiced, professional Marine from California, who had won a Navy Cross at Saipan for heroism under fire while commanding a battalion. As tough as any traditional Marine, he was nevertheless smooth-mannered in peaceful surroundings and as sharp at administration as at tactics; in civilian clothes he had the air of a business executive. In combat fatigues his rugged face and prominent nose were emphasized, however, and he became the definitive picture of a hard-driving regimental commander, though in a straightforward way and with no bizarre traits or poses. With a regiment under him he should have been a full colonel, but his promotion hadn't caught up with him yet. He wasn't the type to worry about it.

Murray had a way of keeping on the move in battle, and it was, as a matter of fact, unusual for him to pause long enough to pitch a tent as he had today. He usually traveled in a jeep with two other men: a driver who doubled as a radio operator, and his orderly. His staff often found it hard to keep up with him and also thought he put himself into unnecessary danger by not staying put somewhere further to the rear.

Scarcely two weeks before, his Regiment had faced the enemy in this same general area in what was known as the First Battle of the Naktong, and on that occasion he had watched them chase North Koreans across the river and up another ridge, so that from his hillside vantage point the swarms of Communists in flight seemed "like a bunch of ants." The Marines shot at them with small arms and their tankers turned huge 90-mm. guns upon individuals and picked them off as though potting at game with rifles. It was a complete victory on that occasion, and at one point Murray found himself jumping up and down and rooting as though at a football game.

Now, at Second Naktong, the Marines and the Army's 9th Infantry Regiment managed to push the North Koreans back again, and with a couple of days had them on a ridge known as Obong-ni. Then Murray received telephoned orders that he would be relieved immediately by a single Army Battalion. Withdrawing a regiment was a complicated business and he spent most of the day making plans and seeing that they were carried out. That night the Army lieutenant colonel whose battalion was to take over the sector came into Murray's tent out of a drenching rain and after conferring briefly with Murray, sat on a folding stool with his head in his hands as though to say to himself: "What have I done to deserve this?"[10]

His battalion was less than a third the size of Murray's regiment. It would be facing most of a North Korean division —a depleted division, to be sure, but one that still outnumbered him in alarming proportions. He didn't know about the Inchon plan—at least not officially—so he couldn't soothe himself, as Murray could, with the knowledge that weakening the line now, when the enemy had just been pushed back again, was part of the huge gamble MacArthur had entered upon in his decision to turn the course of the war once and for all.

Murray did know about Inchon. He'd been alerted to prepare his regiment for amphibious operations two weeks before, just after the First Naktong battle, when he'd withdrawn to the town of Masan, near the coast, where the Marines stayed when in reserve. There they pitched their tents in the fields of a former soybean farm they called the Pea Patch. And there, on a sweltering August afternoon, a Marine liaison officer from Tokyo had brought Murray the word about Inchon, telling him the date and leaving him a map of the port city. Murray's immediate reaction had been to say to himself: "For God's sake, what do they think they're doing?" His main objection was the short time they'd have to prepare for a major amphibious assault—under conditions that looked pretty formidable, come to think of it, what with the tides, the sea walls, the tiny landing areas, and the dangerous city to be fought through after the landing.

But orders were orders and the thing had to be done. Now, whenever he could spare time from whatever immediate battle was on his hands, he pored over the map of Inchon, often late at night in his tent, and tried to puzzle out a workable plan for putting the battalions of his regiment ashore. There simply wasn't room to land them all at once on the narrow beach assigned to him, and they would have to fan out somehow, afterward, to take the various objectives in the city itself. He sketched in blocks and arrows and military symbols in various ways to see if he couldn't figure out a method to land his Regiment without losing it.

That last night on the Pusan Perimeter, Murray stepped out into the drenching rain and watched as his tent was taken down. He had one last quick conference with the Army lieutenant colonel whose battalion was moving in, discussing some of the equipment the Marines would leave behind, and then received a gratifying report that the withdrawal had worked like clockwork and that the Marines were ready to go back to the coast.

He boarded a truck for the jolting, uncomfortable ride south to Pusan and knew that neither he nor anyone in the Regiment would get much sleep that night. Only Murray and his staff officers realized that instead of going back to rest, they were on their way to gamble their lives in an amphibious landing some of the Joint Chiefs of Staff members in Washington still regarded as an impossible, hairbrained scheme. . . .

And that was how matters stood in the fortnight just before the landing at Inchon . . . Walker at the Perimeter, plugging holes . . . Lieutenant Clark reconnoitering under the enemy's nose from an island near Inchon . . . a Marine regiment deliberately withdrawing from the Perimeter to board ships and sail to Inchon where it would act as one prong of the projected amphibious assault.

Perhaps hard-pressed Johnny Walker in the Perimeter asked himself now and then why this dramatic landing, far in the enemy's rear, had to be undertaken anyway. Seventy thousand troops would be involved in it, and with such reinforcements he could no doubt break out of the Perimeter and start pushing northward. Perhaps this thought didn't occur to him—he never gave voice to such an idea and instead did his best to carry out MacArthur's orders. But the thought certainly occurred to others, and very definitely to some of the high-ranking planners in the Pentagon. Until the day of the landing they were not averse to stating their objections.

How had the necessity for this dramatic long end run, this wide and deep penetration come about? Indeed, was it such a necessity? Was it the only probable way to victory or was it all planned and executed primarily because this was Mac-Arthur's flamboyant way of doing things? Any answers to these questions will have to be generously larded with suppositions, what-ifs, and might-have-beens. To understand it all you have to go back, briefly at least, to the events that led up to the landing—to the beginning of the war that caught everyone off-base two months and three weeks earlier.

NOTES *Chapter 1*

1. Interview author—Vadm Hahm Myong Soo, R. O. K. Navy. The basic account of Clark's reconnaissance is from Karig, Walter *et al. Battle Report,* Vol. VI, *The War in Korea,* New York, Holt, Rinehart and Winston, Inc., 1952, and interview Canzona—Soper 16 Aug 54 in Historical References, Hq USMC. Admiral Hahm has supplied additional data, especially from the Korean viewpoint.
2. Interview author—Lt Gen W. H. Sterling Wright.
3. Interview author—Dr. David Holly, and Holly, "The ROK Navy," *Proceedings of the Naval Institute,* Vol 78 #11, 1952.
4. Interview author—Lt Gen Edward M. Almond.
5. Like Patton, Walker died in a jeep accident. Allergic to dust, he always urged his driver to speed over Korea's dirt roads and leave the dust behind. He lunched with several officers, Brigadier General Farrell among them, one day in mid-December, and during the meal happened to remark, "I always thought it ironic that Georgie Patton, who lived the kind of life he did, died the way he did." Two hours later Walker's jeep, with its special handrail that enabled him to stand while traveling, crashed head-on with a weapons carrier and Walker was dead. Interview author—Lt Gen Francis W. Farrell.
6. *Ibid.* Later, in Seoul, General Walker received a surprise serenade one morning from the R. O. K. Army band whose members, like so many Koreans, were musically talented and played extremely well. Walker turned to Farrell and said, "Hell, if I'd known these guys were around they'd have been the Eighth Army reserve back in the Perimeter!"
7. Interview author—Almond.
8. Author's recollection.
9. Appleman, Roy E. *South of the Naktong, North of the Yalu; The United States Army in the Korean War,* Washington, D.C., Department of the Army, 1961, pp. 479–81.
10. Interview author—Maj Gen Raymond L. Murray, USMC.

2

"I see perfectly."

THERE WERE A LOT OF EUPHEMISMS IN THIS WAR. WHAT MOST Americans thought at first was just a simple little police action had exploded into a nasty conflict of frightening size. Back in the United States, newspaper readers had followed the retreat of American forces and their allies down the peninsula and into their last-stand Perimeter with the uneasy suspicion that this was defeat, even though nobody was calling it that.

The term "police action" was still being used, even though large, bloody battles, with tanks, artillery, planes and all the trimmings, were being fought. Retreats were usually called withdrawals or maneuvers for position. And the force that had been hastily thrown into Korea, primarily a United States Army in force and influence, was still stoutly and doggedly referred to as the United Nations force because of the R. O. K. Army and a few attached units from various other nations.

In that short summer of 1950, everything happened so quickly that hardly anyone had a chance to catch his breath, let alone find proper names for things. At the end of World War II, Japan had been occupied, and that was the main job in the Far East, but Korea had been part of Japan's Empire, a reluctant auxiliary, to be sure, but nevertheless nominally Japanese territory. Thus the peninsula nation had to be occupied, too. The Soviets had declared war on Japan in the closing hours of World War II in order to share in the spoils, and at Potsdam they clamored for Korea, which was after all on the Asian mainland and could logically be said to lie within their sphere of influence. After much haggling, it was agreed that Russia would occupy the northern

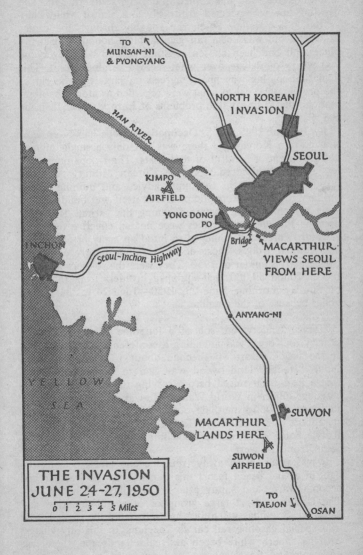

TO
MUNSAN-NI
& PYONGYANG

NORTH KOREAN
INVASION

SEOUL

HAN RIVER

KIMPO
AIRFIELD

YONG DONG
PO

Bridge

MACARTHUR
VIEWS SEOUL
FROM HERE

INCHON

Seoul-Inchon Highway

ANYANG-NI

YELLOW
SEA

SUWON

MACARTHUR
LANDS HERE

SUWON
AIRFIELD

THE INVASION
JUNE 24-27, 1950

0 1 2 3 4 5 Miles

TO
TAEJON

OSAN

half of Korea, and the United States the southern half. The dividing line was selected arbitrarily and almost whimsically as the 38th parallel, which ran roughly through the center of Korea, but was not a fair geographical boundary in many places. (It had been chosen at a late session when everyone was weary of debate over what seemed a minor point. This demarcation line was finally agreed on largely to be rid of the problem and get to what were regarded as more important matters, that is to say, the problems of Europe rather than the Far East.)

By June of 1949, U. S. Occupation troops had been withdrawn from Korea, and there was left only a small military aid group and a handful of diplomats. The troops numbered less than five hundred from the Korean Military Advisory Group. Their job was to supply advice and training to the military forces the Republic of Korea itself was building, and their personnel were scattered among the various R. O. K. units so that they themselves were not an effective force.

South Korea had managed to build an army of about 65,000 combat troops, most of them rather poorly equipped, by the early summer of 1950. They were the soldiers who first faced around 89,000 well-equipped invaders from the north on Sunday morning, June 25, 1950—June 24 in the United States because of the dateline.

Horace Underwood, son of a longtime Presbyterian missionary to Korea, was attending a conference of missionaries at the beach resort of Taechun about 135 miles south of Seoul. "Hedbe" Underwood was glad to be back in Korea where he'd been raised before serving the U. S. Navy as a language officer in World War II. He was a somewhat stocky, snub-nosed young man, devout at heart, but not at all the stereotype of a missionary. He lived in the large brick colonial-style home of the Underwood family on a hill overlooking Seoul from the west.

It was good to get away from the city and especially delightful at the beach resort this morning as the weather had become warm and sunny after several days of heavy rain. The Underwoods, a large group of other missionaries, and a few U. S. embassy families had left Seoul the night before in a special gasoline rail car to Taechun. In this tiny village, with its superb white beach and calm landscape, there was no electricity, no telephone, and not even a radio. Everybody considered that part of the charm.

Hedge Underwood, splashing in the surf, hadn't the vaguest premonition that within a few weeks he'd be serving again as a language officer in a war, that his services would prove of great value to Douglas MacArthur's most spectacular end run and amphibious landing, that in this operation he would come under fire and narrowly escape with his life, and that the big brick house on the hill would be among the tens of thousands of structures demolished.

The missionaries spent all that Sunday quietly unaware that war had begun. The next morning, before daylight, a Seoul Embassy official, Frank Barnhardt, who was himself the son of a missionary, set out in a rickety car over the rutted and washboarded back roads to Taechun to warn the people there and bring them the sad news that they wouldn't be able to return to Seoul, since everyone expected it to be captured momentarily. It was now more than twenty-four hours since the North Koreans started down from the parallel, only about thirty miles north of Seoul, and the earliest reports made it plain enough that they were not being significantly delayed.

In Seoul itself, one of the first Americans to get word of the North Korean advance was the Ambassador to the Republic of Korea, John J. Muccio. A quiet, career foreign-service officer from Rhode Island, Muccio wore horn-rimmed glasses and looked more like an advertising executive than a diplomat. He was a bachelor and had no particular preference as to where he might be sent; thus he had become the State Department's odd-job man in the Far East, and had held important posts in China before World War II. His assignment to Seoul in August of 1948 had given him his first ambassadorial rank.

Muccio was finishing his breakfast in his residence at about eight o'clock that Sunday morning, when the phone rang and he heard the voice of his first counselor and deputy, Everett Drumwright. "Brace yourself for a shock," said Drumwright. "The Communists are smashing through all along the front."

Muccio dressed hurriedly and rushed into town where the chancery of the Embassy, for lack of better quarters, was situated in an upper floor of the Banto, Seoul's largest hotel. As he entered the hotel he saw Bill James, a United Press correspondent, coming out. James's nose for news twitched. "What are you doing down here this early on a Sunday, Mr. Ambassador?" Muccio said, "Well, Bill, there've been some reports of a breakthrough up north. You might look into it."

James did, indeed, look into it, and Ambassador Muccio was later chagrined to learn that the U.P. dispatch, in the clear, got to Washington twenty minutes before his own message, which had to be coded.

Upstairs, Muccio found out that sporadic reports of the invasion had been coming in from various KMAG advisers with the South Korean units since about seven that morning. As he sent his cable, he realized that Washington, half a world away, would be inclined to caution in accepting his reports, but in his own mind he was convinced that it was an all-out offensive. The North Koreans had been prodding and probing along the 38th parallel for two and a half years. That Sunday morning there had been four very definite heavy attacks across the parallel, and even a landing on the east coast below it.

In Tokyo at the moment there was at least one man to share Muccio's deep alarm over the situation, and this was John Foster Dulles, who had been swinging through the Far East for the past week as a special assistant to the Secretary of State. Dulles was now in Japan to lay the groundwork for the Administrative Agreement that would take the place of the Occupation, returning Japan's sovereignty, but providing for U. S. troops to remain as protection. He had just spent several days in Korea, making the usual sight-seeing trip to the 38th parallel, where he'd been photographed gazing across the strip between North and South Korea. North Korean propaganda releases made much of this photo, and their descriptions implied that Dulles was looking covetously northward as the South Koreans readied themselves for an attack. In Seoul, Dulles had talked to Ambassador Muccio and had shown deep interest in his feelings about the danger of an attack from the north, seeming to agree with him that it was more likely than most officials in Washington thought.

Now the attack had come, and for the moment there wasn't much for Muccio to do but to put into effect the evacuation plan for Americans he'd had the foresight to establish many months before. There was still a day or two in which he could function. The reports now seemed to show that the South Korean units up near the parallel, though smashed, battered, and in many cases enveloped, were not surrendering and were doing much to heroically delay the North Korean advance.

The next day Muccio received an eyes-only cable from Dean Rusk, then Assistant Secretary of State for Far Eastern Affairs. There'd been rumors that Muccio wanted to stay in

Seoul and Rusk thought he'd better leave while it was still possible. The reports, Muccio replied, were erroneous; he had no intention of staying and would leave ahead of any Communist arrival as soon as he could be sure all other Americans under his jurisdiction were evacuated.

Altogether it was a busy three days for John Muccio. He spent most of Sunday talking on the Armed Forces radio station to all Americans in Korea in an effort to calm everyone and acquaint them with the facts of the invasion and the evacuation plan. Early Monday morning, he saw that all American women and children in the Seoul area were taken to Ascom City, a large military supply dopot about halfway to the coast at Inchon, by State Department buses. To his own staff at the Embassy, he issued orders that everyone must travel lightly, taking only what could be conveniently carried by hand. He was pleased to see that no one rebelled at this, and the corps of women who acted as secretaries, stenographers and clerks in the Embassy refused to rush away, but insisted on staying and assisting until the last possible minute. Nevertheless, he wired Tokyo for an airlift for the women, and asked that it be increased to take care of all the U. S. mission, plus the United Nations diplomatic corps and other allies.

Muccio himself planned to head southward to Taejon, ninety miles below Seoul, toward which President Syngman Rhee had already fled. The seat of South Korea's government would be there, and that was where he belonged. He sent Drumwright and other key Embassy officials ahead of him early on Tuesday, and made arrangements for himself to ride with Major Holland, a KMAG officer in charge of the evacuation, and Don MacDonald, an Embassy official.

The last bus left shortly after noon on Tuesday. At his residence, Muccio called in his Korean household staff, told them to help themselves to the food and beverage stores, and then to leave quickly and not be found around the Embassy when the Communists arrived. He told Chung, his chauffeur, to put his own family in the official Embassy Chrysler and meet Muccio, who would be in his own Mercury, at the bridge later.[1]

Muccio now checked at the chancery in the Banto Hotel, where he found all communications to Tokyo cut off. In the code room Sam Berry, the senior cryptographer, was grunting and cursing as he tried to move the huge, typewriterlike SIGABA coding machine.

"I can't lift this thing," said Berry. "Let's take it in the bathroom and try chemicals on it. Got to be destroyed."

Muccio shook his head, said there might be danger of fire, and then both men, grunting and sweating, carried the huge device downstairs and out into the parking lot. Muccio looked at his watch and said to Berry. "Sam, you've got five minutes to run upstairs again and clear your room." Berry was back in three minutes. "It's already cleared," he said. "The looters got in there."

Looters were all over town by now. The streets were choked with people trying to get out of the city, most of them streaming toward the bottleneck at the one bridge that led south across the broad Han River.

Muccio now went to KMAG headquarters where, among others he found Archbishop Patrick Byrne, the Apostolic Delegate to Korea, and a KMAG officer who spoke Korean. The officer thought everyone had better hurry because he'd heard talk that the bridge across the Han River was going to be blown up.[2]

Also at KMAG headquarters was Colonel Sterling Wright, a suave, able officer, who had already served his time in Korea but had been asked to stay over a short time as acting chief of KMAG until a new commander arrived. Wright had been in Tokyo putting his family on a ship to precede him home. Hearing the news, he had rushed back to Seoul by air.

The two men stepped briefly into an office for a quick final conference, and at that moment there was an engine snarl and the sound of machine guns outside. Through the windows they saw two Russian-made Yaks strafing the streets. As the next pass came, everyone in the office prudently dived under desks. Wright said, "Mr. Ambassador, I think we'd better get out of here." They agreed to meet south of the river if they became separated.

The ambassador finally headed for the bridge at about 3:30 P.M. on Tuesday, a little earlier than he planned, driving his own Mercury and accompanied by the KMAG major, Second Secretary Don MacDonald and code clerk Sam Berry. Just as they got across the bridge, another Yak came scooting along the river and tracers started to crisscross in front of them. Muccio, a career diplomat, turned to the only military man on hand and said, "Well, what am I supposed to do now?"

"Oh, that's friendly fire," said the major, grinning, and

pointing to two F-80's that were coming along on the tail of the Yak.

The small party drove south to the next town of any size, Suwon, where there was an airfield that would later become an important U. S. fighter base. At the railroad station Muccio found South Korea's Minister of Defense and now acting Prime Minister, Shin Sung Moh, sitting rather ruefully on a bench in the waiting room eating a bowl of fish, cabbage and rice. Muccio was so hungry that he asked for some, got it, and ate it with relish.

That night Muccio, who hadn't slept in three days, looked for a place to rest and found some old bungalows previously occupied by a U. S. aid mission. It had begun to rain heavily, and there was a loud tattoo of drops on the metal roof, but this, Muccio decided, wasn't going to disturb the sleep he was looking forward to. He was optimistic about that sleep. He had scarcely arrived at the bungalow when the Korean Foreign Minister's chauffeur came in and said excitedly that General MacArthur wanted to talk to him on the telephone.

He went out and drove through the rain to the Suwon post office, where one of the few operable telephones in town was situated—an ancient French- style model on the wall. All the power was off and candles were flickering in the building.

Instead of General MacArthur's deep baritone, he heard a female voice when he picked up the receiver. "This is Molly Lee, Mr. Ambassador! I'm still here in Seoul at the International Switchboard!" He knew Molly, a Hawaiian of Korean descent who had been born in Korea and was not a U. S. citizen. He told her to get her two children and somehow make it down to Suwon the next morning if she could; he'd try to do something for her.[3]

Then the connection to Tokyo was plugged through and it turned out to be not General MacArthur, but his ubiquitous Chief of Staff, Ned Almond. "General MacArthur will fly to Korea Thursday and personally size up the situation. He'd like Syngman Rhee on hand as well as the Korean military leaders and the KMAG people. Where shall he land?" Muccio said for MacArthur to come in at Suwon.

The next morning he managed to confirm the intelligence that South Korea's President, Rhee, was in Taejon, another sixty miles to the south, and he decided to contact him personally and at the last moment, fearing Rhee might let out the news of MacArthur's arrival. Muccio knew that Rhee, who spoke excellent English and had a benevolent, wrinkled appearance, plus a flare for the dramatic, had been built up into something of a hero by the press so that the American public regarded him as the George Washington of Korea, but most of the diplomatic community in Seoul always felt that Rhee was not so much interested in developing South Korea's economy, as in keeping U. S. troops to insure his political position, which at times bordered on dictatorship. At the moment, however, Muccio was only worried about Rhee's penchant for making dramatic and immoderate public statements which might break security.

He flew to Taejon in an L-4, a light liaison plane of the type used by sportsmen and private pilots, found Rhee, but did not yet tell him that MacArthur would be in Suwon. He gave the Prime Minister instead some fast doubletalk about the U. S. Air Force having been ordered to support his South Korean armies and asked him to return to Suwon to discuss it. At dawn Thursday, Rhee got into an L-5, Muccio returned with his pilot to his own L-4, and the two small planes took off for Suwon.

Minutes later, Muccio noticed that both airplanes were flying dangerously close to the ground. He sat behind the pilot and there was no intercom. He was about to lean forward and ask why the low flying, when he spotted two Yak's overhead, crisscrossing the country like hawks. He understood, leaned back, and hoped that everything would be all right. Presently the runway at Suwon appeared and the liaison planes slanted toward it. Muccio breathed a sigh of relief.

General MacArthur and his retinue landed at ten. After a long visit with President Rhee, the Supreme Commander called a purely military conference and some of Muccio's loyal assistants felt ruffled when the Ambassador was not invited, but Muccio himself understood the situation and did not expect or desire to attend.[4]

Colonel Sterling Wright was at this meeting of some fifty officers; he'd finally managed to make it out of Seoul before the bridge had been blown at 0230 Wednesday morning. By now he'd received a flamboyant message in a radio-equipped truck from MacArthur himself: "Repair to your former locations. Momentous decisions are in the offing. Be of good cheer."

He watched as General MacArthur paced in a small room near the airfield and outlined his plans to the KMAG staff. It was a gripping speech, full of rolling MacArthurian phrases, and Wright saw the general on this occasion as a cavalier from another age. Like many others, he was not entirely fooled by MacArthur's way of greeting an individual. MacArthur would grab your hand when he met you, take your elbow with his left hand, and then draw your hand in close to his body say, "Well, well, how are you?" with studied warmth, and Wright was sure he was briefed beforehand whenever someone was ushered into his presence for the first time.

As MacArthur stalked back and forth, talking, in that room at Suwon, he continually punched at the air with his corncob pipe. There was no stenographic record of the talk, but Wright remembered that MacArthur said, in effect: "I've seen the situation. I think the Korean Army can be reorganized. I'm going to recommend to President Truman that we send air support and ground units. It will be about a week before we can send help from Japan. Until then, gentlemen—" a dramatic pause, a lowering of the corncob pipe and of the deep voice almost to a whisper—"you will hold the line!"[5]

As he gestured, the pipestem fell from the corncob and hit the floor. MacArthur didn't appear to notice and went on talking. No one else dared notice. Then, some minutes later, he was finished and turned to go. Wright, senior officer present, called "Ten-*hut!*" as the general stalked out. The moment he left the room there was a mad scramble as everybody dove for the pipestem. Wright never did learn who finally retrieved it as a souvenir.

It was now approaching 5 P.M. and MacArthur, who had had his conference with Syngman Rhee, turned to the old man and Ambassador Muccio and said "How are you getting back to Taejon?" Muccio said they'd return in the same light planes. MacArthur then directed that they be sent back in a twin-engine Beechcraft that was on hand.

The twin Beech's props were turning when they stepped into it and buckled themselves in. It surged forward in takeoff and then, halfway down the runway, suddenly swerved violently and came to a halt. The sergeant in the cabin cried, "Jump! Get out of the way!" The Ambassador and the aging Korean President scrambled from the plane and dove headfirst into muddy rice paddies beside the field. Strafing Yaks came roaring overhead, making two passes.

General MacArthur was all apologies, and now realized that the F-80 jets which flew from Japan were limited by fuel capacity to staying over the field only fifteen to twenty minutes at a time. The Yaks must have been sizing up the situation and had made their quick strafing run in one of the short intervals when there was no air protection.

Late that night, Ambassador Muccio, still weary from lack of sleep, would find himself driving Syngman Rhee back to Taejon in his personal Mercury, but only after General MacArthur borrowed the car at about 2:00 P.M. for a quick trip north to the Han River where the hectic evacuation of Seoul was still taking place. MacArthur told Muccio there was no point in his coming along and exposing himself to possible danger; Muccio agreed, not so much on account of the danger, but because he was still tired.

The small motor convoy heading for the Han breasted a current of refugees streaming south. Colonel Wright was with MacArthur, along with high-ranking members of MacArthur's Tokyo staff. On the trip up, MacArthur remarked that he believed the situation definitely called for the commitment of American troops to Korea, and he would wire Washington to that effect this evening.

By the time they arrived at the south bank of the Han, Seoul was already being shelled by approaching North Korean troops. The refugees were still swarming across the river on their rafts. Around the city great clouds of yellow dust were rising as the artillery shells struck. The party stepped from the car and MacArthur gazed toward the north.

Douglas MacArthur, the hero of Bataan, of Leyte, of so many places, was already seventy years old in the summer of 1950, long past the age when most generals are retired, and only the closest of observers knew that occasionally his hand trembled when he held a paper (as it had, slightly, aboard the *Missouri* in Tokyo Bay during the Japanese surrender ceremonies), for he was still full of grandiloquent vigor and he managed to conceal any signs of age—perhaps deliberately, perhaps casually; no one ever really knew—by his erect posture, by the crumpled, braided general's hat of his own design, by the corncob pipe, by smoked glasses on occasion, and perhaps most of all, by his lofty and supremely confident manner, which lacked only a sense of humor to bring it to true greatness.

He stood there on the south bank of the Han and stared north. That was where the threat was coming from. But a military threat to Douglas MacArthur was merely another opportunity to shine with brilliance. Few men of advanced age received such a second chance for greatness.

"Would you like to use my binoculars, sir?" said Colonel Wright, offering them.

MacArthur looked at the handsome colonel coldly. "Not at all, young man," he said. "I see perfectly."[6]

The glory . . . the bittersweet glory of the days that followed. It is never easy to die in battle, but it is most difficult when you know the battle you're dying in is already looked upon as lost—was, indeed, given up for lost before it was ever enjoined.

There were dozens of such battles as the Communist army, a stolid, impervious robot, marched down the length of the peninsula that long, hot July of 1950. The first major conflict between the United States forces and the able, modern North Korean columns must have been the easiest to enter, for there was still hope. False hope, to be sure: four hundred men swiftly airlifted from Japan on the first day of July took a train north from Pusan, marched up the road that came down from Seoul, dug in where the highway passed between two hills, and blanched not at all when they saw what seemed to be an endless tank and infantry column approaching, for there was in all of them a dangerous belief in the myth of American invincibility, and an unspoken notion that civilization, which to most of them meant technical superiority, sprang from their side of the world and that these troublesome Asians in this quaint land that smelled of burning charcoal and night soil were little more than brigands to be routed out of the hills so everyone could relax and go about his business.

The battle began on the morning of July 5. The force, known as Task Force Smith, for its commander, Lieutenant Colonel Charles B. Smith, now numbered around 540, and they'd brought along a few howitzers, recoilless rifles and bazookas, but had limited ammunition, and as it turned out, some of the fireworks had deteriorated with age. They were eight miles below Suwon, where MacArthur had landed and conferred, and which the Communists had calmly taken on July 4. At about 8 A.M. they sighted the first tanks, and the trucks streaming back out of sight behind them, and opened fire. Their shells bounced off these treaded, Russian-built monsters known as T-34's; even their 105-mm. howitzers couldn't stop them at 150 yards, and from their ambush position all morning they managed to immobilize only four tanks out of thirty-three.

Then hordes of enemy infantry came along and the men of Task Force Smith retreated, but with no panic. Oddly enough, they fought well that day, though there were only a sprinkling of battle-blooded noncoms and officers from World War II among them. One hundred fifty men were killed, wounded or missed; the men of Task Force Smith regrouped to fight again, and now other units began to arrive from Japan to join them.

The Japan-based division handiest to Korea was the 24th, commanded by Major General William F. Dean. Tall, crew-cropped, open-faced, Dean was to command his division at the hopeless task of delaying the enemy advance, and before the month was out he was to become the enemy's most famed captive and spend long, bitter days in their brutal prisoner-of-war camps. Other divisions would be on the way, all from the Eighth Army, commanded by the doughty little Texan, General Walton H. Walker, who now had the primary job of fighting the invaders of South Korea.

But it all took time; troops had to be moved, their supply lines had to be filled. Airlift was not yet significant and the only available port was Pusan at the tip of the peninsula. The Far East Air Forces, commanded by General George Strate-meyer, Asian veteran of World War II, leapt in to help with planes taken from storage, and with the excess joy peculiar to flyers in war, began, in those first days, to shoot up everything in sight, including friendly troops and installations. They plastered Suwon while it was still occupied by KMAG men, shot up thirty friendly trucks and killed two hundred R. O. K. soldiers on another occasion, and attacked R. O. K. Army headquarters no less than five times. Brigadier General John H. Church, temporarily in command of the more or less troopless American effort at this point, sent a violent protest to Tokyo asking that air attacks be kept north of the Han River where they'd be sure to hit the enemy only. This problem was solved in time when air strikes were better coordinated by means of ground observers and spotter planes, and from the first FEAF—primarily the Fifth Air Force and attached units—dominated the skies over Korea. Their support was welcome, but as it turned out, hardly decisive, and the North Korean armies pushed on.

Down the peninsula, at one roadblock after another, Americans were thrown hastily into battle at Pyongtaek, the Kum River line, Taejon—each point a little further southward—and the public back home watched in surprise as the arrows symbolizing the enemy advance pushed closer and closer to the last exit port of Pusan.

By now young Hedge Underwood, warned at the resort beach the day after the war broke out, had made his way with the other missionaries back to Pusan, where he'd been swiftly accepted into active duty as a Navy lieutenant and promptly sent up to Taejon as an interpreter on General Dean's staff. John Muccio stayed with the Republic of Korea government, as his duty directed, as it moved first to Taejon and then to Taegu, in the Perimeter.

By early August the United Nations Forces, as they were called, consisting primarily of the Eighth United States Army and the Republic of Korea Army, all under the command of Johnny Walker, were in an upright rectangle, fifty by ninety miles, on the extreme southeastern tip of Korea. They were to stay more or less in that position for the entire month, fighting desperately, while MacArthur in Tokyo planned the great flanking movement that hardly anyone thought would work; but now, at least, it was a stand, not a delaying action, and there was a purpose—"they shall not break through!"— even if it was a negative purpose, and perhaps that made it a little easier to die.

Headquarters was at Taegu, South Korea's third-largest city, inland fifty miles from both the south and the east coasts, the enemy already pressing almost into its western outskirts and, before the month was out, destined to brush toward it with probes from the north. The line looked neat on the map, but battle fronts, like weather fronts, are broad areas of turmoil, swelling and receding as the days go on, filled with dents, pockets and open places. Except for air supply, everything poured into the Perimeter through Pusan, the second-largest city of South Korea, ten thousand tons a day during July and, after the arrival of a 100-ton crane in August, half again as much. On the last day of July, came the first troops directly from the United States, the 9th Infantry Regiment of the 2nd Infantry Division, and on the third of August, a provisional Marine brigade came in from San Diego to take a position at the extreme southwestern edge of the Perimeter.

In a private ninety-minute conference on July 27 in Taegu, attended only by MacArthur, his Chief of Staff and General Walker, Walker was told that from here on in withdrawals must cease.[7] Two days later Walker passed the word on to the staff of the 25th Division, and his paraphrased remarks were picked up by the press and reported as a grim "stand-or-die" order. What he'd really said, in effect, was "If some of us must die, we will die fighting together. Any man who gives ground may be personally responsible for the death of thousands of his comrades."[8]

But as the press reported it, the order had an even more salutary effect, shocking everyone into a realization that this was indeed a serious war, not a police action, and that it might well result in shameful defeat. On August 2, Hanson Baldwin, military expert of *The New York Times,* put it very well when he called Walker's order a "well-merited rebuke to the Pentagon, which has too often disseminated a soothing syrup of cheer and sweetness and light since the fighting began."[9]

It was a hot, dry summer in Korea in 1950, with drought all over the brown land and rugged hills. Along the Perimeter men fought, sweated, died, and the living cursed the arena into which they'd been thrown. The general feeling was that if you had to have a war, well, by God, this benighted peninsula, no damn good for anything else, was the place for it. There were hills and ridges, ravines and gulches everywhere. The saying throughout the army was that if you rolled Korea out flat it would reach back to California. At night, flying over the battle area, pilots could see wormlike squiggles of fire along the ridges and in the day there were low-lying acrid clouds of smoke.

In Tokyo, General of the Armies Douglas MacArthur calmly presided over everything, attended by his faithful Chief of Staff, Major General Edward Mallory Almond. Almond was of less than medium size and dwarfed in many ways by the towering presence of MacArthur. A VMI graduate with a fine combat record from World Wars I and II, Almond had a pleasant, handsome appearance that lacked the startling character marks of the eaglelike MacArthur or the bulldoglike Johnny Walker; it was receptively mild and at times seemed almost bland. His manner, when not commanding men, was almost courtly—he might well have been an admiring disciple of Robert E. Lee, unconsciously emulating the air of that great soldier.

But Ned Almond's blue eyes could snap when he wanted them to, and he was possessed of an almost photographic memory for details. Each day, he went through the controlled routine he'd established for himself as MacArthur's Chief of

Staff. He would arrive at the sixth-floor office of the Dai-Ichi Building, just across a broad park from the Emperor's palace in Tokyo, at 8:30 every morning and get his early paperwork in order. MacArthur would make his daily ceremonious entrance around 10:30 and then he would often stay until midnight, and Almond would remain until he departed.

Almond was MacArthur's buffer. Only the most distinguished of visitors—the Emperor of Japan was one—could get to MacArthur without seeing Almond first. No communications other than cable or radio messages could go to MacArthur without passing under Almond's eyes, with the possible exception of the college football scores MacArthur demanded each morning of the season. As each radio message or cable came into headquarters, two copies were made by the Signal Officer, one for MacArthur, one for Almond. If Almond could take action on a document. he would do so immediately. Otherwise he would wait for MacArthur, and by the time the Supreme Commander arrived, would usually have all the necessary information corollary to any communication already assembled. Almond would give MacArthur about thirty minutes to get settled after he arrived, and take everything in at about 11 A.M.

The olympian MacArthur was never really close to anyone in his official family, not even the favorites he'd brought along with him from the Philippines, but Ned Almond in those days probably stood in his presence for longer periods of time than anyone else in the headquarters, and he would be treated to bits of the MacArthur philosophy with greater frequency than others. MacArthur, as the guiding light of the Occupation, talked to Almond many times about the mores and customs of the Japanese, as he saw them. Once, when the question of birth control was being discussed, he said to Almond, "Don't ever let yourself get mixed up in how the Japanese will make love or things of that nature—you'll be outside your function as an occupation soldier."[10]

Like most professional soldiers, Almond, in his heart, would have preferred to command men in battle, a function in which he'd already proved his worth as commander of the 92nd Infantry Division in Italy during World War II. In World War I, as a junior officer, he had led a machine-gun battalion in action and had been wounded and decorated for bravery. Now he was fifty-eight, and a thoroughly loyal chief of staff—in a sense, an executive secretary on a high plane— and as such he had to contain his self-confident ego which, in battle, had been not so much a fault as a great strength. There was no way he could properly point out to MacArthur that he was a most able combat tactician and a thorough student of both Napoleonic and Civil War campaigns; he could hardly explain that in combat he would show boldness tempered by thorough knowledge of his craft, and most of all, he didn't dare even hint that now that a shooting war was going on across the straits, he simply wanted to be in it.

MacArthur perhaps knew all these things. Before two weeks were out, he was to pick Almond to head the most daring major amphibious landing in history, not as huge in scope as the Normandy landing, but one planned and mounted in an unbelievably short time and carried out against the greatest natural odds that ever faced an attacking force from the sea. It was the landing MacArthur believed had to be made to keep the Perimeter from turning into another Dunkerque, or at the least, a dreary, drawn out counterpush. It was the pet idea that had been growing in his mind since early July, and now, in the face of opposition from Washington, had become almost an obsession with him.

Later, there were stories in both press reports and current histories that MacArthur at the outbreak of the war had stood on a rise below Seoul and conceived the landing then, perhaps on the day when he'd stiffly declined to borrow Colonel Wright's binoculars, but at that time even the eagle-eyed MacArthur couldn't have gazed far enough into the future to see the need for his favorite strategy of an amphibious end run. In fact, he was to consider the possibility only tentatively as late as the middle of July, and even then have several places in mind as potential landing sites.

The final decision to outflank and to do it at Inchon was MacArthur's, but the plan itself grew in the mulch of his busy headquarters after he had unconsciously dropped its spore.

It was taking visible shape as that dry, hot July of 1950 came to a close.

NOTES   *Chapter 2*

1. Chung unfortunately tarried and arrived at the bridge after the Ambassador had gone. The guards would not let him cross. Later, in news photos, Muccio saw the captured offi-

cial Chrysler in parades in Pyongyang, the North Korean
capital. Chung survived the war, however, and migrated to
the United States afterward. As for the American women
and children in Seoul, 682 were evacuated from Inchon on
the only ship available, the *Reinholt,* a Norwegian fertilizer
ship. Interview author—Ambasador John J. Muccio.

2. The bridge was blown up at 2:30 the following morning,
possibly by the order of the controversial South Korean
Army Chief of Staff, General Chae Byong Duk, known to
most Americans as "Fat" Chae, stranding many civilians and
KMAG soldiers who later made their way across by makeshift raft. Chae was a big burly fellow with cauliflower ears
he'd acquired as a *sumo* wrestler in earlier days. Later,
MacArthur, visiting the front south of Seoul, saw Chae
sleeping in a chair in the midst of all that desperate activity
and remarked, "We ought to get rid of that fellow." He was
presently replaced as Chief of Staff. He finally met his
death while almost single-handedly trying to defend a roadblock below Seoul. Afterward the rumor persisted that he'd
been executed for prematurely blowing up the Han River
bridge. Actually it was the R. O. K. Army's Chief Engineer
who, after a court of inquiry, was executed for the "manner"
in which he prepared the bridge for demolition. In fairness
to Chae, it should be mentioned that the court also found
some strong indications that the Vice Minister of Defense,
not Chae, had ordered the Han River bridge destroyed early.
Interviews author—Muccio, Wright, Farrell, Dr. Horace
Underwood and Brig Gen Mun Hui Sok, ROKA (Ret).

3. Molly Lee didn't make it, but later Muccio found her in
Seoul when it was retaken; she had survived the North
Korean occupation largely by concealing her identity. In-
terview author—Muccio.

4. *Ibid.*

5. Interview author—Wright.

6. *Ibid.* Later that day Yaks strafed near the party and everyone dove for cover—except MacArthur who sat calmly in
place and watched.

7. Interview author—Almond.

8. *25th Div G-3 Journal,* 29 Jul 50.

9. *The New York Times,* 2 Aug 50.

10. Interview author—Almond.

3

"There'll be no defensive moat. . . ."

IN THE SMALL ROOM BETWEEN MACARTHUR'S AND NED Almond's offices, there were maps on the wall. MacArthur liked to vary his compulsive pacing by coming in here and frowning at them, usually keeping up a monologue that amounted to thinking aloud. In early July he did this several times in Almond's presence, and Almond could almost see the theme in his mind take shape. "A landing in their rear," MacArthur would say, musing. "Something to cut off their supply line. If I had some other force to use as an enveloping element far to the rear I could do it. . . ." These, more than once, were approximately his words, as Almond would remember them later.

He was probing the idea now. He mentioned it at a meeting of Army, Navy and Air Force representatives as early as July 4, before the first real battle between Americans and North Koreans was fought, and out of this came a hasty plan for landing the 1st Cavalry Division somewhere in the rear, with a Marine Corps amphibious expert, Colonel Edward H. Forney, to give them training in amphibious techniques. This plan was given the name "Operation Bluehearts" and assigned a tentative target date of July 22. The place was perhaps to be Pohang-dong, on the east coast of Korea, or Kunsan on the west coast, but before the planners could so much as adjust their thinking caps, the North Koreans pushed forward and there was a more immediate need to delay their advance.[1]

Strangely enough, at least one unit in Japan was already in the midst of amphibious training, begun the day the war started. That was the 5th Regiment of the 1st Cavalry Division now going through beach exercises on the broad shores

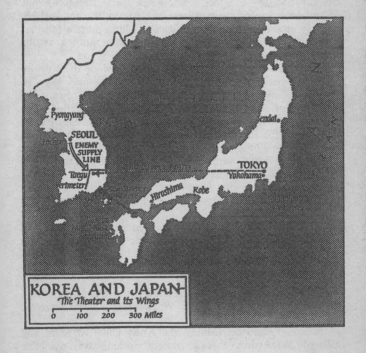

KOREA AND JAPAN
The Theater and its Wings
0   100   200   300 Miles

of Chigasaki, a little south of Tokyo, one of the areas that had been marked as an invasion point in World War II before Japan's abrupt surrender. There was much for an ordinary foot soldier to learn if he was to attack from the sea. Something about ships and boats had to be known, there was the matter of waterproofing combat equipment, safety practices that applied even in shallow water, the business of climbing down nets from ships, a little knowledge of tides and currents, the difference between reading maps for land and charts for water—in effect, a whole new specialized technique.

And, not so strangely, there was within the total U. S. military establishment an organization whose precise business it was to attack from the sea. They were known as the United States Marine Corps.

Marines had been in virtually every war since the Revolution, and because of their participation in World War II, they were involved in the Occupation of Japan. From the beginning of the Korean War, their flyers were called upon to assist the Navy in its various strikes and missions. Marines throughout the Pacific were organized under what was called Fleet Marine Force, Pacific, with its headquarters in Hawaii.

The FMFPac Commander was Marine General Lemuel Shepherd and, like most Marines, he wanted to get into the war. He dropped into MacArthur's headquarters on about the 9th of July, primarily to see if all was well with his units in Japan. While he was waiting to be ushered into MacArthur's presence, he chatted with Ned Almond, whom he'd known as a cadet at VMI, and from the 6th Marine Division that had been under MacArthur at Okinawa.

"I wish we could get more Marines out here," said Shepherd.

Almond said, "Well, General MacArthur has asked everybody for any kind of troops. We were told there were no more Marines available."

General J. Lawton Collins, the Army Chief of Staff, had assured MacArthur that absolutely nothing was available when MacArthur had earlier specifically asked for Marines, and doubtless, from the viewpoint of world commitments, this was true enough at the time.

Shepherd said, "Well, I can get you a division of Marines if you'll just ask for them."

Almond raised his eyebrows. "You can? How long would it take?"

With almost no hesitation Shepherd replied, "I can get a

division assembled three weeks after you ask for them, and in another three weeks I can put them anywhere in the world you want them."

This was the kind of talk Almond liked to hear. "Lem," he said, "you'd better tell that to General MacArthur."

"All right, I will," said Shepherd.

He was closeted with MacArthur perhaps twenty minutes. When he came out again he was grinning and said, "By God, the General's all for it!"

"Fine!" said Almond. "You put your thinking cap on and I'm going in there and tell him to ask for what you said you could produce, and we'll have a radio out of here by tonight!"

Almond went into the eagle's nest and found MacArthur also elated. He was looking from the window, pipe in hand, and he turned immediately, smiling, as he heard Almond come in. "Shepherd tells me he can get me a division!" he said. "That's not what Collins has been telling me!"[2]

At 2 P.M. MacArthur's G-3, Major General Edwin K. Wright, a hard-working, cheerful officer whose reddish hair and fresh complexion had given him the nickname of "Pinky," prepared the cable to Collins, and—most fortunately, as it turned out—gave Shepherd a copy and sent another information copy to Admiral Forrest P. Sherman, Chief of Naval Operations, who was Shepherd's ultimate boss. It was the correct administrative thing to do, and a small matter on the face of it, for these information copies might well have been left out without materially altering the basic idea of transmitting a request, but for once clean paperwork and good administrative manners paid off, and it was the copy to Admiral Sherman that in the end did the trick.[3]

In Washington the Joint Chiefs of Staff met, General Collins dutifully reported the cable he'd received, and drawing on what was the best of his knowledge, said it was, of course, out of the question. But Admiral Sherman said he didn't think it was an impractical idea at all. Collins looked surprised, asked for details, and when he had them, sent a quick message back to MacArthur saying his request had been discussed in a meeting of the Joint Chiefs and that everything possible would be done to fulfill it.

Up to this point researchers and planners had been working hard to find all the places where an amphibious landing might be possible, to study them, and translate their material into comprehensible form. MacArthur's G-2 section had begun a landing plan for Inchon that was called "Operation Bluehearts," but before they had worked on it for more than a day or two, Walker's situation at the Perimeter called for a more immediate landing at a place called Pohang on the east coast. "Operation Bluehearts" thus became the Pohang landing instead—an amphibious transfer of troops near the northeast corner of the Perimeter on July 18. Although mounted and equipped as an assault landing, it turned out to be unopposed. Meanwhile, the planning staff kept what little intelligence they had gathered concerning Inchon and continued to look into Inchon's possibilities. The bulk of this early research was being done by a naval force known as Amphibious Group 1, commanded by Rear Admiral James H. Doyle, a tall, spare, untalkative but quick-minded naval officer who had taken part in amphibious warfare at both Guadalcanal and Tulagi in World War II.

It was almost as though the Inchon landing had been preordained. Doyle and Phib Group 1, as everyone called it, had come to Japan in January of 1950, in the normal course of peacetime military operations, specifically to train army troops in the mystique of amphibious operations, and casting about for examples, had already examined some of the problems that might be encountered in what was regarded as an extremely hypothetical landing at Inchon, and had even discovered one of Admiral Nimitz's old plans for World War II for a Korean invasion.

At the moment when MacArthur began to have hope of getting a Marine Division, Phib Group 1 had momentarily laid aside considerations of an Inchon landing and was busy with the more immediate problem of setting up a ferry system for troops and supplies into the port of Pusan.

But Admiral Doyle was on hand with exactly the talent MacArthur needed, both at this stage and later. Phib Group 1 was a group of naval experts who had been together a year and a half planning practice landings in Hawaii, the west coast of the United States, Alaska and other points. They did their work on the command ship *Mt. McKinley*, a vessel about the size of a large transport at the moment anchored in Tokyo Bay, but presently they would continue their feverish researchers, with an expanded staff, in the Dai-Ichi Building itself.

They were actually deep in plans for four landings; the 1st Cavalry at Pohang on the east coast (which they did not know would be unopposed), a possible landing at Wonsan, also on the east coast but further to the north, one at Kunsan, many miles south of Inchon, and an Inchon landing itself.[4]

MacArthur had been briefed on all the various plans as they developed, usually in digested fashion through Ned Almond, and shortly after Lem Shepherd's visit, when Collins had cabled there might be a Marine Division available after all, he called Almond in, waved the message, and said there would now definitely be a strike at the enemy's flank. "If we make this operation, this will be the eleventh amphibious operation I've commanded, and the largest one. The objective is Seoul. Have the staff make a study of the possibility of a strategic landing in the rear of the enemy." He went to the map and his pipestem touched Wonsan, on the east coast. "Maybe here."

Almond leaned forward and pointed out the distance across Korea to Seoul, some 160 miles. "Well, General MacArthur," he said, "Inchon is much closer to your objective."

MacArthur nodded in agreement but said he still wanted data on all possible sites.

The task of continued planning now was passed along to one of the unorthodox cells in the great honeycomb of MacArthur's headquarters, JSPOG (pronounced "Jospog") or the Joint Strategic Plans and Operations Group, a collection of several officers from each of the four branches of the armed forces. It was headed by the tall, deliberate, somewhat studious Colonel Donald H. Galloway, who had been a West Point cadet when MacArthur was superintendent, and who had served in VI Corps with Ned Almond in World War II. A year before, MacArthur had been under pressure from the Joint Chiefs in Washington to set up a joint staff in his Far East Command. His staff was mostly composed of Army men whom he knew, and in whom he had confidence; he didn't care for the idea of replacing them with men from other services who would be strangers to him. So he set up JSPOG, a kind of staff within a staff, and put it under his G-3 section, a move that quieted down the demands from the Pentagon.

Colonel Galloway, the JSPOG chief, now received through Almond a note in MacArthur's own handwriting: "Prepare plans for an amphibious landing in the vicinity of Inchon on or about September 15."[5]

Galloway called a quick meeting of his personnel. They were select people, carefully picked by each service to represent it in the joint group, and in the opinion of Pinky

Wright, the G-3 under whom they worked, "a highly competent group, and I doubt that their like has ever been assembled elsewhere."[6]

After Colonel Galloway explained the need for an Inchon landing plan, immediate objections came from the table. The Navy men at once called attention to the great tides—thirty feet or so at high water—and the swift currents at Inchon, to say nothing of the rocky surroundings and narrow channel. Both Army and Marine officers, speaking of the troop assault over a narrow beach into a hilly city of 250,000 used the word "Impossible!"

But it would be done, Galloway reminded them, and with Almond, a hard driver for all his courtly manners, on their necks, it would be done damned soon. When Galloway had asked when the plan was wanted, Almond had snapped, "Have it tomorrow," and Galloway still wasn't sure that he hadn't meant it literally.[7]

There was still the day-to-day war to be run in Korea, and that took most of everybody's time in MacArthur's headquarters, but the plan for an amphibious invasion was now an undercurrent running through everything. General Collins's trips from Washington to Tokyo became more frequent, and he seemed to regard the Inchon idea as an uncomfortable risk the more he learned about it. He was quite right, of course; it was a risk. The only real question was whether or not to draw a deep breath and take it. Possibly because of Collins's lack of complete enthusiasm, MacArthur each day became more firmly attached to the notion of Inchon as a landing site.

Ned Almond attended briefings almost daily as new material was brought to light on all the possible landing points; occasionally MacArthur himself would listen in, but for the most part Almond reported to his Chief what he'd learned. General Collins was being closely advised, too. He cottoned toward Kunsan, a hundred miles below Inchon. On one visit he said to MacArthur, "Well, Kunsan is a suitable place because of the difficulties at Inchon—particularly that tide."

MacArthur said, "But if you land at Kunsan you merely extend the west flank of General Walker's army. You do not *envelop* the enemy."[8]

But General Collins was beginning to be aware of some of the truly formidable obstacles to a successful landing at Inchon. When the Navy's Phib Group 1 had been told to drop the Inchon plan temporarily to concentrate on more immediate matters, most of its members had felt relieved, and one officer, Lieutenant Commander Arlie G. Capps, summed it up piquantly for all the history books by saying, "When we were ordered to stop work on the Inchon invasion on July 10 we all breathed a sigh of relief. We had done enough research to realize its dangerous potentialities. We drew up a list of every conceivable natural and geographical handicap—and Inchon had them all."[9]

Place, time and tide—these were the problems, though not necessarily in that order. Take the tides first. The bigger landing ships needed twenty-nine feet of water to get in, and there would be that much only on September 15, October 11, or November 3. But the tides would rise to this height only twice on each date, and stay high for about an hour each time, although there was no real slack water. That meant two separate landings some twelve hours apart, each to be accomplished with incredible speed.

Time? Well, MacArthur wanted the earliest date, not only to relieve the Perimeter as soon as possible, but for political reasons, to return the capital of Seoul to South Korea by the end of September, only ninety days or so after it had been taken. By the time Inchon was definitely decided upon, that left a bare thirty days in which to get ready for it; no major amphibious landing in history, and not even Phib Group 1's practice landings, had been planned in less than six months.

And finally, place. Inchon was a city in enemy hands. Traditionally, you landed on wild lonely beaches, not city waterfronts. There were sea walls all along the waterfront that would have to be scaled, Inchon harbor itself was dominated by a high, small island, Wolmi-do, connected to the mainland by a mile-long causeway, and Wolmi-do was a natural fortress. At that, the invasion fleet might never even reach Wolmi-do. The approach through the mud flats, extending in some places two miles out to sea, was through a winding, narrow passageway of six to ten fathoms known as Flying Fish Channel, in which a capital ship wouldn't even be able to turn around under its own power, and a few well-placed mines could put a stop to everything.

That much at least was known about Inchon at this stage in the game. But it wasn't nearly enough knowledge, and all over MacArthur's headquarters, which in the natural course of things had become an unwieldy echo of the mazelike Pentagon, planners and experts and near-experts and honest men assigned to jobs for no reasons they could discern were trying to find out more, often duplicating each other's efforts, often stepping on each other's toes, frequently eying each other suspiciously, or quarreling over who had charge of what and for how long.

The main planning for Inchon was being done by JSPOG, but later much of it would be the province of a Special Planning Section that would grow into X Corps, the landing force. The specialists of Admiral Doyle's Phib Group 1 were continuing their studies from the naval viewpoint. Pinky Wright in G-3, Plans and Operations, sat on top of it all, and under him the supervisors were supervising the supervisors.

Lieutenant Commander Jack Lowentraut, Assistant Operations Officer for Employment, Phib Group 1, had tried to contact Wasington for information on Inchon and Washington had replied, in effect, "Our information on Inchon is all boxed up somewhere in a warehouse in St. Louis and it will take us six months to get it out."[10]

Lowentraut and his colleagues scoured Japan for people who might know something about Inchon. He found an Army warrant officer, W. R. Miller, who had operated harbor craft in Inchon harbor for a year or so just after World War II. Lowentraut used aerial reconnaissance photos to glean information from Miller on Inchon. Here were the tidal basins where ships were floating after the tide ran out. Were they usable? Did the gates work? Did the tides run the same on one side of Wolmi-do as on the other? What were the surface conditions on the causeway leading to Wolmi-do? What were the beaches like when dry? Could you drive a truck on them? And so on, with time ticking away.

There were charts and tide and current tables available, as there are for most places in the world, but they were several years old, and the swift waters around Inchon constantly changed the contour of the bottom. If they didn't know exactly what it was like, a destroyer or an LST could promptly ground itself during the landing, and become a sitting duck for shore fire.

Admiral Doyle, Phib Group 1's commander, was to become a staunch supporter of the Inchon gamble, but when he saw the roughed-in total plan for the first time in Colonel Galloway's JSPOG office, he said, half in jest, "Don, if you think a plan like that would work, you ought to have your head examined."

Galloway laughed and said, "Better check with General

MacArthur, Admiral. Maybe his head better be examined, too."[11]

In Boston, a good-looking young Marine of Irish descent, Sergeant Patrick P. Byrnes (no relation to the apostolic delegate to South Korea), was, as he told it afterward, "sittin' on my haunches" in the Navy Yard, with the duty of chauffering some colonel around. He'd been a tanker in World War II and his Military Occupational Specialty (MOS) was still 1811, tank crewman. He was following the war in Korea and wishing he could be in it. Somewhere, in some headquarters, the file cards were flipping and before long his MOS number and then his name would be picked.

In San Diego, Corporal Joe Maize was just readjusting himself to Marine life with the First Marine Regiment. Joe was a stocky, friendly, dark-skinned young man whose father was a full-blooded Kiowa Indian and whose mother had been a Mexican refugee from the Porfirio Díaz revolution. Joe had originally joined the Marines during World War II and had learned, among other things, how to box, studying under a Marine named Lee Rodak, then featherweight champion of the world at San Diego.

Joe Maize enjoyed a certain small fame throughout the tight fraternity of the Marine Corps, having supplied its scuttlebutt sessions with one of its favorite stories. He'd taken part in the amphibious invasion of Okinawa, and on a rainy night just after the landing had been sent back to the beach to assist the unloading detail. He got lost in the rain and darkness on the return trip, and suddenly was pounced upon by a sentinel patrol of the United States Army. Joe, a Pfc., was wearing old fatigues, no chevrons, and was carrying neither dog tags nor ID card. Now it happened that Joe had taken a six-week course in Japanese at Norman, Oklahoma, before going out to the Pacific, and when, in the darkness, he heard the rifle bolts of the Army patrol clicking, he thought they were Japanese and called out: *"Chotto-matte ku-dasai!"* ("Hold on—wait a minute!"). When he was captured, they took one look at his darkish skin and Kiowa features and rushed him to the prisoner-of-war compound. There he was questioned all night, until finally, when he said he was from Texas, they brought in an officer from Texas who threw a test question at him. A real Texan would know about football scores. "Who won the Southern Conference?" asked the officer. Joe answered that there was no Southern

Conference in Texas, just a Border Conference, and that cleared him.

After World War II, he'd worked at odd jobs and done a bit of boxing, but in his heart he wanted to be back in the Corps. Then he read an article in *Leatherneck,* the official Marine magazine, entitled "Once a Marine, Always a Marine," and that did the trick; he went to the recruiting office the next day and asked to be recalled to active duty.

Joe was assigned to the 1st Marine Regiment, which was just being taken over by Colonel Lewis B. "Chesty" Puller at Camp Pendleton, California. Chesty Puller was a Marine legend. A career Marine since World War I, he wore more combat decorations than any other Marine in the Corps, and carried marks and scars to match. His nose was mashed at the bridge, his voice was growling and gravelly. He walked with his shoulders thrown back tightly and his chest sticking forward in exaggerated pride. In the field he had contempt for comfort and his idea of a regiment command post was a foxhole with a radio operator somewhere nearby. A pipe smoker and pipe collector, he always took one short-stemmed pipe into combat with him; it was easier to carry and handle.

Sergeant Byrnes in Boston, Corporal Joe Maize in San Diego, and Colonel Chesty Puller would all be taking part in the Inchon landing along with several thousand other Marines now scattered throughout the world—along with other thousands of young men who weren't even Marines yet, but were being recruited feverishly.

When General MacArthur had asked for more Marines, the Joint Chiefs of Staff had passed the request along to the Commandant of the Corps, General Clifton B. Cates; he'd replied that the only way to bring the 1st Division up to wartime strength was to call in the Reserves. President Truman authorized the call-up and Congress approved. Cates began to pick at the Marine detachments in embassies all over the world for experienced personnel. He went as far as the Mediterranean, where Marines were serving with the 6th Fleet, for additional units.

The goal was to have a wartime-strength division in Korea by the middle of August. It was sent in two increments: a Provisional Brigade in the middle of July, with the rest to come along when they were properly organized and trained— if the activity of those few weeks could be called proper training.

Experienced NCO's like Pat Byrnes and Joe Maize sometimes had their doubts. They worked hard with the fresh-faced youths that came pouring in and hoped that by the time they first heard shots fired in anger they'd have more than short haircuts to show that they were Marines.

So MacArthur's Marines were on the way, or at any rate, half of them were. But things were too critical on the Perimeter for him to hold them in reserve until it was time for the landing; Walker needed extra manpower as soon as he could get it, and it was just as important for Walker to hold as it was for the landing itself to come off successfully.

Brigadier General Edward A. Craig, USMC, arrived in Tokyo July 19, four days after the Provisional Marine Brigade he commanded left San Diego by ship convoy for Japan. The 4,713 Marines aboard didn't know that before they were halfway across the Pacific, they'd be ordered to go directly to Korea rather than to Japan.

In modern military organization, a brigade is, in a sense, not a standard unit, just as a Brigadier General (a "buck general" to GI's) dwells in a kind of purgatorial rank and is usually given odd jobs until such time as he earns his second star. The Navy, indeed, ignores the one-star rank, which it calls Commodore, except in a time of declared war, and ordinarily jumps its men from their captain's eagles right up to the two stars of a rear admiral. In land forces, the basic unit is the regiment containing three battalions. Each battalion in turn is made up of about three companies, although various special companies to handle specific needs, such as artillery, reconnaissance, transportation and administration, are sometimes attached. When two or more regiments are put under one command it is called a division, and the divisions themselves make up armies. It never works out this neatly of course, and fighting forces are organized in wars or campaigns according to the needs that arise.

The First Provisional Marine Brigade was really the 5th Marine Regiment augmented by a number of attached units. Lieutenant Colonel Murray's 5th had the usual three battalions, but the brigade itself also had sixteen other units of varying size, from a military police detachment to the 1st Reinforced Battalion of the 11th Marine Regiment. There were service, signal, ordnance, military police, and combat service detachments; there was a medical company, and tank and anti-tank companies. For artillery there was a 4.2 mortar and a 75-mm. Recoilless Rifle company. There was an engineer company and a reinforced amphibious tractor battalion. A unit of Corsairs for air strikes was also included.

The hard-pressed Johnny Walker, on the Perimeter, must have watered at the mouth to know this formidable force was on the way. In a few days, however, he would learn that MacArthur had these Marines in mind for an amphibious landing—nothing one hundred per cent definite, for approval from Washington was still needed, and there were some signs that such approval might not be forthcoming—but the gist of the thing was that Walker could only have the Marines until early September, when he might have to find a way to do without them.

Brigadier General Craig, arriving in Tokyo by air with the principal members of this staff, reported immediately to General MacArthur. He received a cordial greeting as most MacArthur visitors did, along with the double-armed handshake, the smiling but penetrating gaze, and a few well-placed personal remarks out of the quick briefing before the visitor appeared. MacArthur chose the subject of the United States Marines themselves as the utensil for his buttering-up technique this time.

There were those, he told General Craig, who had inferred that MacArthur didn't like the Marine Corps, but on the contrary he was a great admirer of Marines, had commanded them in the South Pacific in World War II, and would like to have them fighting for him at any time. He then lit his pipe and sat down to discuss the business at hand.

General Craig explained that the provisional brigade was now at peacetime strength, as were all the Marine Corps units, but he felt that they were nevertheless well-equipped and armed, and to make it even better, they had their own air unit, commanded by Brigadier General Thomas Cushman. The brigade had trained extensively with this unit and knew its ways; they were, in other words, an effective fighting team. MacArthur frowned at this a little, and asked about the other Marine units being gathered from all over the world to come to Korea to augment the brigade and form the 1st Marine Division. These, too, said General Craig, were at peacetime strength.

MacArthur immediately called Ned Almond in. He wanted a dispatch sent to Washington right away requesting that all Marine units he was to get, including the brigade, be brought up to wartime strength.[12]

Craig was particularly concerned to know who would

command his precious air wing; he'd heard rumors that all air effort in Korea and Japan was to be under General Stratemeyer's Far East Air Forces. Like most Marines and Army officers, and as a matter of fact, like many combat GI's at the front, his private opinion was that Air Force pilots lacked the extra push and daring that meant so much in ground-support missions; airmen didn't even care too much for the term "ground support," since it implied a secondary role. They preferred long-range strategic bombing or interdicting enemy supply lines in the rear.

Indeed, the Air Force, while often giving valuable support in the ground fighting, had struck at mistaken targets or friendly forces enough times to earn an uneasy reputation. At the outbreak of war they had strafed Suwon when the KMAG officers were there and shot up several retreating South Korean columns. When the enemy had harried Ambassador Muccio's small plane and bombed and strafed near MacArthur himself, MacArthur had called Stratemeyer, who explained that the Japan-based planes had only enough fuel to stay over their Korean targets for short periods. MacArthur had then told him to go ahead and bomb the enemy wherever he could.[13] Stratemeyer had taken this to mean that FEAF's primary mission was to hit the enemy behind their lines. It was never really cleared up as to whether MacArthur had actually meant this, and it was one occasion, at least, on which this great professional soldier slipped and gave an ambigious directive. In the Perimeter, Air Force planes ripped up a British unit when Panel signals became mixed, so that General Walker personally apologized to the British commander.[14]

All in all, it was understandable that Marine General Craig wanted to work with his own air power. General MacArthur assured him that he'd control Marine air as long as he was under MacArthur's command and immediately sent a directive to the Far East Forces to that effect. Craig always felt afterward that this had an important bearing on the subsequent success of Marine combat operations in the Perimeter.

MacArthur also told Craig that he was determined to carry out an amphibious landing at Inchon. Until now it had been only a possibility, a dream that could be abandoned if it proved unfeasible. As late as July 10, when Galloway's JSPOG planners had given a presentation on Inchon during one of the almost daily briefings on amphibious landing possibilities, MacArthur had said, "Of course we can't execute this right now, but keep it available."[15] Since that date, however, he had spoken increasingly of a flanking movement as desirable, and of Inchon as the optimum site. By the 19th of July, apparently, it was firm in his mind, possibly because the actual presence of his Marine commander, at last, with a brigade of amphibious fighters on the way, jelled it all into absolute reality for the first time.

"This landing," he told General Craig, "will bring the war to an end."

"I left General MacArthur's office," General Craig wrote later, "feeling much better regarding the whole situation. He impressed me with his efficiency and confidence and was most friendly. I felt that here was a man who I would work for to the limit."[16]

Fully briefed, therefore, General Craig arrived in Korea by the 26th of July. The day before, Pinky Wright had told him he'd conferred with Washington by radio telephone and that the 1st Marine Division and Marine Air Wing would be brought up to war strength. In Taegu, Craig went to General Walker's scholhouse headquarters, was briefed again by the fiery little armored cavalryman, and was lent Walker's personal plane for a thorough reconnaissance of the battle area. He found Walker also most cordial, as well he might be, for here was help at last; over four thousand Marines ought to be in his front lines by the first week of August.

While in Taegu waiting for his Marines, Craig also did a little preliminary research on the upcoming landing. He looked up Harold Noble, an economic aid man in Muccio's embassy, who had stood with Colonel Wright and General MacArthur on the south bank of the Han the day MacArthur refused the binoculars. Noble had learned a great deal about the Korean countryside, and was particularly familiar with the beaches at Inchon. There was also on duty with the embassy a Marine Corps sergeant who had been an amtrac driver and had explored Inchon harbor. Craig found their information rather discouraging: the tides ran out swiftly, exposing long mud flats; the sea walls were nearly fifteen feet high; the city of 250,000 was filled with narrow streets and dotted with hills and rises from which a defending force could pour superior fire upon any invaders. Craig frowned, and had his G-3 jot down bits of this information on a map of Inchon. He was not discouraged—he had confidence in MarArthur—but he saw that the operation might be tougher than he'd thought. He wrote later, "Of course I did not have a real opportunity to study the Inchon situation thoroughly or I might have changed my mind."[17]

As night was falling on the 3rd of August, Lieutenant Colonel Raymond L. Murray and his 5th Marine Regiment watched from the decks as their transport came alongside the dock at Pusan. They were in combat gear, ready to step ashore, and their rations and ammunition were already laid out on the deck.

Murray, tall and tough looking, stood at the rail as the ship came alongside the dock. Suddenly, he saw his new commander below, Brigadier General Eddie Craig. Craig called up, "Did you get our dispatch?"

"No sir, what dispatch?" said Murray.

Craig smiled a little. "You're to leave right away for the front lines!" he called.

Murray grinned and nodded; as far as he was concerned, something like that was par for the course in this Marine business. He ordered the rations and ammo on the dock issued to the men and then conferred with Craig further, getting detailed orders to take his 1st Battalion toward a place called Masan by truck and there await the rest of the regiment, which would travel by train. The whole movement, Murray reflected, had about it an air of haste and off-the-cuff maneuvering. He and the 5th Marines had left Camp Pendleton in California on the 10th of July with no written orders and only the vaguest understanding that they were to proceed to Japan and stand by for an amphibious operation; then, in mid-Pacific, the ship's radio had received an order that they were to go to Pusan in Korea instead. He wondered if there'd be enough of South Korea left to accommodate his regiment as he looked around in the lowering dark and saw the forms of ships everywhere, all over the harbor and along the docks. He'd followed the news by radio on the way across the Pacific and it had seemed to Lieutenant Colonel Murray that there might not be a Perimeter left by the time he arrived.[18]

Then the trucks arrived and the men of the 1st Battalion clambered in and jolted some thirty miles down a badly kept road to the west, stopping just short of Masan near a few scattered houses that bore the village name of Ch'angwon. There the Marines, self-contained, broke out their tents and C-rations and bivouacked for the night. The next morning they moved into headquarters in a nearby bean field that was to be known to them ever afterward as the Pea Patch. Army elements were in contact with the enemy less than five miles away, and they could hear the rumble of gunfire quite clearly. Within three days that gunfire would be directed at them, and they would be returning it.

The Marines who had come to Korea were cocky, as Marines are expected to be, and like the first American battalion to face North Koreans only a short month ago below Seoul, they were to a man confident they'd push back this Asian rabble in short order. Their favorite slogan as they moved ashore was, "Tell Mac we're back!" Their first mission was to join the Army's 5th Regimental Combat Team in a two-pronged attack directly westward. A few miles beyond their bivouac the road was forked; they were to take the left-hand fork, the Army the right. Coincidentally, however, just as this attack out of the southwest corner of the Perimeter was launched in order to relieve the pressure on Pusan, the North Korean 6th Division was starting its own drive down the same two roads, and the opposing forces ran headlong into each other. That wasn't the worst of it. The North Koreans, that early August, began furious blows all around the Perimeter in a desperate effort to break its defenses once and for all and drive the Americans and South Koreans and their allies into the sea.

Yokohama harbor was glassy and still on the morning of August 6, as a big gray transport from Oakland, California, was pushed gently toward a pier by a couple of Army tug-boats. Leaning on a rail for his first close look at Japan was Second Lieutenant Jesse F. Van Sant, a platoon leader in C-Company, 73rd Tank Battalion, United States Army. Although he wore a shavetail's gold bars, young Van Sant had already seen a bit of war and a great deal of military life. He had enlisted as a Marine in World War II, served as a diesel mechanic and instructor on tank engines, then had come back to finish college at the University of Kentucky, and had promptly entered the Army, determined to make a career of it. Van Sant was of medium build, less than medium height and quite fair in both hair and complexion. His coloring was perhaps a throwback to his original Dutch ancestry. The sixth child in a family of ten, Van Sant had the agreeable nature of one raised among a gaggle of siblings, and in neither appearance nor personality did he give the impression of a formidable fighting man. But buried somewhere within him he had a fine, instinctive talent for the military art.

Jesse Van Sant was delighted to be approaching the shore

of Japan this fine morning, for he'd heard all the tales of the pleasurable life there, but he was a little puzzled as to just what sort of assignment he'd receive or why someone of his particular background was needed in an Army of Occupation where there was a shooting war going on not far away. Because he'd been a Marine and because his tank outfit had taken part in several important amphibious exercises, he was considered partly an amphibious expert and it seemed to him that knowledge like this ought to be useful somewhere in Korea. All that he and the men of his company knew at the moment was that they were to debark here at Yokohama—at least, so they thought. En route from Oakland the ship's radio had received a long operational message which apparently referred to the tank outfit aboard, but no one had been able to decode it, so they decided to wait until they arrived and then find out what it said.

As Van Sant watched from the rail, some sailors threw a line to the pier, and then suddenly a port official with his retinue came along and ordered the line thrown back again.

The ship's bullhorn sounded with the voice of the skipper from the bridge. "Hey! What's wrong? Wrong pier?"

The port official had his own bullhorn. He lifted it and everyone aboard heard him say, "Hell, no! Wrong port!"[19]

The message they'd been unable to decode had directed them to Pusan, Korea, where they arrived the next day. General Walker had been desperate to get this 73rd Tank Battalion and all their M-26 Pershing medium tanks with their 90-mm. guns. Until now he'd been pitting light tanks with 75-mm. guns against the monster, Russian-built T-34's, and the light tanks had been getting the worst of it.

Debarking at Pusan, the battalion was immediately split up and its units sent to the various points on the Perimeter where they were needed. Jesse Van Sant and C-Company were transported promptly to the front lines only a few miles from General Walker's Taegu headquarters, where it looked very much as though the enemy was about to break through.

A good commander looks ahead, and General Walker, masterfully shuttling units back and forth along the Perimeter wherever they were needed, was a good commander. His former boss, George Patton, had once called him "the best corps commander in World War II." Like Patton, Walker was impatient with headquarters protocol and always resented having to go through Chief of Staff Ned Almond to get to MacArthur. Among his many busy projects in these madden-

ing summer days when the temperature in South Korea sometimes reached 112° was to have the Eighth Army engineer
start preparing a last-ditch defense around the city of Pusan.
He hoped, of course, it wouldn't be necessary, but as a good
commander, he was looking ahead.

Word of the project floated in to MacArthur. He was
furious. "We won't put a spade in the ground!" he said.
"There'll be no defensive moat around Pusan!" He promptly
sent a cable to Walker to that effect—[20] and continued to plan
for Inchon, come hell or high water.

NOTES *Chapter 3*

1. Manuscript review comments for author, Almond, 8 May 67.
2. *Ibid.*
3. Interview author—Capt Jack L. Lowentraut USN; letter Vadm James H. Doyle to author 13 Oct 66.
4. Interview author—Col Donald H. Galloway.
5. *Ibid.*
6. Letter Maj Gen Edwin K. Wright to author Sept 66.
7. Interview author—Galloway.
8. Interview author—Lowentraut.
9. Karig et al, p. 161.
10. Interview author—Lowentraut.
11. Interview author—Galloway.
12. Memorandum Lt Gen Edw A. Craig to author Oct 66 (here-after Craig memo).
13. Interview author—Farrell.
14. Interview author—Lt Gen Alonzo P. Fox.
15. *Ibid.*
16. Craig memo.
17. *Ibid.*
18. Interview author—Maj Gen Raymond L. Murray USMC.
19. Letters Lt. Col. J. F. Van Sant to author, 1 Apr & 4 May, 67.
20. Interview author—Lt Gen James Polk.

4

"When a guy gets killed you . . . treat him as a hero . . . ."

AT THE END OF PIER 2 ON PUSAN'S BUSY WATERFRONT, ONE day in mid-August, Commander Michael J. Luosey and Lieutenant David C. Holly, USN, were bustling about in a small office to make it presentable for a visit by no less a personage than Syngman Rhee. Luosey, a tall, energetic, positive man, and Holly, a former instructor at Johns Hopkins University who looked upon war and the world with an air of mild astonishment, presided in this office over a somewhat shabby empire, but one with at least a resounding title. They were the chief U. S. advisors to the Korean Navy, and as such, their designation was DEPCOMNAVFE, or Deputy to the Commander, Naval Forces, Far East. There was a crude sign over the office door to that effect. There was a similar sign on a battered old Dodge sedan an embassy attaché had brought to Pusan in the flight from Seoul and loaned them for official use.

Syngman Rhee entered the office flanked by several South Korean admirals and generals, greeted the two young naval officers with smiles and kind words, and at least pretended not to notice the dusty, bare-walled room with its helter-skelter collection of furniture scrounged from a dozen sources since Luosey and Holly had occupied the office several weeks before.

Rhee was seventy-five years old; his moon face was a mass of wrinkles, but he could still move about in sprightly fashion and his mind was alert, his prejudices deep-rooted and stubborn. He'd suffered once from frostbite and whenever he became agitated, would rub his hands together vigorously. He had first been elected to the presidency of Korea in 1919, and left the country to head the government in exile during World War II. He returned in 1945 and was elected president in 1948.

With his perfect command of English and knowledge of western ways, Rhee enjoyed a high level of communication with his U. S. allies. His earliest education had been in a Methodist mission school in Seoul; he had become a Christian and married an Austrian wife. Before 1910, he had studied at George Washington, Harvard and Princeton Universities in the United States. Upon returning to Korea, he had resisted Japanese rule and had been forced to flee to Hawaii where he directed the Korean Christian Institute until 1939. The unification of North and South Korea, with himself as leader, was an obsession with him, and he was tragically willing to use any means to bring it about, suppressing the slightest opposition with iron police-state law and urging attacks anywhere, even at the risk of starting World War III, in order to bring the two Koreas together. The general feeling among old Korea hands was that he welcomed the North Korean invasion and the opportunity to fight back that it afforded.

But he was most congenial in person, and protocol at the moment called for the two young naval officers to honor him as an ally and the head of a friendly state. Rhee walked to the nearest chair to sit and Lieutenant Holly stepped forward to warn him that its seat, from which the springs had been removed, sagged unduly, but it was too late and Syngman Rhee sank deeply, all but losing his balance. With a look of surprise he rose again and took another chair, making no comment.

His visit was to discuss with the American advisers an amphibious landing being planned by his South Korean Navy. Luosey and Holly had been in their seedy office in Pusan most of July and the first part of August now, working round the clock at their mission of running the Korean Navy and encouraging it to grow. In addition, they had the responsibility of getting Pusan's naval facilities in order so that supply ships could begin pouring in, and on the side, they acted as naval liaison officers with Walker's Eighth Army in the Perimeter.

The two Americans had the feeling that the South Korean plan for an amphibious landing a little to the west of Pusan had been approved in higher headquarters as an activity that would keep the R. O. K. Navy busy and stop them from bothering MacArthur and his staff with trivial matters. Any-

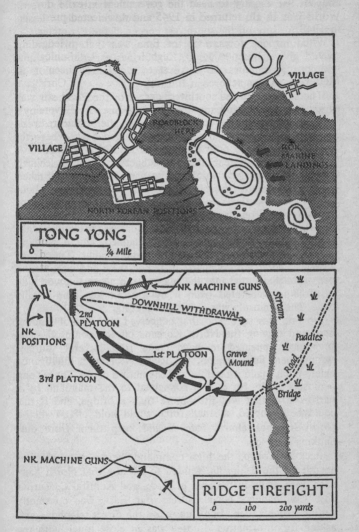

way, it had been approved, and the truth was it didn't seem a bad idea at all; if it succeeded, it would do much to lessen enemy pressure on the southwest corner of the Perimeter.

What no one foresaw at the time was that this landing would give about 600 R. O. K. Marines experience in amphibious operations and make them a valuable addition to MacArthur's assault force at Inchon.

The situation in the southwest corner of the Perimeter was this: The North Korean 6th Division, one of the enemy's finest, was hammering at the line there, attempting to break through and take Pusan. As the line surged back and forth, they were at times only thirty miles from the vital port. A little to their own rear, they were backed up by the North Korean 7th Division, which had reached the coast and taken up positions there. Just off the coast at this point, and about twenty miles southwest of Pusan, was the big fertile island of Koje-do, an irregular shape some twenty miles long and twelve wide, known for its farms and dairies. It could sustain an army, had good ports, and if occupied, would outflank Pusan and even neutralize it as a supply point. The North Koreans weren't on Koje-do yet, but they had occupied a peninsula that jutted into the sea and ran along the west side of Koje-do, separated from it by a strait less than a mile wide. The peninsula was called Tong Yong.

No one was sure who first conceived the idea of landing here and driving the North Koreans off the peninsula. The suggestion appeared to have come from several sources, among them Spike Hahm, the R. O. K. Navy's intelligence chief. What made it feasible was the nature of the Tong Yong peninsula itself, for it was connected to the mainland by a narrow strip that was little more than a bridge, and if this could be occupied, a small force could hold off advancing North Koreans almost forever and keep them from outflanking Koje-do.

Back in Tokyo, the high command, before approving an assault on the peninsula, wanted to be sure that North Koreans were really in the area in force, and Admiral C. Turner Joy, Commander, Naval Forces Far East, was constantly getting Commander Mike Luosey on the direct telephone and asking for information. Luosey was in close touch with the Korean Navy which supplied a great deal of intelligence about the enemy situation, its small boats making runs to points all over the peninsula, usually at night, its officers and men infiltrating easily into places where Caucasians would have been conspicuous.

South Koreans were able to supply MacArthur's G-2 (Intelligence) section with a major portion of its knowledge of the disposition of enemy troops, and much of it came to Colonel James Polk, the Executive Officer for Intelligence under Colonel Charles Willoughby.[1] Polk, a rather earnest career intelligence officer, was the great-grand nephew of the famed Bishop Leonidas Polk, who fought as a colonel for the Confederates in the Civil War, and like most staff men in Tokyo these days, he was working hard on the Inchon landing project, running agents into Korea through the lines and on the coast, searching the U. S. military establishments for men of Korean extraction, and overseeing the interception of North Korean radio messages in a dozen listening posts strategically placed near the battle zones. He had a rule that any piece of information had to be corroborated by at least five agents before it was considered first-class data, and many of his spies were double agents, originally sent from the North Korean side. "You don't shoot spies," he would say. "You double them and send them back."

There was a personality clash between the quiet Polk and his flamboyant boss, Colonel Willoughby, and often a disagreement as to methods between them. Willoughby was a firmly ensconced member of MacArthur's palace guard who was given to forming strong opinions and holding on to them stubbornly, often not letting himself be sidetracked by facts. Once Willoughby wanted to send a systems-analysis team to Korea to find out why tanks were being lost. He recommended a computer section in each tank battalion to compute losses. Polk discussed this with Major General Doyle O. Hickey, Far East Command Deputy Chief of Staff, a forceful no-nonsense officer, who said, "Let's recall Nathan Bedford Forrest in the Civil War. When a bugler asked to join his cavalry he said, 'We need more shooters and less tooters.' Well, right now we need more shooters and less computers."

Once, when Polk dared to say too firmly he thought Willoughby was wrong, the intelligence chief had thrown three books at him. A few days later he'd come up to Polk and asked, "Are you still mad at me?" Polk had said, "Yes, sir, but I'll take that as as apology."[2]

Ordinarily, therefore, it was the Koreans who reported what was taking place behind enemy lines, but when the R. O. K. Navy proposed a landing at the Tong Yong peninsula, Admiral Joy wanted some information reported by his own people and Commander Luosey decided to send Lieutenant Holly on a special junket to the area. Schoolteacher Holly had been somewhat amazed all along at the way everything was done with verbal orders—and pleased at the speed with which things got done this way—and on this occasion it was no different. A few phone calls managed to bring a destroyer to the docks at Pusan, its captain in receipt of verbal instructions to take Holly wherever he wanted to go. Holly directed the ship to a shore village called Son Champ-po a little west of Pusan, and of Chinhae, the site of the R. O. K. Navy's principal base. The destroyer anchored in deep water far offshore, and Holly and his Korean interpreter took a whaleboat in. In the town he found no North Koreans, but talked with civic and police officials who gave him their estimates of the nearby enemy positions, and seemed to confirm the intelligence that there was a garrison of nearly a thousand men on the Tong Yong peninsula. Holly headed further inland, and after about fifteen miles of travel over narrow roads in the dark, he reached an advance Observation Post of the Eighth Army's 25th Division in a schoolhouse near a village. (Schoolhouses were always favorite places for Command and Observation Posts all through the Korean War, possibly because they afforded conveniently laid-out buildings without residents; General Walker himself used one in Taegu for his Eighth Army headquarters.) The soldiers at the OP were astonished to see Holly and his interpreter, and assured him that he had walked through enemy lines to get to them, although Holly assured them in return that he hadn't seen any enemy. In the morning they set out to return to the coastal village, and on the way, from the crest of a hill, saw what appeared to be a North Korean Command Post or supply point less than a mile away in a shallow draw, with soldiers moving about a number of oil drums. When Holly finally got back to his destroyer he reported this location, and an air strike was sent to demolish it. The 25th Division OP he'd visited was overrun by the enemy shortly after he left it.[8]

Because the supply point had been destroyed, Holly felt his nominal run behind enemy lines had accomplished some good, even if he hadn't managed to bring back any startling new intelligence. Anyway, the amphibious landing at Tong Yong was scheduled to come off on August 19, and he and Luosey would watch with much interest to see how their protégés would fare. Neither knew of the plans for an Inchon landing at this time, although like everyone else they'd heard rumors and had even had direct questions from their Korean friends about such a landing. Preparations for it had begun to generate furious activity in a number of places, principally in Japan, which was perforce filled with North Korean spies, and it was a hard secret to keep.

In the small but excellent harbor of Chinhae, just west of Pusan, where the R. O. K. Navy was now principally based, Commander Lee He Chung was readying PC-703 for the attack on the Tong Yong peninsula, and drawn up beside it were the Republic of Korea's two other patrol boats, PC-701 and 702. Lee, the man who took Clark to the island off Inchon about ten days later, was commander of the entire expedition, and Spike Hahm was acting as skipper of his boat at this time. An LST (Landing Ship, Tank), left over from World War II, was being loaded with South Korean Marines, most of them newly recruited, some of whom had never so much as fired a practice round with their pieces, old Springfields supplied by the U. S. Army.

Gunnery Sergeant Chu Dong Han, of A-Company, 1st Battalion, was one of the few who did know something about soldiering. He'd joined the R. O. K. Marines a year before when they were more closely attached to the Navy. His 1st Battalion, since the outbreak of the war, had been engaged in flushing out guerillas on the big island of Koje-do, and he had trained a bit near Pusan firing the M-1 rifle for the first time. He was a lean, tall, hard Korean with slightly northern features, although he had actually been raised around Pusan itself.

He crouched with his comrades somewhere in the hollow confines of the R. O. K. Navy's only LST as it moved out of the harbor and into the severe chop of the open sea. The big, boxlike landing ship was designed to put tanks ashore, not ride the waves, and Sergeant Chu and dozens of others became violently ill. He spent the rest of the day wishing he were dead as the tiny fleet pushed on toward Tong Yong and reached it at nightfall.

Just ahead of the troop-carrying minesweepers, the three patrol craft began to bombard the narrow peninsula with their three-inch guns. PC-703's bombardment was so enthusiastic that Spike Hahm was later censured by his superiors for using more than the planned amount of precious ammunition. The LST pushed heavily into a beach, dropped its bow ramp, and the Marines went ashore.

The met enemy fire from heights inland as soon as they hit the beaches. Sergeant Chu was surprised to find that when firing started, and he heard the not-too-distant reports of small arms and saw an occasional comrade fall, he was not as frightened as he thought he'd be, although he was by no means enjoying the experience.

There was a large, ridgelike hill in the middle of the peninsula, Won Mun Hill, and on the other side of it, the town where the North Koreans were garrisoned. The first fire they met came primarily from outposts and pickets on the hill. Lieutenant Colonel Kim, commanding the battalion, led it northward along the foot of the hill to the point where the peninsula narrowed and connected with the mainland. Meanwhile, small parties with radios fanned out to the crest of the hill, set up observation posts there, and looking down into the North Korean camp, directed fire from the ships. The little South Korean Navy craft had by now taken positions on either side of the peninsula and were shelling from both the right and the left.[4]

All through the darkness of the next morning, the North Koreans tried to slip through the line the Marines had formed across the neck of the peninsula. A few made it, but many more were shot down or bayoneted in brief hand-to-hand combats. There was a story that grew up afterward in the R. O. K. Marines, and was repeated with interest by their U. S. allies, that they had felt for heads in the darkness and if the heads were shaven, their owners were North Koreans and should immediately be bayoneted. But Sergeant Chu never believed this romantic tale, because even in the dim light on the night in question you could tell friend from foe at a distance of a few yards, and besides, many of the R. O. K. Marines, enthusiastically emulating their U. S. Marine mentors, had procured short haircuts, right down to the skull, for themselves.

In the morning the North Koreans attacked the thin line across the peninsula neck in more organized fashion. By now the positions on the hill had been augmented and strengthened, and from these a murderous flanking fire was poured down on the enemy troops.

The North Koreans fell back. Those who were unable to flee the trap holed themselves up in mine shafts on the western slope of Won Mun Hill. It now became a kind of siege, with the R. O. K. Marines unable to storm those strong positions. Word of the situation came back to Commander Luosey in Pusan. It semed to him that an air strike was the only way to neutralize the enemy in the mine shafts, and he got on his single telephone and called for one, naturally from his own Navy.

There were aircraft carriers up and down the Korean coast —the *Valley Forge*, the *Philippines Sea*, the *Sicily*, the *Badoeng Strait*, and the British carrier *Triumph* among them. Marines fighters flew out of southern Japan to come in for strikes when called upon. (In cocky pride the Marine pilots of the *Sicily* had painted "U. S. Marines" in letters three feet high on their wings and fuselages so they wouldn't be mistaken for anyone else by ground troops.)

But on this occasion, no naval or marine aviation was available; they were busy with missions all around the beleaguered Perimeter and the little sideshow at Tong Yong didn't seem to have any desperate strategic or tactical importance. Luosey had to go to the Air Force, though it much offended his pride. Besides, he hated the U. S. Air Force with a grand passion. The R. O. K. Navy ships were not well marked and lacked good communications, so in recent weeks Air Force planes had shot up several of them at sea; the situation became so bad that Luosey, a mere commander, had been bold enough to send a message directly to Admiral Joy's COMNAVFE headquarters say, "The ROK Navy will cease to operate if the USAF does not desist its bombing of ROK ships."[5]

The Air Force came through magnificently this time, bombing and strewing napalm on the side of the hill at Tong Yong and making it possible for the R. O. K. Marines to secure the peninsula. As a matter of fact, now that the war had progressed, their reputation for hitting friendly troops was no longer deserved, and an overall system of air control had been worked out that did much to prevent such mistakes.

Still, in these days of the Perimeter, when Johnny Walker was holed up in his tight rectangle at the southeastern tip of Korea, the Air Force seemed a bumbling arm, eager to help, but not quite the weapon for this kind of in-fighting, with the opposing armies in what amounted to a clinch. At the moment their most valuable work was in airlift, but this was an unglamorous job that didn't attract notice. Their fighter squadrons based in Japan, using primarily F-80 Shooting Star jets, did their best to fly ground support missions, but were hampered by the distance which allowed them to be in the target area only a few minutes before it was necessary for them to return. Huge B-29 bombers, the type that had brought Japan to its knees in the closing days of World War II, were also standing by and all but inventing missions to get themselves into the act.

It went back to World War II—a different kind of war—when General "Hap" Arnold had fought to make the Army Air Forces an independent arm and when evaluation after the war showed that his AAF had indeed contributed materially to victory by its strategic long-distance bombing in the German rear. After the war the AAF became the USAF, with many air tasks assigned, but geared primarily to long-range bombing. As the youngest of the services, the Air Force lacked its own traditions and history, and began to try too hard to build an image for itself. When its new blue uniforms came out, pilots were sternly admonished to keep the grommets in their hats and not try to look like the flop-topped cavaliers of World War II who had softened hats to allow for the bands of earphones when they flew. In Korean War bombing missions, aircrews no longer scrambled with *élan* toward their waiting planes but lined up formally before climbing aboard, received their final instructions, and saluted the airplane commander. Small matters, to be sure, and no one complained much about the insistence on military discipline—but it was all reflection of the almost pathetic desire of the Air Force to convince the other services that it could be just as military, just as important, as anyone else.

Important they were, if only to be on hand and available for another long-distance war, should it start. They were valuable on many occasions when their jets and World War II prop-driven Mustangs flew well-directed ground support. Heroic they could be, like any other group of individuals in a war. But the thinking of their generals was still tuned to the long-range bomber mission as the basic job of an air force and this war was confined to a dirty little arena where the distant bomber targets were too few, too insignificant.

Three days before the Tong Yong landing, nearly a hundred B-29's clobbered a battlefront area seven and a half miles long by three and a half miles wide in a "carpet-bombing" strike widely hailed by the press. It happened because the enemy was threatening to break through at the northwest corner of the Perimeter near Walker's Taegu headquarters. The pressure, in fact, had become so bad that on August 18

Syngman Rhee moved the seat of his government south to Pusan, though Johnny Walker would stay in Taegu, which was filling up with refugees so that its population had risen from 300,000 to about 700,000.

It was apparently MacArthur's own idea to saturate the threatening North Korean wedge with bombs from the air; there is no precise record of who first suggested it, and it was the sort of dramatic, unorthodox move that MacArthur liked to make. On August 14 he called in General Stratemeyer, commanding the Far East Air Forces, and Major General Emmett O'Donnell, Jr., who headed the Far East Bomber Command. O'Donnell, nicknamed "Rosie" because of his somewhat florid complexion, was a stocky, fighting airman from World War II who had informal Irish charm and was regarded by those who served under him as genial but tough.

MacArthur wanted to know if O'Donnell, with the B-29's available to him, could decimate a small area of land—say, a three-by-five mile patch—and practically blow it out of existence. O'Donnell wouldn't quite go so far as to say it could be annihilated, but he thought his ninety-eight planes, some based in Japan and some on Okinawa, could do a relatively good job.

The area MacArthur had in mind was only thirteen miles northeast of Taegu. This was where the enemy was breaking through, and where, according to intelligence reports, the North Koreans might have as many as four divisions plus several armored regiments, altogether around 40,000 men.[6]

Two minutes before noon on August 16, the B-29's began to strike, and in twenty-six minutes dropped 960 tons of bombs from an altitude of 10,000 feet. The bombs were five hundred pound and one thousand pound general purpose bombs. Rosie O'Donnell himself went along and tooled around the target area for more than two hours. He reported that there was no sign of enemy activity in the area.

There was so much smoke and dust that for a whole day ground troops observing from nearby hills were unable to determine results, but when the dust settled the next day, patrols went forward to take a look and were promptly driven back by enemy fire. Later, after prisoners had been interrogated, it developed that the enemy hadn't been precisely in the bombed area after all and that the strike probably hadn't killed a single North Korean soldier.

After this both General O'Donnel and General Walker

were against ever trying carpet bombing again, and General
Stratemeyer personally had to talk MacArthur out of a second
scheduled try for the 19th of August.

But the Inchon landing was coming up less than a month
from now and Air Force planners felt that at least they'd be
able to do some valuable work on that operation, which more
nearly came under the heading of their specialty of striking
behind the lines. As matters developed, they were to be left
out of the Inchon operation, but they didn't know it this
mid-August.

Sergeant First Class Roy E. Collins, United States Army,
had been in this discouraging war for quite a few weeks, and
he knew it was more than a matter of driving a few ragtag
and bobtail bandits out of the hills. He was the lean, tough,
laconic leader of the second squad in the second platoon of
Company A, 1st Battalion, 34th Infantry Regiment. He was
not pleased to know there was another jump-off this morning
of August 15, just after daybreak. He was not pleased to be
exposing himself to enemy fire again, although that was his
job and he'd do it when told to, but he was especially apprehensive about the platoon itself which included twenty-
four replacements who had belonged to it only three days,
and nine men without the slightest combat experience. He
also had a few doubts about his young platoon leader, Lieutenant Edward L. Shea, who had proved himself in combat
and whose courage was unquestioned, but who, in Collins'
opinion, still had a few things to learn about tactics. But
then, that went for all the other platoon leaders and also for
the company commander, himself a lieutenant, Albert F.
Alfonso.

Company A moved forward this morning as part of what
was a general attack up and down the line, although Sergeant
Collins at the time didn't know the entire picture. This movement was part of a general counterattack being mounted by
three regiments of the 24th Infantry Division in a sector of
the Perimeter about halfway up in its western boundary
where, a week ago, thousands of North Koreans had begun
to cross the Naktong River, which formed a huge bend here,
making a kind of bulge along the Perimeter. It was only one
of the desperate situations the harried General Walker was
trying to cope with, as blows fell upon defenses on both the
northern and western lines. One counterattack had already
failed. They were going to try again this morning.

Company A's small part in this attack—small to everyone but its members—was to take a ridgeline four hundred feet high and about one and a half miles long. The Communists were holding it with at least one machine-gun nest atop a low, rocky cliff on one of the ridge's crests.

Collins glanced at his platoon mates as they assembled on lower ground southeast of the ridge where a narrow dirt road ran through some rice paddies and then along the foot of the ridge beside a stream. They were still far enough from the objective not to draw any fire and somewhat protected by the natural, wavelike rises in the ground on the way to the ridge. He felt, as he watched the men deploy into a loose formation for the advance, that there were only a few present who could be regarded as combat-tested and dependable. Among them was Master Sergeant Willie C. Gibson, the platoon sergeant who, as Collins understood it, had known combat in World War II. Most of the others were either unknown factors or completely green. Like Pfc. Edward O. Cleaborn. Cleaborn was a Negro, loose-jointed and athletic looking, and he'd seemed sensible and pleasant enough when he'd joined the outfit, but Collins, who had no special prejudice against Negroes, was nevertheless aware of the sickening reputation of the 24th Regiment whose members bugged so shamefully when the mortars began to thud. His feeling was that there wasn't much he could do about it, so he might just as well forget Cleaborn was there, at least as far as expecting any performance out of him was concerned. And that went for most of the others too.

Now, as the sun came up dimly through murky weather behind them, Company Commander Alfonso outlined the method of his attack to his two platoon leaders, Lieutenant Melvin D. Schiller, of the 1st Platoon, and Shea, of the 2nd. Company A was leading off the attack for the whole battalion, and the 1st Platoon would be the spearhead for Company A. The 2nd Platoon would come along behind it. That was where Collins and his second squad would be.

Back in the reserve area, Collins had had a chance to read *Stars and Stripes,* published and printed in Tokyo, rushed by air to Korea, and distributed free to the troops there. With its experienced and talented staff and fine facilities in Tokyo, it looked and read just like a first-class stateside metropolitan daily. Frequently it would show, along with the current news item about the war's progress, the map of the Perimeter, which wasn't changing much from day to day during this hot

August, with a neat line drawn to show the front between the U. N. defending force and the enemy. The line just wasn't that neat out here in the dust and jagged hills. What the front amounted to was an irregular, uneven area where units down to company size had command posts in various places, in villages, in draws, on hilltops, sometimes several miles from the nearest enemy troops, sometimes within sight of their positions. These units were not always necessarily in contact with each other. They might be separated by a matter of miles or yards. Outside the command post, usually forward, but often to each side and sometimes to the rear, were stretches of land not controlled by either side, and according to orders, you went out into these zones from time to time to take objectives—hilltops, ridges, villages, crossroads. There were attempts to keep everyone informed as to the overall situation, but it was impossible to communicate to each G. I. the purpose of each maneuver every day. The one thing they all knew was that it was rough all along the Perimeter and that as soon as the enemy was stopped or slowed down in one spot, he would hammer at another, not only on this western line where the Naktong River made a natural boundary for much of it, but along the line north of Taegu from a point fifty miles inland out to the east coast of the peninsula.

Well and good. There was a job for Company A this morning. Take that ridge.

The 1st Platoon started out along a road and, walking slowly in broken combat formation—one squad on the point many yards ahead, the other following cautiously—came to the southeast corner of the ridge. Here they slanted off and started across fields and rice paddies in an oblique line toward where the ground began to rise. The 2nd Platoon came along behind. Altogether, the column of the entire company stretched back perhaps a little less than half a mile.

There was a separate hump of high ground before the ridge itself began to rise steeply. Lieutenant Alfonso, the Company Commander, brought the squad leaders of the 1st Platoon here and pointed out the objective and the general route toward it. They were near the southern tip of the ridge; several peaks rose from it as it ran northward, and if the first peak could be taken they'd be in a good position to advance toward the others.

The enemy was undoubtedly up there somewhere. For

concealment he had rocks, gullies and scrub foliage. At the moment there was no sign of him.

Alfonso used his back-pack radio to call in a barrage from the mortars stationed on another rise some distance to the east, out of sight. Moments later the shells came, exploding in great, curling cabbages of smoke and flame at various spots along the ridge. It sounded much like blasting in a nearby quarry, except that the explosions were more frequent. The barrage lasted for fifteen minutes. Then Alfonso requested a halt to it and sent the 1st Platoon forward, heading northeast, and up the ridge.

It was perhaps a mile to the first peak, possibly a little less. Moving forward at a wary crouch, the men of the 1st Platoon, led by Schiller, made their way upward about a quarter of the way. Suddenly there was the sound of two enemy machine guns from the higher ground to the left, and the ground began to spurt where the bullets hit, while chips flew from boulders that were struck and the whine of ricocheting slugs embellished the chatter of the guns. There were no tracers and it was impossible to tell exactly where the fire was coming from. The men of the 1st Platoon hit the dirt and found what cover they could. The machine guns stopped firing momentarily.

Lieutenant Alfonso called Lieutenant Shea of the 2nd Platoon over to him, along with his squad leaders. "Ed," he said, "take your platoon up through the stalled unit there and continue to advance."

Shea nodded and said okay, but he and Sergeant Collins looked at each other doubtfully. It was not so much the situation—platoons had advanced under enemy fire before—as the composition of their unit: one third of the men were green, the other two thirds had never worked together as a team before.

Lieutenant Shea said, "Come on, let's take a look at it," and started up the hill. Nothing happened until he came within spitting distance of the men of the 1st Platoon, all crouching in cover over a small area, bunched in small groups, and then the machine guns opened again. The men of the 2nd Platoon hit the dirt, too, and Shea, peering upward and forward, saw Lieutenant Schiller, fifteen or twenty yards above him, crouched behind a dirt grave mound about four feet high and covered with neatly trimmed grass.

Collins stayed where he was, behind the dubious cover of some humped ground, and watched the two platoon leaders confer. Every once in a while one of them would raise his head to peer over the grave mound toward the source of the machine-gun fire. Occasionally there would be short bursts. Just above the two platoons and near them was the first peak of the ridge, a kind of rounded eminence. As the ridge continued northward, there was a saddle formation for perhaps four hundred yards and then another more jagged peak with a small rocky cliff forming one of its sides. The machine-gun fire seemed to be coming from their left and toward the second peak.

Lieutenant Schiller, the 1st Platoon leader, raised his head for another look. A machine gun stuttered and he fell. At first Collins was not sure whether he'd ducked or been hit. Then as he watched he realized that not only Schiller but his own platoon leader, Lieutenant Shea, had been wounded. He learned later that it had been a freak accident: a slug had struck Schiller's helmet, penetrated, followed a wild course around the interior of the helmet, severely cutting and bruising his head, then had passed through his shoulder and struck Lieutenant Shea in the thigh just above the knee. One bullet had taken out both platoon leaders.

Remarkably, neither man was unconscious and now they motioned for the men in the platoons to fire in the general direction of the machine-gun positions. As about sixty men sent slugs in rapid fire toward the machine guns, a medical aid man ran and crawled up to the two lieutenants, and the company commander, Lieutenant Alfonso, made his way upward from below and by motions directed both platoons forward in a leap-frogging maneuver, one platoon firing while the other advanced a few yards. As the first two platoons moved forward, the third, which was the reserve unit, came along behind them.

By this method the whole company, in another fifteen minutes or so, gained the first peak of the ridge, where they crouched behind a kind of natural embankment that faced north over the long saddle leading toward the next peak. Occasionally they could see the dim and flitting figures of enemy soldiers in the vicinity of that next peak. On their own rise there were a few freshly dug holes, but no other signs of the enemy.

Collins checked his ammunition and saw that he still had plenty left. Some of the new men, he thought, had fired too often and too wildly, wasting ammunition they might later need. Before they'd started out, each man had loaded himself with two bandoliers and a bull bolt of M-1 clips, altogether 176 rounds, and most men carried one or two hand grenades.

Master Sergeant Willie C. Gibson now inherited the leadership of the 2nd Platoon. Lieutenant Alfonso told him to take his men forward and get the cliff four hundred yards away, across the saddle. The 1st Platoon would stay behind the embankment and cover his advance with their fire.

Gibson nodded, lined up his four squads, and told Sergeant Collins to stay at the rear of the line and make sure all the men moved out. Collins looked at the men, and understood the precaution. They were white, nervous, scared. Collins had to admit to himself that he was scared, too, but the difference was that he wasn't showing it.

And then suddenly one of the platoon's recent replacements, a cocky, stock corporal named Lee M. Brennen who, Collins knew, had fought in the Pacific in World War II, jumped forward, pulled the pin partly out of a grenade and slipped the ring over his finger so that the bomb was ready to throw, and said, "I'll be the first man to go—the rest of you guys follow me!"

Before anyone could think further, Brennen jumped over the embankment and began to run along the saddle toward the cliff. Other men who had been hesitating and staring fearfully at the objective a moment ago began to follow him, one after the other, each about fifteen yards apart. Collins remembered looking at his watch at this point. It was 8:45 A.M.

Led by Brennen, the men ran a little to the right of the saddle's high point, just below the crest, to protect themselves from fire that might come from the opposite side. As the fourth man in line jumped from the embankment, the machine guns opened up from the rocky cliffs in several short bursts. The unexpected always happens in combat, and this fire struck none of the advancing men but, queerly, caught two members of the 1st Platoon behind the embankment, hitting one in the eye and the other in the neck, killing both. It now seemed more fearful than ever to the remaining 2nd Platoon men to leave the embankment and run forward, but to a man they did, impelled by that strange desire of most combat men not to flinch before their peers, and now the running line was strung out along the ridge, the men crouching, dodging, making a zigzag progress forward, and those behind the embankment blasting away at the rock cliff.

When all but two men were out, Corporal Joseph H.

Simoneau rose to follow in his turn and bullets struck him in both the leg and shoulder. The force knocked him backward and he cried out, "I'm hit!" Collins jumped forward, pulled him in behind the embankment, and yelled down the line for a medic. Then Collins himself went over the top.

As Collins tagged along at the rear of the line, he saw that the wildly brave Brennen, far ahead, had already reached a point near the rock cliff. At this proximity, Brennen could see three North Koreans in their dusty, faded khaki sitting around their machine-gun tripod, looking oddly relaxed, as though they were merely having target practice on a range. They were only about twenty yards away. He tossed his armed grenade at them. At is exploded, he suddenly noticed from the corner of his eye a second machine gun, just below the cliff, partially concealed by some boulders and scrub, but even nearer to him than the first. Desperately he swung his M-1 in that direction and fired an entire clip. Simultaneously, the second machine gun swung toward him and opened up. A bullet slammed into his leg, knocking him down. There was no pain in that first instant; it was as though someone had swung a huge two-by-four and knocked his underpinnings from him. He rolled and slid down the steep hill on his right until, a moment later, he was in a protected spot and out of the line of fire.

Now there was firing, confusion, yelling and the screams of the wounded all along the saddle. It was impossible to fix attention on any individual action, but the general situation was that the men of the 2nd Platoon had stopped running forward and were crouched just below the crest of the ridge on its eastern side. Enemy fire had now begun to come from its western slope.

Collins inched his way forward. He, too, carried a grenade at the ready, the ring over his index finger. He saw that several men were wounded and that each, after he was hit, tended to slide back down the ridge as Corporal Brennen had done. So there was a growing group of wounded down there, and for some reason Master Sergeant Gibson, the acting platoon leader, was helping the medics care for them when he should have been up on the crest still leading the platoon. It wasn't cowardice, for Gibson had already run the gamut of fire, but it was one of those faintly irrational moves men often make in the confusion of combat.

Collins took over direction of the platoon, running along

crouched just below the crest of the ridge, moving men back and forth as needed to make a more even firing line.

At one point he moved upward a little too much, exposing his head to the opposite slope. He heard the hollow cough of a burp gun on his left. Glancing that way he saw a North Korean, quite close, firing at him. He tossed his grenade and threw himself flat. Over the crest he saw the explosion of the grenade and the burp gun flying up into the air. He rose to a crouch again. Another North Korean was picking up the fallen burp gun. Collins raised his M-1, snap aimed, shot, and saw the man fall backward.

Like so many other Americans who had sallied forth along the Perimeter to meet these strange, swarming Asian soldiers, he was wondering where they all came from. The ground seemed to be breeding North Koreans like maggots. They were swarming over the other side of the ridge; the fire was hot and heavy all along the saddle, and even back at the first peak where the 3rd Platoon was holding in reserve. Collins didn't know it at the time, but the 3rd Platoon was pinned down by heavy fire.

There were now dead and wounded men all along the ridge. The wounded were yelling for medics. Nearly everyone was yelling for more ammunition. Collins grabbed a nearby private and told him to run back to the Company Commander and get more ammo, especially grenades to toss over the ridgeline. The private looked greatly relieved and took off in a zigzagging run.

Then Collins began to go along the line and collect ammunition from the wounded or the dead, parcelling it out to those who called for it.

In less than ten minutes the runner was back again. He gave Collins a note from Lieutenant Alfonso. It said, "Pull out."

At that moment, up near the rock cliff, a corporal named Joseph L. Sady yelled toward Collins: "Hey, they're pulling a machine gun up here! Gimme a grenade!"

Collins tossed the note away, ran forward and handed a grenade to the corporal. He tossed it over the ridge and said, "There—that'll take care of them!"

The grenade exploded, partially out of sight. A moment later a North Korean popped up from the ridgeline ten paces away from Corporal Sady and shot him in the head. Someone nearby immediately shot the North Korean.

The right of the line seemed to be holding as well as could

be expected, and Collins now made his way back toward the other flank. Abruptly another Sergeant First Class, Regis J. Foley, who had come up from the 3rd Platoon to join the fight, came sliding down the ridge with his helmet knocked off and bleeding from the head, apparently hit by a ricochet. Collins bandaged him quickly and told him to go back to the Company Commander and for God's sake get more help. He didn't know why he was ignoring the lieutenant's note to pull out. It just didn't seem the time to let go of things yet.

The fight continued while the wounded Foley worked his way back. Again it was a gaggle of fire, shouts and screams. More men were yelling for ammo. Some men were beginning to fix bayonets.

Sergeant Roy Collins was in the midst of a tiny action that would be reported in a cold line or two up at division headquarters, and possibly not even specifically mentioned back in Taegu where General Walker was running the entire army, but he was sharing now with the highest-ranking generals the experience of the frightening moment of decision when, in the space of several seconds, scores of imponderable factors must be weighed, and a decision made. It seemed to him that the platoon would never get extra ammunition in time, for it would take the founded Foley at least five minutes to reach the company Command Post, and at least another five minutes before it could be sent along. All around him men were either dropping as casualties or firing their last clips. There was no way to control their fire now, and in his heart he couldn't blame most of them for squeezing off a whole clip when one or two shots would have sufficed—he'd known that same panic in his own first experience in combat. "Okay!" he yelled, moving up and down the line to be sure everyone heard. "Come on—let's get out of here!" and looking down the slope, he saw Master Sergeant Gibson still with the wounded and shouted for him to get them out, too.

Then, in the middle of the firing line along the saddle, Collins saw the Negro soldier, Pfc. Edward O. Cleaborn, standing tall almost on the crest and firing furiously at a group of North Koreans who were trying to set up a machine gun a short distance down the other slope. There was something magnificent and defiant about him there as he ignored cover, kept firing, and between clips yelled things like, "Come on up, you sons of bitches, and fight!" The heat of combat was upon him.

"Get down, Cleaborn! Get down!" Collins yelled at him.

Cleaborn turned and looked at Collins with a deliberate calm that seemed almost absurd. "Sergeant," he said, "I just can't see 'em when I get down!" Then he turned and continued firing.

Collins sighed and bent over to take the ammunition belt from another dead man.

Much to his astonishment, a North Korean soldier suddenly jumped over the ridge, ran past Cleaborn and threw himself at Collins, grabbing him tightly about the waist. He was unarmed and Collins was at a loss to understand his action. He struggled and spun to throw the man off, but the North Korean continued to hold on tightly. Cleaborn, from the crest, saw this and rushed toward Collins to help him. When the North Korean saw Cleaborn coming he kept shifting himself to the opposite side of Collins, and suddenly it came to Collins that his man wanted to surrender. He waved Cleaborn away and shoved the prisoner back down the slope toward Master Sergeant Gibson who was still evacuating the wounded along a gulley that led down to the foot of the crest.

A man with a bandaged head came running toward him from the left of the line and Collins saw that it was Sergeant Foley whom he'd sent for ammunition. Foley had another note from the lieutenant. Withdraw, get the hell out.

There were six men left at the ridge line, Cleaborn among them. Collins yelled at them to pour one last volley toward the enemy, then pull back with everybody else. The dead were all around Collins—of the thirty-five men in the platoon, only ten were unhurt. The men at the ridge fired their volley, then turned and began to run back.

All except Pfc. Cleaborn. "Just one more clip!" he yelled back to Collins. He stepped back to load it. A bullet struck him in the head and killed him.[7]

Second Lieutenant Jesse Van Sant sat in a tank in a narrow valley only twelve miles north of General Walker's headquarters in Taegu. It was night, the 21st of August, and it was dark in this long flat corridor of land between two mountain ridges that swept up to 2,500 feet or more. The valley was less than a mile wide in most places and extended in a straight line for several miles, forming a classic terrain feature that might have been constructed in a sand table at a tactical school—"Here, gentlemen, we have a typical narrow-valley situation"—and in the past week or so, it had been dubbed "The Bowling Alley" because the rounds from the

North Korean tank guns came down it at night like so many fiery bowling balls.

Van Sant's platoon, attached to a battalion of Lieutenant Colonel John H. Michaelis's 27th Infantry "Wolfhound" Regiment, had been sent into the Bowling Alley as part of a maneuver to stop the enemy at this key point, before he broke through and took Taegu. The movement was another of Johnny Walker's quick shuttling of units to points where they were needed.

The entire 13th North Korean Division was ready to attack down the valley and along the bordering ridges this evening, and as their advance units were spotted moving forward, their assault was no secret. An outpost telephoned back that nineteen enemy vehicles, tanks and self-propelled guns were coming down the road, full tilt, and Jesse Van Sant and his platoon of five tanks sat in their blocking position and waited quietly for them.

It was dark, of course, and the American gunners wouldn't be able to sight on the enemy tanks as they approached. Van Sant had therefore made "range cards" the day before, in which the proper azimuth and elevation settings were given for various points on the road and the surrounding terrain. The range cards were helpful, of course, but Van Sant knew that the only sure way to knock out T-34's was to hit them from as close as possible, for only then could their more vulnerable spots—the throats of their turrets, for example—be picked out and hit.

And there would be visibility of a sort as soon as the North Korean tanks were near. They were up the road somewhere, right now, hordes of infantry advancing along with them, and American battalions and their artillery on either side of the road had already begun a confused duel with them; explosions, tracers and flares were lighting the valley in a great firework display.

Suddenly Van Sant and the men of C-Company's 4th Platoon could see the forms of the approaching tanks by the light of a flare or explosion, momentarily, as in a throb of lightning. "Hold it," he cautioned over the radio, reminding his men of his strict instructions before night fell. "Hold it, now." The moments were agonizing as the first of the T-34 tanks barreled down upon them. "Hold it!" The lead tank was but thirty feet away. The infantrymen coming along beside it were also at that distance.

Van Sant himself fired the first round from the 90-mm.

gun in his tank and that was the signal. That little road through the valley erupted in flame and explosion for the next two minutes. The lead enemy tank was destroyed, and dozens of North Korean infantrymen were mowed down by machine-gun fire. The column drew back, badly stung. All through the valley that night, a five-hour battle raged, and when morning came the enemy had lost 1,300 men and seven tanks. Among the decorations passed out later to individuals for their various parts in that night's action was a Silver Star for Second Lieutenant Jesse Van Sant in recognition of the courage he displayed in holding his fire until it was certain it would be effective.[8]

Van Sant and his combat-tested companions would be called upon shortly to add their knowledge to the assault upon Inchon and the drive inland. General Walker, still hemmed in at the Perimeter, would not enjoy losing them, but MacArthur's mind was made up, and it was at Inchon that his more shining resources would be gambled while Walker did the best he could with whatever was left.

Bravely, bravely they held on in the Perimeter during those hot, humid, hellish days of August. R. O. K. divisions held the northern line. U. S. divisions stood firm in the northwest corner where Taegu was perilously close to the line, where the North Koreans at times managed to push to within seven or eight miles of Walker's schoolhouse headquarters. Along the western border of the Perimeter the line was held as divisions, regiments, and task forces were shifted back and forth according to need. Somewhere on this line Sergeant Collins had seen his platoon all but decimated on an un-named ridge, and on another part of this line, where the Naktong River formed a wide bend known as the Naktong Bulge, the enemy managed twice to cross the river and penetrate the Perimeter, but each time the Marine brigade sallied out of the pea patch in Masan, farther south, to march to the north and throw them back. The line held at its southwest corner where it came to the sea and where the great port of Pusan was threatened.

The Air Force had finally taken hold, and its strafing and napalm strikes were doing much to help hold the line. Eight fighter squadrons operating out of southern Japan mounted over seven thousand sorties in August, directed by T-6 Mosquitoes—advanced trainers from World War II—that flew out of Taegu in relays and maintained almost constant daylight cover over the battlefront. A tactical air-control center in Taegu directed the pilots by radio, so that the bombing and strafing of friendly troops lessened, and men on the ground began to welcome the appearance of planes. They were always friendly planes—the Fifth Air Force had complete control of the skies over the battlefront. B-29's, meanwhile, were hitting bridges, railyards, docks, and industrial plants up north, but the good effects of this effort would not be felt for some time yet.

The reinforcements kept pouring into Pusan. In the Perimeter, General Walker now had at his disposal three infantry divisions and one cavalry division, totaling around 61,000 men, plus the R. O. K. Army of about 91,000, a British infantry brigade of 1,500 and well over 4,000 Marines.

There were hundreds of actions like the fight on the ridge by Sergeant Collin's platoon. As in all wars, American soldiers in their first combat embroilments showed fantastic bravery and quickly became veterans, hardened and battlewise, and if they had any weakness it was in the well-meant but awkward fumbling of their junior officers and in their lack of training when they first arrived.

The cocky, professional Marines—many of whom were also without adequate training—looked upon the Army men when they moved into a sector as troubleshooters. Lieutenant Nicholas A. Canzona, in later years an official historian of Marine action in Korea, moved along with Lieutenant Colonel Murray's 5th Regiment as part of an engineer platoon, and cast a cold, professional eye on the discrepancies he saw. A tough Marine, but at times intellectually inclined, with a deep voice and a boxer's nose, Nick Canzona was interested in all aspects of tactical science, and as he moved forward to the First and Second Naktong battles, he noted young soldiers carrying carbines but supplied with .45-caliber pistol ammunition; he saw tanks used without infantry support, and he observed men moving out on patrol with their rifles slung rather than held ready. Once he came across a small detachment, in the forward area, that the night before had crept under a bridge to sleep out of the rain. He found them slaughtered, for the enemy always looked under bridges when they came to them, and there was no sign that they'd posted any guards while they rested. It saddened him. He could not bring himself to feel smugly superior and later he would shrug and say, "When a guy gets killed you have to treat him as a hero no matter what he did."[9]

There was something eternally jaunty about the Marines, part of their carefully nurtured *esprit de corps*, no doubt. In the midst of everything, they would find time, as Canzona did, to collect several score of North Korean motorcycles they found in a valley where an enemy motorcycle regiment had been destroyed; they had a field day driving them around for the sheer hell of it, and some even managed to get the vehicles back to the Pea Patch. They were most disappointed later when they learned they wouldn't be able to take the bikes with them to Inchon, and at that point sold them to Koreans or to members of other services as souvenirs. They also found a Russian jeep, a Ford, in good running order, that had been lend-leased to the Russians in World War II. This fetched fifty dollars which, with the motorcycle money, went into a platoon fund that eventually bought things like engraved souvenior lighters for the men.

Sergeant Pat Byrnes, the tank crewman who had been sitting on his haunches in Boston when the war broke out, had by now joined the 5th Regiment. He'd been culled separately early in August and flown directly to Pusan as an individual. On his arrival at the Marine bivouac west of the port, he had happily run into an old commander of his, Captain Max English, who had Company A of the 1st Tank Battalion, and who pointed to a tank and said, "Go ahead and take over A-4-2. It's yours." Byrnes was a tank commander at last.

Twice during August and the first few days of September, the Marines fought where the Naktong bulged on the western part of the Perimeter, twice they put the enemy to flight, and then, much to their disappointment, were called back again.

They were not happy about it. But General Walker, harried hourly with his myriad problems in Taegu, was even unhappier. MacArthur had just told him that now it was time to pull the Marines out and use them for the Inchon landing.

It was the first of September. The heaviest Communist attacks of the Perimeter campaign were hitting the line from all directions. Walker called Tokyo and said to Ned Almond: "If you take the 5th Marine Regiment away from me now I won't be responsible for what happens here at the front!"[10]

NOTES   *Chapter 4*

1. After the Inchon landing when one of the first Chinese officers was captured with North Korean troops near Pyongyang during the push north, a language officer, Lt. James Lampe, was flown from Tokyo to interrogate him. Willoughby simply would not believe he was Chinese, and when he finally accepted increasing evidence of Chinese participation in the war, continued to underplay it in his reports to MacArthur—"hedging his bets," one of his staff members said until the sudden appearance of the Chinese force at the Yalu border in November of 1950. Interviews author— Underwood, Polk; Appleman, p. 764; Gugeler, Russell A., *Combat Actions in Korea,* Chap 2, Washington, D.C., Combat Forces Press, 1954.
2. Interview author—Polk.
3. Interview author—Holly.
4. Interview author—Hahm, Mon and Lt Col Chu Han Dong R. O. K. Marine Corps.
5. Interview author—Holly.
6. *Air University Quarterly Review,* Vol IV, # 3, Spring 51.
7. Appleman, p. 307; Gugeler, *Combat Actions in Korea,* Chap 2, 24th Inf Div War Diary, 16 Aug 50.
8. Letter Van Sant to author, 1 Apr 67 General Orders # 377, 25th Inf. Div., 23 June 51.
9. Interview author—Lt Col Nicholas A Canzona.
10. Interview author—Almond.

"The Command, Ned, is yours."

HARD-BITTEN ARMORED CAVALRYMAN, MAJOR GENERAL DAVID
G. Barr was champing at the bit up in northern Japan, where
his 7th Infantry Division was stationed on Occupation duty.
He had assumed command of the Division in Hokkaido,
Japan's northernmost island, and later moved it down to
Sendai, a picturesque port on the Pacific Ocean north of
Tokyo. On the 4th of July, before the Perimeter began to
form, General Walker dropped up to see his old friend Dave
Barr and told him he was going to Korea to direct the Eighth
Army from the combat area. Barr said, "Why don't you let
us go with you?" and when he'd pressed the point, Walker
had become angry and told Barr to shut up. Someone had to
garrison Japan, and the duty had fallen to Barr's 7th Division.
They were both soldiers, Walker felt, both old pros, and they
both ought to recognize that decisions to commit major bodies
of troops came from higher headquarters which, in their case,
meant MacArthur.

Dave Barr was indeed an old pro, a crusty, fire-eating old
pro, his troops thought, who operated in the tradition of
Stonewall Jackson, living with Spartan denial in the field,
traveling light, moving fast and hitting hard. He was originally an infantryman and had earned his commission at the second Officer's Training Camp run in World War I. Barr came
from Alabama where his father, who had political connections, might have been able to send him to West Point, but
he had been impatient to get into the war. After two weeks
at the camp, Dave Barr had his first taste of army life and
said to himself, "This is for me." He had remained in the
Army ever since. In World War II he switched to armored
cavalry, a fast-moving corps that better suited his tempera-

ment. Just after World War II he'd gone to China with one of the first post-war Military Advisory Groups, and when the Communists had overrun China in 1949, he'd been virtually the last American to fly out.

He hadn't gone home, but had reported to MacArthur in Tokyo. MacArthur had said, "Dave, I have a top staff position for you."

Barr had said, "Sir, I don't want to retire without commanding anything."

MacArthur had said, "I know exactly how you feel. All right, you'll get a division."[1]

He'd gotten his division, but now, with the war nearly two months old, it was still doing Occupation duty in northern Japan. But the Occupation was virtually finished—John Foster Dulles had set up the machinery for its termination when he visited Japan the week the war started—and the 7th Division had little to do. Barr wanted to use this time to give his men combat training, but as Occupation units they were "scattered from hell to breakfast," as he liked to put it, all over the Japanese landscape and down to one-third strength, which meant around five thousand men, so that when you boiled it down he didn't have much of a command after all. As the final drop of gall in the whole bitter pot, MacArthur was now picking at his division to find a unit here and there to transfer to Johnny Walker's Eighth Army.

In mid-July, General MacArthur sent for Barr, dispatching a plane to bring him from Sendai because floods had made the railroads there inoperative. At this conference Barr heard that there would be an amphibious landing, probably at Inchon, and MacArthur assured him that his division would be brought up to strength to take part in it. The rough idea, as Barr understood it, was to assemble a corps which would consist, hopefully, of his own 7th division and of one Marine division to make the landing. But weeks passed, and instead of adding to the 7th, MacArthur robbed it, like an old junk heap, for spare parts.

Finally, however, in the heat of August, as the situation on the Perimeter was growing darker, the 7th Division was moved down to a huge training area near Yokohama, and a trickle of personnel began to come in from the States. In later years Barr was able to regard it all with perspective and even a little amusement, and said, "They promised me the world and gave me nothing," but at the time he was truly disgusted. One part of him understood that the immediate

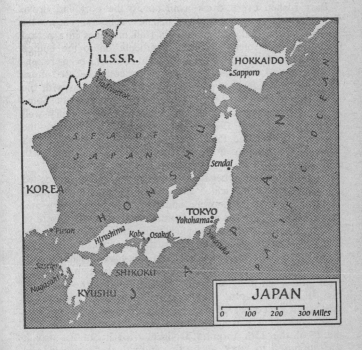

demands of the war itself dictated everything, but the other part of him was snorting like a war horse held deliberately and maddeningly in check.

When the first major augmentation to his division finally came, it was close to the worst disappointment of all. They were not Americans as he'd expected, but about 8,600 South Koreans. On the 18th of August Ned Almond called him on the phone from Tokyo. "Dave, your replacements are arriving in Yokohama, and two more ships are coming in."

Barr rushed every truck available to the port and drove there himself to get a look at his new soldiers. They were part of a plan that had evolved in staff meetings in a period of only a few weeks—Korean Augmentation to the United States Army (KATUSA). The original idea had been, roughly, that the 84,000-man R. O. K. Army could be used more effectively to defend their homeland in conjunction with the U. S. forces than they were being used independently. Some of the Korean divisions at the front had fought very well indeed, and it was they, primarily, who were holding the northern line of the Perimeter. With U. S. units under full strength, the thing to do seemed to be to augment them with Koreans.

The augmentation began in August as a movement called the "buddy system," which was widely reported in the press. South Korean soldiers were added to the 1st Cavalry and 2nd Infantry Divisions at the front. Exactly how they were to be employed was left largely to division and regimental commanders, but the general idea was that they were to be scattered throughout the units and fight side-by-side with Americans, while their American "buddies" took time, presumably with bullets whistling all about, to give them on-the-job training. It seemed a pipe dream to many officers. Perhaps, in part, their preconceived notions kept the plan from working well. Perhaps it was unworkable from the start. Two regiments of the 25th Infantry Division tried it out the way it was supposed to work by putting individual Americans and Koreans side-by-side, while the third regiment bunched the recruits into separate platoons with American officers and NCO's. The 24th Division separated them entirely, assigning their own officers to command their platoons and squads, then attaching them to American units.

It didn't work out in combat. The Korean recruits simply didn't have time to leap the language barrier and adjust themselves to a vastly different environment. As many KMAG officers already realized, American military terminology was particularly difficult for the Koreans. There wasn't time to explain fully such subtleties as the difference between "delay" and "defend," or the fine concepts of "zone," "corridor," and "boundary." Colonel Sterling Wright, who commanded the KMAG in Seoul when the war broke out, once ordered the preparation of a military dictionary but finally gave the project up when he saw that it led to nothing but long-drawn-out semantic disputes.[2]

Ned Almond, during one of his many hectic trips to Korea as MacArthur's Chief of Staff, once visited the front and fell into step with a sergeant walking down a dusty road and chatted with him. He asked him how the R. O. K. troops in his outfit were getting along. "They're not worth a goddamn," the Sergeant said. "I've been all night walking along my platoon keeping these gooks awake." Almond himself—one of MacArthur's most loyal staff men—felt doubtful, when toward the end of July, MacArthur said to him, "The 7th Division is useless, isn't it? Try to get enough manpower from Korea to bring it up to strength."[3]

Second Lieutenant Robert K. Sawyer commanded a platoon of Korean recruits in the Reconnaissance Company of the 25th Division. He was a keen and unbiased observer, and he later wrote an account of South Korean participation in the war.[4] His recruits had had a few days training in their own replacement training center and some brief schooling from the company's first sergeant on methods of attack, and they were thrown into combat. They did not like the American food they were given, plus a huge, steaming plate of rice for each man. (Korean food is some of the hottest in the world and even children can mouth a red-peppered stew that would burn out the lining of an occidental mouth. U. S. soldiers of Mexican descent admitted in Korea that even their own chile-flavored cuisine did not prepare them for this.) They never seemed to understand that one cardboard box of C-rations was meant for one full day, and would promptly eat several days' supply as soon as it was issued. They fell asleep on guard. And, perhaps most annoying of all, when in bivouac near the enemy—when everyone was trying to be quiet—they'd infuriate their American buddies by following the Korean custom of greeting the morning with a song.

Major General Barr had heard some of these stories by the time he drove to Yokohama to greet the first of the Korean reinforcements for his division, but he'd also heard how trained Korean soldiers had fought well and sometimes with fanatical bravery along the Perimeter. He was hoping that his new troops would be at least potential soldiers.

The half-disorganized group that stepped off the LST at the pier seemed to be a shocking mob in his eyes. They were supposed to have had the rudiments of basic training, but somehow, in the eagerness at lower levels to carry out the recruiting order, the matter of training had been overlooked, and indeed, a large proportion of the recruits were civilians who had actually been impressed in the streets of Pusan—shanghaied was the only word for it. Many of them were surprised to find themselves in Japan, and hardly any knew where they were meant to go next. Among them were boys still carrying their schoolbooks; one poor man had simply stepped out of his house in Pusan to get medicine for his wife when he'd been grabbed by several South Korean military policemen who were doing the recruiting and rushed to the ship—he still had the bottle of medicine with him.[5]

Barr thought it shameful and howled loudly about it. For political reasons he could not have the more unwilling recruits returned, for it was the South Korean government that had engineered the thing and it was not proper for a division commander to criticize an ally or countermand his actions. He felt ever afterward that Ned Almond knew all along how inadequate these recruits would be, but this was probably unjust, for Almond himself had gone along with the plan with no more than an obedient sigh.

Barr took his new troops, more of which now began to arrive in succeeding ships, to the 7th Division training areas and did his best to make soldiers of them. He was pleasantly surprised to find most of them cooperative, although few spoke English and most needed separate messes for Korean food. Their biggest worry was about their families, and this remained the greatest morale problem, though Barr tried to solve it by easing mail channels between Japan and Korea. The first necessary step in making 7th Division soldiers out of them, he found, was to delouse them, for somewhere along the line, perhaps in the ships, they'd become infested to a man; they all had to run through disinfectant baths, sprinkle themselves with DDT powder, and burn their old clothing.

Dave Barr felt a little like a neglected orphan in MacArthur's military family. The old man was so busy with so many things that somehow Barr was seldom completely informed as to what was going on, and shortly after the arrival of his 8,600 South Koreans, he was called at the last minute to another conference in Tokyo which he found attended by most of the high-ranking generals on hand and some visitors from Washington. He had not been prepared for such a high-powered meeting and he was angry and embarrassed. The conference took place in the map-filled war room at the Dai-Ichi Building, and it was here that Barr first learned that Inchon was definitely decided upon as the landing place and heard the detailed general plan for the operation. He listened carefully, heard of all the natural obstacles to such a landing, and then, when he had cooled off a little, remarked to one of his fellow officers, "It's so wrong that it's right. That element of surprise will be great."[6]

MacArthur's self-assurance was of course an expression of his genius, but it was one of the traits that irritated those who had to deal with him from a nominally superior level, such as the Army Chief of Staff, the Chairman of the Joint Chiefs of Staff (for the U. S. Military by now had undergone a shuffling called Unification which, in fine Orwellian fashion, really meant the complete separation of all the services), and the Army and Defense Secretaries; moreover, as would become shockingly evident the next spring, it became irritating to the President of the United States himself. It was difficult to deal with MacArthur as a subordinate because he was already a living legend and a national symbol. The most powerful men in the land somehow felt they should address him as "sir." As the desire for a dramatic end run to Inchon grew upon him, he managed to advise Washington in a general way of his probable intentions and there was a technical and traditional necessity to obtain their approval—though no precise law or regulation requiring it—but from Washington's viewpoint it never seemed very clear whether he actually meant to go ahead with this potentially hazardous scheme. Washington's approval was necessary, not only because it was such a major undertaking, but because the Pentagon controlled the additional men and equipment MacArthur needed for the landing. All the Chiefs of Staff—J. Lawton Collins, Army; Admiral Forrest Sherman, Chief of Naval Operations; Hoyt Vandenburg, Air Force—would make frequent trips to Tokyo to find out what was going on, but somehow it was always difficult to get them together in one time or place. Collins would trot north to Hokkaido, where Barr's 7th Division was

the principal Army unit in Japan; Sherman would go down
to the big naval base at Yokosuka, fifty miles south of Tokyo;
and Vandenburg would make for Nagoya in central Japan,
where the fifth Air Force was headquartered.

So, in a general way, the chiefs in Washington knew what
MacArthur was up to, and in a sense had approved of it, but
by mid-August they still hadn't given their entire blessing.

To Ned Almond MacArthur gave the job of setting up a
Special Planning Staff to work specifically on the Inchon plan,
under the code name of Operation Chromite. They were
activated by a special order on August 15 and on that day
consisted of only five officers (including Almond) and twelve
enlisted men to assist them. They were at first all intelligence
officers, but within a few days others joined them to begin
personnel, operations and supply plans. On August 16, they
assembled in an old airplane hangar known as Building AP-1,
in the motor pool in downtown Tokyo, to hear an initial
address by General Almond. As his own chief of staff, Almond had been given able, energetic Major General Clark L.
Ruffner, who relieved him of much of the drudgery as the
planning staff, in time, grew into a full corps. As the days
went on, Almond spent more and more time with the Special
Planning Staff, although he retained his title as MacArthur's
chief of staff and worked in the Dai-Ichi Building at least
part of the day.

MacArthur always referred to this special group as "X-
Force." It grew like protoplasm, and within a week additional
officers and men were streaming into its headquarters in the
motor pool. By that time it had somehow become evident to
MacArthur that this "X-Force" was his nucleus for the
corps that would carry out the landing and he called Almond
in, told him this, then said, "What shall we call this corps?"

Almond knew his MacArthur history. He remembered
how, in World War II, MacArthur had flown from the Pacific
battlefront to Honolulu for a grand conference on the taking
of Japan itself, with President Roosevelt at the head of the
table. At that time the other top military planners had
wanted to climb toward Japan through China, Formosa and
the Philippines, but MacArthur pushed for amphibious attacks on Okinawa and the Bonin Islands so that they might
be used for bases in the final jump. President Roosevelt had
been intrigued by MacArthur's plan and had invited the
general to ride back from the conference with him. There
MacArthur had sold him on the idea of an amphibious ad-

vance, and before the atomic bomb brought about Japan's surrender and made it unnecessary, great plans had been formulated for Operation Coronet, the proposed invasion of Japan. Oddly enough, Coronet included a plan for a landing at Inchon. For Coronet, MacArthur had planned to form the group of divisions he would call "X-Corps"—pronounced "Tenth Corps."

Almond now said, "How about X-Corps?"

MacArthur nodded. "Yes, that's a good idea."[7]

X-Corps it was then, but for the moment it existed only as the Special Planning Staff in a hot, musty, high-ceilinged structure where men worked far into the night at desks and tables that were becoming increasingly strewn with maps and documents.

Adequate map coverage, as a matter of fact, was one of the major problems when it came to Inchon. There were standard maps of all of Korea in the usual sizes, but of Inchon itself there was available only a map with a scale of 1:12,500, which gave not nearly enough detail. This had to be supplemented by photo-map coverage as quickly as possible. Larger maps were available, but they were not all constructed according to the same mathematical scheme— for there are several methods of depicting a portion of earth's surfaces, by definition curved, on a flat area—and some were what is called polyconic grids, while others were Universal Transverse Mercator Grids (UTM's).[8] Whatever maps and studies became available, meanwhile, had to be reproduced and for security reasons they were taken in portions to four different Japanese printers for the rush jobs.[9]

Just about everybody in MacArthur's GHQ had a finger in the Inchon plan. In Japan only a blind idiot with no interest in military matters could fail to know that something was in the wind. Correspondents were beginning to poke around for details and to speculate among themselves about a probable planned Inchon landing, which they called "Operation Common Knowledge." General Wright, MacArthur's G-3, later wrote: "It was of course impossible, in an Asiatic area, to conceal the fact that something big was in the making, the increase in shipping, the increase in Japanese manufacture of materials and matériel for the U. S. forces. The Japanese islands, particularly Honshu, had many dissident Koreans. It was impossible to hide the fact that . . . South Koreans had arrived in Japan for training with the 7th Infantry Division. We realize that this was all another part of the calculated gamble. The only recourse was to do everything possible to mislead the Communists as to where the big attack was to take place. It must be realized also that the Soviet Embassy in Tokyo was an ever-present concern. Probably our biggest ace in the hole was the fact that it looked impossible to mount a large force without reducing the strength in the Pusan area and it did not take a crystal ball to see that any large scale reduction from the Eighth Army would be disastrous."[10]

Two or three days after the Special Planning Staff was ensconced in its old airplane hangar, General Almond was in MacArthur's office reporting on the progress of their plans and said that now that everything was becoming firm, he thought it was time to appoint a commander for the X-Corps that would make the landing. Much to his surprise, MacArthur smiled at him for a moment, then said, "The command, Ned, is yours."[11]

Ned Almond, like the old man himself, already wore several hats in that well-bonneted headquarters. MacArthur was at once SCAP (Supreme Commander Allied Powers), CINCUNC (Commander in Chief, United Nations Command), CINCFE (Commander in Chief, Far East), and CGFEC (Commanding General, Far East Command). Through these various titles he was running the Occupation of Japan, the ultimate deployment of U. S. troops in places like Okinawa and Taiwan, the use of allied troops in both Japan and Korea itself, the naval forces in the Far East, the air forces stationed there—altogether, anything military that was taking place in this part of Asia. As his chief of staff, Ned Almond had a hand in all of it. But for the next few weeks, all his attention would be devoted to building a corps and girding it for a major amphibious landing. Almond's desk near MacArthur's office in the Dai-Ichi Building couldn't go unmanned, however, so the various deputy chiefs of staff sat in from time to time, principally Major General Doyle O. Hickey, the Far East Command Deputy, and Major General Alonzo P. Fox, deputy for SCAP and the U. N. Command.

Alonzo Fox, a quiet and rather earnest soldier whose forte was staff work, was one of those caught by the outbreak of the war who felt obligated to stay on for a while. He'd been scheduled to go back to the States in early July and his household goods were already on the boat when the Communists marched south. For most of July and the first part of August, Fox had trotted off to Taiwan to make a survey of the supply and manpower requirements of Chiang Kai-shek's Chinese Nationalist Forces there, for it was another dream of MacArthur's to use these troops in Korea, a notion that eventually horrified State Department policymakers and became part of the conflict that led to MacArthur's removal by President Truman the following spring. When Fox returned to Tokyo in mid-August, he learned through General Almond's aide-de-camp, Captain Alexander M. Haig, who also happened to be Fox's son-in-law, that the plan for Inchon was in full swing.

Fox was among those who had some doubts about the wisdom of the plan. He once dared, in MacArthur's presence, to say—softly and diplomatically, of course—that Kunsan, one hundred miles down the coast, might be a better target, both because it had no major city to be taken and did not have the frightening depth of the Inchon end run; MacArthur had nodded and said, "But we would still have to climb uphill from there." Fox was beginning to understand that the real objective was Seoul, the capital of Korea, and that once this city was taken the war could be symbolically won and its progress after that, even if slow, essentially didn't matter.

The great headquarters chess game produced a new move for General Fox. Using Dave Barr's 7th Division as part of the landing force meant stripping Japan itself of troops, especially up in Hokkaido which, incidentally, was the area nearest Russian territory and the most logical place for a Russian invasion of Japan. With the uneasy fear of World War III flaring up from the sparks in Korea, such an invasion was not considered at all a remote possibility. Now, part of the mission entrusted to the Occupation troops in Japan was to defend the islands from any attack, and the Japanese themselves had adopted a new constitution—under MacArthur's prodding and bearing more of MacArthur's thinking than their own—which specifically forbade that they maintain a military establishment. But MacArthur was not at all above employing sophistry when it suited his purpose, and so he told Alonzo Fox to get busy and organize a Japanese "police force," ten thousand strong, to be equipped with light weapons and to garrison and patrol Hokkaido. This later became the nucleus for the present-day Japanese "Self-Defense Forces," which, theoretically at least, exist only to defend Japan from direct attack on the homeland, and thus, to everybody's satisfaction, do not violate the Japanese Constitution.

This became Fox's primary job, but at the same time he was helping to cover the chief-of-staff desk while Almond was busy in his airplane hangar. Presently MacArthur came to him and said that when the Inchon landing succeeded (he always said "when," never "if"), he would set up a forward headquarters in Korea, a kind of advanced command post, with Fox at its head, so he'd better start planning for that, too.[12]

General Fox, busy and a bit harried like everyone else in headquarters, worried about the lack of security attending the Inchon plan. One day, as he sat at the chief of staff's desk, the telephone rang and the Japanese civilian overseas operator, who spoke English, said it was a long-distance call from Tennessee. It turned out to be a radio-station newsman who wanted to speak to MacArthur, and Fox had to spend several minutes assuring him that this was out of the question. Then he asked the caller what he wanted to speak to General MacArthur about. "We understand General MacArthur is about to land on the coast in Korea," said the newsman, and Fox's every muscle, as he sat there, turned to ice. For another few minutes he tried to talk calmly and say as little as possible. He could not flatly deny there was such a plan, for a negative story that would have repercussions later could be made out of that alone. At the same time, by not flatly denying it, he would tacitly admit its possibility. For once the relative anonymity enjoyed by anyone who clustered about the shining star that was MacArthur was useful, and Fox put the inquirer off with some fast doubletalk, the essence of which was that he, Fox, was only a staff man—he made it sound like some kind of office clerk—that he wasn't involved in such matters as high military planning, and therefore could tell him nothing. Finally the man said, "All right, thank you, General. By the way—our conversation has been on the air. Goodbye."

It seemed to most of the planners in MacArthur's headquarters that the North Koreans must by now surely have strong suspicions that an attack would fall upon Inchon. If so, the element of surprise that Dave Barr saw as the plan's principal merit was gone and the whole operation could turn into a disastrous fiasco. Not only were the rumors flying about, but special equipment for the landing was being ordered in great quantity from Japanese manufacturers, primarily because they were there and could deliver on time. There were the scaling ladders, for example. Until now amphibious landings had been made upon flat beaches and the table of equipment hadn't called for ladders. But the sea walls at Inchon were nearly sixteen feet high, and so it was decided that the landing craft would nose right up to them, then the attackers would throw up their ladders and scramble over them, probably in the face of heavy enemy fire. A contract was let to a Japanese firm in Kobe to make aluminum ladders hooked at one end, and to make them in about two week's time. (They did not come through on time, as it worked out.)

In the great naval base at Yokosuka, a little south of the Tokyo-Yokohama complex, the shops and drydocks were lit through the night as amphibious craft and equipment were put into operating shape. Not all of the Japanese workers had had a complete security check. There were undoubtedly home-grown Communists and actual North Koreans among them. To most occidental newcomers to the Orient, Japanese and Koreans (and Chinese for that matter) at first look alike, but there are ethnic differences of which Orientals themselves are easily aware, so that Japanese usually spot Koreans and vice versa. On the other hand, some Koreans can pass physically for Japanese—just as some Japanese resemble the Korean type—and Japan was filled with Koreans who had lived there for many years, spoke Japanese perfectly, looked and acted Japanese, all of them with adopted Japanese names. Undoubtedly hundreds of them worked for the United States Forces as everything from chauffeurs to the housemaids of general officers. It was, in short, a spy's paradise.

Then there was the matter of the thirty-nine rickety, leaky old landing craft that belonged to the Japanese. They were turning out to be one of the luckiest accidents in favor of the landing, like the naval amphibious planning group that had been on hand at the outbreak of war.

When Brigadier General Edwin K. "Pinky" Wright joined MacArthur's staff early in 1949 as G-3, Plans and Operations, he had been at first mildly confused to find himself wearing two hats: one for SCAP, which dealt with civilian matters springing out of the Occupation, and the other for the Far East Command, which was purely military. There was often conflict betwen the two commands and Wright occasionally found one viewpoint in direct opposition to the other. Now, it so happened that SCAP had turned over to the Japanese thirty-nine wartime LST's—big, boxy, seagoing vessels that could be run up on beaches to disgorge troops and tanks from their bow ramps and also had a huge cargo-carrying capacity. Japan lacked water transport at the war's end and the LST's were meant to provide her with coastal commercial traffic until she could build ships of her own. The LST's were given Japanese skippers and crews but maintained by the U. S. Navy. They needed plenty of maintenance and the Navy found this an annoying load. It was anxious to scrap them, and SCAP was pushing the Japanese to hurry and build their own small craft so this could be done. Shortly after General Wright arrived, the Japanese managed to finish enough of their own ships to sustain the coastal traffic and the plan to scrap the old LST's was sent up through the staff for final approval.

". . . the matter was presented to me," wrote Wright, "as G-3 FEC for clearance, and for this I will always be thankful. Our missions centered on providing for the security of Japan and, while we did not know we would be in Korea the next year, there was always such a possibility. With the poor road network in Japan we *had* to have the capability of getting into the small Japanese harbors, of shifting military supplies and troops quickly."[13]

Wright talked it over with Major General George L. Eberle (G-4, Supply), who agreed that the old LST's ought to be kept, even if the Navy did find it a burden to keep them running. He also sent some inquiries to Washington and other places and learned that nowhere in the world, at the moment, were there any other leftover LST's in better shape or available for replacements. He prepared a firm recommendation that the LST's be kept, even with their Japanese crews, and took it to Almond, who approved it. Thirty-seven were destined to be used at Inchon. "Without this lift," said Wright, "it is doubtful if the Inchon assault could have been initially supported."[14]

But now LST's were being hastily repaired and even modified in the Navy shops and dockyards, and their Japanese crews were receiving last-minute briefings and training for an amphibious landing. There were two potential breaches of security here: first, that word of the landing itself would leak out, and second, that the public would learn of the employment of Japanese nationals in the Korean War, a move certain to draw a howl from the grimly peace-oriented

Japanese government and from the Communist world, mainly Soviet Russia, that supported the North Korean side.

General Wright, who had been Deputy Director of the CIA before joining MacArthur's staff, was particularly conscious of security, but he saw all these leaky spots as ". . . another part of the calculated gamble."[15]

Major General Oliver P. Smith, USMC, stepped from the plane at Haneda Airport on southern Tokyo Bay in midafternoon, August 22, 1950. He was the tall, white-haired, slender and somewhat precise Marine who was to command the 1st Marine Division in the upcoming landing. As a colonel and brigadier general in the Pacific in World War II he had known considerable combat experience, including amphibious operations. He had served in joint operations with the Army before and had been cited for his "tact, understanding and warm, friendly personality" in a Legion of Merit decoration for Marine-Army activities. Of all the Marine officers available, Oliver Smith was probably the ideal choice for a Marine amphibious operation that was to be carried out in cooperation with the Army. He thought it rather odd that at this moment he did not know either the date or the hour set for the landing.[16]

Smith had been hastily rebuilding his 1st Division at Camp Pendleton, California, when the still somewhat vague instruction to make a landing for MacArthur reached him. It had all been hasty, frantic, but Smith was a man who liked to proceed calmly and refused to get rattled. Just before the Korean War's outbreak, he'd had a division of almost 7,800 men, then suddenly, in early July, it was stripped down to less than 3,400 to provide the men of the Marine Brigade now fighting on the Perimeter. In addition, around 1,500 Marine airmen were taken from the 1st Marine Aircraft Wing, also based in California, to form Marine Aircraft Group 33, the brigade's air arm. Following this, there had been a furious build-up, with recruits and recalled reservists pouring into Pendleton.

General MacArthur, who at first had entertained only a slim hope of being given enough Marines, was now scheduled to get them in spades. The 1st Marine Division would consist not only of the brigade now in Korea, but of the 1st Regiment under hell-roaring Colonel Chesty Puller and the 7th Regiment under Colonel Homer Litzenberg which, as it turned out, arrived about a week after the initial landing and assisted in the push toward Seoul.

General Smith was met at the airport by Rear Admiral James H. Doyle, the amphibious planner who had been assigned to command the naval elements of the actual attack force until they got ashore, various naval beach units, and a swarm of over 150 ships, ranging from transports, destroyers and cruisers, to the rickety LST's resalvaged from the Japanese. Even this formidable flotilla was only part of the Joint Task Force, headed by Vice Admiral Arthur D. Struble, the Seventh Fleet Commander, and which included the carriers, the support and screening destroyers, the patrol and reconnaissance force and the various logistical vessels. At any rate, Admiral Doyle had the word and he passed it on to Marine General Smith in the crowded planning compartment aboard the U.S.S. *Mt. McKinley*, the command ship now berthed in Tokyo harbor. The date would be September 15, and there would be two landings, morning and evening, when the tide was high enough to allow the LST's to clear the mudflats and the gunfire support ships to move in close enough to do their work.[17] He learned also that the entire landing force, with both a Marine and Army division, would be known as X-Corps and commanded by Major General Edward M. Almond. He was about to meet Almond. He had an appointment with him and with MacArthur himself at 5:30 P.M. Doyle had him rushed by car to the Dai-Ichi Building.

Smith was ushered into the conference room between MacArthur's and Almond's offices, and a few moments later Almond appeared and greeted him. It was the first meeting in what was later to prove a strained relationship, apparently the result of a simple but unfathomable personality clash, for Almond had gotten along well enough with other Marines, and Smith had often worked in harmony with Army officers, particularly as deputy chief of staff with the U. S. Tenth Army on Okinawa. At this first meeting, Almond was buoyant and energetic as usual—perhaps Smith thought that his manner bordered on the effusive. Smith was somewhat reserved, as always, and this struck Almond as being slightly cold. Although neither man knew the other well, Smith quite unconsciously saw in Almond a superficial extrovert, and Almond saw in Smith a by-the-book soldier and a cold fish. Both were wrong of course. But it was unfortunate that two men who would work so closely in the difficult and bloody assault on Seoul after the landing could not more naturally be in harmony, and it was to have its effects.

Almond explained that MacArthur hadn't arrived yet, and went into details about the general's unorthodox day with its long afternoon break and late night sessions. General Smith carefully noted his prompt arrival and the subsequent wait in his diary.

The two men began to discuss some of the tactical problems to be faced at Inchon, and here they were on common ground. At about this time MacArthur arrived, sent for Almond briefly, and then asked that General Smith be brought in. The Supreme Commander greeted Smith warmly. The war could be won in a month after Inchon—the 1st Marine Division would win it. He realized that the Marines were perfectionists and this landing had been planned most hastily, so perhaps everything wouldn't be neatly in place. But there was no doubt of victory, and the credit for it would accrue to the United States Marines.

General Smith made no judgments, one way or the other, about the great man, quietly accepted his cordial farewell and then went off like a good Marine to do his job.

NOTES *Chapter 5*

1. Interview author—Gen David G. Barr.
2. Interview author—Wright.
3. Interview author—Almond.
4. Sawyer, Robert K. *Military Advisors in Korea: KMAG in Peace and War,* Washington, D.C., Department of the Army, 1955.
5. Interview author—Barr.
6. *Ibid.*
7. In great excitement one day early in July, General Wright, the G-3, had come into Almond's office waving a thick document and saying, "We've found a plan from World War II for the invasion of Korea!" It had apparently come up originally from MacArthur's headquarters in the Philippines and had been in the files all this time. It was part of the old Operation Coronet, the invasion of Japan, and it was helpful but not of sufficient detail to be used as a basis for Inchon. Interview author—Almond.
8. Hq X-Corps War Diary, 16 Aug 50.
9. Late in August, Willoughby's G-2 section received a scare when a Japanese magazine writer came to ask if he could

study "the old Pacific War Plan for the invasion of Inchon."
The Counterintelligence Corps was put upon him immediately and probably no writer ever received such a thorough
background check in so short a time. As it turned out, he
was doing a most innocent historical piece, but he never
did get to look at the old Operation Coronet plans. Interview
author—Polk.

10. Letter Wright to author, 10 Oct 66.

11. Interview author—Almond.

12. The forward GHQ in Korea was never established, probably,
thought Fox, because MacArthur decided he didn't want to
be too closely involved in the complications of Korean
politics, but he appears to have considered it up until the
landing, for Fox was invited to a grandstand seat on the
U.S.S. *Mt. McKinley* to observe the Inchon operation. Interview author—Lt Gen Alonzo P. Fox.

13. Letter Wright to author, 28 Sept 66.

14. *Ibid.*

15. ". . . . my good friend Charlie Willoughby (G-2) and his
entire staff looked upon me with a jaundiced eye for at least
a year when I became G-3. That I maintained some slight
connections with my old outfit may be taken for granted."
Letter Wright to author, 10 Oct 66.

16. Maj Gen O. P. Smith, *Chronicle,* Manuscript File, Hq
USMC G-3 Historical Section.

17. Even at this point the information given General Smith
was not complete. In his own words: "At the time of my
reporting aboard the USS Mt. McKinley the question of a
morning landing was not firm. The slow-moving [landing
ships] could not make an approach . . . through the tortuous
and mud-lined channels to the transport area. After considerable discussion . . . it was agreed that sufficient shipping
. . . fitted with radar . . . could be provided . . . for the
morning landing on Wolmi-do . . ." Manuscript review
comments for author, Gen. O. P. Smith, 24 Jun 67.

6

"Take no counsel of your fears . . . . "

THEIR FACES WERE PAINTED GREEN AND BLACK, SOME HAD grown beards, and they were dressed in tennis shoes, dungarees and Marine fatigues. This moonless night at 1030 hours they gathered, all forty of them on the fantail of a small, fast transport called the *Horace A. Bass,* which was approaching a strip of Communist-held coast in North Korea.

The voice of Lieutenant Commander Alan Ray, skipper of the *Bass,* came somewhat softly over the battle telephones. "Coast five thousand yards . . . will arrive in anchorage in fifteen minutes."

Marine Second Lieutenant Dana B. Cashion checked his watch and ran his eyes, as best he could in the darkness, over the tiny detachment of a half-dozen Marines he would take ashore. Cashion was young, earnest, agreeable, anxious to please, new to the Marine Corps, new to war. He hadn't at all expected, upon arriving in the Far East, to be made part of a forty-man raiding outfit that operated exactly like the bizarre commandoes of World War II. Like all brand new second lieutenants or their equivalents since perhaps the time of Caesar and the Gallic Wars, he was doing his best to be unobtrusively on hand and let his experienced non-commissioned officers work out the details, but at the same time maintain the dignity of his commissioned rank.

The ship's engines began to slow down, then abruptly stopped, and there was near silence broken only by the rattling sound of the anchor running out. In the darkness the men who were to go ashore took their final drags from the cigarettes in their cupped hands.

Young Cashion's part in all this was to take his handful of Marines in after his colleague, Second Lieutenant Phillip D.

Shutler, landed with another small group and began a probing reconnaissance in the darkness. The point of landing
would amount to a miniature beachhead, and here Cashion
would set up a perimeter defense.

There were some twenty-five underwater demolition experts
of the United States Navy in this raiding force. They were
known as "Utes," a condensation of the official designation,
'Underwater Demolition Team," and they were trained to
work below the surface in face masks, flippers and black
neoprene suits; their principal weapon was an explosive known
as C-3 which worked under water and could be handled
roughly, or even struck with a bullet, without exploding, although a tracer slug would usually set it off. Their junior
officers were Lieutenants (jg) Edwin P. Smith, P. A. Wilson
and George Acheson III, a nephew of the Secretary of State.

This melodramatic outfit of raiders was the personal crea-
tion of amiable and deceptively mild Admiral C. Turner Joy,
commander of Naval Forces, Far East, who had an almost
grandfatherly air about him, and whose own son was a lieutenant (jg) on duty in this sudden war. He wanted a raiding
team for two purposes: to supplement the ship-to-shore bombardment and air strikes on the various roads, rail lines and
supply points up and down the coast, and to keep his naval
planners supplied with intelligence about the coastal portions
of enemy territory. He had called up Marine Major Edward
P. Dupras, who had led raiding parties in China in World
War II, to form the team, and Commander Seldon Small to
lead the overall attack force, with Lieutenant Commander
David F. Welch at the head of the Navy underwater demolition men.

This tiny group worked out a technique of amphibious
strikes that was similar, even in its command structure, to the
operation of a major landing force of the kind scheduled for
Inchon on September 15—provided the chiefs of staff in
Washington would finally authorize the daring maneuver. But
also, as in so many campaigns and battles, one small and almost unnoticed operation by this team of raiders was to have
its effect in the mahogany-paneled conference room between
General MacArthur's and General Almond's offices on the
sixth floor of the Dai-Ichi Building.

The name of the target location on the night of August 21
was Posung-myon. There was a long beach and, a little inland, some scattered houses, but nothing that could really
be called a village, and, in fact, on most maps and charts

JOHNSON
AIR BASE
USAF

CAMP DRAKE
(U.S. ARMY)

YOKOTA

USAF

TACHIKAWA

EMPEROR'S
PALACE

TOKYO

DAI-ICHI
BUILDING

HANEDA AIRPORT

CAMP ZAMA
(U.S. ARMY)

ATSUGI
NAVAL
AIR
STATION

T O K Y O
YOKOHAMA
B A Y

YOKOSUKA

BOSO-
PENINSULA

S A G A M I
B A Y

TOKYO AND
VICINITY

0   5   10 Miles

the name of this spot on the coast, only about thirty miles below Inchon, was not even noted. Ordinarily the team's objective was to damage or destroy when it went ashore. Tonight the instructions were primarily to look around, see what they could find, then bring back a report.

They had no way of knowing it, but Rear Admiral James H. Doyle, the amphibious expert who headed Phib Group I, and had been chosen to command the attack force at Inchon for the landing phase, had been thinking seriously about this stretch of beach at Posung-myon ever since he'd noticed it on the charts.

For the raiders aboard the *Bass*, the mission began like several others they'd already carried out, in particular a spectacular strike on the east coast at a place called Tanchon a little more than a week before. There they'd been part of the strategy to keep the northeastern wall of the Perimeter secure, for the Communists were attacking furiously here, and their effort was well-supplied by a major rail line that ran down the east coast of Korea from Manchuria, where it connected with the Trans-Siberian railway. In places this rail line ran along the sea. Naval guns had bombarded it from offshore, but at Tanchon it was protected by two tunnels, themselves connected by a bridge, within fifty yards of the sea.

"Our job," said Major Dupras, in briefing his men, "is demolition, not fighting. Avoid any fire fights, if you can. If you run into interference, or if you're detected, get out fast."

The raiders spent the day before the assignment aboard the *Bass* studying their target area and going over their own movements again and again until a split-second teamwork plan had been worked out. The transport would anchor offshore, but would lower a square-bowed LCPR (Landing Craft, Personnel, Ramp) that would go in a little closer, hover about like a mother duck, keep communications with the ship, and watch the raiders make their approach in five inflatable rubber-boat loads. (The boats were really plastic, but were called rubber boats as a generic term.)

The LCPR was lowered with its engine already turning over. The raiders scampered down the cargo nets into their rubber boats. The "PR," as they always called it, towed them to within five hundred yards of the shore, and they paddled for the beach. Second Lieutenant Shutler, in Boat Able, went in first. His task was reconnaissance, and he had fifteen minutes for it.

That night at Tanchon, Major Dupras, in the "PR," called

him several times on the walkie-talkie, received no answer, and after about twenty-five minutes began to go, as he said, "raving crazy."

Ashore, Shutler had approached the first railroad tunnel cautiously and to his surprise found a formidable-looking concrete pillbox at the southern end. With his dozen or so men, he sneaked along the beach to the northern end, and found another pillbox. Both pillboxes seemed quiet and perhaps were empty. He crawled toward the northern one on his belly. When he came close he heard, through the tiny concrete slits, what seemed to be the sound of breathing.

Now Shutler moved in a crouch around the corner of the pillbox to its entrance, which was open, and beamed his flashlight inside. He had been ready to spray the interior with fire from his carbine, and no doubt this would have been the proper precaution, but something on this occasion caused him to hold off and shine the flashlight first. In its beam he saw four ragged civilians, two middle-aged men, one scrawny woman and a wide-eyed, ten-year-old boy. They had been working their way down from the north to flee the Communist regime and had taken shelter for the night in the pillbox.

Shutler finally called the Marine major back on the "PR" with his walkie-talkie. "I have four prisoners," he said. "What'll I do with them?"

Dupras relayed this back to the *Bass* where Commander Small wondered what he'd done to find himself with the necessity of making a decision like this, and finally solved matters by saying that the civilians were to be tied up tight enough to keep them from interfering with the demolition preparations, but loose enough to let them escape afterward.

And so it was done, and the charges of C-3 planted, and the raiders brought back in a scramble to their rubber boats and once more toward the small landing craft lying offshore. The explosion came twenty minutes later in a great blue sheet of light and flames that leapt 150 feet high. The rubber boats shook in the water. The tunnels had been demolished.

Another night at Kunsan, about one hundred miles below Inchon, the raiders had been fired upon as they were withdrawing and Lieutenant George Acheson III had had the bill of his baseball cap split by a bullet, though he himself was unharmed.

Tonight, however, at the wide beach of Posung-myon, everything went most smoothly, and young Lieutenant Cashion, alert, tense, and not so much afraid of enemy fire as of the possibility of his goofing through lack of experience, decided he'd learned one important thing about combat. You never really knew exactly what was going to happen. They'd been prepared for opposition here, and they found none at all. It was surprising that the Communists apparently hadn't seen fit to post some kind of guard along these ideal landing beaches. That was all it meant to Cashion—surprise; it would mean a great deal more to both Admiral Doyle and Marine General Lem Shepherd when they received this information back in Tokyo.[1]

In Tokyo, on August 21, Admiral Doyle studied the reports on the beaches at Posung-myon, and in the crowded compartment of the U. S. S. *Mt. McKinley* showed his estimate of the situation to General Shepherd. Like everyone else involved in the planning, Doyle knew that MacArthur had his heart set on Inchon, and if MacArthur's mind couldn't be changed he would go along with Inchon—he'd storm Gibraltar and try to do a good job of it, if ordered to—but he still saw Inchon as something less than the ideal landing site, and he considered it his duty to pass along to MacArthur as much of his own expert knowledge and accumulation of facts as the old man had time to assimilate.

His feelings about Inchon were summed up in a statement he made less than a year later. "Besides the hardships imposed by the tides, Inchon had other objectionable features. For example, we lacked complete information about how much and where dredging had been done in the harbor. Another obstacle was the limited facilities there, even after we won it. Its pier and dock space was small, and the harbor wasn't big enough ever to make it a real logistics base through which we could supply and maintain a big army. The available landing points were spread over a four-mile stretch of waterfront and consisted for the most part of piers and sea walls. So we had to plan on improving the existing facilities in order that unloading could proceed at an acceptable rate."[2]

Doyle believed that with the necessary experienced forces an amphibious landing could be made anywhere, even at Inchon, if the commander was willing to accept the risk. He had studied Iwo Jima where it had been known from the start that the losses would be high, but where the rewards had been considered worth it. It seemed to him that any commander, including Douglas MacArthur, would "naturally prefer to make a landing at a place where probable losses would be minimized, if the same strategic and tactical objectives could be accomplished."[3]

He liked Posung-myon. It had beaches, as opposed to Inchon's sea walls. It was sparsely inhabited; the Utes and Marine raiders had gone ashore there virtually unnoticed. Aerial photographs showed many gun emplacements around Inchon, and there wasn't so much as a toy cannon at Posung-myon. Posung-myon was also fairly near to the final objective of Seoul—a short drive inland, indeed, would bring troops to the main highway leading north to Seoul—and quite near the point where that slim battalion of American troops had first met the Communists driving south. This was now the North Korean main supply line. A stroke here would cut it neatly and put the attackers in perfect position for a shot at Seoul. This ought to take care of MacArthur's principal objection to a spot other than Inchon.

It would mean a slight delay, of course. More intelligence would have to be gathered on Posung-myon. Fortunately, the tides were not critical here—another advantage—and the landing wouldn't have to be made on a specific date or be put off until the following month. So the slight delay shouldn't be significant. He felt that Posung-myon at least ought to be considered even though "there was no opportunity to make a detailed study . . . because it was obvious that General MacArthur's mind was made up on Inchon."[4]

Doyle wanted to be very sure that MacArthur understood Inchon's disadvantages as well as himself. He approached General Almond and suggested a detailed briefing. General Almond answered that General MacArthur was not interested in details. But it so happened that on the next day, August 23, a major briefing was scheduled anyway, primarily for Admiral Sherman, the Chief of Naval Operations, and General J. Lawton Collins, the Army Chief of Staff who had flown to the Far East this time to find out what was going on. Collins, in particular, felt "somewhat in the dark" about precisely what was intended at Inchon.[5]

And so Doyle was given his chance to take several selected experts from his Phib Group I planning team and have them tell both MacArthur and the chiefs of staff exactly what Inchon would mean. "Actually," he wrote, "it would have made no difference whether I 'believed' in Inchon or not. The decision was General MacArthur's and I would have executed it successfully if it was humanly possible to do so."[6]

Still, he was the expert—the only flag or general officer on

MacArthur's staff with intense amphibious warefare experience, he felt, and in good conscience he had to pass on his opinion and the cogent reasons behind it to the great man himself, even if it meant risking his anger. He was not alone in thinking that Posung-myon's beaches might be a better site. General Shepherd, another amphibious expert, the commander of the Fleet Marine Force, Pacific, now out on a visit to see how his Marines would be used, had looked over the available data and agreed with him.

While Doyle was showing the results of his studies to Shepherd, the Chief of Naval Operations, Admiral Forrest Sherman, was in southwestern Japan, far from Tokyo, conferring with Vice Admiral Arthur D. Struble, commander of the Seventh Fleet. Struble had his flagship cruiser, the U. S. S. *Rochester*, moored in the big naval base at Sasebo in Kyushu, Japan's southernmost main island, on a shore that looked across the straits toward Korea.

(To all but the members of MacArthur's GHQ themselves these interlocking commands and relationships often seemed confusing and the basis for an unnecessarily wide dispersion of responsibility. There was even a feeling that offices and commands were created and passed out so that all the high-ranking officers would feel they had something important to do—a kind of many-chiefs-few-Indians situation. New arrivals to GHQ would sometimes be there several weeks before it became absolutely clear who had charge of what. It was common to all the services, but in the case of the Navy, the command structure, unraveled, was this: Admiral Joy was overall commander of Naval Forces, Far East, which meant not only Japan and Korea but such places as Okinawa and Taiwan. The main fighting seagoing unit under him was the Seventh Fleet, commanded by Struble. Struble would also command the task force that was being formed specifically for the Inchon landing; it would include most of the Seventh Fleet. Admiral Doyle had been the specialist commander of the study and training organization, Phib Group I, but now he had been drafted to head the attack element, Task Force 90, under the larger Joint Task Force 7, which Struble would command.)

Since the outbreak of the war, the Seventh Fleet had been busy helping to keep Walker's beleaguered Perimeter army supplied, and its carrier planes had been providing air support in the target area while its ships were bombarding points on the coast. Struble had been so involved in these matters that he hadn't been included as often as some of the other commanders in the Inchon plans.

On August 22, in Sasebo, aboard the *Rochester,* Admiral Sherman brought him up to date as far as the thinking in Washington was concerned. Struble had been Sherman's deputy in Washington before taking over the Seventh Fleet and the two men were on friendly terms. Sherman explained that he and the Army's chief of staff had come to the Far East, this time specifically to hear MacArthur's final justification for the Inchon plan, which they still had the power to disapprove, even though the preparations for it were now going along full tilt. "Rip" Struble (they all had nicknames for each other) was to command the seaborne part of the operation if it went through. "Go to Tokyo," said Sherman, "and get the plan done as soon as possible. It's very important for the Navy to have a good, sound plan."[7]

Struble was not among the doubters concerning Inchon, possibly because he had not yet studied the site in great detail. He realized that there were some obstacles but decided he would "not waste five seconds" debating whether the landing should be at Inchon or Kunsan, and afterward, when he was quoted in the press as saying that Inchon had been a great gamble, he was disturbed and certain he'd never said anything of the kind.[8] He felt that his own amphibious experience in the Philippines, working with MacArthur, was closer to the Inchon project than the experience of some of the experts; he had also worked with the Army in amphibious operations in the great Normandy invasion.

After Sherman left him that night, Rip Struble sat down for three or four hours and made the notes that would eventually become the Navy's Inchon plan. He called one of his two carrier admirals in, Rear Admiral Edward C. Ewen, a senior man whose competence he admired, outlined his brief schedule—some of it not yet on paper—and then told Eddie Ewen he would command the fast carrier group, which would consist of the *Philippine Sea,* the *Valley Forge,* and the *Boxer.* He would leave for Tokyo in the morning, and his flagship would follow as soon as it could get away.

Doyle, meanwhile, was enlisting a new ally to his position that perhaps the Inchon site did not offer the best buy. Marine Major General Oliver P. Smith had arrived to command the Marine Division that would be landed at Inchon, and aboard the *McKinley* in Tokyo harbor he was now getting a closer look at the assault scheme. "When I first looked at Inchon," he recorded later, "I thought it was preposterous. The city was poison. It was risky because the enemy had splendid opportunities for defense while the ability of my troops to spread out quickly and gain sufficient ground to secure the beachhead was restricted, and once we got ashore we'd have only a very short period of daylight in which to gain a foothold, capture our objectives, and organize for the night."[9]

How much of this feeling on the part of his key naval and military commanders MacArthur knew or sensed is not known, although some of it would shortly become evident at the big conference being readied, but the important men to be sold on Inchon were General Collins and Admiral Sherman. It was not only that they had the power to disapprove. They had to be fully behind it. They had to feel, as MacArthur did, that out of several possible moves it was by far the best. They had to commit themselves, as MacArthur had, to the point where they couldn't possibly back out at the last moment.

August 23, 5:30 P.M. Generals with their glittering silver stars and admirals with their gold shoulder boards filed into the relatively small conference room between MacArthur's and Almond's offices. It was a dignified and somewhat old-fashioned room, erected originally by the big Japanese insurance company that had built the Dai-Ichi Building; polished wood panels covered the walls, and columns were lined like sentries along one side.

A large chair with a high back had been put into the room for General MacArthur. He sat at a front table, his back to everyone except the briefing officers and their charts. A number of his pipes had been laid out on the table before him.

Behind MacArthur, on ordinary chairs, were Collins, Sherman and Lieutenant General Idwal H. Edwards of the Air Force, representing its top Washington command. They were the distinguished visitors. From MacArthur's command itself were General Almond with the general officers of his staff, and General Ruffner, who would be his X-Corps Chief of Staff, Admirals Joy, Struble and Doyle, plus the Far East Air Forces commander, Major General George Stratemeyer.

These men and their immediate assistants filled the small room, so the briefing officers stood outside in General Almond's office, waiting to go on as though they were performers in the wings.

General Wright, the G-3, opened with a brief outline of the basic plan, then turned the meeting over to the naval experts. It was the fourteenth briefing Phib Group I had given on an amphibious landing. It was the fifth major conference at which Inchon was dicussed. The officer in charge of the briefers, Captain Norman W. Sears, USN, sat at the open door to Almond's office, rather like a stage manager in full view of the audience.

The briefers had nine subjects—navigation, hydrography, intelligence, weather, military aspects, beach study, the pontoons and causeways, ship-to-shore plans, gunfire and air support—and each was alloted about ten minutes for his presentation. Young Lieutenant Commander Jack Lowentraut, who gave the presentation on beach study, shared the opinion of his colleagues that Inchon might be a tough nut to crack. Since mid-July they'd been working furiously on plans for no less than three landings—Inchon, Wonsan, and Kunsan—and they were probably as familiar as anyone in the world with the characteristics of these three locations. Even so, they'd given themselves last-minute rehearsals on Inchon so that each briefing would be concise and to the point. The listening time of so many generals and admirals was not to be wasted.

MacArthur sat quietly, puffing his pipe, as the briefings began. In battle it was his trademark to take dramatic risks, to dare all for the absolute reward, and then to emerge triumphant with everyone but his supremely confident self in a cold sweat. Now he was acting with this same audacity in that other important battlefield of war—the conference room. He had agreed to hear Doyle's briefing; he could not help but know that the briefers would conscientiously point out every possible obstacle to an Inchon landing. It was their job to do so. But there was a very real danger that Forrest Sherman would be impressed by this information and refuse to give his moral or perhaps even his actual support. MacArthur was willing to risk this, because after the briefings, he would have the perfect opportunity to present, in one stroke, his side of the case and make it forever clear why he was determined on Inchon.

As the briefing went on, the picture of a most formidable undertaking, indeed, began to emerge. It seemed that every aspect of the plan was hung with one or more little bells of discord. They were all beginning to ring with an annoying clamor.

The LST's needed twenty-nine feet of water to clear the mudflats as they came in, and they'd have it only for short periods that day, near sunset and daybreak.

Between tides the water would move in and out fast—as much as six knots in some places—vastly complicating the necessarily slow approach of larger ships, drastically cutting down the speed of the smaller boats that would be bucking the current.

The only approach would be up through Flying Fish Channel, a trench in the mudflats that led to Inchon, and there was no room here for the larger ships to turn.

The fire-support ships would have to anchor in the channel to keep from being swept away by the current, and they would be sitting ducks for the shore batteries.

The stand-by ships out in the Yellow Sea would be about thirty miles off; this would interfere with voice communications and perhaps even make them impossible.

After each high tide the water would ebb somewhat more slowly than it had come in and there would be a period of perhaps three hours when troops and supplies could be put ashore, once in the morning and once in the evening. That was not a great deal of time—unheard of, as a matter of fact, for a major amphibious landing—and thus every minute would have to count and there would be no margin for even the slightest of errors. It was possible that the landing force might be stranded until the next high tide. The LST's would almost certainly be stranded; you could just about count on that. They'd be fine, fat targets for shore batteries, there on the mud by the sea walls.

Flying Fish Channel would probably be sown with mines. (Admiral Struble, who supported the Inchon plan, himself worried more about mines than any other single factor; he felt the Russians might well have supplied the North Koreans with their particularly dangerous "ground mine," a coffinlike affair of cement that sinks in forty or fifty feet of water and explodes as a ship passes over it, by far the most destructive type of mine. It was impossible, in the time allotted, to mount a reconnaisance that might detect their presence. Struble told MacArthur that "barring Russian intervention, the worst thing that could happen would be to find the Inchon channel loaded with modern ground mines." (The channel was beautifully adapted to them.)

All this would have been bad enough upon an unpopulated or undefended shore. Inchon, however, was guarded by a small fortified island hill that stood just off the harbor, connected to the mainland by a mile-long causeway. This was called Wolmi-do, and from its crest all the harbor and waterfront in every direction could be seen. A number of gun emplacements had already been photographed by aerial reconnaissance on Wolmi-do. Wolmi-do could be knocked out by aerial and naval gun bombardment. But this job would take more than a few hours in a single morning (it would take ten days, one of the naval briefers opined), and if you hammered at it too long, there went the element of surprise —the principal virtue of the landing.

MacArthur's own researchers in JSPOG had come up with the belief that two days of barrage ought to be enough to knock out Wolmi-do. They thought a one-day preparation might be even better to preserve the element of surprise. This call for a ten-day bombardment began to sound like hyperbole, and a cold, hard, concise briefing was no place for colorful figures of speech. Besides, the briefing had been going on for about an hour now, and some of the high-ranking officers were fighting yawns. The briefer seemed to be overstating his case for Admiral Sherman's benefit.

Pinky Wright happened to glance at Admiral Sherman. He thought he saw him frown. Until this moment Wright had considered the briefing excellent, "sound, objective and clearly consistent with the serious problems involved," as he later said. But the briefer holding the floor at the moment seemed to be talking down to Admiral Sherman, himself scarcely a novice in naval combat operations. Ever afterward General Wright felt that "Admiral Sherman at this point began to question some of the other aspects of the Navy staff objections to the JSPOG plan."[10]

And that was where the MacArthur luck came in. An over-enthusiastic junior officer, undoubtedly sincere in his own beliefs, hardworking and all wrapped up in his own expertise, at the end of a long, hot August afternoon, began to faintly annoy the Chief of Naval Operations, just enough to have him start thinking that maybe all of the objections were a little narrowed, a little focused, a little too subjective. Maybe. He still wasn't ready to whistle with joy over Inchon. But he might start considering some of its advantages now and weighing them against the disadvantages, some of which had already lost weight in his own mind. He knew that alternate sites existed at Kunsan and Posung-myon, but these would not be discussed in detail unless Inchon was dismissed.

The briefing was done. Admiral Doyle rose and turned to General MacArthur. "General, I have not been asked for my recommendation on Inchon, nor have I given it. However, the best I can say about Inchon is that it is *not* impossible."

MacArthur nodded, and said, as though musing, that if the landing force got to Inchon and found it couldn't get ashore, then it would withdraw.

"No, General," said Doyle—and it was like damning the torpedoes and going ahead to throw a flat "No" at MacArthur —"we don't know how to do that. Once we start in, we'll keep going."[11]

There was a pause and a stir. MacArthur, still in his chair, still facing the wall where the charts hung, still with his back to everyone else, reached for another pipe, and then in his low, deep voice, in his measured, full-blown phrases, with nary a vocal edit, began a forty-five minute monologue that no man in that room would ever forget.

It was a soliloquy that should have ben recorded verbatim for history. Those who were there remembered the substance of the remarks afterward, and there were phrases that stuck in their memories, but most of the actual words seeped into the dark mahogany walls of that conference room and were lost.[12]

Seoul was the target, said MacArthur; Seoul, the capital of Korea, captured by the Communists when they began the war not quite two months ago. A landing at Inchon would make possible the recapture of Seoul only ninety days or so after it had been taken. That was important. It would seize the imagination of all Asia and win psychological support for the United Nations cause in Korea.

The enemy, MacArthur pointed out, had now concentrated ninety percent of his forces around the Pusan Perimeter, where they were still trying to drive Johnny Walker back into the sea. To take the troops earmarked for Inchon and give them to Walker to fight his way northward out of the perimeter would cost a hundred thousand casualties.

He pointed to Inchon on the map before him. A force would land there and take Seoul. It would control all the territory in the rear of the main North Korean army. "It will be the anvil," he said—and all present remembered in particular this image—"upon which General Walker will smash the Reds from the South!"

Then he discussed one of the alternatives that had been mentioned, the landing at Kunsan, one hundred miles below

Inchon, that seemed to be favored by General Collins. The idea was good, he remarked diplomatically, but the location was wrong. A landing there would not sever the North Korean supply lines, which came out of Seoul and then swung southeastward to the Perimeter. Also, the landing area at Kunsan was extremely limited—the map showed a narrow river leading up to Kunsan and swamps all about—and the exit routes to the interior were marginal. No major communications center such as Seoul was available as the end target. True, a landing at Kunsan would remove some of the objections to an Inchon landing. But from a strategic viewpoint, the taking of Kunsan would not be a decisive stroke. It would just be another landing.

The amphibious landing was a powerful military device, said MacArthur, and it should not be wasted, but employed properly. To use it at Inchon would be to strike deep and hard into enemy-held territory. To land elsewhere would open the possibility of a long and bitter winter campaign in Korea.

And then there was the element of surprise. The North Koreans would consider a landing at Inchon impossible. Something like this had happened before, strangely enough in mid-September, at Quebec, in 1759. The British general, Wolfe, had sailed from England to take Quebec from the French, and he had put a flanking force ashore at the base of a steep cliff, the last place the French expected it, taking the city swiftly and with a minimum of casualties. He had done this with the help of the British Navy, as MacArthur had carried out his own landings in World War II.

"The Navy has never let me down," said MacArthur.

He still hadn't turned to look at those behind him. It was masterly—the feeling was not that he was talking to them, but that they were sharing his deepest thoughts. It could not possibly have been contrived. It was the MacArthur touch.

His voice dropped almost to a whisper.

"We shall land at Inchon and I shall crush them!"

"There was not a dry eye in the place," said one of the young briefers, remembering it afterward. Everyone had been caught up with MacArthur's emotion, dazzled at his way of saying words that in the mouths of other men might sound like sentimental oratory and out of another century, at that.

Filing out of the room with the others, Admiral Sherman sighed and said, "I wish I could share that man's optimism."[13]

Sherman was just about won over. Yet he realized he'd been swayed not entirely by cold logic, and to be quite sure about everything, he conferred with MacArthur privately the next day for nearly one and a half hours. After that he was ready to gamble, although he still wished that the odds could be better.

General Collins was not entirely sold. Everybody else seemed to be going along with MacArthur's plan, and he had to agree that it had its merits, but he still wasn't convinced it was the best plan, all things considered. It seemed to him that sound military practice called for stronger alternative moves to be ready in case something went wrong. Remaining in Tokyo the next day, he questioned Ned Almond closely about the other possible site at Kunsan. Almond went over the map with him, pointed out the narrow river leading inland, and explained that only one LST at a time would be able to make the approach in such close quarters. Collins also worried about enemy opposition at Inchon, but Almond assured him that Willoughby's G-2 reports, estimating no more than six to eight thousand North Korean troops in the area, were reliable. Collins was still not precisely won over to the plan, but he was running out of objections that could not be met.

Almond's VMI classmate, Lem Shepherd, came to MacArthur the day after the conference in an apparent last-minute effort to get him to change his mind. Shepherd liked the plan Jimmy Doyle had suggested—the landing at the undefended beach of Posung-myon, thirty miles south of Inchon. True, the area hadn't received the intense study already given Inchon and Kunsan, but it looked well worth some further investigation.

MacArthur was adamant.

"I shall land at Inchon . . . and I shall crush them!"

Collins and Sherman went back to Washington and presented MacArthur's detailed plan, as they now knew it, to the Joint Chiefs of Staff, and the messages began to go back and forth.

The partial text of JCS Message 89960, sent to MacArthur on August 28, is interesting and typical: "We concur in making preparation for executing a turning movement by amphibious forces on the west coast of Korea, either at Inchon in the event the enemy defenses in the vicinity of Inchon prove ineffective, or at favorable beach south of Inchon if one can be located. We further concur in preparations, if desired by CINCFE, for an envelopment by amphibious forces in the vicinity of Kunsan. We understand that alternative plans are being prepared in order to best exploit the situation as it develops."

The language is almost legalistic, and what they really seemed to be saying was, "Go ahead, if you must—but don't blame us if it fails."

And one of MacArthur's return messages in this exchange began. "Take no counsel of your fears. . . ."[14] Only Douglas MacArthur could speak to the Joint Chiefs of Staff in this manner and get away with it.

His message of September 8 reiterated his convictions. The JCS had asked him if he wouldn't reconsider the whole question. "I regard [the Inchon landing's] chance of success," said MacArthur, "as excellent. I go further and believe that it represents the only hope of wresting the initiative from the enemy and thereby presenting an opportunity for a decisive blow." The message continued a little further on, "Caught between our northern and southern forces . . . the enemy cannot fail to be ultimately shattered . . . the embarkation of the troops and the preliminary air and naval preparations are proceeding according to schedule. . . ."

And the answer to this message, almost like a short sigh, was simply, "We approve of your plan and the President has been so informed."

There would be no backing out now. The commanders in MacArthur's headquarters, the ragtag and bobtail Seventh Army Division training desperately just south of Tokyo, the Marine Brigade fighting in the Perimeter, a Marine regiment still at sea and on its way, the ships of the Seventh Fleet, all would meet at Inchon at dawn on September 15. The obstacles had all been considered, the dangers noted, and they would be braved.

But far, far to the south in the Pacific Ocean, somewhere off the Philippines, a new natural obstacle was being born. Two of them in fact. And these were obstacles that the skill and spirit of the finest amphibious task force in the world would not be able to overcome.

These were the typhoons Jane and Kezia, the tenth and eleventh massive storms of the season noted by the weather observers and given their alphabetic female names. Jane was already discernible as a tropical storm swirling in a hundred-mile circle, drifting slowly northward. Kezia was a mere pocket of low pressure just beginning to form elsewhere in the trackless Pacific waste. It was too early to say exactly just what these storms would do, but the general pattern of such huge meteorlogical cataclysms in this part of the world and at this time of the year was to work up toward Japan, gathering force all the while, and a definite possibility was that Jane might hit just as most of the attack force was embarking from Japan and Kezia might come along through the Yellow Sea the very day of the landing.

NOTES   *Chapter 6*

1. Letter D. B. Cashion to author, 17 Nov 66.
2. Karig *et al,* p. 162.
3. Letter Doyle to author, 12 Oct 66.
4. *Ibid.*
5. *MacArthur Hearings,* 82nd Congress, June 51, p. 1295.
6. Letter Doyle to author, 12 Oct 66.
7. Interview author—Adm Arthur D. Struble.
8. *Ibid.*
9. Karig *et al,* p. 163.
10. Letter Wright to author, 10 Oct 66.
11. Letter Doyle to author, 12 Oct 66.
12. MacArthur himself reconstructs the words of his talk in his *Reminiscences,* pp. 348–50. He remarks that during the pause before he spoke, Almond "shifted uneasily in his chair." Almond remembers this pause and remembers stirring, for before the conference he had said to MacArthur, "General, do not let them talk you out of it." Manuscript review comments for author, Almond, 8 May 67.
13. Interview author—Struble.
14. Interview author—Polk.

7

"Thank God for that little bulldog ... "

ERNEST HEY WAS GETTING NO SLEEP ON THE DARK MORNING of September 3, in the great port of Kobe on Japan's southern coast. One of the many civilian experts working for the U. S. military forces occupying Japan, he was a husky man who looked like the port boss and dockmaster that he was. He was a simple, no-nonsense man who seldom used unnecessary words and dressed plainly. Some of his co-workers kidded him about the cheap $6.50 rummage sale watch he wore when fine Swiss models could be bought at bargain prices in the tax-free PX's. He worked with tough men and he himself was tough, but with special knowledge of intricate port problems learned the hard way. The Kobe port commander was Army Lieutenant Colonel R. L. Blust, but it was Hey, his principal civilian assistant, who ran things at the operating level.

This morning it looked as though things were going to need some pretty special running, if they weren't to fly entirely out of control. There were more than fifty major ships in the harbor, and the biggest typhoon of the season was screaming its way toward Japan, its center expected to pass directly over Kobe at ten o'clock that morning. Hey knew that typhoons could toss the largest ships around as though they were corks, and all night he and his men had been working to double two-and-a-half-inch chain steel mooring lines. But now the wind and rain had increased, and as Hey glanced up anxiously now and then, he wondered if the unpredictable typhoon hadn't decided to come in ahead of schedule. Typhoons often did things like that in spite of the best weather predictions.

Hey knew that damage to the ships now lying-to in Kobe

harbor might be disastrous to the United States war effort across the straits in Korea. For every one of these vessels was marked to bring troops and supplies—primarily those of the 1st Marine Division—to a landing at Inchon on September 15. Only a few days ago, the big transports had waddled into Kobe with about 12,000 Marines and their gear, and this combat force was scheduled to jump off again in a week— provided they still had their ships, Hey thought darkly, as the heavy rain began to come in almost horizontally and struck everything like steel shot.

Strictly speaking, Hey probably wasn't supposed to know about the top secret plan for an Inchon landing, but of course he did know about it, as did practically everyone else in Kobe, and he understood the desperate importance of the maneuver. His boss, Colonel Blust, had learned about it on August 25, when he'd attended a meeting at nearby Atami airfield, where he had been briefed by high-ranking officers of the Japan Logistical Command who had flown down from Tokyo specifically to give him the word. The word had been passed on to Hey. Marines from the United States would arrive about August 28. By September 11, they would have to be ready to sail again in assault ships to make the three-and-a-half-day trip to Inchon. They and their gear would have to be unloaded, the equipment stacked, inventoried and loaded again, about thirty thousand tons of it, all in less than two weeks.

It was unheard of. But then so was almost everything else about this landing plan.

The first thing Hey needed was space, and so the quartermaster, who controlled port facilities, was instructed to turn over to him three additional piers and warehouses "for the duration." That gave him six piers, each 1,270 feet long, which meant twelve docksides at his disposal. He had also three half-piers for smaller vessels, and eight buoy sites in the harbor. Loading and unloading would be speeded by eight floating cranes, ranging from thirty to two hundred tons.

On August 28, the first influx had arrived: the transports *General Buckner* and *Butner,* filled with Marines and equipment. The following day the *General Weigle, President Jackson, American Patriot* and *Oglethorpe* pulled in. These were the major ships. They brought in the various Marine units that, added to the 1st Provisional Marine Brigade already fighting in the Perimeter, would form the 1st Marine Divi-

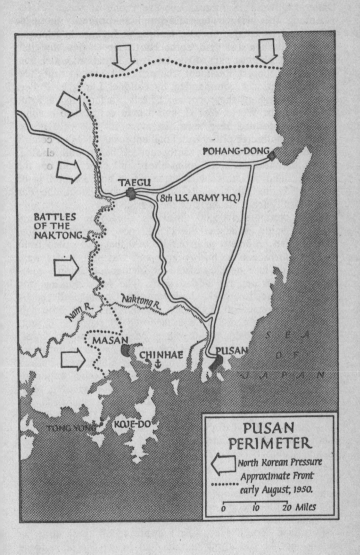

PUSAN
PERIMETER

North Korean Pressure
Approximate Front
early August, 1950.

0   10   20 Miles

sion under the command of the scholarly, precise Major General Oliver P. Smith.

Among the arrivals was Corporal Joe Maize, the half-Kiowa Indian amateur boxer, who between wars had longed for the Marines and had come back just in time for this assignment. He was part of the 1st Tank Battalion, which was attached to the 1st Regiment, the principal combat unit. The 1st Regiment was commanded by Colonel Lewis B. Puller, known throughout the corps as "Chesty," a flamboyant fighting veteran of World War II, and a man destined to become the most decorated Marine in history.

Although the absolute and final approval of MacArthur's plan did not arrive until exactly a week before the landing, all the preparations were going ahead full blast, and not the least of them was this swift organization and assembling of the 1st Marine Division, its units converging upon the Far East literally from all parts of the world.

There were nearly 5,000 Marines already in Korea, and to them would be added the 12,000 now arriving in Kobe, plus another shipment of around 5,000 that had sailed from the Mediterranean in mid-August and was still on its way. The brigade in Korea consisted of Lieutenant Colonel Murray's 5th Marines and added units. The force coming into Kobe was, so to speak, built around Chesty Puller's 1st Marines, a regiment of nearly 4,000 men. Both Murray's and Puller's regiments were augmented by portions of units that sometimes belonged together. Murray, over in Korea, for example, had Company A of the 1st Engineer Battalion, but the rest of this battalion had come along with Puller's force. Tank, Ordnance, Signal, Medical and other battalions were split the same way. Thus, for the big show itself, Murray Puller would be commanding not straight regiments, but larger forces known as Regimental Combat Teams—RCT-5 for Murray, RCT-1 for Puller. These two forces would go ashore first. They would be followed by still another Regimental Combat Team, RCT-7, commanded by Colonel Homer Litzenberg, but not scheduled to arrive until several days after the beachhead was secured. This would give the entire Marine division three of these Regimental Combat Teams for the capture of Seoul, a project that might turn out to be bloodier and more difficult than the landing itself.

Port boss Ernest Hey wasn't aware of all these strategic details, but he did know that he had to get the main force of Marines on its way to Korea by the 11th of September or there wouldn't be any landing, and just as in the old want-of-a-nail story, the Perimeter would be breached and the war lost.

On the first day of the Marines' arrival, Hey and his men unloaded 6,000 long tons of cargo from the transports (one long ton=2,240 pounds). It was hasty, frantic and not neat. Everything had been loaded in California in such a rush that nobody knew where any particular group of items might be; in many cases it was simply a matter of putting unmarked crates to one side, and hoping they'd be reloaded in the proper places. The job was done by over a thousand Japanese workers divided into fifty-six teams of around twenty men each, and with each team four United States officers and ten enlisted men. Work went on around the clock, the lights glowing in the harbor waters all night, every night.

Port workers unloaded not only cargo but personnel, and processed them for their brief stay in Japan. The largest portion of the Marine force fanned out to nearby Army posts to continue their combat training—many were fresh recruits who had barely learned the manual of arms. Hey and his staff managed to arrange for a firing range at sea for the Marine amphibious tractor unit so its men could sharpen their proficiency. About 3,000 of the Marines remained in the port of Kobe to assist as stevedores, and they were kept quartered aboard the transports, regarding their accommodations as rather plush for Marines.

As the typhoon approached, Hey thought of these 3,000 men living on the docked ships. They were infinitely more important than cargo.

All night of September 2, and all through the morning of September 3, the stevedores and Marines worked furiously to prepare for the typhoon. Gear and supplies already on the dock had to be doubly lashed. Many of the supplies were still in the holds of the ships and had to be moved ashore quickly. There was a great deal of ammunition and ordnance still unloaded. Corporal Joe Maize worked with the rest, and he was pleased to see his company commander, Captain Philip Morrel, an ex-schoolteacher recently called back to active duty, laboring with the rest, his shirt soaking wet with rain and sweat. This was one of the reasons why Joe liked the Marines; by tradition, Marines cussed their officers and pretended they hated all officers, but when the chips were down, Joe thought, Marine officers were always right there with their men, taking the worst of it.[1]

Just before dawn, Hey got the report from weather that the typhoon was four hours ahead of schedule and would pass over Kobe at 6 A.M. instead of 10 A.M. He hardly needed the report—he could see that most of its fury was already upon them. It was very dark. Even the big lights glaring along the docks didn't entirely penetrate the thick, whiplashing rain. The waves beyond the breakwaters were rising to heights of forty feet and the immense and unbelievable power of the seas in the harbor itself was kicking the huge vessels around as though they were bathtub toys. The mooring lines that had been doubled during the night, snapped in places, and Hey sent teams racing through the storm and along the piers to triple them. They were tripled, and began to snap again. They were quadrupled. Some of them still snapped.

All around the dock area, houses were toppling and up-rooted trees were flying through the air. The winds were rising to over a hundred knots. The waves were picking huge eight-by-four concrete blocks off the breakwater and tossing them aside. The sea, pushed into the shore by the typhoon, had come up to cover the docks so that the water in some places was knee deep.

It was a man's life to go out into it, but men did just that, including Hey himself, inching along the piers with lifelines around them to reach a winch or a bollard where a line had snapped, to secure a pile of cargo about to topple.

The sternline of a transport called the *General Meigs* snapped and she swung hard toward a parallel pier to slam the side of another transport, the *Whiteside,* and crush her plates. Once a ship got away, there was nothing much that could be done about it but let her swing, and before the day was over seven vessels altogether were to snap their lines.

By the clock it was daylight, but still almost as dark as before dawn. Hey, making fast an extra line near the end of one pier, suddenly saw several of the Army port men rushing toward him, waving and shouting. Their sickening news was that one of the 200-ton cranes had broken loose completely and might go tossing through the harbor to smash everything in its path. Hey jeeped to the spot immediately, fighting his little car through the wind and the rain. The crane was against the dock, at the moment more or less pinned there by the wind, but rubbing and pounding and already doing damage to the dock itself. Hey knew that as the typhoon passed the wind direction would change, and eventually send the monster off.

The big crane was a ship in itself, with spaces below in its hull, and the several members of its Japanese crew had already gone below, possibly to get out of the storm, possibly resigned to fate. Several Marines leapt aboard the tossing hulk to fetch them and help them ashore.

"There's only one thing'll hold that baby," said Hey. Steel line would snap and most manila line was too weak. But he knew where there was a coil of manila ten inches in diameter. It was in a storage space three and a half miles away.

A Marine sergeant volunteered to get it. In the excitement, Hey didn't catch his name. There was a two-and-a-half-ton truck nearby that Hey thought might be heavy enough to drive through the typhoon. The Marine sergeant jumped into it and took off. He could make headway only in first and second gear, and before he returned, the terrible winds had blown out his windshield, bashed in part of the truck's side, and crumpled the hood. It was about an hour before he got back with the line.

The coil of ten-inch line was arranged on the dock; Hey took another small line for hauling it in his wake, poised himself at the edge of the dock, waited for the right moment, and leapt aboard the deck of the crane as it surged on the upswing. For a moment he lost his balance and to the horrified watchers on the shore it seemed that he might be thrown by the heaving deck against the pier and crushed; then suddenly he was on his feet again and making his way to a main girder where the line could be made fast.

At that instant the wind and rain abruptly subsided. The eye of the typhoon was passing over them. In the center of the huge moving doughnut of cloud and storm, it was suddenly ominously quiet; the hot, still, sticky air seemed some poisonous substance in which everybody was being immersed. Hey affixed the giant line to the crane.

In the relative quiet of the typhoon's eye—though the seas were still heaving—Hey and his workers rushed about to make other lines fast to the crane. Their respite did not last long. Presently the other circular wall of the storm was bearing down upon them, and now the wind had changed direction and was blowing the 200-ton crane away from the dock. As they watched in agony it jerked, bobbed and tugged, and suddenly the ten-inch manila line snapped and it was free.

With Ernest Hey and four Marines aboard, the crane began to rush, berserk, around the harbor. Its deck would disappear under water, then suddenly reach upward on the crest of a wave. They clung and tied themselves to girders. Abruptly a huge cargo hook, itself weighing several hundred pounds, broke loose from its fastening and began to swing on its cable like a terrible mace, slamming and crashing all about the men on deck, barely missing them at times.

The wind and waves carried the crane swiftly toward another pier. Hey was gauging distance and wondering if they'd be able to find an opportunity to leap ashore, when suddenly a huge wave picked up the entire floating 200-ton monster and crashed it atop the dock, where it made a deep crater in the concrete and steel plates. Hey and the Marines leapt from it.

He had just about regained his breath when a smaller, 30-ton crane broke loose. He rushed to the spot and saw that it was bobbing a few yards away from the dock—just far enough to make a leap impossible. He tied a line to his waist, jumped into the heaving sea, swam to the crane and crawled aboard. He then hauled out a heavier line, made it fast, and the crane was winched back to the dock.

It was past noon now. The storm was still raging, reaching its second period of maximum fury. Suddenly, on one of the docks, a stack of 55-gallon drums containing 115-octane gasoline broke loose, fell and burst, and the volatile fluid began to stream into the wild sea, making the water a color that Hey remembered afterward as a "sickly yellow." The fuel was not far from one of the many piles of ammunition in the area.

Hey held his breath and waited. There wasn't much else he could do.

At about 3:30 P.M., the winds began to lose force and the rain started to fall more nearly in a vertical line. The typhoon had passed and all that was left was mere gale winds and heaving waters. Everyone was dog-tired and in need of hot coffee. Teeth chattered and knees trembled, mainly in relief. Twenty-nine hulls had been damaged. Precious stores had been ruined; the docks themselves had been battered in places. But there was still plenty of matériel left for the landing, and more important, no lives had been lost.

One of the Marines came up, looking ruefully at his own ruined expensive Swiss wristwatch and asked Hey for the time. Hey glanced at his $6.50 watch. It was still running. That pleased him more than any other single fortunate outcome of the entire day.[2]

At Fleet Weather Central in Yokosuka, the naval base south of Tokyo, the meteorologists frowned at the charts in their big osprey's nest atop a steep hill facing the bay. Typhoon Jane had passed, cutting viciously across central Japan, and was now losing itself somewhere in the Japan Sea. They'd stopped looking at Typhoon Jane. They were looking at Tropical Storm Kezia which was coming to life somewhere down near the Marianas, and which might grow and follow the customary northward track just in time to smash into the convoy that would be on its way to Inchon.

In Pyongyang, the capital of North Korea, Mr. Jae Duk Hahn was watching with particular interest the news reports that came in by wireless from the various correspondents with the People's Army in the south. He had sent several special queries to the man stationed with the small garrison in the port of Inchon, following up rumors that had floated in to him there in the offices of the government-controlled Central News Agency.

Hahn was a tall, dark North Korean with aquiline features that gave him the look of a Sioux Indian. He was chief of CNA's Pyongyang bureau and in this position saw most of the news as it came in, before it was censored and passed out to the North Korean people. He knew, for example, that the Perimeter line around Taegu and Pusan was still holding and not yet virtually broken as the official news releases said. He knew that the losses of the People's Army were high as a result of the reckless tactics of their generals in sending masses of soldiers forward in old-fashioned charges.

He was worried about this business of using plain soldiers for fodder, because his seventeen-year-old son was presumably somewhere down there where the fighting was going on. In early August, all the boys in his son's high school had suddenly been rounded up one day, forbidden to send word to their homes, and told they were to march toward the front lines far to the south. Hahn learned later that the sons of top Party officials hadn't gone to school that day. Word of the impressment spread swiftly through the city, and within hours most of the parents were at the bridge south of the city to watch their children march off. Some boys managed to break away from the guards; most were simply forced to continue.[3]

Along with a number of his journalist colleagues and even a few government officials and high-ranking military officers,

Hahn in those first few days of September felt that the Inchon area bore watching. Scores of North Korean spies, both official and unofficial agents, had reported elaborate preparation in Japan that pointed to an amphibious landing. One of the principal agents, whose Japanese name was Yoshimatsu Iwamura, but whose cover name was "Sekisan," had managed to put together what he said was a complete plan for a strike at Inchon—operational details, troop numbers, supply lists, all in great detail. But through other sources there was similar intelligence that seemed to indicate an assault at Wonsan, on the west coast.

Hahn knew the high command would be bickering over this intelligence right now. They were always bickering. In the Communist hierarchy, which he found increasingly distasteful, everyone's prime motivation seemed to be to fix blame on others for past mistakes and to keep from getting involved too deeply in any plans that might turn out to be future mistakes.

He and many others who dared to discuss such things privately believed that the march to the south at the end of June had been a gross mistake in the first place. Communist agents in Seoul, who didn't dare send negative reports back, had deceived everyone into thinking that the inhabitants would welcome the North Koreans with open arms; they'd been quite surprised to meet stiff resistance, and after that surly stares, from the populace. They had also thought that the United States would not try to defend South Korea. Now they had a tiger by the tail.

At any rate, Hahn was particularly interested in the Inchon-Seoul area because his good friend, General Sung Yap Lee, had been named its commander. Lee, a tall, handsome, soft-spoken, scholarly man, was a fanatic Communist, but this didn't interfere with their friendship. Hahn and Lee, as young men, had known each other in Japan during World War II, when they'd both been forced to join the "Yamato Juko," a patriotic society of Koreans loyal to Japan. Most recently, Lee had been director of the Kum Kang institute, North Korea's school for spies in Pyongang, operating under the guise of an institution training personnel for foreign ministry service. In spite of Lee's fierce and dedicated Communist beliefes, Hahn found his old friend charming in person and enjoyed his company. Lee at least was not quite as ascetic as some of the other Communists. He was a bachelor and rather noted for his success with the ladies.

Hahn had the feeling that with Sung Yap Lee in charge at
Seoul, an excellent defense could be set up there if they'd give
him enough troops to meet any assault from the sea. Unfortunately Kim Il Sung, North Korea's premier, and his top
generals at the moment seemed blindly and emotionally determined to break the Perimeter defense line at Taegu and drive
the so-called United Nations Forces into the sea. They discussed Inchon; they looked in that direction with worried
frowns, but no one wanted to take the responsibility of saying that troops ought to be sent there immediately. If someone did, and it turned out to be the wrong move, he would
surely be executed for sabotaging the war effort and for
spoiling Kim Il Sung's pet scheme of bringing about another
Dunkerque at Pusan.[4]

In the offices of the Central News Agency, the radio tele-
type transmissions of western world news services were received as a source of news along with the copy that originated
behind the bamboo curtain in either Soviet Russia or Red
China. Detailed war news, as seen from the North Korean
side, came from correspondents attached to the troops, men
who held military rank, usually as junior officers, and were
considered to be more like intelligence officers than newsmen. There was a Lieutenant Lee fulfilling such a function
with the small garrison at Inchon, and Hahn sent queries to
him almost daily in the early days of September asking if he
noticed any signs of enemy activity. The correspondent reported merely the usual small commando-type raids here and
there along the coast, and insisted that otherwise things were
quiet. Hahn did not have to send any special queries to Wonsan on the east coast, for the reports from that small city
were already telling of naval bombardment and air strikes in
the vicinity.

Wosan, across the peninsula, facing the Japan Sea, seemed
a likely place for an assault. At Wonsan there were no formidable tide problems and plenty of beaches where invaders
could land without exposing thmselves to a city or exceptionally fine defensive positions. If the United States and its allies
should land at Wonsan, there would be no great problem in
using the North Korean armies already at the northeast corner of the Perimeter for its defense, and even in the case of
a successful landing, about the most the enemy would accomplish would be to enlarge the Perimeter somewhat.

Journalist Jae Duk Hahn, about as well-informed as anyone in Pyongyang about the true progress of the war, and

with the added advantage of non-party objectivity in his thinking, did not consider Inchon the likeliest landing site; it was more a remote possibility that ought to be watched just to keep everything thorough. But he was certain there'd be a landing, or a strike, or a counterattack of some kind somewhere. He knew many people in Pyongyang, particularly Christians, who listened to the short-wave radio (a forbidden act, of course) and who were now constantly muttering among themselves that "a liberation was coming."

Many Koreans now in the southern half of the peninsula —and indeed, squeezed into the tiny fifty-by-eighty mile Perimeter, were, like journalist Hahn, originally from the north. The northern people were thought to be taller, tougher and more martial than the southerners, and there was a popular belief that the R. O. K. forces, which belonged to the south, were made up primarily of northerners. This wasn't true, of course, but there were enough men from above the parallel to make it seem that way.

R. O. K. Marine Major Kil Hun Koh was one of these transplanted northerners. Although he'd been a soldier since he'd been drafted as a recruit in the Japanese Army in World War II, and although he was a complete professional who loved the trade of soldiering, he was a slender, quiet youth with a mild, unruffled manner—not at all a fire eater. Perhaps because of this, he was having gratifying success in his assignment on the big, fertile island just off the tip of South Korea known as Cheju-do. He'd been sent there to recruit a new battalion of R. O. K. Marines, and in two weeks he'd gathered over a thousand young men, most of them farmhands and high school students.

When the R. O. K. Marine Corps had been founded only a year before, Army personnel like Major Koh were sought out to be its officers. Koh was one of the few officers of lower or moderate rank who had a college education and enjoyed the added prestige of speaking good English; he had worked for a while in Seoul for the U. S. military government as a translator. When he transferred over from the Army to the newly formed R. O. K. Marines he received a promotion, but at times he wondered whether it had been worth it. His new battalion of about a thousand completely green recruits was about as ineffective a military force as he had ever seen. Among the new Marines there were genuine volunteers, but there were also a few hundred who had been more or less impressed into joining. Major Koh and his assistants had been told to come up with a thousand men, and in one way or another, they had done so.

The big island of Sheju-do, virtually a prefecture in itself, had not been touched as harshly by the war as the mainland, and it was still relatively rich in both natural resources and manpower. Now, according to the word from the high command, the Republic of Korea was girding itself for the march back, and its armies needed all the young men who could be found. Major Koh wasn't certain just where the march back would begin, but he had his suspicions. This new emphasis on Marine personnel meant, he believed, an amphibious landing somewhere, and among the rumored sites was Inchon, but he thought it likelier that the actual assault would take place at some more remote location.

Major Koh took his thousand recruits by small ship to the naval base at Chinhae where they were quartered in makeshift tents and barracks, and there began to put them through basic training without actual weapons. The teen-agers were so confused by military life that they seldom knew to which squad, platoon or company they belonged, and whenever they met an older man—a man past his mid-twenties—they'd ask which was their outfit. At each roll call the composition of the squads would change, and this, along with the natural duplication of Korean names (huge majorities of all Koreans are named either Kim or Lee) led to utter confusion.

Americans helping with the training of Major Koh's 1st Marine Battalion began to call it the "Damned-near-lost battalion" and when this was translated, the recruits took it good naturedly and shared in the joke. They were given Springfield rifles, the bolt-action weapon that had been the U. S. Army's standard piece in the First World War and was now supplanted by the Garand M-1. At Tong Nae, a range just east of Pusan, each man was permitted to fire five shots.

Afterward, they were considered trained. Major Koh was told to stand by and be ready to board a transport in Pusan harbor. There was definitely going to be an amphibious landing. He wasn't told where, but the strongest rumor was that it would be at Kunsan on the west coast, some hundred miles below Seoul and Inchon. At any rate, they'd all learn where they were going once they were aboard their ship and on the way.

The U. S. Marines of Lieutenant Colonel Raymond Murray's 5th Regiment were fighting like hell in the action that came to be known as Second Naktong. It was in an area about in the middle of the western wall of the Perimeter, where the Naktong River curved toward the North Korean forces. A little less than a month before, the Marines had helped throw back a Communist spearhead that had crossed the river and penetrated this bulge. Now they were back again, doing the same thing.

Sergeant Patrick P. Byrnes, just out of chauffering duty in the Boston Navy Yard, moved up toward the fighting area in the tank he now commanded—A-4-A. In Company A of the 1st Tank Battalion there were twenty-one tanks, five to a platoon. Each tank crew consisted of five men; this was later cut to four. Byrnes's platoon had been ordered to go up and support the 3rd Battalion of the 5th Regiment, and now they were moving in single file along a winding, dusty thoroughfare, making what tankers call a "Road march."

Night fell and they rolled the tanks into a small village—no more than a few dozen ramshackle houses at a spot in the road. As Byrnes understood the situation, infantry held a ridge of high ground nearby, and although enemy units were certainly in the area, there was, at the moment, no contact.

A thin, bony woman of forty or so came into the road as they were parking the tanks and began jabbering and gesturing. With the platoon there was a Marine who knew a little Japanese, and since all older Koreans had learned Japanese when their country was annexed by Japan, he and the woman achieved a rough level of understanding. It seemed that all the men of the village were gone and she was acting as village chief. She did not want the tanks in her village. She felt they might draw an attack and that in the firing, the village would be damaged or destroyed, and its inhabitants killed or wounded. Unfortunately, the village offered the concealment they needed and the platoon lieutenant insisted that the tanks remain.

As darkness closed in, each tank put one man on watch while the other crewmen slept either on the tank or near it. Pat Byrnes stretched out on the engine doors. At about 2 A.M. a Sergeant Moore was on watch, and Brynes awoke to hear him yell, "Hey, there's some gooks out there!" The next sound he heard was the leopard cough of the .50-caliber sky-mounted machine gun.

After firing a burst toward the scrub trees where he

thought he'd seen enemy soldiers, Moore ducked back into the turret and took the co-ax .30-caliber machine gun. Byrnes dove in after him and took a bow gun. Peering through the slits, he saw that there were indeed enemy soldiers moving upon the village. All the tanks sprayed them with machine-gun fire. The noise, as in any firefight, was deafening.

The fight lasted almost an hour. At times the North Korean soldiers got within grenade tossing distance of the tanks, but none managed to throw the hand bombs that might have done serious damage; most of them were not equipped with grenades. When the attack finally subsided, there was still occasional sniping fire for a while so that Byrnes and his platoon mates had to remain inside the tanks. There they stayed until dawn.

In the morning light all was quiet; the enemy detachment had apparently withdrawn. But scattered over the road and fields, near the tanks, were the bodies of about 120 dead North Koreans. The old woman was very upset, marching up and down, wailing, waving her hands, and crying desperately for them to leave the village. This time they obliged her.

They were only a few days at Second Naktong. The Marines were called back and told to go to Pusan for embarkation just when they believed they had the enemy on the run again. In his headquarters in Taegu, stubborn, energetic, bulldog-tough Lieutenant General Walton H. Walker had the same belief. He was furious at the prospect of losing his Marines.

In Tokyo, the planners met: Admirals Joy, Struble and Doyle, Generals Almond, Ruffner, and Wright, and Marine General O. P. Smith. General Wright pointed out the dilemma they suddenly faced: Without the Marine Brigade, the Perimeter might not hold, but also without this experienced Marine force, the Inchon landing might not be made successfully. It was Admiral Struble, a Navy man, who finally made the suggestion that solved the problem. He suggested a compromise in which the Marines would be taken from the Perimeter, but a regiment of General Barr's new 7th Infantry Division sent as a floating reserve to replace them.

Everyone but Johnny Walker was happy with this arrangement, but that was how it was decreed, and Pinky Wright immediately flew to Walker's headquarters to advise him that the 5th Marines would be relieved at midnight on the 5th of September, no matter what they happened to be doing at that moment.

General Wright later looked at it this way: ". . . the real big gamble of this whole affair was getting the Eighth Army to break out of its predicament. It was on defense everywhere and when it was to be deprived of a Marine unit and the Marine close-support air it was asking a lot. Thank God for that little bulldog Johnny Walker. . . . It was originally planned for the Eighth Army to attack on the same day as the date of the landing because we felt that word of the landing would get to the North Koreans along the Eighth Army front immediately. About the 6th of September General Walker submitted to GHQ the Eighth Army attack plan and a few days later I went over to see him and suggest a few minor changes in the plan. At that time he asked for a reconsideration on the matter of taking the Marines units away from him, as it was true that he had absolutely nothing which could be called a suitable reserve. . . . He also requested that the date of the Eighth Army attack be one day later than the date of the landing and this was agreed to."[5]

An odd situation—another of MacArthur's gambles, in a sense. The hope was that the momentous news of the landing would take some time to filter down to the North Korean armies at the Perimeter and cause further delay in any movement they might make to bring opposing troops up to the Inchon-Seoul area.

First Lieutenant Sam Jaskilka, commanding E-Company of the 5th Marine Regiment's 2nd Battalion, was sitting in pouring rain with his back against a stone wall somewhere in the Naktong bulge sector when he got the word from a runner to withdraw. He was both disappointed and puzzled. Until this pouring rain they'd had the enemy on the run, and he wanted to wait for the clouds to lift so he could keep up the pursuit.

Sam, of Ukrainian descent, came from the mill town of Ansonia, Connecticut; he was a slim, agreeable, soft-spoken former University of Connecticut basketball star who had made the Marine Corps his life. As a child he had been raised in the Greek Orthodox Church, although his family later became Roman Catholics. Once, when a chaplain had asked him his religion, he'd smiled and said, "I'm a Marine."

Sam was clad in a poncho with no insignia of rank showing, while he rested against the stone wall. A moment before, he had been heartened at overhearing a conversation between two Marines who had slogged by in the mud, paying little attention to him. One of them said, "Know what makes the Marine Corps so good? Our officers are always with us."

His company had just finished a two-day battle that resulted from a "meeting engagement"—a kind of accidental clash of units. During the battle they'd dislodged the enemy from a hill with the help of air strikes, and Sam had thought all the air support excellent but he knew the men cheered when Marine F4U came in, and said among themselves, "All those Air Force pilots must be married." It did seem to him that the Marine pilots were more daring and came in closer, but he was ready to admit that this may have been his natural pride in the corps.

Anyway, Sam was now ordered to pull back, with the rest of the regiment, and that was a shame, just when they had the North Koreans really on the run, but orders were orders. He picked himself up and went on to pass the word down through the company.

One of the things plain troops on the Perimeter were worrying about was beer. Ever since the war started, American soldiers had received, along with their candy bars and cigarettes, several free cans of beer a week. Administratively, the beer was part of their food rations, regarded as a supplement to the field messes.

It was H. L. Mencken who said that a puritan was a person with the lurking suspicion that someone, somewhere, was happy, and back in Christian America the puritans got busy on this one. Church and temperance groups howled mightily about the free beer and deluged Congress with protests. One Congressman, sympathizing with the troops, made a widely quoted comment when he said, "Water in Korea is deadlier than bullets." That really had nothing to do with the issue, but it cheered the fighting men who wanted their beer. Unfortunately, the issuing of free beer did break regulations, and in the strictest legal sense, there was nothing to do but cease the practice. The order was issued that as of September 12, beer would have to be purchased, like other comforts, at the PX's.[6]

Sergeant Pat Byrnes, pulled out of the Naktong bulge and returned to Pusan to await embarkation for the landing. As he waited in bivouac near the port while the tanks of his platoon were fitted out with fording gear, or big metal ducts to allow them to move in eleven feet of water, somebody in the outfit managed to scrounge a "skid" of beer—144 cases—from the Army. The Marines iced it down in 55-gallon drums, drank it and enjoyed it.

Lieutenant Colonel Raymond Murry, the regimental commander, was now in Pusan, too, trying to perfect his hasty plans for the landing at Inchon, the matter had been occupying his spare time between attacks ever since he'd been advised of the projected assault. His troops had been moved into warehouses near the Pusan waterfront, and he himself had been given a small office at his command post. There were no real living facilities in the warehouse, and the Marines were going in relays to the ships in the harbor to take showers. Meanwhile, most of the units had been brought up to strength with new arrivals, and in order to integrate them, companies were holding training sessions at an area in the Pusan race track. By now everyone knew there would be a landing and Murray had the feeling that most of them suspected it would be at Inchon. He didn't see how the Communists, too, could help but know it, and he was pretty sure there'd be some extremely tough opposition staked out among the high sea walls and in the winding streets and hills of the city.

He thought he had his landing plan worked out, though. The 5th Regiment would be going in at a narrow beach, where it was impossible to land battalions abreast. On the other hand, once the landing was made, they'd be pushing forward into a broadening front, as though they'd entered a funnel the wrong way.

Murray's regiment was composed of the usual three battalions and ordinarily two battalions made a two-pronged attack, with the third battalion in reserve. That was the book method used under most conditions. At Inchon, one of his battalions—the 3rd—would make a landing in the early morning on Wolmi-do, the fortified island in the harbor, and if all went well, would be on this island with its mile-long causeway to the mainland about twelve hours later when the second installment of the landing was made on the city's beaches at the height of the evening tide. They might or might not be available as a reserve by that time. What it boiled down to was that Murray would in reality have only two battalions for his main landing. In spite of the narrowness of the beach, he decided to land them abreast, in two columns, company by company, so that each company, as it came ashore, would be able either to push directly forward or fan out toward its objective. To keep each battalion under control and perfectly integrated, he decided to land them from separate ships, even though they would be going in abreast and at the same time.

If not unorthodox, the scheme of maneuver was unusual; the timing would be delicate, and there was infinite room for error. In that respect, Murray's reverse-funnel landing tactic resembled the entire operation to take Inchon. The plans were sound enough; all the obstacles had been taken into consideration. It was just that there wasn't much room for bad luck.

NOTES *Chapter 7*

1. Interview author—Maize.
2. Griffin, SFC W. J. K., "Typhoon at Kobe," *Marine Corps Gazette,* Sept 51.
3. Hahn's son was taken to North Korean Army advanced positions near Taegu but stayed in reserve and instead of a weapon was given a sharpened, spearlike pole. After suffering a minor leg wound from shrapnel he broke away and walked alone all the way back to Pyongyang, keeping to the hills to avoid soldiers. He arrived in Pyongyang in early October 1950, when it was ready for evacuation, and was given a pistol for the march north. He remarked that though he'd been a soldier, this was the first weapon he'd ever owned. In this evacuation, Party officials promised Hahn his family would soon follow, but never kept that promise, and it was this act that finally crystallized Hahn's determination to defect as soon as he was able. Interview author—Jae Duk Hahn.
4. *Ibid.* Immediately after the U.N. capture of Seoul, General Sung Yap Lee was praised for his dogged defense of the city, but in November of 1952, he was suddenly arrested and accused by Kim Il Sung of working as an agent for the U. S. and "deliberately planning the bloody battle of Seoul" in order to decimate the North Korean People's Army. His success with women was also held against him, and he was charged with frivolity and moral turpitude. In the purge, he and thirteen other original top party fanatics were executed.
5. Letter Wright to author, 10 Oct 66.
6. There is some evidence that ways were found to pass out

beer in spite of regulations. The *Pacific Stars and Stripes*, 14 Sept 50, the day before the Inchon landing had a front page headline: MEN AT FRONT WILL HAVE BEER. . . . The story quoted MacArthur's headquarters as saying the ration would continue.

8

"I'm going on a little operation . . . "

COLONEL LOUIS B. ELY WAS TRAINING A SPECIAL DETACH-
ment of about 124 men in a tucked-away seashore camp
about fifty miles south of Tokyo. The official designation of
this detachment was the Special Activities Group, and he
had been assigned to it after arriving from the Pentagon early
in July.

Except for his physical trimness, Colonel Ely had the look
of any middle-class breadwinner, with a plain, pleasant face
and a slightly hawkish nose; there was nothing about him
to suggest his training in the arcane sciences of guerilla warfare and espionage. The men of the Special Activities Group
were the forerunners of the Special Forces, or "Green
Berets" of Vietnam. Ely himself was an intelligence officer
steeped in all the techniques of the secret agent, and he had
been told to make the group ready to gather information by
means of swift reconnaissance strikes behind enemy lines.

For over a month now, the men of his group, under the
command of a Major Weir, had spent long days and nights
hardening themselves physically, and sharpening their prowess
in hand-to-hand combat and in the use of various light weapons. It seemed at times that headquarters had forgotten their
existence, but now the planners in Tokyo had come up with
two important missions for these hand-picked men, both of
which were vital parts of the Inchon landing operation.

Ely was relieved, at last, to have something important to
do. When he first arrived in Tokyo, no one quite knew where
to put him. He had been an intelligence officer specializing
in unconventional reconnaissance—you could almost call it
espionage—since World War II, a career he entered by a
curious accident. Serving as G-3, Plans and Operations, with

141

a combined Army-Marine force under Marine General Howland M. ("Howlin' Mad") Smith, he had complained so bitterly one day about the lack of good intelligence that Smith had said, "Okay, Ely! You're the intelligence officer from now on. Let's see if you can do any better!" Intelligence had been Ely's field ever since. Because of his close association with the Marines, he had become something of an amphibious expert.

When he received his assignment to MacArthur's headquarters, Ely thought he might be getting back into Plans and Operations work and was rather looking forward to it, but upon arriving, he discovered that his old acquaintance Pinky Wright was the G-3. Ely was senior to Wright in years of service, so it wouldn't quite do to have him work under Wright, who was now a brigadier general—it was a possible source of conflict. None of this was said aloud, but Ely had the feeling that it was one of the considerations affecting his assignment.

In the web of organizational lines emanating from MacArthur's headquarters, Ely's tiny command was theoretically right under MacArthur himself, but he was also considered to be both on Willoughby's G-2 staff and part of Admiral Doyle's Phib Group 1; thus he was able to circulate rather freely through headquarters during the planning for Inchon, and to find out what was going on, although no one told him exactly how his group would be used. No one, in fact, knew. But somewhere along the line, it occurred to someone that it might be nice to have a small, commando-like force on hand in case it was needed, and so the Special Activities Group had been formed. But Admiral Joy's team of Marine raiders and Navy frogmen—similar in size and purpose to the Special Activities Group—was doing most of the reconnaissance on the coast of Korea, and Ely was beginning to feel that he and his men had been forgotten.

Suddenly, on the night of September 8, Ely was called to Tokyo and, to his surprise, ushered into a highly secret conference of top-ranking general and flag officers in the paneled war room between General MacArthur's and General Almond's offices. He heard the plan to use his group in a double-barreled mission discussed, and he was given verbal orders to carry it out.[1]

The next night Colonel Ely and his 124 men were boarding three special cars attached to a troop train headed from Tokyo to the port of Kobe on Japan's southern coast some

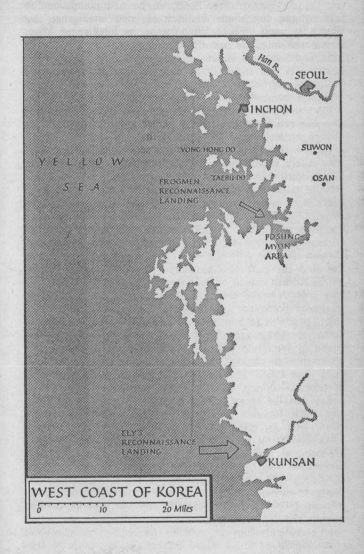

Han R.

SEOUL

INCHON

SUWON

YONG HONG DO

TAEBU DO

OSAN

YELLOW

SEA

FROGMEN
RECONNAISSANCE
LANDING

POSUNG
MYON
AREA

ELY'S
RECONNAISSANCE
LANDING

KUNSAN

WEST COAST OF KOREA

0   10   20 Miles

three hundred miles away. They had loaded all their amphibious landing gear—rubber boats, weapons, ammunition. Ely said nothing to the men about where they were going and what they were supposed to do when they got there. Upon arrival in Kobe, he had the three cars detached from the train and left on a siding—the men and their supplies still in the cars and restricted to them—while he walked down to the waterfront to see if he could find the ship he was supposed to meet there.

Ely's small force had been chosen to go ashore at Kunsan a day or two before the Inchon attack, and to carry out their assault with enough noise and violence to make the Communists believe that it might be the major landing they were now surely expecting. It was the old device of a feint and demonstration by a small force, a favorite gimmick of adventure tales since perhaps the times of the Medes and the Persians. It would be one of several feints taking place in Korea. The Fifth Air Force was already increasing intensive bombing and strafing attacks within a thirty-mile radius of Kunsan. Far to the north of Inchon and fairly deep in North Korean territory, a British task force was lobbing naval gunfire into the port of Chinnampo, itself a gateway to the North Korean capital of Pyongyang further up the river. The idea was to make the Communists think that MacArthur might be bold and unorthodox enough to make his strike there. Nor was Inchon, the real target, being neglected. Both destroyers and naval aircraft were hammering at its guardian island of Wolmi-do with a devastating bombardment. It was all reverse psychology, in which the reasoning went something like this: "The Reds surely suspect by now that an invasion is coming, and they must have overwhelming evidence that the target is Inchon. All right, we'll make them think that Inchon's so obvious we must be trying to fool them. And for good measure we'll bewilder them with attacks and feints at other points." The battleship U. S. S. *Missouri*, arriving in the Far East in the second week of September, was ordered to shell Wonsan on the east coast of Korea. (The great, waddling "Big Mo," on which the Japanese surrender had been signed, would be the last battleship used by the United States in any war; aircraft carriers became the capital ships after Korea; cruisers became either fleet command ships or vehicles for guided missiles, and technological advances added increasing importance to submarines. For the moment, however, the war in Korea was being fought with what were basically the weapons of World War II, which meant the only weapons on hand in a nation that hadn't been prepared for another war, a nation that had so naively believed World War II would settle things.)

Arriving at the Kobe waterfront in the dark of early morning, Colonel Ely looked about for the ship he was to meet, the British frigate, H. M. S. *Whitesand Bay*. He found a set of offices at one of the piers, a minor headquarters manned by a sleepy clerk who had no knowledge of any British frigate, and even less of Ely's mission. From this office he made several phone calls to various duty officers, but none of them knew anything either. So much the better, thought Ely. His own little plan seemed a better-kept secret than Inchon itself.

Ely stared out into the darkness toward the harbor and then, beyond the breakwater, detected the lights of a ship at anchor. It occurred to him that this might be the *Whitesand Bay*. Another phone call to a sleepy duty man in the harbor master's office confirmed this, and Ely went down to the dock's edge where a launch was making constant trips back and forth to and from one of the ships marked for the Inchon landing and now serving as living quarters for a group of dock-walloping Marines. He found a young naval officer supervising the launch trips and managed to convince him that it was in the best interests of the United States to get him out to that frigate beyond the breakwater.

On the frigate he found a pleasant, handsome and rather reserved British skipper, Lieutenant Commander J. J. Brothers, Royal Navy. Commander Brothers knew only that he was supposed to "pick up some outfit or other from Kobe," and seemed mildly disturbed that everything was being done by word of mouth, and so vaguely to boot. Nevertheless, he was cooperative. "There's only one difficulty, Colonel," he said. "You've got supplies to load and we can't get pier space. Harbor's full."

At that moment both men glanced shoreward and saw a ship wearing away from her space at the pier and heading out of the harbor. A ship was supposed to have permission to take a vacant pier space, but Commander Brothers didn't wait for it, weighed anchor, and the frigate docked immediately.

Ely now returned to where he had left the three railroad cars with his company and its special amphibious landing gear and supplies. They were a good mile from the loading point, and there was no way to get the detachment to the

ship. In the railroad yard, he spotted an engine with steam
up, and immediately called one of the company's lieutenants
who spoke Japanese. Ely and the lieutenant went over to the
locomotive, and by some fast doubletalk, managed to convince its Japanese driver to pull the three cars to the pier.

All through the harbor men were busy loading and unloading from transports to invasion ships, but no one seemed
to notice the transfer of some 124 men and their gear from
three railroad cars to a British frigate. Ely was pleased that
his mission was still secure.

By morning the frigate nosed out of the harbor, men and
supplies aboard, and headed into the seas that were already
beginning to kick up from the approaching Typhoon Jane.
The ship was smaller than the average destroyer, and there
was no space below for the men. They huddled on the decks,
covering themselves with blankets and ponchos against the
spray and increasing rain. The ship began to pitch and toss
in the rising seas.

At a chart table on the bridge, Ely pointed out the target
to Commander Brothers—Kusan, this river mouth lined with
beaches about one hundred miles below Inchon. Brothers remained polite but looked puzzled and faintly pained, as
though wondering how the United States ever accomplished
anything, operating this way without written orders and with
only the vaguest of instructions. Ely explained that they
would be landing in inflated boats, jumpy little craft that
could hold ten men but could be handled by four. These
boats were difficult to paddle, so Ely would appreciate it if
the Commander would put into shore as closely as possible.
"Yes. Quite," said the Commander, and frowned.

Ely considered himself lucky to have the boats. When he'd
first arrived in Tokyo, and had been directed to form a
raiding team, nobody had known where the rubber boats
were. A supply sergeant in headquarters with a reputation as
a first-class scrounger had finally located them in a near-
forgotten warehouse near Tokyo. Much of the time in camp
had been spent by Ely and his men checking and repairing
the surplus boats.

The swells had subsided somewhat when, two days later,
the H. M. S. *Whitesand Bay* stood off the west coast of Korea
in the darkness. Commander Brothers correctly felt that the
charts showing the rocks and shoals were not entirely accurate, and he approached the shore with great caution.

"Much closer than *he* liked," Ely said later, "but much farther than *I* liked."

Ely and the troop commander, Major Weir, gathered the men on deck and gave them their final instructions. The main force would land on the longest stretch of beach while eight British sailors would make a reconnaissance of another beach a mile or so away to find out what the landing conditions were. Several times Ely reiterated his most important instruction: "If you meet any opposition you're to withdraw immediately. You must understand that this is a pure feint, and its main purpose is to make the North Korean troops in this vicinity think we might be the spearhead of a division."

Secretly Ely wondered how his handful of men could possibly pose as part of a division. And he hoped that once they were ashore they'd be able to get back again. During the secret conference on September 8, he'd heard the intelligence estimates of enemy strength along the west coast of Korea, and as he understood it, three North Korean People's Army divisions were deployed in the general area, all within fifty miles or less of Kunsan. They were situated on either side of the main highway that ran south from Seoul through Taejon and then swung in an easterly direction toward Taegu. These were the North Korean 3rd, 13th and 10th Divisions; any of their elements could reach the west coast quite rapidly. It was not known exactly how large a garrison sat in Kunsan itself, but aerial reconnaissance had shown definite military installations and gun positions. Kunsan was at the relatively wide mouth of the Kum River which ran into the sea from an almost horizontal east-west direction; the town itself was sizeable, but the shores all around it were not heavily populated. Ely's landing was to be within a few miles of the town.

It was pitch dark and shortly after midnight when the rubber boats were inflated on the deck of the frigate and then lowered into the water. The men scrambled into them. They rowed nearly two miles to the shore, the main group of boats heading northward and to the left, the eight British sailors toward the right and to the south. It was a rocky approach and the beach itself offered broken terrain, but the boats all landed with no major difficulty and the men fanned out to explore the beach before deciding whether to push further inland.

Suddenly, some six or eight hundred yards to the north, machine guns from concealed positions somewhere just back of the shore began a stuttering blast and greenish tracers flew wildly over the rocks and sand. It caught the several men who had moved that way by surprise; in the first volley two were killed and another man seriously wounded. This small party turned back quickly and ran in broken formation for the landing area. All the others who had fanned out were hastily recalled; the entire detachment returned to the rubber boats. Afterward, some of the raiders said that they were disappointed; they felt they could have stormed and taken those machine guns, but their officers had stuck to Ely's firm instructions: no fighting, pull back immediately if fired upon.

The entire group returned to their rubber boats and rowed back to the frigate. The British skipper politely said it had been a good show, but Ely knew that not much had been accomplished, and he was also disappointed. Still, his basic purpose had been to disturb the North Koreans in the area and make them think a landing might come at Kunsan, and he supposed the raid had achieved at least that much.

But perhaps a little more could be done. Ely asked Brothers if he could make some sort of demonstration. Brothers considered a while, then said, "Why, yes. I believe I could." Shortly after darkness the men of the *Whitesand Bay*—much to their own entertainment—began a fireworks display that consisted of shooting up flares, then potting at them with their 20-mm. anti-aircraft guns. Explosions filled the air and bursts and tracers filled the sky. Ely and Brothers both hoped it would alarm the Communists as much as it amused the Jack Tars of Her Majesty's frigate.

And so Ely's first mission was accomplished. He wasn't so sure the second task would be as easy to carry out, for he had been told to make a landing just north of Inchon on September 14, the night before the big assault, march inland about twelve miles, and seize the vitally important Kimpo Airfield near Seoul. Once Kimpo Airfield was in friendly hands, additional troops and supplies could be brought in very quickly from Japan. In many respects, Kimpo was the key to Seoul.

Ely frowned whenever he thought about it. Only 124 men to take a major airfield near a capital city! It seemed a weird pipe dream, even though he'd been assured in Tokyo that only a handful of superannuated or poorly trained troops guarded the runways. But that assurance had come several days ago; by this time a regiment or more could have moved into the area. Ely could see Commander Brothers' well-bred astonishment when he heard of the plan. But he was, of course, quite willing to go along with it, and with a bit of a sigh, commented that at least this time he wouldn't have to bring his ship too close to the shore and risk putting it aground.

Brothers considered the waters and the terrain. At a point among the many islands west of Inchon—a good ten miles at sea—the *Whitesand Bay* would meet two of the Korean Navy's ubiquitous patrol boats, and these would bring Ely and his men to a spot from which they could be launched to paddle ashore. Where they would be landed, however, about eight miles north of Inchon, the mud flats extended five or six miles out and were exposed at low tide. Only during high tide could they be negotiated, even by rubber boats, and the high water would be there for only about two hours, which meant that Ely, Major Weir and the raiders would have to be sent shoreward at exactly the right time or not at all.

The special force would then march overland at night through strange territory with only inadequate and outdated maps to guide them, and some time the next day, presumably, if they still had the energy left, storm a huge airfield on flat terrain that offered very little in the way of a concealed approach.

"Rather a job," said Commander Brothers.

"Yes, isn't it?" said Ely, who was falling into the spirit of British understatement.

The only thing that made Ely feel better about it was the obvious importance of taking Kimpo. Having it in friendly hands would ease much of the strain on the troops pouring into the cluttered bottleneck at Inchon—if, indeed, they managed to gain the beachhead there.

That, at any rate, was how Colonel Ely understood it. Almond's last words to him before he boarded the train for Kobe had been, "You will go and take Kimpo Airfield." Clear enough. But during the conference, there had been serious objections to the plan and Ely had the feeling that by now it was either partially disapproved or even about to be cancelled. Presumably word would come to him, probably by radio, if the plan indeed was cancelled. But Ely was enough of a soldier to know that sometimes communications fall down, especially in the midst of a big, hectic operation when high-ranking planners have on their minds more important things than a 124-man raiding team on a mission somewhere out in left field.

He went over the conference again in his mind. Marine General O. P. Smith had been there, along with Admiral Doyle and Generals Almond and Hickey. The commando-type raid on Kimpo airfield was Almond's idea. He was certain that once the main assault on Inchon's waterfront got under way, all available troops in the area would be rushed there to meet it by the North Koreans. The last intelligence estimate was that no more than six or eight thousand troops guarded the entire area near Seoul and Inchon. At Kimpo Airfield itself it was believed there were a bare five hundred potential defenders, many of them technicians and service personnel rather than soldiers. All of them were thought to be second string reserves—recruits, old men and boys. Ely's small force, he believed, ought to be able to take and hold the airfield easily.

Tall, white-haired General Smith was against the idea. The coolness between the quiet, deliberate Marine general and the mercurial Army general, Almond, was beginning to become evident to observers. Smith, at the conference, tried to explain his objections as factually and diplomatically as possible, but it seemed evident that he regarded the plan as rather dramatic nonsense. Ely's raiders, he pointed out, would have to paddle against or across extremely strong currents of three or four knots, and that was about the speed the rubber boats could make, which meant they might find themselves paddling furiously and getting nowhere. Any radios they could carry would have only a four-mile range and they'd be out of touch with any command or observation posts. Naval gunfire or aerial support for them would be impossible.

Ely himself had objected that his force was too small to take and secure an airfield, and Almond had told him it would be augmented with a hundred Marines. What Ely didn't know was that after his departure from Tokyo, Almond had ordered these extra Marines, first by a phone call, then by a follow-up message, and Smith had immediately replied with a dispatch urgently requesting reconsideration. The Brigade in Korea had suffered battle casualties so that it was now below strength, and the Regimental Combat Team in Kobe, now embarking, had had its numbers reduced by about five hundred men. These were Marines seventeen years of age or under who, by sudden and special direction of the Secretary of the Navy, responding to public pressure, were being left behind. Besides, Smith added, most of the Marines Almond wanted had already sailed in the transports and LST's for Korea. When General Lem Shepherd, Almond's old VMI classmate, added his support to Smith's objections, Almond had finally given in. But somehow Colonel Ely hadn't been informed of all this, and there he was, aboard the H. M. S. *Whitesand Bay*, going ahead with his plans to take the airfield.

In the skipper's cabin of the frigate, Lieutenant Commander Brothers gave the colonel a drink and stared at him quietly as though feeling sorry for him, but wishing him luck. Ely thought it very civilized of the British to permit liquor aboard their naval vessels.

On September 6, Typhoon Kezia had been only a swirling disturbance in the Pacific near the Marianas Islands. Then Typhoon Jane had struck Kobe and gone on its way. Typhoon Kezia, gathering force, becoming a great, swirling circle of wind, storm and cloud with a diameter of more than a hundred miles, was following in Jane's wake and moving slowly on a steady course toward the tip of Korea. Its highest winds were already more than a hundred knots. Even the largest ships are scarcely comfortable in a typhoon, but the waddling LST's heading for Inchon might be seriously damaged and in some cases even sunk, taking tons of supplies and perhaps battalions of Marines to the bottom with them.

The best estimate was that if the typhoon held its present course, it would strike the invasion fleet just as it was turning northward into the Yellow Sea and on the last leg to Inchon. Even if, by some rare luck, no ships were seriously damaged or sunk, the timetable would be upset and the critical date of September 15, when the tides would be just right, would be lost; there could be no invasion, then, until the following month. It wasn't certain Johnny Walker could hold out in the Perimeter that long. It was probable the North Koreans would scrape up a more formidable defense for Inchon by that time. All in all, if the landing couldn't be made on the 15th, it might as well be forgotten.

As he prepared to leave Tokyo for the landing, General MacArthur was perhaps the least ruffled of anyone in the face of this news about the approaching typhoon. Some of the older members of his staff recalled what had happened aboard the U. S. S. *Missouri* in Tokyo Bay during the Japanese surrender ceremonies on September 2, 1945. That morning the bay had been cloud-covered, and as the signing of the surrender documents took place, the few officers who knew the script for the ceremony reflected that the clouds would spoil the effect of a flight of B-29's scheduled to roar overhead immediately after the signing. At the conclusion, MacArthur had looked up and intoned, "These proceedings are closed." At that moment the clouds parted, the sun shone through in long beams that the special effects department of a major Hollywood studio could not have duplicated, and the planes passed over the *Missouri*. Those who remembered were wondering now if MacArthur had the same influence over typhoons and could somehow, by his stern desire, turn Kezia away.

Early on the morning of September 14, Mr. Jae Duk Hahn came into the editorial offices of the Central News Agency bureau in Pyongyang, the capital of North Korea, and was excitedly handed a radio dispatch that had just come in from Lieutenant Lee, the CNA correspondent at Inchon. It said, "Heavy bombardment started. Airplanes and warships. I hope my death will be worthwhile. I do not wish to die without reason. Long live the labor party! Long live the People's Republic!"[2]

It amazed Hahn that in the midst of a bombardment Lieutenant Lee could find time to fill his message with patriotic encomiums and slogans. He personally rushed the dispatch over to military headquarters. Everyone was busy there and merely glanced at it—they had apparently received their own messages with the same news. Before he left, the news item was put on a "secret" distribution list for the eyes of less than twenty people. He rather wistfully asked if he might get out a story saying that some activity had been reported at Inchon, and was tongue-lashed furiously by a major general for even daring to think of anything like that.

Hahn sighed, returned to his office, and listened carefully to the radio in the hope of further news.

What had prompted the dispatch from Inchon was the bombardment of the tiny island of Wolmi-do, the prelude to the landing. This little cone of an island, 351 feet high, was part of the curious toy landscape that made up the immediate environs of the port of Inchon, surroundings that might strike a tourist as quaint and picturesque. The city of Inchon was on a short, fat peninsula about two miles wide that jutted westward into the sea for perhaps two miles. There was high ground on the peninsula, but beyond it, looking landward, were low stretches where the sea was let into vast pans, or beds, and then dried for its salt. Wolmi-do was just off the westward edge of the peninsula; it was an island less than a thousand yards in diameter, most of which formed a steep, conical hill with a small flat portion on the northern part. This island was connected to the mainland by a thin causeway less than a mile long, running southwest from the center of the peninsula's broad tip. At the extreme southern edge of Wolmi-do a skinny finger of land jutted out to form a breakwater enclosing the harbor; like a spatula at the end of this finger was a rocky eminence called So-Wolmi-do.

Guns on Wolmi-do could be aimed at anything approaching Inchon from the sea. Aerial reconnaissance had located some artillery on Wolmi-do, although the fliers felt they had seen more empty emplacements than guns. Colonel Willoughby's G-2 estimate, based on various sources, was that no more than 500 troops were manning the little fortress of Wolmi-do; the bulk of Inchon's garrison was in the city. But some of Lieutenant Eugene Clark's reports, radioed in from his camp on the nearby island, seemed to indicate rather stiff defenses. His reports over the past several days had said, in part: "Two anti-aircraft guns are located on Wolmi adjacent to the former U.S. Communications Building . . . three large guns on So-Wolmi-do, one gun, size unknown, at south end of breakwater. Four or five machine guns on west side, two on southwest side. Infantry trenches are a few feet back from the waterline. . . . There is a gunfire observation post in the tower of a large red building on Wolmi-do. . . . Twenty-five machine guns and five 120-mm. mortars have been located on So-Wolmi-do by observing their fire. . . . Wolmi-do has twenty heavy coastal defense guns placed on island's seaward side. Extensive concrete trench and tunnel system combs island. Estimated 1,000 troops on island which is restricted; only laborers admitted."[3]

Whatever the exact nature of its defenses, Wolmi-do had to be knocked out if an invasion was to take place. The two methods of bombardment would be from naval guns and from the air, but for the sake of keeping the element of surprise, the bombardment could last no longer than two days. It would be the overture to the show MacArthur would watch from the bridge of the *Mt. McKinley.*

In Tokyo the Air Force had been badgering MacArthur's command to tell them what their part in this dramatic operation would be. As the G-3 planner, Brigadier General Edwin K. Wright spent many anxious hours trying to determine just how to convince the air generals that their power would best be used in continued ground support at the Perimeter, and in the valuable bombing and reconnaissance missions they were flying deep in North Korea. Inchon, however, was a brilliant master stroke that would make news, and the Air Force was not above having their efforts favorably publicized. They wanted to share, like everyone else, in the glory of Inchon.

The trouble was, the operation simply didn't call for air power in the accepted sense, at least not the sort of air power that cuts enemy sources of matériel and shows its beneficial effects at some future date. The Air Force was already doing its part by patrolling and, in the process, controlling the skies all over Korea; in this war GI's could look up, see planes, and have no doubt as to whom they belonged. Finally, late one night, as Pinky Wright was poring over the accumulated plans, he realized that every major operation connected with Inchon was centered in one relatively small area and that it would be most efficient and least confusing to have one air arm—namely, Marine and Navy airplanes—taking the entire responsibility for that third dimension of the campaign. He took a draftsman's compass, put the point at Inchon, and swung a thirty mile arc around the city. He labeled this the "Objective Area," and in a day or two, after suitable conferences, a directive went out from MacArthur's headquarters that the Navy alone would conduct air operations within this circle; the Air Force was authorized, as part of the operation, to act anywhere outside it. Wright felt that this kept everyone happy, and if the Far East Air Force planners were disappointed, at least they didn't say so.[4]

The commander of one of the Marine regiments to be put ashore at Inchon, Colonel Chesty Puller, was fighting seasickness aboard a wallowing, boxy ship on its way to Inchon, and telling himself it wouldn't do for the troops to see the old man succumb, even though practically everyone aboard, including most of the naval officers, was green and miserable by now.[5]

Typhoon Kezia was heading in the general direction of the straits betwen Japan and Korea, but it hadn't yet quite arrived. Nevertheless, the seas were rolling and pitching in a genuine storm, one of the roughest the skippers of the various transports and LST's heading for the invasion site had ever seen.

Admiral Doyle had taken one look at the approaching typhoon, and in this whole atmosphere of chance-taking had made his own gamble. He'd ordered the slower ships out of Kobe one day early, on September 11, in the hope that the typhoon would veer to the right and pass behind them. The faster ships would come along just behind the path of the typhoon so that, in effect, the groups would be staggered with the full force of the typhoon passing between them—a maneuver that called for neat timing and more luck than a man had the right to expect. It was only a matter of dodging the typhoon; the fleet had to arrive off the invasion point at the same time, and the loss or absence of key vessels on September 15 could upset the entire plan. The vessels were in two main groups: those taking Chesty Puller's Regimental Combat Team from Kobe in Japan to Inchon, and those carrying Lieutenant Colonel Murray's similar outfit from Pusan in Korea. To complicate things, other important vessels were embarking from Yokohama, at the eastern end of Japan, and from Sasebo on the extreme west. An attack transport (AKA) and four LST's, for example, were bringing Army engineers and a field artillery battalion from Yokohama; a vital Pontoon Movement Group of seven slow ships was in Sasebo, lying over. The command ship itself, the U. S. S. *Mt. Mc-Kinley,* would leave Kobe, stop at Sasebo long enough to pick up General MacArthur (who would fly that far), then join the rest.

It was done by a series of rendezvous points that were no more than spots in the sea defined by latitude and longtitude. The first, Point Iowa, was about 180 miles south of the Korean peninsula. Most of the ships from Japan would assemble there, if they could. Another hundred miles along the route, which now began to curve northward toward Inchon, was Point Arkansas where the vessels from Pusan would join the others. And there would be a final rendezvous at Point California, about fifty miles southwest of Inchon itself. There were, of course, no landmarks to aid in piloting, and many of the rickety, salvaged vessels had no modern radar navigation gear; taking sights on heavenly bodies at dawn or dusk would also be out of the question, in most cases, because of the cloudy skies. It meant dead reckoning for many of the ships—pointing the vessel toward the rendezvous point and hoping it got there—and to bring a ship within fifty miles of an imaginary spot on the ocean by this method is always a minor miracle. The winds and rough waters didn't help at all.

On one of the ships in the slow, storm-battered convoy, Corporal Joe Maize, the half-Kiowa Indian, was trying to keep up the morale of some of the younger Marines who had never known combat. He was an agreeable fellow, not at all the traditional tough, barking NCO, and the recruits all looked up to him, though he was only in his mid-twenties. The men all knew by now that they were being shipped to the Far East to make a landing somewhere, but no one had yet been told officially where.

They had just finished their long voyage from San Diego to Japan and the short layover at Kobe. Now, on this last leg to Korea, the routine of shipboard life continued as much as it could under the crowded conditions. The men cleaned their weapons, attended lectures, and after they were told of the target, studied maps. General Quarters were sounded each day and they practiced getting into formation at designated places along the deck. Pamphlets on Korea were passed out. There was no chaplain aboard Joe's ship but two officers with religious leanings, one Catholic and one Protestant, conducted services.

Joe noticed that most of the NCO's had more or less adopted a special recruit or two whom they would advise and encourage. His own protégé was an eighteen-year-old whose family he'd met back in San Ysidro, California; he'd promised them he'd take care of the lad. The big question the kids were always asking was: "How does it feel to kill someone?" That was a little hard to answer. One night he found his protégé in his narrow bunk, his face turned to the wall, crying. "Look, kid," said Joe, "don't be scared. It ain't all that bad when you get in it, and it don't last as long as you think." The boy smiled a little, shook his head and said, "I'm not scared." Suddenly Joe realized he wasn't. He'd been crying because he was plain homesick.

Joe was fascinated by the Japanese officers on the bridges of the LST's. With the gold braid on their caps and sleeves, they looked to him like admirals, and he wondered that the United States was now using its former enemies to help fight this war in Korea. In a sense it was, for there hadn't been time to find U. S. Navy skippers for all the landing craft, and their Japanese officers and crewmen had been retained. Joe didn't realize it, but this was one of the great secrets of the Inchon operation; there would have been all sorts of political howls from the Japanese and the Soviet bloc of the United Nations, if the fact had been made public.

Major Kil Hun Koh and his battalion of young recruits from the agricultural island of Cheju-do were aboard the U. S. S. *Pickaway,* one of the four transports taking the Marines from Pusan to Inchon. The last exercise he gave his troops before embarking was a session of climbing down nets on the side of a transport and into smaller landing craft; he still wasn't sure they were all proficient at it. They were still learning the rudiments of military life here aboard the crowded transport. As they embarked, the rumor was that they were all going to Japan for further training. The first day out at sea, Major Koh had a tape recording played throughout the ship, and from this his men learned that they would be helping the U. S. Marines to make a landing at Inchon.

The transport was so crowded that there wasn't enough drinking water to go around, and Major Koh had to institute a system of rationing. American food was plentiful, but both Koh and his men missed their fiery Korean *kimchi.* Almost to a man they were seasick. There was a bad stink all over the ship, and it kept rolling and pitching as though it would never cease.

Koh had a way of stopping to chat now and then with individual men he encountered. He ran into a seasick recruit in a passageway on the second day and asked him how he felt about making a landing under fire. The young man gulped and said he'd be glad to get his feet on land again under any circumstances. Koh laughed and decided this was probably as good a motivation as any.

Typhoon Kezia, which had been heading for the straits near the tip of Korea, suddenly began a slow right-hand turn to the north. It headed up between Japan and Korea, and also between the two elements of the invasion fleet, just as Admiral Jimmy Doyle had gambled it would. He was aboard his amphibious group flagship, the *Mt. McKinley,* now steaming toward Sasebo to pick up General MacArthur. He breathed a sigh of relief as he saw the haymaker swing on the typhoon missing its mark, even though the *McKinley,* a top-heavy ship, was rolling sickeningly in the twenty-five-foot swells.

Admiral Struble had wanted MacArthur to attend the invasion aboard the *Rochester*, the cruiser that was the flagship of his Seventh Fleet. Rip Struble was one of the few men who could argue with MacArthur—in private, of course—and he'd maintained that it was wrong for the Supreme Commander to travel in a junior ship, but MacArthur had said, "I'm sorry, Rip. I'm already committed to the *Mt. McKinley*."[6]

The *McKinley* was better equipped to handle communications and large numbers of surplus personnel. And there would, of course, be room for the press. On the 11th of September, MacArthur had called in all the major correspondents in Tokyo and briefed them in the Dai-Ichi Building. "I'm going on a little operation," he had said, "and I'd like to have you boys with me if you'd like to go. I say a little operation—it's a big operation. You will leave . . . at 6:30 Wednesday morning. I've got a new plane and I'll follow you in that." He pointed his pipe and laughed. "But you bums will go in my old plane, the *Bataan*."[7]

It was one of the few recorded MacArthur attempts at humor. His new plane was the SCAP; the *Bataan* was the four-engined C-54 transport in which he'd originally landed in Japan on August 30, 1945.

Typhoon Kezia had caused a reshuffling of all schedules, and MacArthur decided to leave Tokyo on the afternoon of the 12th instead of the 13th. He would board his plane at Haneda, the airfield on the southern edge of Tokyo, fly to southwestern Japan, and at the U. S. naval base of Sasebo board the *Mt. McKinley* and proceed at flank speed to the invasion site. He gathered his immediate party together: Generals Almond, Wright, Fox and Whitney, and Marine General Lemuel Shepherd. Their departure at Haneda, set for 3:00 P.M., was delayed thirty minutes while a condenser in the right outboard engine of the SCAP was replaced.[8]

The SCAP landed in a pelting rain at 5:50 P.M. at Itazuke Air Base. The naval base at Sasebo was several hours distant by auto. As the party transferred to waiting jeeps and staff cars, General MacArthur remarked to General Wright that he seemed to have forgotten his gloves and raincoat in his hurried packing. MacArthur's pilot, Lieutenant Colonel Anthony Story, gave him a raincoat, while General Wright supplied a pair of gloves. MacArthur wore these gloves all through the Inchon operation, and returned them later to Wright, who hung them in his den as a treasured souvenir.

At 9:20 A.M., the party arrived in Sasebo to learn that the

Mt. McKinley had been delayed by typhoon-ruffled seas and was not in yet. They all sat down for coffee and sandwiches at the Officers' Club Mess. The conversation in this brief interval did not center particularly upon Inchon; the plans had been made, the dice thrown, and there really wasn't much to talk about now—nothing to do but let it roll and see what would happen. By midnight, the *Mt. McKinley* was in. The party of generals, tired but excited, boarded and were assigned their cabins. MacArthur had his own cabin, but the other generals doubled up; Alonzo Fox and Pinky Wright, for example, found themselves together in one small cubicle with double bunks.

By this time the eight correspondents selected to be aboard the command ship were in place, and at thirty minutes after midnight Captain Carter A. Printup gave the order, and the Amphibious Force Flagship, U. S. S. *Mt. McKinley*—an AGC in Navy terminology—headed into the rough seas for the largest amphibious operation by the United States since Okinawa in World War II, and perhaps the most improbable major amphibious landing in military history.

NOTES   *Chapter 8*

1. Col. Ely says there were no written orders. Karig *et al* in *Battle Report* quotes from an order for the operation: "Conduct beach recon and amphibious landing Kunsan during the period September 9–14. Purpose this plan is to obtain essential beach information, to disrupt coastal communications, and to hamper enemy reinforcements in the Kunsan area." Such orders are often written afterward to confirm verbal orders. Interview author—Col Louis B. Ely.
2. Interview author—Hahn; *Personal Notes*, J. D. Hahn.
3. Karig *et al*, p. 198.
4. Letter Wright to author, 28 Sept 66.
5. Interview author—Lt Gen Lewis B. Puller USMC (Ret).
6. Interview author—Struble.
7. Carl Mydans in *Time*, 25 Sept 50. Interview author—Frank Gibney.
8. *Personal Notes*, Lt Gen Edw. M. Almond.

9

"I don't see how I could be better."

THE DESTROYERS WERE THE FIRST TO GO IN.

Rear Admiral John M. Higgins, a naval officer known for his swashbuckling red mustache, was directing the destroyers from the cruiser *Toledo,* lying offshore. It was the morning of September 13. Six destroyers broke from the main fleet seven to ten miles southwest of Inchon and nosed into the narrow Flying Fish Channel that led to the port in single file. Their job, which they shared with the air attack element, was to knock out the island of Wolmi-do.

Among the destroyers was the *Mansfield* (which had carried the Japanese surrender party out to the *Missouri* in Tokyo Bay almost exactly five years before), the *De Haven,* the *Swenson,* the *Collett,* the *Gurke* and the *Henderson.* They started toward Inchon seven hundred yards apart. On the bow of the *De Haven* were half a dozen dummies, straw shapes clad in shirts and dungarees. It was hoped that they might draw enemy fire which would give away gun positions on the shore. The destroyer skippers were not nearly so worried about fire from the shore as they were about mines, however. On each vessel, men were keeping a sharp lookout for floating objects.

Junks and fishing boats dotted the approaches to Inchon. As the destroyer squadron passed the scattered offshore islands, they could see astonished civilians gathered on the beaches to watch, many of them in traditional white silk Korean robes.

In the radio room of the *Mansfield* a Korean interpreter, monitoring some of the enemy frequencies, heard a hasty message saying that vessels were approaching Inchon and warning the coastal defense gun positions.

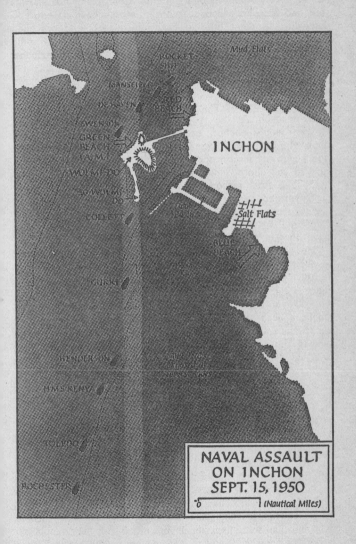

Even this destroyer operation, two days preliminary to the landing, was something of a gamble. Admiral Higgins and his staff had held long, soul-searching discussions in an effort to determine the best time to begin the attack, and they had finally decided upon the somewhat dangerous course of going in at low tide, just before the incoming flood. Although this increased the danger of grounding, it would perhaps give them an opportunity to spot mines, since mines are ordinarily anchored to the bottom, and at high tide, hang below the surface. There were two more tactical advantages to a low-tide approach. As they began to gun shore positions the destroyers would anchor, and the incoming tide would swung them about so that their bows were pointed seaward for a quick getaway if necessary. This would also turn them broadside to the shore, enabling them to bring all their guns to bear. The final reason for the maneuver was to allow the destroyers to depress their guns sufficiently to hit many of the shore targets. "At the peak of a 30-foot-high tide," said Captain Paul C. Crosley, Higgins' chief of staff, "we couldn't have hit 'em."[1]

The squadron began its slow crawl up Flying Fish Channel at about 7:00 A.M. Presently they were moving past the lighthouse on Palmi-do where Lieutenant Clark was to light the lamp two nights later. On the *Swenson* was young Lieutenant (jg) David H. Swenson. The ship had been named for his uncle, a hero of World War II. Swenson was standing by to direct the fire of the quadruple 40-mm. mounts. Swenson was one of those able, handsome young men who seem born for a naval career; he graduated second in his class two years before at the Academy; he had been a football star and brigade commander, and upon graduation had received a sword as an award for leadership. This was to be Dave Swenson's first taste of combat.

For more than four hours the destroyers moved toward Inchon. At 1145 hours the port lookouts on the *Mansfield* suddenly called: "Mines off the port bow!" Officers on the bridges of all the ships swiftly trained their binoculars on what looked like a group of roundish, lumpy objects just outside the narrow channel in muddy, shallow water, perhaps eight hundred yards away from the course line. No one could be sure whether they were actually mines. Admiral Struble, who had had some experience with mines, felt the channel was a perfect mine field, and that if *he* were on the North Korean side, he would certainly put up a mine defense. Yet barely two weeks before, the British cruiser *Jamaica* had done some shelling in the area and had found no mines. But it was possible that the Communists had, in the interim, scattered a few mines in case the *Jamaica* decided to return.

The destroyers in the lead immediately began to fire at the suspicious objects with their 40-mms., and one minute later a shot from the *Gurke* scored a hit; a mine exploded in a great, black and grayish plume of smoke and muddy water. Captain Halle C. Allan, commanding the squadron, told the *Henderson* to hang back, destroy the mines, then follow the others at high speed toward Inchon. The tide was coming in so swiftly that the *Henderson's* guns were able to explode only four of the twelve mines sighted before all were covered by the rising waters.

Wolmi-do, rising some three hundred odd feet, greenish with scrub foliage, pockmarked by the tiny ochre blemishes of foxholes and gun emplacements, was clearly in sight now, and details of the island's topography could be made out through the binoculars. Everything seemed very quiet on the island. Sailors could see the busy populace of the area working or playing on the shore—fishermen mending nets, swimmers bathing for sport—carrying on as though there were no war anywhere, certainly not at their doorsteps. Wolmi-do was the prime target today, but there were also orders to lay a few shells on some of the narrow strips of waterfront chosen for the landing. The presence of these presumably innocent civilians—among them sightseers who had evidently come down to the shore to see the warships come in—greatly disturbed Captain Allan and his destroyer skippers. Admiral Struble, in issuing his order for the operation, had written: "The Seoul-Inchon area is inhabited by our South Korean Allies, and our forces plan to utilize facilities in this area. Unnecessary destruction will impede our progress. Bombing and gunfire will be confined to targets whose destruction will contribute to the conduct of operations—accurate gunfire and pinpoint bombing against specific targets, rather than area destruction, is contemplated."[2] Despite these good intentions, however, the civilians were there and this was war, and Allan realized that some would have to be hurt. Their presence was even more significant in that it indicated that the North Korean high command evidently did not suspect that Inchon would be attacked, since the populace had not been warned or evacuated.

The sun was bright now. The *Gurke* was in the lead and

the swift, incoming currents carried her to a point about eight hundred yards from Wolmi-do. At 1242 hours, her anchor clattered down into the murky water; she swung about slowly with her bow to the tide and hung tightly on her anchor chain.

Eleven minutes later, the *Collett* came along and anchored, her navigator noting in her log: ". . . *30 fathoms of chain to starboard anchor, mud bottom, following bearings: Syaku Yaku light 011°T; Suto light 025°T, Wolmi light 060½°T, and breakwater light 078°T.*"

On the decks of all the destroyers, handy for immediate use, were grenades and submachine guns. There was a possibility that troops might come out from the shore and attempt to board a disabled or grounded destroyer. If so, it would be the first time in about a century that the ships of the United States Navy rang with the classic order: "Prepare to repel boarders!"

The signal to fire was given by flags flying from the destroyers' halyards. As they came in, the combination indicating, "Execute assigned mission," was hoisted, and the signal to open fire would be the lowering of these flags. Lieutenant Arthur T. White of the *De Haven* fired the first shot. Before he depressed the firing key, he had seen North Korean soldiers scrambling toward a gun pit, and that was his target. At the first blast the gun pit went up in dust and disappeared.

All the destroyers began to fire now, but slowly and with careful aim. The straw dummies on the bow of the *De Haven* caught fire from the muzzle blasts and began to burn.

At first the shore batteries did not respond to this bombardment. Captain Allan, jubilant, radioed back to Admiral Higgins: "Not even a pistol has been fired at us yet." Barely seconds after the message went out, the guns on Wolmi-do began to echo through the harbor, and the artillery duel was on. *Swenson, Collett* and *Gurke* were nearest the island. The North Koreans concentrated their fire on these three destroyers. They bracketed at first, the initial volley passing over the ships, the next volley short. On the third try they found the range, and at 1306 hours, a 75-mm. shell struck the *Collett* forward on the port side, exploding in a crew compartment. The next shell, a larger projectile, caught the destroyer at the waterline, opening a two-foot hole. Minutes later the *Collett* was hit again with a dud shell that penetrated, failed to explode, and ended up on a sofa in the wardroom. The fourth shell to hit the *Collett* wounded five men and knocked out her firing computer. Then she was hit a fifth time. Only the *Collett* had been hit so far, and as her skipper, Commander Robert H. Close, said later, "It was obvious that they had us boresighted." The *Collett* moved out of range.

Now all the destroyers began to receive counterfire. The *Gurke* was struck thrice, amidships, and two men were wounded. Shell geysers appeared all around the *Mansfield* but somehow, miraculously, she was not touched.

An enemy projectile exploded in the sea near the *Swenson*. It was a clean miss, doing no significant damage to the ship itself. But on deck at his post was the young and promising Lieutenant (jg) David H. Swenson. A fragment whizzing through the air caught him and killed him. He was the only man to lose his life among the attacking forces in this two-day bombardment.

From the hilltop building of Fleet Weather Central at the Yokosuka Naval Base just south of Yokohama came the report for D-Day, September 15: "Typhoon Kezia no longer a threat and no new typhoons brewing. Weather to be clear, visibility at least 10 miles, wind six knots from the northeast. Some cloudiness by midmorning and perhaps a moderate squall by late afternoon."

On the *Mt. McKinley,* now nearing Inchon along with the more than two hundred ships of the entire attack force, General MacArthur gathered the correspondents in Admiral Doyle's cabin and said, "The history of war proves that nine out of ten times an army has been destroyed because its supply lines have been cut off. That's what we are trying to do.

"Everything the enemy shoots, and all the additional replenishment he needs, have come down through Seoul. We are going to try to seize that distributing area so that it will be impossible for the North Koreans to get any additional men or more than a trickle of supplies into the present combat area."

That same day, in casual remarks to General Fox and others of his staff, he commented, "We're going to go ashore and we're not going to get our noses too bloody. If we have to pull out, the only thing that will be lost is MacArthur's military reputation."

When he looked at Wolmi-do and saw it blackened and devastated by two days of aerial and naval gun bombardment he said, "I don't think we'll have a hundred casualties going in there."[3]

In the dark of morning, on the deck of a pitching vessel, Marine Corporal Joe Maize heard the roar of bombing as the attack on Wolmi-do continued. The recruits were nervous. He and the other NCO's were directed by the officers to keep them busy.

Dawn broke, gray and cool. Joe Maize looked around the sea and the dim land to the east. It seemd to him that there were millions of ships; he had never seen so many in one place in all his life. (Joe would have been interested in the exact count if he had known it. There were 194 U. S. ships, 32 Japanese [perhaps illegally on hand], 15 South Korean, 12 British, 3 Canadian, 2 Australian, 2 New Zealand and one French vessel—261 altogether. In addition, there were several hundred smaller boats being readied for the actual trip to shore.) The officers went up and down the line and saw to it that everyone's haversack was loosened so that it would come off easily in case its wearer fell into the water.

And now it was D-Day, September 15. The attack plan allowed for three beaches to be taken, Red, Green and Blue. Red was on the mainland just north of the causeway that went out to the island of Wolmi-do. Green was on Wolmi-do itself, on the northern finger that was its only flat land. Blue was further south, somewhat separated from the other two beaches, just below the tidal basin with its locks where ships remained in deep water when the tide ran out, and in a flanking position that offered an entry into the city from the southeast.

Green Beach, on Wolmi-do, was to be taken first, in an initial and separate landing during the period of morning high tide. Red and Blue Beaches would be hit that evening when the tide came in again. It was, as a number of professional officers reflected, the only amphibious landing in history ever to be made in two installments.

There was logic in the method, of course. The island peak of Wolmi-do first had to be blasted into a charred heap, and then secured by actual troops before the real penetration of the mainland could begin. The 3rd Battalion of Murray's 5th Marines, headed by Lieutenant Colonel Robert D. Taplett, had been chosen for this job.

The men of the 3rd Battalion were aboard five ships: an LSD (Landing Ship, Dock), the *Fort Marion* and three des-

troyer-transports: the *Bass,* the *Diachenko* and the *Wantuck.*
As dawn began to break, they clambered down landing nets
and into the smaller craft that would take them ashore. All
this time the bombardment of both Wolmi-do and the mainland was continuing, and to the naval guns, aerial bombs and
napalm was added a rocket barrage from three LSMR's
(Landing Ship, Material, Rockets) each about two hundred
feet long, squat and square like most landing ships, and this
morning in use for the first time in any combat operation.
On each rocket ship were ten continuously fed launchers. By
the end of the day, they fired 6,421 rockets.

The world seemed filled with noise—"the fire from the
ships like the sound of slammed doors," thought *Time-Life*
correspondent Frank Gibney, as the first wave of Marines
started toward the shore in LCVP's (Landing Craft, Vehicle
and Personnel)—289 of them from the *Bass* alone. They
tooled about in the sea near the transports for a few moments
to get organized, and then in a group left the LOD (Line of
Depature), about nine hundred yards offshore. There were
seventeen of these LCVP's, filled to the gunwales with Marines, and there were three somewhat larger LSU's (Landing Ship, Utility) waiting to bring nine tanks ashore. The
tanks had been modified for the landing at about the time of
Sergeant Pat Byrnes's big beer party between battles in Pusan; three of them were now equipped with bulldozer blades
for going through barbed wire barriers and filling in dugouts
or caves, which were all over the mound of the island; another three were armed with flame throwers.

The rocket barrage was still going on as the seventeen landing ships, maneuvering about behind the starting line like so
many sail yachts minutes before the starting gun of a race,
waited the word by radio to head for the shore. Wolmi-do
was now a blackened mound wrapped in a wooly shroud of
smoke. Since 0500, eight Marine Corsairs had been hitting it
from the air with bombs, napalm, and machine-gun strafing.
The first two of these planes on the scene, in the dimmest
light of dawn, had spotted an armored car trying to run across
the causeway from the island to the shore and had stopped
it and set it afire after several machine-gun passes.

By this morning of September 15, Wolmi-do, in fact, had
been suffering from heavy blows from both sea and air for
nearly five days. Marine planes had attacked it with napalm in
sixty-five sorties on September 10; the six destroyers had blasted
at its gun emplacements at close range, and on that same

occasion, two heavy U. S. cruisers and two light British cruisers had lobbed shells into the mound from positions further out at sea. On September 14, planes from all the carriers in the task force had struck at the island. Simultaneously, the heavy cruisers had made a second attack. It was hard to see how anything could still be alive on Wolmi-do. But the older Marines, who had made other amphibious landings, knew man's astonishing propensity to survive and decided to hit the beach and move on cautiously.

In the grayest part of the dawn, on that morning of September 15, while the final bombardment of Wolmi-do from the air was beginning and lighting up the immediate horizon with great sheets of flashes, filling the area with thundering sounds and the ammonia smell of explosives, the command ship, the U. S. S. *Mt. McKinley,* with MacArthur and the other top commanders aboard, steamed into Flying Fish Channel to move toward Inchon. Captain Carter W. Printup, on the bridge, was suddenly notified by one of the lookouts that a strange, tiny craft was approaching.

He turned his binoculars upon it quickly. There were several figures in a putt-putting motor sampan about the size of a lifeboat, and they looked like Koreans, although one of them was tall and seemed to be wearing an old suit of fatigues. This taller man was standing atop the sampan's small cabin waving his hat. At times it looked suspiciously like a U. S. naval officer's hat. Printup supposed that the North Koreans, like the Japanese in World War II, might be capable of spectacular suicide missions, and he didn't like the look of the approaching craft. He grabbed an electric bullhorn, rushed to the wing of the bridge, and called out, "Stand off! Stand off, there!" He saw that the small craft had cut its engine. An LCVP was lowered and sent toward it.

A young ensign commanded the LCVP. As he moved toward the sampan he saw that the tall figure in green fatigues and Navy hat was a Caucasian with a heavy four-inch beard. He pointed a submachine gun at him and called, "Who the hell are you?"

"I," said the apparition, "am Lieutenant Eugene Clark of the United States Navy! And put down that gun before you hurt somebody!" Clark had spent the night in the lighthouse, but, seeing the Navy ships at dawn, had decided to join them.

About ten miles west of Inchon, between two islands, and

within hearing distance of the bombardment, Colonel Louis B. Ely was in the captain's cabin of H.M.S. *Whitesand Bay*, arguing with two South Korean naval officers, while the frigate's skipper, Lieutenant Commander Brothers RN, looked on with polite interest. The Koreans commanded the two R. O. K. Navy patrol crafts that had pulled up to the *Whitesand Bay* and made fast, one on either side.

Communication among everyone there was at a minimum. Not only did the entire conversation have to go through an interpreter, but the Korean skippers, like Ely and Brothers, had apparently received only the vaguest of instructions: meet the British frigate at such-and-such a point where there will be some American colonel and about a hundred men; they will need your help, take them wherever they want to go. Ely, still unaware that his mission had been cancelled, was trying to explain that he wanted to be taken to the shore eight miles north of Inchon. Not all the way in, but to the edge of the mud flats where it was too shallow for the British frigate to approach. From that point on he'd take the rubber boats.

The Korean skippers were not at all attracted to the idea of approaching the mud flats. It wasn't that they feared enemy resistance; it was the nature of the coast itself. The Han broadened out and emptied into the Yellow Sea in a kind of estuary just north of Inchon. When the tide was in, there was perhaps thirty feet of water in the deepest parts, but between high tides there were nothing but vast mud flats barely covered by water; this was why the capital of Seoul itself was not a port, and why Inchon, though not at the mouth of the river, was its entry and exit point to the sea. The Korean pointed out that they could go partway toward the shore during the high morning tide that was about to rise, but that the tide would run out again in a couple of hours and they'd never be able to make it back. Besides, there were rocks. Ely showed them aerial photos of the area taken at low tide and tried to point out that there were no rocks. They shook their heads. He tried to play one man against the other and at one point had one of them agreeing to try it if his partner would. But the partner was adamant.

The argument went on until suddenly everyone realized that the tide was now at its height and that it was definitely too late to carry out the mission. Ely sighed deeply and asked the British commander to take him and his unit back to the *Mt. McKinley* just off Inchon harbor. Maybe they'd remember him there on the command ship, and still have something useful for him to do.[4]

At 0625, September 15, 1950, the *Mt. McKinley* gave the radio and flag signal to the seventeen small landing craft filled with Marines to head for the beach. The G- and H-Companies of Taplett's 3rd Battalion started forward with I-Company in reserve. Rockets and naval gunfire were still hitting the island as the little ships surged toward it, and the barrage continued until they were no more than fifty yards from shore, with the explosions literally under their noses.

It was the first amphibious assault undertaken by American troops since the landing on Okinawa on Easter Sunday, April 1, 1945. Unlike Okinawa, Wolmi-do was not a semi-tropic place with virtually uninhabited beaches, but a rather pleasant spot that in peacetime was a favorite place for picnics and beach outings. Its conical hill took up the bulk of the island, but just to the north of the hill, where the causeway came to the island, was a lower spit of land with a short, sandy beach facing the sea at high tide, sloping into mud flats at low water. Near the northern tip of this beach was a swimming pool. Between the pool and the hill (marked as 105 meters high on the maps, and therefore known as Hill 105), the Marines had an area no more than 300 yards wide in which to land. Rather, it *had* been 300 yards wide. The bombardment had wrecked and reduced to kindling wood dozens of tiny fishing and pleasure craft that had been beached here, and this reduced the usable landing area to about fifty yards.

The men of the 1st Platoon of G-Company, huddled in the LCVP as it approached, heard the pinging of a few wild shots against the steel hull as they neared the shore. There was apparently only scattered and occasional small-arms fire, probably from the slopes of the hill just to their right. The recruits stirred nervously; the veterans among them made a great show of aplomb and disdain. As the boats coasted in for the last fifty yards or so, the barrage ceased, and the sudden quiet, punctuated only by an occasional distant rifle shot, was startling and a little frightening. The first boats scraped ground. Other boats, behind them, slowed themselves and bunched together in an accordion effect, while they waited for landing room in the narrow area. Marines jumped from the bows and splashed through the last few feet of shallow water to the shore. Within minutes the beach was crowded and everything was in a state of controlled confusion, with NCO's and junior officers assembling and directing their men by voice and hand signals, and with 1st Lieutenant Robert D. Bohn, commander of Company G, making sure that his runner and radio operator were with him, so that as he moved forward, he would still be, in effect, a command post.

It was now 0633; the approach to the beach had taken eight minutes. Bohn, glancing about hastily, saw with satisfaction that apparently no one had yet been killed or wounded, and he noticed that the sporadic small-arms fire they were receiving was coming primarily from the mainland; there seemed to be no resistance at all left on the slope to the right which had been designated Objective 1-A.

The Marines assembled on the beach now turned right and moved forward in broken formation toward Hill 105, and then upward on its slope. Behind them the LSU's nosed onto the beach and disgorged their M-26 Pershing tanks. Bohn, his executive officer, Lieutenant Jaworski, and their radio operator were soaking wet; his boat, on the extreme right and nearest the hill, had hit an underwater obstacle coming in and had been unable to traverse the last few yards to the shore. Bohn had ordered the ramp lowered anyway and the three of them had plunged into the water which they'd thought shallow. To their surprise, they sank; immediately they shucked off all their equipment and swam ashore. The boat, with the rest of its Marines, had backed off and landed at another spot further down the beach.

As the Marines started up the hill, the F4U Corsairs flew in again and sprayed the area ahead of them—no more than fifty yards in some cases—with machine-gun fire. Even the veterans who had worked under Marine air cover before thought it incredibly fine marksmanship to be able to lay down such accurate fire from the air. As the landing craft circled about, waiting for the order to go in, and as the Corsairs were giving the island its final plastering, a Marine in one of the boats shouted: "Hey—save *us* a little of that island!" The ensuing laughter relieved some of the tension.

When the first skirmishers were about halfway up the 300-foot hill, North Koreans began to pop out of their foxholes. They were dirty, blackened by smoke, shabbily dressed and scared. Some were all but deaf after the long bombardment. *Time-Life* correspondent Frank Gibney had learned fluent

Japanese as a naval officer in World War II, and he was able to speak to some of the prisoners. "Are you going to kill us?" asked one. Gibney said no, and the man and his companions seemed vastly relieved. He came across a tall, scrawny man in his late forties who was kneeling and had his hands folded in an attitude of prayer. When this man looked up and saw Gibney and some approaching Marines, he cried out in Japanese, "Don't shoot me; I'm a Christian!"[5]

Hill 105 was smoking and thoroughly devastated. It had been rather thickly wooded with small trees and bushes before the bombardment; now there was literally not a whole tree left: it was a landscape completely filled with stumps and splinters. The North Koreans continued to come out of holes and caves. Each prisoner, as he was taken, was immediately stripped so that he could carry no concealed weapons, and then sent back, usually in nothing but his loin cloth, to the rear. For most of the advancing Marines, it was startling to be moving cautiously forward and suddenly see a man or small group of men pop out of the ground, hands raised in surrender.

The tactical plan for taking Wolmi-do called for definite movements on the parts of the units involved. Lieutenant Bohn took his men up the north face of the hill to secure the crest; Captain Patrick E. Wildman, commanding Company H, attacked across the northern spit of the island—which itself rose to a humplike ridge perhaps fifty feet high—to clear a path to the causeway. Company I, commanded by Captain Robert A. McMullen (the reserve company whose assigned task was to follow in after the spearheads) came along in his wake, and after crossing most of this spit, suddenly swung to the right toward the steepest face of the big hill which looked toward the mainland, and which contained a number of caves. Ironically, McMullen's company ran into the stiffest resistance.

Company I had landed in the fourth wave, almost a half hour after the first landing craft touched the beach. They moved across the broad northern spit and swung right toward the hill. There was a low cliff facing Inchon just ahead of them. Like all the rest of the island it was smoking, scorched and blackened, and it didn't seem possible that any organized unit could be ensconced there. But suddenly North Koreans began to pop up from behind the rubble and toss hand grenades at them—there appeared to be about a platoon of them. The enemy soldiers rose, tossed their grenades, and ducked down again, usually before they could be shot. The men of I-Company scattered for cover. They poured small arms and automatic-weapons fire at the cliff face, but it didn't seem to have any effect. The company's interpreter crawled forward and yelled for the Reds to surrender. They answered with more hand grenades. McMullen got on his radio and called for tanks.

Several tanks clattered up from the beach and stationed themselves in covering positions while one tank, with a bulldozer blade on its snout, moved upward and forward, scooping up earth and covering the foxholes containing the enemy soldiers, burying most of them alive.

At 0655 the 3rd Platoon of G-Company reached the crest of Hill 105, Sergeant Alvin E. Smith tied an American flag to the longest tree stump he could find. It was no accident that Smith, the platoon's guide when it marched, had a flag in his haversack. The Marines, as conscious of style as bullfighters, had issued several for exactly that purpose.

Back on the northern point of the island where the landing had originally taken place, the swimming pool had been converted into a prisoner-of-war stockade, and was now filled with some forty-odd North Koreans. The empty concrete hole seemed as good a place as any to keep them for the time being. Also in this immediate area, follow-up supplies were being landed and stacked on the beach, but now the tide was starting to run out again, and in a very short time the 3rd Battalion and its supporting tanks would be isolated on the island until the larger force could hit the two remaining mainland beaches just before dusk.

For the rest of the day, they occupied themselves with a thorough investigation of the battered island, to find hidden enemy soldiers and any gun emplacements that might still be operational against the mainland landings. Two 76-mm. antitank guns were found on the western face of the hill, where they might have done damage to subsequent waves coming into Green Beach, but fortunately their crews had been so thoroughly demoralized by the bombardment that they no longer had the spirit to operate them. The main part of the island was thus under control, but there was still the long southern finger that went out to the little rock of So-Wolmi-do, and as a squad supported by tanks and machine guns moved toward it, they ran into heavy rifle and machine-gun fire. There was apparently at least a pla-

toon of North Koreans holed up there, ready for a last-ditch
fight.

Lieutenant Colonel Taplett called for air strike. The Corsairs dropped tanks of napalm (flaming jellied gasoline) over
the tiny satellite island. From the rear, a mortar platoon
poured 81-mm. shells into the target. The smoke cleared
away. Marine infantry went forward, tanks still supporting
them with fire, and although the resistance had died down to
an occasional popping of rifle shots, they found the defenders
holed up in caves, and it took them another hour to silence
things completely.[6]

It was 1115 hours. Wolmi-do was thoroughly and without
question in American hands. Seventeen Marines had been
wounded, none killed. One hundred eighty of the enemy had
been killed and 136 captured. A hundred or more had been
buried alive in their holes and caves by the bulldozing tanks.

The thirty-foot tide had receded and Wolmi-do was surrounded by mud flats. The Marines now holding the island
stared at the mainland less than a mile away across the inner
harbor, and noticed that every once in a while a mortar
round came lobbing toward them, as though to remind them
that Inchon itself was still in enemy hands.

Since dawn, General of the Armies Douglas MacArthur
had been sitting on a kind of wing deck just forward of
amidships on the amphibious command ship *Mt. McKinley*,
about two miles southwest of Inchon, watching the capture
of Wolmi-do. He sat in a special revolving chair of the type
used in the pilot houses of capital ships so that their commanders can observe for long periods from the bridge. Near
him was a mounted revolving telescope which he used several times to look toward Wolmi-do, especially during the
eight minutes when the seventeen small landing craft approached the shore, but for the most part smoke obscured
the details of the operation. He wore khaki trousers, a
leather jacket of the kind flyers favored in World War II,
and his famed "Bataan hat" the khaki-billed cap with the
gold oak leaves on its bill and around its sides, patterned
after the headgear of the topmost ranks in the Philippine
Army which MacArthur had commanded.

Everyone had risen with MacArthur at dawn and, without breakfast, gone topside to watch the first assault. Generals Almond, Wright and Fox were with him, as well as
General Whitney, his principal aide, Admiral Doyle and a

group of staff members. MacArthur had, in fact, been on deck before the first real light as the *Mt. McKinley* had steamed toward Inchon from the southeast. He and Admiral Doyle had both noticed the flashing light at Palmi-do, where Lieutenant Clark was still sitting after turning it on. Doyle had said, "They've left their navigation lights on. That's the fourth we've picked up on the way in here this morning."

"That's courtesy," MacArthur had remarked.

And then the dawn came, reddish and bright, fillling the sky beyond the hills behind Inchon.

"Just like Lingayen Gulf," MacArthur said. "But it's quieter and nicer, isn't it?"

Moments later it was no longer quiet; the naval guns began to pound at Inchon, and with fine timing, the carrier planes began to strike at the island between the gun barrages. The carriers offshore were sending in eight F4U's every ninety minutes to fly in close support of the Marines. At the same time, another flight of Corsairs and attack planes was penetrating further inland in a series of deep support missions designed to weaken the enemy's immediate supply lines.

Shortly before 8:00 A.M. there was a terrific explosion from somewhere beyond the city of Inchon. It was so violent that even the *Mt. McKinley,* two miles off, rocked a little. MacArthur looked up, raising his eyebrows slightly. A nearby officer, anticipating the question in the general's mind, rushed aft to go below to the combat operations center and find out what had caused the noise.

Five Corsairs from the *Valley Forge* had been on one of the penetration missions beyond the city, flying at 2,000 feet, watching the roads below for signs of enemy movement. Only a few miles out of Inchon they had spotted two machine-gun nests beside the road and had peeled off to attack them. On the first pass both machine guns were destroyed, and according to several pilots' reports, about ten of the soldiers manning them killed. (One pilot reported ten dead and "clearly visible lying out in the road in their white clothing"; since North Korean soldiers generally wore uniforms, these may have been civilians, possibly forced to work in the area or even man the machine guns.)

As the pilots completed their pass they saw a third machine-gun emplacement down the road a little further, this one unmanned. Across the road from it was a long line of boxes stacked man-high and in orderly rows. The first four pilots were so busy destroying the gun emplacements that they didn't have time to react and realize that this was an ammunition dump. Ensign Eldon W. Brown, Jr., came along at the tail end of the attack. He saw the boxes and sent a burst of tracers into them. They started to flame. He understood suddenly that they were, indeed, ammunition, and that he was about to fly right over the coming explosion.

It called for a split-second decision. If he pulled back on his stick and zoomed upward, he would be directly above the explosion. The best tactic was to keep flying straight and level, and hang on, which he did. In the next micro-second, when he was barely past the ammunition dump, the explosion came. Brown felt his airplane buck and saw the swift, frightening shadow of the shock wave—like an instantaneous heat ripple in the air—shoot past, overtaking him. For a moment he thought he was out of control and then, miraculously, the plane was responding again and still flying straight and level.

He looked back. The dust and smoke cloud was reddish and was beginning to form the mushroom top characteristic of atomic blasts. This was not an atom blast but, thought Brown, was the next thing to it. He was up to 4,000 feet and the smoke was still billowing above him.

Twenty-five miles away, the pilot of a torpedo bomber on another mission felt the concussion.

When the Combat Operations Center aboard the *Mt. McKinley* radioed to find out what had caused the blast, the flight leader called back, without further explanation, "We just exploded some ammunition."

MacArthur, hearing the reply, nodded calmly and continued to watch.

As the smoke began to rise from Wolmi-do, General Almond appeared. "Good morning, General. How are you?"

MacArthur smiled and said, "I don't see how I could be better."

Everyone was watching intently as the landing craft went forward from the LOD (Line of Departure), as they hit the beach, and as the Marines fanned out to take the island. From this observation wing deck on the *Mt. McKinley* no one could see too clearly through the smoke, and the reports that came in from time to time actually gave a better picture of what was taking place. Although it was widely reported afterward that MacArthur saw the flag raised atop Wolmi's hill, the first real news of success came by way of a messenger who brought a dispatch and handed it to Admiral Doyle. Doyle paraphrased aloud: "Admiral Struble reports from the *Rochester* that the landing party is ashore, has advanced inland and the North Koreans have put up the white flag."

MacArthur laughed and clapped his hands together. "Good!" he said. "Now let's go down and have a cup of coffee!"[7]

The party breakfasted simply in the small Captain's Mess at about the time the Marines were sealing the North Koreans in the caves and rubble on the northern face of the hill. Minutes later Admiral Struble arrived in his barge from the *Rochester,* which was anchored further out. He conferred with Admiral Doyle and Marine General O. P. Smith briefly, then said he was going in to take a look at Wolmi-do. He stepped up to MacArthur and said, "If you want to go in, General, I'll take you."

MacArthur brightened and said, "Yes! Yes! By all means!"

The Supreme Commander then went below to put on a warmer jacket, saying he would be ready in about ten minutes. Five minutes later an aide came up to Admiral Struble. "General MacArthur would like to know if some of the correspondents can go along." Struble said they could. He had meanwhile invited Generals Almond and Shepherd for the boat ride.

Somehow it got out of hand. Everybody wanted to go ashore, and when Struble walked to the quarterdeck about fifteen minutes after MacArthur had gone below, he found over thirty people expecting to take the trip. That many wouldn't fit into his barge. (An admiral's small motorboat is, in Navy parlance, always a "barge"; a captain uses a "gig" and lesser ranks a "launch.") Struble asked Jimmy Doyle if he'd break out his own barge and take half the party, and then arbitrarily chose the nearest half to accompany himself. It always amused him in later years to reflect that in the midst of this momentous military operation, the commander of the Seventh United States Fleet had to decide on this minor matter.

The boats, filled with the top management of the Inchon landing operation, started ashore after being lowered. Struble reflected that a couple of well-placed rounds from the shore could take out quite a few admirals and generals at this point, including MacArthur himself. By now the tide was going out and the current was at 3.5 knots, even higher than had been estimated—the recent typhoons, in fact, had thrown

off all predicted tide and current data slightly—and it took
the two barges a good hour to negotiate the two or three
miles to Green Beach.

On the beach, MacArthur looked about a bit and the correspondents found Marines with stories to tell. The sound
of small-arms fire was coming from the other side of the hill
where the attackers were still pressing forward toward that
last pocket of resistance on the end of the southern spit.

MacArthur said, "Let's go around and take a look at
Red Beach."

His high-ranking staff men frowned and glanced at each
other. Red Beach was on the mainland just north of the
causeway where it connected. It was one of the two principal
landing areas that would be hit that evening when the main
body of the invasion force was put ashore. There were defenders in the city—throwing occasional mortar rounds at
Wolmi-do, as a matter of fact—and as it turned out later,
one of the strongest trench defenses was just behind the sea
walls along Red Beach. None of these men was thinking of
his own safety, but rather of General MacArthur's; it was
the old MacArthur pattern again—he had shocked his staff
officers by exposing himself to fire, quite calmly, at Corregi-
dor and a dozen other places. Doubtless he believed he led
a charmed life. Very possibly, thought his associates, he did.

Struble and Doyle directed their barges to a point off the
northern tip of the island from which they could see Red
Beach and the long expanse of mud flat, now exposed, leading to it. General Shepherd was particularly concerned that
fire might be directed from the mainland toward General
MacArthur. Admiral Struble remarked that the Oriental has
a tendency to hold his fire until he is sure and that this
made it a little unlikelier they'd be shot at. There was no
fire, and the two small boats returned to the *Mt. McKinley*
without incident.

The tide was out; the smoke of battle lay flat over everything in the quiet hours that began at midday. MacArthur
and his captains lunched aboard the *Mt. McKinley* and discussed the taking of Wolmi-do in quiet but animated fashion.
They did not yet dare to be exuberant, for the difficult second stage of the landing operation was yet to be accomplished.

Lieutenant Commander Jack Lowentraut, who had
watched the morning strike with the correspondents from a

deck just above MacArthur's, returned to the operations center below to resume the work that had kept him and his colleagues busy on an average of twenty hours a day for the past week. Captain Norman W. Sears, Doyle's chief of staff, returned from an inspection trip to Wolmi-do aboard an LCVP; he himself had not slept for forty-eight hours.

Aboard one of the attack transports, Lieutenant Colonel Murray ate his lunch and continued, up until the last minute, to frown and stew over his plan to land his battalions in bits and pieces on the narrow beach that evening.

On an LST, Sergeant Pat Byrnes fussed over the "gripings" or chains holding down the tank he commanded and would take ashore in a few hours.

On another LST, Corporal Joe Maize assured the recruits that being under fire wouldn't be as bad as they expected.

On the transport *Pickaway*, Major Koh went up and down the passageways to be sure none of the bewildered farm boys in his R. O. K. Marine battalion had gotten themselves lost, and that all would be on hand when the time came to climb down the nets.

The tide was out . . . the mud flats lay exposed, raw and ugly all around Inchon and Wolmi-do, in some places extending almost two miles to the sea. The ships that all morning seemed to be lying in a wide stretch of water now found themselves actually in a narrow stream. One hapless LCM (Landing Craft, Matériel, or "Mike Boat") discovered itself on a mud island nearly thirty feet above the water with cliffs dropping down on all sides.

Some distance to the north was the wreck of an old airplane lying in the mud and now exposed by the disappearing waters. It was an F4U Vought Corsair that had apparently been sunk there in some chance encounter during World War II.

Low tide . . . and a quiet pause. The waters of the sea and the men of the invasion force gathered themselves together for the evening assault.

NOTES *Chapter 9*

1. Karig *et al*, p. 200.
2. Interview author—Struble.
3. *Time*, 25 Sept 50; Interview author—Fox.

4. General Almond was rather surprised to see Ely and his raiding group when they showed up. He told Ely finally to turn his troops over to General Barr's 7th Division and to go back to Japan. Interviews author—Ely, Almond.

5. Interview author—Gibney.

6. Eight defenders were still hiding out on So-Wolmi-do, and that evening when Marine brigade commander General Craig came ashore, he saw their successful break for freedom and watched them swim to the mainland. They were shot at as they swam, but some observers felt the Marines were deliberately letting them go as though admiring their pluck. Craig memo.

7. Events and dialogue aboard the *Mt. McKinley* that morning are reconstructed from a number of eyewitness sources, all of which agree closely. Interviews author—Almond, Fox, Struble, Lowentraut; letters Wright and Doyle to author.

10

"They all got ashore fine."

Major General Oliver P. Smith, USMC, commanding the 1st Marine Division from aboard the *Mt. McKinley*, was quietly satisfied with the morning's events. All the intelligence estimates from Colonel Willoughby's G-2 Section in Tokyo had been quite accurate concerning Woldmi-do, and Taplett's battalion, landing there, had encountered only about four hundred defenders. The resistance, as such things go, had been half-hearted—the mere seventeen casualties among the Marines, all wounded, none dead, attested to that.[1]

General Smith wasn't so sure the big landing on the mainland that evening would be quite as easy. Intelligence said there were only about 1,000 enemy troops in the city of Inchon itself. Assuming this to be true, and it probably was, those few troops held almost ideal defensive positions, and they had had time to build, behind the sea walls, trenches, dugouts or barricades that could make Inchon as bloody a landing as Tarawa in World War II.

At the moment Oliver Smith had charge of that portion of the action that would take place on land. It was his 1st Marine Division that would seize the beachheads and the first series of objective lines in the city of Inchon. After that, they would be joined by Dave Barr's 7th Army Division and the drive inland would begin with Ned Almond, as X-Corps commander, calling the major shots.

The principal units of the 1st Marine Division had meanwhile been shuffled slightly, so that Brigadier General Edward Craig, who had commanded the Marine brigade in the Perimeter, now found himself Assistant Division Commander. If possible, he was to set up the division's first advance command post on the island of Wolmi-do. It would be a complete headquarters organization with men, vehicles, communications and facilities, all in a package and ready to operate moments after it came ashore.

Eddie Craig, himself an amiable man, had nothing but the greatest admiration for General Smith, and long afterwards wrote: "I consider General O. P. Smith . . . the outstanding officer in this operation and the later operations in North Korea including the Chosin Reservoir. His leadership and tactical ability contributed more than anything to our success." But in the entire Inchon operation, where nothing went quite according to the book, Craig, the Assistant Division Commander, hadn't even been able to confer with his boss in person, and wouldn't be able to do so until after the the landing. The nearest thing to a conference with General Smith he'd enjoyed so far had been a personal letter sent to him in Pusan from Smith, in Tokyo, and dated September 8, 1950. It read in part: "Dear Eddie . . . if everything goes all right on Wolmi-do during D-Day I would like for you to go ashore on the evening tide and set up an advanced CP. We will give you a dispatch to that effect sometime during the day of D-Day. I would expect you to function at discretion. There may be decisions to be made which you can best make on the spot. If there is time and you feel that the matter should be referred to Division, do so. In any event keep us advised. In this connection I am thinking primarily of Red Beach. I believe we will be better able to handle the situation Blue Beach from the *Mt. McKinley*. Depending on the situation it is my intention to land on Wolmi-do on the evening tide of D plus 1. We do not want to clutter up the beach and will bring a minimum of personnel.

"I appreciate the beating you are taking coming out of action and mounting out. Only Marines could do what you are doing. We had a narrow squeak in getting you at all." (General Smith was here referring to Walker's attempt to keep the Marines in the Perimeter and the compromise decision to give him a relatively untrained Army regiment instead as a reserve force. A quiet and almost unnoticed action of the overall plan, this was actually one of the more desperate risks of the Inchon gamble; Walker's line might well have broken at about the time of the landing itself. Good generalship—which always includes a certain amount of good luck —kept that from happening.) Smith's letter continued: "The Brigade has done a splendid job in South Korea and we are all proud of you. You have put the rest of us on the spot.

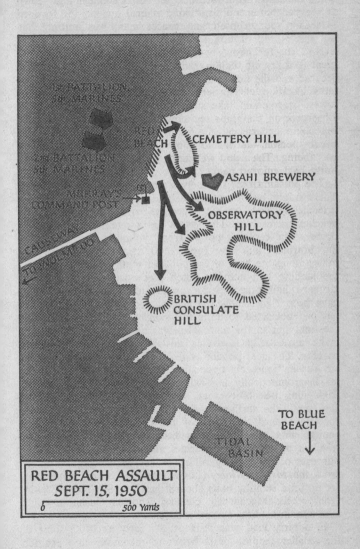

RED BEACH ASSAULT
SEPT. 15, 1950

0   500 Yards

I am confident we can all give a good account of ourselves when the chips are down. I regret that I could not get down to see you but I could not work it in. I am looking forward to seeing you on Wolmi-do. Sincerely, Oliver Smith."[2]

And so, for about two hours, from noon till 1400, the great fleet lay off Inchon, quiet and watching. Wolmi-do was secured and the tide had run out and in effect stranded Taplett's battalion of Marines, since only boats with the shallowest draft could take supply or personnel back or forth. Observers on the ships scanning the mainland through their binoculars experienced the old cliché of so many Indian War cavalry stories—it was so quiet you were certain the enemy was there, hidden and watching; you could feel his presence in the back of your neck.

The planners kept themselves alert for all possible hazards. There might be, for example, undetected mines on the approaches to Red and Blue Beaches, perhaps inland along the beaches themselves. They were again reminded of this obstacle when Taplett reported from Wolmi-do that his exploring Marines had now found 300 cast-iron anti-personnel mines along the base of the hill, just south of the area where the landing had actually taken place; somehow the North Koreans had prepared for an assault here—which would have been right below the heights and militarily unsound—but had neglected to mine the more choice landing area on the sand spit to the noth. This was no guarantee that they'd make an equally favorable mistake on the two mainland beaches. The next possibility that was considered was sudden air attack. True, air opposition in the Korean War had so far been practically non-existent, but there was always the frightening possibility that Russia might get into this war and supply the north with air power. Indeed, naval electronic spotters aboard the ships of the invasion fleet knew well enough that the entire expedition had been stalked and watched by Russian submarines all the way to Inchon. For purposes of the landing, all air strikes were being controlled from the *Mt. McKinley,* but a separate control center was set up on a standby basis aboard the U. S. S. *George Clymer* from where Marine air General Thomas Cushman could take over immediate control if necessary.

Five-thirty P.M. was H-Hour. As early as 1400, some of the smaller landing craft began to maneuver into position around the larger ships, ready to receive their cargoes of assault troops. At 1430 the bombardment began again, this time with the mainland beaches as the targets. Admiral Higgins' four cruisers and six destroyers poured everything they had into the seaport, smashing every landmark they could see and filling the entire stretch of waterfront with blazing fire and billowing smoke. In between the naval gun barrages, the planes dropped bombs and napalm.

MacArthur and his staff took their places on the winged observation deck of the *Mt. McKinley* once more and listened to the dry, metallic radio reports of the various air and bombardment strikes as they were piped into a speaker somewhere overhead. There were ships everywhere, of all sizes, on all sides. Murray's 5th Regiment and its supporting units were in a group of transports and larger landing ships scattered in the area to the north, and Chesty Puller's 1st Regiment team was waiting in vessels a few miles to the south. Just before H-Hour the foot soldiers scrambled down cargo nets and into the smaller LCVP's and similar craft. Tanks, artillery and other heavy support items would come in on the larger LST's and be disgorged from bow ramps in the wake of the first assault troops.

Red Beach was the strip of waterfront that would be the front door into the city itself. It was only three hundred yards wide, its lower end at the point where the causeway from Wolmi-do joined the mainland. Its entire width was one long barrier of stone seawall, fourteen to sixteen feet high. Blue Beach was alomst three miles to the south and led to a factory area on the city's outskirts. It was also just below the neck of the blunt, square peninsula on which the city was situated. Chesty Puller's landing on Blue Beach, therefore, would in effect be a support landing and flanking movement, and his orders were to cut around to the left after landing, heading in a somewhat northerly direction, to either outflank or surround the defenders in the city, and cut their supply lines completely.

Slender, dark-haired, serious Lieutenant Colonel Bob Taplett, his force now in complete control of Wolmi-do, observed the mainland just across the inner harbor with his binoculars. The shore was only about a mile away. He had set up his observation post on top of Hill 105 and here he placed his Shore Party Fire Control Officer, Second Lieutenant Joseph R. Wayerski, to look for targets of opportunity. Wayerski found several, among them trenchworks in which enemy soldiers were moving about halfway up the principal hill in the city; he called in thirty rounds from the 5-inch guns aboard the destroyer *Mansfield,* and the trenches were reduced to smoke and dust. On another occasion, he detected a group of people stirring a little to the south in the area of the big square tidal basin which operated with locks and where ships were kept in deep water when the tide ran out. As the firing began, he suddenly realized that the figures he was watching were merely civilians raiding a pile of rice stores. He called the fire off quickly.

Taplett, meanwhile, kept swinging his binoculars back to Red Beach at the throat of the causeway with its silent walls. No matter how long or closely he looked, he could detect no movement; absolutely none. It was a great temptation, and he radioed the *McKinley* for permission to take his men across the causeway and capture Red Beach immediately. That was just a little too bold and the *McKinley* answered with a firm and definite, "No!"

From 1430 on, the naval and air bombardment increased in intensity. Noise filled the air and smoke hung over the city like a great cloud. Now other low natural clouds began to blow in from the sea. A light, gray drizzle began. The waters became choppy in the rising wind, and the tide began to pour back toward the shore at 3.5 knots—slightly higher than had been expected.

Aboard the *Mt. McKinley,* General Pinky Wright frowned at the squalls that were moving in and cutting down visibility, particularly in the vicinity of Blue Beach, south of the city. His job in planning was done, of course, and he was on hand now largely as an observer, but his emotions were as fervently involved in the success of the landing as anyone else's. It seemed to him miraculous that everything had gone without a hitch so far. It would be ironic to have unexpected adverse weather move in now and interfere with the plan. The clouds themselves were an obstacle, even if they didn't drop much rain. For the landing, perforce, would be at 5:30 P.M., at high tide, and sunset would be only an hour and thirteen minutes later, at 6:43 P.M., so that the landing force would need every possible minute of daylight to secure the beaches and advance toward their first, limited objectives. The rapidly thickening overcast might cut down the minutes of daylight to a critical point, and could upset the entire, closely interwoven scheme.

He glanced at MacArthur, still sitting in his swivel chair on the starboard side of the observation deck, and wondered if the Supreme Commander was also disturbed at what he saw. MacArthur, as always, radiated Olympian calm.

In the ward room of one of the attack transports hovering just off Red Beach, 1st Lieutenant Sam Jaskilka of Ansonia, Connecticut, was drinking coffee and listening to a record his fellow officers were playing over and over again. It was titled *"They'd Better Have Seven League Boots and Invisible Gabardines When They're Foolin' Around with Marines."* The song did not particularly amuse him, and he remarked dryly that he hoped the enemy believed its message.

It was well after 2:00 P.M. now and the barrage had started up again outside. Eight-inch guns from the cruisers . . . five-inchers from the destroyers . . . 40- and 20-mm. chattering in obbligato . . . and in between the blasting of air bombs. It could be heard easily even here, inside the ship. In moments, Sam and his Company E of the 2nd Battalion in Murray's 5th Regiment would go down the cargo nets, over the side of the transport and into the small boats. There they would wait for hours, perhaps, until they got the radio signal to cross the line of departure and go forward. So much of war, Sam reflected, was waiting for the signal to go. It was one of the worst aspects of combat; it gave men too much time, sometimes, to think about what they might be getting into. On the other hand, Sam didn't think the battle-tested men of his company, who had been through so much and done so well on the Perimeter, were particularly nervous about the upcoming assault. He'd seen the wooden faces of men in combat and he knew from experience that each man believes the *other* guy might get it, but never himself. In spite of this, he'd noticed that no one in the ward room had eaten much at lunch. He himself hadn't had a great appetite, but that may have been because lunch consisted of cold macaroni and ham, which he found not especially tempting.

The loudspeaker barked some orders and Sam went topside to join his men who were forming on the deck. They watched as the LCVP's with their Navy coxswains maneuvered alongside, fighting the slight chop that was bouncing them a bit. At the next signal the men scrambled down the nets and into the boats, which were 36 feet long and carried about 36 men apiece. At Sam's side was a huge, bearded Gunnery Sergeant, Robert Barnett, who would pass on his orders to the men.

Time-Life correspondent James Bell was also going along in Sam's boat. Just before he went down the net Sam paused and suddenly said, "Oh, God, I almost forgot!"

"What?" asked Bell. He wondered if Jaskilka had left behind something vital, like ammunition.

"The football season opens tomorrow. We'll be playing Yale." He meant the University of Connecticut, which he'd attended. Actually his dates were a bit mixed and Yale and Connecticut were not scheduled to play untl the following week—but at the moment this seemed the most important thing on his mind.

The LCVP's began circling for position. At about 4:45 P.M., the naval gun and aerial bombardment suddenly halted and the rocket ships moved in, three of them altogether, and began to send in high, curving arcs the first of six thousand rockets that would fall on Red and Blue Beaches. Smaller craft dotted the waters near the shore like a swarm of waterbugs. There were nearly 200 LCVP's, 70 larger LCM's, 12 LSU's, nearly 200 LVT's (Landing Vehicles, Tracked) and from the big, 300-foot seagoing LST's tiny little amphibious craft called DUKW's were emerging, 85 of them altogether.

The smaller ships would go in, eight abreast, in a series of ten or more waves on each beach. The Marines they brought would attempt to hold the shore. In previous landings in World War II, such initial assault troops had been able to move inland, if only a few yards, and dig into positions for their foothold; this time, on both Red and Blue Beaches, they would have to go over walls—and there was no doubt in anyone's mind that the enemy was waiting and dug in behind those walls. The landing ships that followed the smaller assault craft would grow larger until, about an hour after the first wave—providing the beach was held—would come the big LST's with their tanks, trucks and major supplies.

This was another wild gamble. The LST's would be stranded high and dry when the tide ran out in a couple of hours and they would be there on the beach all night, sitting ducks for artillery fire from the heights in the town. One of the eight LST's (about all that could be accommodated on the narrow front) to land at Red Beach was an ammunition ship. Another, LST-898, was the first beached field hospital in any amphibious operation. It contained an operating room and three doctors, Lieutenants John T. Egan, Jr., Rudolph B. Stevens and Henry A. Sparks. The eight

LST's—if they weren't blasted to kingdom come—would make the initial assault force about as self-sufficient as it could be during the first long night when they'd be partially stranded ashore by the receded tide.

At 5:22 P.M.—H-minus-8 (Hour minus 8 minutes)—the first wave of eight LCVP's started forward, four boats on the left carrying two platoons of Company A in the 1st Battalion of Ray Murray's 5th Marine Regiment. Upon landing, they were to push forward toward a low rise in the town known as Cemetery Hill, and by seizing this high ground, anchor the left flank of the assaulting force. In the next four boats, were platoons of Lieutenant Sam Jaskilka's Company E of the 2nd Battalion. They would fan out somewhat to the right and take, as the first objective, the small hill on which the British Consulate stood. In succeeding waves, detachments of the 1st and 2nd Battalions would follow side by side, each arriving group automatically reinforcing its own battalion which, presumably, would be moving forward toward its first objective. This was how Murray's plan of feeding in the two battalions by bits and pieces worked. His 3rd Battalion was being held in reserve and would come along in the wake of the first two.

Leading the first platoon to go in was a big, amiable Second Lieutenant named Edwin A. Deptula, and Sam Jaskilka was particularly fond of Deptula's cheerfulness and complete reliability under fire. He was a large man with a slow grin, who always called Jaskilka "Skipper."

The rocket barrage from the boxy LSMR's ceased suddenly as the tiny landing craft reached a point about halfway to the shore. Corsairs and Skyraiders took over and began to make strafing passes on the sea walls. In a remarkable exhibition of flying, they continued to hit the target accurately with machine-gun bursts until the first wave was no more than thirty yards from the beach. In the meantime, the Marines who had taken Wolmi-do that morning poured in additional support fire from the island with machine guns, mortars and the guns of their M-26 tanks.

Literally tons of metal and high explosive were being thrown at the sea walls and the enemy troops behind them by this barrage, yet portions of the sea walls remained standing. Where they were blasted, even the rubble made a formidable obstacle for foot soldiers.

As the eight LCVP's churned through the last few yards to the beach, bullets fired by unseen defenders began to zip into the water all around them, each making an angry little hiss as it struck, and other slugs began to ping on the bow ramps and metal sides of the landing craft. In the bow of each boat, two Marines held a scaling ladder ready. The Japanese manufacturers who had contracted to make aluminum ladders hadn't been able to deliver most of them on time and they were using hastily built ladders of wood with hooks of metal piping on their ends, most of them put together by Navy carpenters and machinists, and some even made aboard ship on the way to Inchon.

The four boats on the right, carrying Ed Deptula's platoon, crunched ashore over an unexpected stretch of rock and rubble extending from the walls out to the sea. The walls were approximately fifteen feet high, and since the bows of the landing craft were about five feet high, there remained ten feet of wall to scale. The ladders were slammed against the walls. At the same moment, two men behind the Marines raising the ladders hurled grenades over the walls. Then everybody started up and over the ladders. Bullets were still crackling everywhere. By some unexplained miracle, nobody in that first wave was yet hit.

Deptula saw the ladder, imperfectly made, begin to wiggle and slip as the men mounted it; the hooks atop it didn't quite fit the sea wall. He sighed and threw his own two-hundred pound bulk up the rungs. The ladder swayed precariously, but he kept going and in a moment had vaulted the wall and dropped to the other side. Before him was a stretch of several hundred yards, a railroad track, and then the high ground of Cemetery Hill beyond it. In this stretch were both trenches and craters left by the shelling, but no enemy soldiers seemed to be in the trenches. Further back, as the hill began to rise, there were pillboxes. Here on the right flank he was not receiving heavy fire, but from the left, where Company A's platoons were landing, there was a flurry of small-arms explosions, and he knew they were running into resistance.

On the left, about 300 yards away, only three boats had landed. Boat 1, on the extreme left, had had a sudden engine failure and was drifting a short distance offshore with its Navy crewmen cursing and working over its power plant. The men from the other three boats, led by platoon guide Sergeant Charles D. Allen, went over the wall in the face of heavy fire and saw a bunker directly ahead. Four Marines were hit as they went over the wall, dropping on either side;

medics would be along to attend to them eventually, but for the moment, the job of anyone not wounded was to keep going forward.

Boat 3 came up against a hole in the sea wall. In it was the platoon comander, Second Lieutenant Francis W. Meutzel, with a squad of men. Through the gap they could see a pillbox inland, little more than a hundred yards away, and the muzzle of an enemy machine gun sticking out of it. Whoever was behind that gun was holding his fire for the moment. The fighter planes came in again and strafed only fifty yards ahead of them. Only a few feet from the sea wall was a long trench that seemed empty. They jumped into it. Two Marines crawled toward the pillbox and tossed grenades. The hand bombs exploded; spurts of smoke came from the apertures of the pillbox. Seconds later six shabby North Koreans, most of them covered with blood, ran out, their hands in the air.

The assault wave on the far left was stopped cold by heavily manned bunkers and trenches beyond the sea wall. First Lieutenant Baldomero Lopez, leader of the 3rd Platoon, came ashore in the second wave, scaled and leapt the wall, and, covered by the rapidly firing Marines all around him, rushed toward the bunker with a hand grenade. Several others moved along with him. As he pulled the pin and drew the grenade back, ready to throw, he was suddenly hit in the shoulder and chest by machine-gun fire. He fell and, still conscious, rolled over the grenade, letting it explode under his body so that none of the men near him would be killed.

First wave . . . 1731. The little boats spewed out their Marines quickly at the sea wall and backed off, getting out of the way for the second wave.

Second wave . . . 1733.

Third wave . . . 1740

Deptula's men, on the right, had already started into the city. The left was still pinned down. And ahead of everyone was the sharp, almost cliff-like rise of Cemetery Hill where the last-ditch defenders were dug in.

Waiting and watching in his boat some 2,000 yards out, Sam Jaskilka turned to the correspondent with him and said, "I wonder if we're strong enough to give Yale a good game." Dark purple smoke rose from the shore and Sam's boat started forward. Sam, tall, lean, friendly, remarkably calm, turned to Gunnery Sergeant Barnett and said, "Get 'em ready, Gunner."

Barnett nodded, his reddish-yellow beard touching his chest. He turned to his men. "All right! Lock and load! The runners go out first! You people know what to do. Keep your goddamn heads down!"

Sam also addressed his men. "There's a ditch on the other side of the wall. Roll over the wall into the ditch, then get up fast and make for the right side of the beach. Good luck!"

There were two ladders in Sam's boat, one of the aluminum devices made in Japan, the other a makeshift wooden ladder. Both went up in the bow. The boat, on the right of its wave line, slammed hard into the sea wall. The ramp fell, but the sea wall kept it from going all the way down. (This happened to a number of landing craft, from the small LCVP's to the big LST's with their trucks and tanks, and one of the reasons was that the recent typhoon, although it did not pass near Inchon, made tides throughout that part of the world slightly higher than expected.)

Sam and his men went over the sea wall. There wasn't any ditch on the other side, at least not in this particular spot. Sam motioned for everyone to follow him and then ran to a tiny, wrecked shack, some kind of storage building, near the point where the causeway from Wolmi-do joined the mainland.

He found his company executive officer, who had come in a previous boat, already there. This was 1st Lieutenant Gilbert R. Hershey, son of draft director Lewis B. Hershey. "Hello, Skipper," said Hershey. "They all got ashore fine."[3]

The regimental commander himself was coming ashore in the fifth wave on a free boat so that he'd be able to set up a command post where the causeway joined the mainland, and where, in a short time, the battalion that had taken Wolmi-do would cross and link up with the main force.

As the little boat neared the shore—and as all the world, it seemed, sounded with the steady din of explosions and small-arms reports—Murray looked to his right and saw a long, shallow concrete ramp coming down the causeway, probably built there for the launching of fishing boats. It seemed an easier landing place than the rubble-strewn beach in front of the sea wall, and he directed his coxswain there at the last minute.

It was nearly dark now. On the railroad line just beyond

the beach, several oil tank cars were burning and Murray considered this a bit of luck, since they gave good light at a crucial point in the battle. Tall and businesslike, his figure no doubt inspiring confidence in those who could see him, Murray strode onto the causeway, scarcely getting his feet wet, and moved forward to a point near a burning shack. There he set up the command post of the 5th Regiment— physically a trunklike field desk, a portable switchboard, and a back-pack command radio with its operator. At his side was his loyal orderly, Corporal Bob Oswald, a buttermilk-fresh young man from Minnesota whom Murray regarded as his strong right arm. Back at the Perimeter, Oswald had always insisted on sleeping across the entrance to Murray's tent, refusing to leave when Murray told him to go somewhere else and be comfortable, and in battle he was always trying to place himself between Murray and the sources of enemy fire so that Murray had even had to speak to him sharply on occasion to keep him from getting underfoot.

Murray spread his map before him as the messages began to come in from his battalion and company commanders, forming a picture of the action. The assault seemed to be stopped momentarily on the far left where defenders were dug in on a low rise known as Cemetery Hill.

It was here that Lieutenant Lopez had fallen on his own grenade to save the men near him. His platoon was pinned down now, its men huddled behind whatever sparse cover they could find, and when any showed themselves, fire came from several positions on the sharp rise, anywhere from one to two hundred yards ahead of them. This was a city waterfront area, and there were some small open areas, but there were also plenty of structures to afford cover for the enemy.

Cemetery Hill was on the extreme left, facing the actual landing beach, its base about two hundred yards inland. Just a little below it, and about 450 yards inland, was the sprawling Asahi Beer Plant, a large compound of a number of shedlike buildings where this excellent Japanese beer was produced for Korea. Company A's 2nd Platoon, under 2nd Lieutenant Francis W. Muetzel, had landed somewhat nearer the center and they had been able to advance all the way to the beer plant. They wound it a shambles, smelling of burnt explosive and spilled beer.

When the commander of Company A, Captain John R. Stevens, came ashore moments later, he saw the dead Lieutenant Lopez's platoon pinned down, and called Muetzel's platoon back from the brewery. He wanted Muetzel to add his fire power to the frontal assault on the low cliff at the the base of Cemetery Hill.

Muetzel started back from the brewery. He had only moved a hundred yards or so when suddenly he realized that he himself was receiving no flanking fire from the hill they were all trying to take. He was just south of the hill, practically at its base. Muetzel seized the initiative, radioed for quick permission, then turned sharply toward the hill, trotting and leading his men up and across the incline toward a concentration of Red trenches and pillboxes. As his platoon neared the crest of the rise, the ground suddenly seemed to grow North Koreans—scores of them—who, evidently realizing that they were completely outflanked, popped up with their hands raised in surrender. They were members of the 226th North Korean People's Army Regiment, a whole mortar company and attached units. To a man, they were dazed and half deaf from the terrific pounding they'd taken from aerial bombing and naval gunfire all that afternoon. They were quickly put under a guard detachment and marched down to the base of the hill where they were stripped.

Cemetery Hill was taken, but it was only one of three. On the extreme right, about 600 yards below the point where the causeway joined the mainland, and where Murray had set up his regimental command post, was the small, round hill on which the British Consulate stood. This was Sam Jaskilka's objective for his Company E, and Ed Deptula's platoon was moving toward it, down the railroad tracks that ran along the shore, and meeting no resistance.

In the center, more or less facing the causeway, was Observatory Hill, the widest and highest of the three, an irregular promontory with spurs coming out of it like the star revetments of an ancient castle, and with several peaks on its crest like low turrets. The Marines had reached the base of this hill, but the greater part of Inchon's defenders were still dug in on its heights. It had to be taken. Other waves of boats were still scheduled to come in with tanks, ammunition and other supplies to support the beachhead. They could easily be clobbered and rendered ineffective from the 200-foot heights of Observatory Hill.

Under Murray's landing plan of two battalions, in column and abreast, a company from the 1st Battalion was to take the northern half of the hill, and a company from the 2nd

Battalion the southern half. Specifically, these were Company C, 1st Battalion, and Company D, 2nd Battalion. But somehow portions of both these companies had landed at wrong sections of the beach, and in places Marines were crouching by the walls, bewildered, looking for the rest of their units, their leaders trying to establish radio contact in the already cluttered air. The commanding officer of C-Company had been delayed when the skipper of his landing craft, over his furious objections, had decided to tow in another boat that had stalled in a previous wave. By the time he reached his company and tried to organize it, some twelve minutes late, succeeding waves had poured in and everything was completely confused. A little further down the beach, First Lieutenant H. J. "Hog Jaw" Smith's D-Company managed to get itself organized, but for some reason Smith and his men were under the impression that Sam Jaskilka—who was far down the railroad tracks taking the knoll on which the British Consulate stood—had already taken Observatory Hill. So the men of D-Company promptly began a march up a rising street toward its crest. Incredibly, they reached that first peak, where no enemy troops were dug in, but as a lead element continued along the road toward the second peak, they suddenly ran into heavy machine-gun fire from an enemy squad positioned on the right of the street. The Marines threw themselves into the rubble on the left of the street and began to return the fire.

It was now 1830, and time for the eight LST's to come in, whether Observatory Hill was cleared or not. The rain was falling lightly, and visibility was decreasing with every passing moment. Corporal Joe Maize, on an LST waiting for its signal to go forward, went up and down the ranks of the recruits in his squad, showing them how to loosen their haversacks so that they could get them off easily in case they fell in the water. At that moment there were several excited shouts from the edge of the deck and Joe rushed there to behold at least a dozen Koreans who had swum out from the shore toward the invasion ships. Several Marines yelled not to take them aboard—they might be booby trapped. Joe doubted it; they looked like plain, scared citizens who had taken the only way left to them of escaping the fire and bombardment ashore. Ladders and lines were put over the side and the Koreans were hauled aboard, wet and terrified but not booby trapped.

Maize went back to his squad. The younger men were still frightened, although they were holding it in very well, he thought. They could see by now that there was plenty of enemy fire in the area where they were to land. Joe's company had been brought across the Pacific as part of Chesty Puller's 1st Regiment, which was now making a somewhat easier landing about three miles to the south on Blue Beach (although Joe did not know at this time that the Blue Beach assault was virtually unopposed), but in the quick reorganization that preceded the landing, elements of the tank battalion to which Joe belonged had been attached to Murray's 5th Marines, and here he was, about to step into the thick of things. His job, when he got ashore, would be to stand guard over the additional communications gear that would be brought for Murray's regimental command post.[4]

On another LST nearby, Sergeant Pat Byrnes was in the galley calmly pouring himself a cup of coffee when the loudspeaker barked with the order to take battle stations. He took a hasty sip, burned his lips a little, set his coffee cup down and stepped out of the galley. At that moment there was a deafening crash and explosion behind him and a great shock wave threw him momentarily off balance, although it did not knock him down. When he turned, scared and startled, he saw that a mortar shell had caught the galley house and exploded. If he had been inside he would have been killed. It was the first time, he reflected, he'd ever been glad to hear an order to saddle up and get moving.

He went down into the hold and started to remove the "griping" chains from his tank. The blowers of the ship began to hum so the bilge would be cleared of fumes when the tanks started their engines.

He climbed in with his crew. The LST was heading for the shore, but Byrnes, down below its slabbed sides, couldn't see the approach. Moments later he felt a jolt and heard a crunch as the huge 300-foot craft jammed itself onto the beach. The tide had receded a little, and because of the way the mud ran in this particular spot, this LST was halted a few yards out from the sea wall. The bow ramp fell open, letting a big square patch of gray evening light into the hold. Almost immediately machine-gun fire came from the hill beyond the wall, and the slugs started to sing, bounce and ricochet inside the vessel with fearful whining and pinging sounds. Byrnes ducked, and the bow ramp came up again, shutting out the furious fire. He wondered now if he'd be able to get his tank ashore, after all.[5]

Eight big LST's had nosed ashore by now, but several had been unable to drop their bow ramps in the face of the fire from Observatory Hill. Some were shooting toward the heights with their 40-mm. and 20-mm. cannon. In all that purple smoke and confusion, the gun crew of one LST went wild and began to shoot indiscriminately at the walls and across the beach, killing one Marine and wounding 23 others. The crew of another LST found the ancient guns aboard the resalvaged tub so worn and pitted that they couldn't be fired at all.

Directing the LST's from its position offshore was the attack-transport, *Horace A. Bass*, that had carried the Marine raiders and Navy frogmen on reconnaissance probes in the weeks preceding Inchon. It began to radio the skippers of the various LST's asking if anyone could see the source of the enemy fire, and several quick opinions came back, locating the gun positions on the heights. The *Bass* relayed this information to the fire control ship further out, and a naval barrage began within a few minutes. This barrage also fell among Marines fighting to take the hill, but fortunately killed none.

Most of the LST's carried such volatile cargo as gasoline, lubricating oil, napalm for flame throwers and ammunition stores. As LST-973 came in, a mortar shell from the shore fell and exploded among a number of gasoline drums stowed on the port side forward. Gasoline began to flood the decks. Shrapnel had made holes in the decks and the fuel began to drip into the hold. Damage-control teams worked furiously to shut off electric motors and patch some of the holes while enemy bullets continued to ping on the sides of the ship. Any one of them could touch off an explosion, and why they did not, no one aboard LST-973 ever knew. It was one of those small miracles that made up the improbable overall success of Inchon.

When LST-973 finally started to lower her ramp, the skipper found that it wouldn't go all the way down because the ship was hard against the sea wall. Marines started to pour out of the opening anyway, and one, jumping six feet to the beach, broke his leg.

LST-898, the hospital ship, kept sliding away from the beach and back into the water. One of its officers was suddenly struck with an inspiration, asked a bulldozer to dig its blade into the beach, then looped the heavy ship's lines around the vehicle.

On the LST-898 was the first mobile surgical team ever to

be brought right up to the beach during a landing. They were literally within shouting distance of the front line. LST-898 had been manned and equipped in frantic haste in order to be ready in time for the landing. Three Navy doctors, a Medical Service Corps officer and ten corpsmen had come aboard her in Japan late in August to find her dirty and neglected, and their proposed operating room a 10-by-15 foot space containing nothing but a washbowl. The three elements the surgeons needed were an operating table, a sterilizer and operating lights. Her crew took her to Koke where her Medical Service Corps officer, Lieutenant (jg) Leslie H. Joslin, managed to get some needed biological supplies from an Army hospital in nearby Osaka, but still nothing for the operating room. The night before she was scheduled to sail, he desperately canvassed the other ships in the harbor, and aboard one transport that was not yet operational, he found a complete operating room containing everything his team would need. Somehow he got the transport's security guards to part with the equipment, signing a simple receipt for it on a scrap of paper, and then he found workers to transfer the equipment to LST-898. The sterilizer and operating table were still being welded to the deck of 898's operating room as the ship cast off and headed for Inchon.

Now, at the beach, Lieutenants Egan, Stevens and Sparks, the doctors, waited for patients. Egan was an internist, Stevens had just finished his internship and Sparks was an obstetrician. Today they would all be surgeons.

On Observatory Hill, the men of Company D were winning their fight. Several had worked forward far enough to toss grenades. One Marine was dead, three wounded. The fight had been going on for about fifteen minutes, when suddenly the few enemy soldiers left in the machine-gun nest left their positions and ran. Observatory Hill was taken.

The bow ramp of the LST carrying Sergeant Pat Byrnes's tank came down again and the tanks rolled forward. Other bow ramps lowered. There was no fire. The tanks and supplies could come ashore and the assault inland could continue.

At his command post in the light of the flaming tank cars, Lieutenant Colonel Ray Murray consulted his maps again. Almost the entire 2nd Battalion under Lieutenant Colonel Harold S. Roise had reached its first objective, a curved line running through the center of the city like a bow drawn and aimed at the enemy; this was designated Objective-A line. During the advance, signalmen had run a telephone wire forward so that Hall Roise's field phone was in contact with Murray's small switchboard.

Roise himself was suddenly on the phone. He'd reached O-A, was meeting no resistance, and thought he'd be able to push on further, or at least send patrols to take a look, possibly as far as the next morning's objective line, O-I, which ran across the fat throat of the peninsula. Murray was proud of Roise and of his Marines in general. In World War II, in the Pacific, you simply hadn't moved in the dark, but now, with the evening well advanced, Roise still wanted to go forward. Murray told him, "All right, send the patrols out, but meanwhile dig in where you are."[6]

A little less than three miles away, Chesty Puller's 1st Regiment was assaulting an equally narrow strip of waterfront known as Blue Beach. The initial waves had started toward the shore at the same H-hour, 1730, but Puller's men had gone to the beach in LVT's. These were as much land crawlers as they were boats, and they were not too efficient for either purpose. Like many other pieces of matériel in this landing, they were being used because they happened to be available. They were, in fact, Army rather than Navy boats, many had inexperienced crews, and none had compasses or radios installed as permanent equipment.

The plan was to lead these LVT's in with Navy guide boats, but by 1730 the gathering clouds had concentrated on Blue Beach more heavily than they had on Red Beach to the north, and the weather, the drifting smoke and lowering dusk left very little visibility. Occasionally the boat skippers heading for the shore could see no more than a couple of hundred yards ahead.

Colonel Puller, stubby pipe in his mouth, bulldog jaw jutted forward, shoulders squared and racked back almost painfully, knew that he was commanding a hastily thrown together regiment and that they'd had very little chance to rehearse this landing, even in theory. He fully expected a mix-up of some sort within the hour. He therefore decided to land personally with the third wave, to be in close control of everything.[7]

He also wanted to be in close touch with his troops. There were veterans of World War II among them, of course, but unlike Ray Murray's 5th Regiment, his men had not had what

Chesty Puller considered the advantage of the recent Perimeter fighting. "No troops," Puller liked to say, "are any good until they've been blooded. On the first day of battle casualties among replacements are two times those among veterans. Not that they lack courage; they just don't know how to take care of themselves."[8]

Nine armored LVT's brought the first wave of Marines ashore on Blue Beach, surging forward on schedule at H-Hour, 1730. They carried part of Lieutenant Colonel Alan Sutter's 2nd Battalion.

Blue Beach was actually subdivided into two beaches, Blue 1 and Blue 2, of about equal size and separated from each other by a drainage ditch. On the aerial photos this drainage ditch seemed to be some kind of road leading up from the beach, over which the tractored vehicles could crawl ashore.

The men in the first wave, landing on the left on Blue Beach 1, discovered soon enough that it was a drainage ditch and, in effect, separated the two battalions of the landing force from each other. Fortunately, there was no enemy fire until the assault forces moved a few hundred yards inland.

The plan was for the first waves to oppose any enemy fire they encountered, keep their toehold on the beach, and wait for the rest of their units to come ashore so everyone could be organized into squads, platoons and companies before pressing further forward. The advance elements of both the 2nd Battalion on the left, and Lieutenant Colonel Thomas Ridge's 3rd Battalion on the right met no serious fire as they landed, so they waited, although Ridge and his executive officer made a short, personal probe to the far right to explore a kind of cove that had originally been designated Blue Beach 3, but subsequently left out of the landing plan.

The second wave of eleven boats managed to reach Blue Beach at H-plus-1, but several boats had drifted too far to one side and were grounded on the mud about three hundred yards offshore. The Marines aboard them waded to the beach, men occasionally falling into potholes, many of them losing communications equipment and other valuable gear.

The third wave, Colonel Puller aboard, got ashore at H-plus-4. On Blue Beach 1, there were now 30 tractors and more than 600 men. It was getting crowded. Lieutenant Colonel Sutter, in order to clear the beach, ordered some of the tractors over to one side against the low wall of a big salt bed that lay there, and then he waited to signal the next waves to swing over that way and keep the beach clear.

The fourth and succeeding waves didn't appear; they were out there somewhere in all that smoke and dust trying to find their way.

But in the darkness and general confusion, the upcoming waves of boats were either seriously delayed or lost. The confusion, indeed, had begun fifty minutes before H-Hour, as the first waves of LVT's milled around the control vessel, U. S. S. *Wantuck*, waiting for the signal to advance. Mortar fire began to fall among them out there, hitting no boats, but destroying their formation. A destroyer shortly silenced the shore battery, but the scattered boats never got back into position.

They were slow, clumsy boats, these vehicle-like LVT's; their line of departure was 5,500 yards or about 3.2 miles from the shore, and the entire trip from there to beach would take each one about forty-five minutes. They did not cut through the water well, and the unexpectedly swift current began to carry many of them off course. A number of their skippers, in the smoke and haze, couldn't see the Navy guide boats that were supposed to bring them in.

On Blue Beach 2, on the other side of the drainage ditch, elements of the 3rd Battalion had come ashore, scaled the sea wall, and were pressing forward in the face of moderate small-arms fire. Six LVT's carrying Captain George C. West-over's G-Company nosed into the drainage ditch. They managed to progress a few dozen yards, and then the lead vehicle bogged down in the mud and stopped all the others behind it.

The troops scaling the walls found that their aluminum ladders bent and buckled under the strain. They waited until engineers came ashore and threw cargo nets over the walls, anchoring them on the opposite side with steel picket pins driven into the ground by sledges. Chesty Puller, from the first, hadn't been too sure the ladders would work and had ordered the cargo nets readied, just in case.

Most of the opposing fire was coming from an enemy machine gun in a tower about five-hundred yards inland. The LVT's turned their fire on it, silenced it, and the first units began to push out from the beach, some fanning out on a road that led up toward the city, others moving straight ahead. They plunged into a jumble of winding streets and burning buildings.

Three miles offshore, in the smoke and thickening darkness, and with the strong current sweeping them off course, dozens of LVT's were unable to make their way to the control ship to get their visual signals to go forward. There was no radio contact. Many of the boats headed for shore anyway, sometimes alone and sometimes in small groups, hoping they'd arrive at the right places in time to do some good.

They finally did get ashore, most of them on the wrong beaches, but somehow, in the next half hour or so, they were assembled into units and deployed by Colonel Puller and his battalion commanders. The 1st Battalion was the reserve unit and was scheduled to come in at 1815 hours, or H-plus-45. It departed in LCVP's, the same type of boat that had brought the first waves ashore on Red Beach to the north, and the coxswains were to follow a searchlight beam the control ship sent out toward the beach. For some reason the beam got pointed in the wrong direction, a good 45 degrees to the north, and the advance party of the 1st Battalion, in two waves, reached the wall of the tidal basin some distance above the landing area. They had actually begun to debark before the error was discovered, and they finally pushed off again and headed for Blue Beach.

As at Red Beach, equipment, vehicles and support personnel would follow the first waves of foot soldiers. Among the tanks to accompany Puller's 1st Regiment were those of C-Company, 73rd Tank Battalion, U. S. Army, the unit that fought so well at the Bowling Alley and on other points along the Pusan Perimeter. Eventually these tanks would go back to the Army, as soon as the 7th Division landed in a few days, but for the moment they were part of the Marine assault. (Actually, a number of units had been shuffled back and forth in the frantic, last-minute preparations, and Chesty Puller was already grumbling that Lieutenant Colonel Murray had his choice tanks; the Army tanks and their combat-blooded crews had evidently been given to Puller to mollify him.)

Second Lieutenant Jesse Van Sant and his 4th Platoon were in one of the LST's and Van Sant was on deck watching the show—what little he could see of it in the smoke and lowering darkness—and marveling at how everything seemed to be working out in spite of what appeared on the surface to be utter confusion. As his lumbering LST groped for the shore, a Marine amphibious tractor loaded with troops suddenly came too near, was caught in its wake, and then suddenly, somehow, snagged by the bigger ship's port screw. The LST's Japanese skipper immediately shut off the engines and the

LST drifted sideways into the shore coming to rest with no real harm done to anyone.[9]

In spite of all the mix-up, the various units of Puller's 1st Regiment pushed forward toward their first objectives. Sutter and the 2nd Battalion headed up the road in a northerly direction toward the city. Ridge's 3rd Battalion pushed straight forward, inland. Lieutenant Colonel Jack Hawkins' 1st Battalion finally got ashore in the pitch darkness and made its way inland about half a mile to an assembly point along some railroad tracks.

They moved out and fought until near midnight. The 2nd Battalion, in its advance, lost one man and nineteen wounded. They killed about fifty of the enemy and took fifteen prisoners.

By midnight Companies D and F of the 2nd Battalion reached a hill a thousand yards inland and just southeast of the Inchon city limits. From here they dominated the main highway to Seoul and could fire on any enemy units either attempting to flee the city or enter it to reinforce the garrison there.

In the morning the Marines of each prong, the one that held Red Beach and the one that held Blue Beach, would move forward to the next series of objective lines and then be on their way to Seoul itself. It was their job to keep moving— Seoul was the real final goal and the reason for the entire landing. Aboard the *Mt. McKinley*, just offshore, the division commander, Major General Oliver P. Smith, absorbing the reports as they came in, was pleased that resistance in Inchon itself had been relatively light, but he knew that within the next day or two, the Communists, who had evidently been completely deceived, would have time to rush troops to the area and put up a stiff defense somewhere between Inchon and Seoul. The worst part of the battle was yet to come.

The Marines, then, were to continue to push forward as soon as it was light, but in the meantime troops and supplies would continue to pour ashore behind them, so that within about forty-eight hours, a sizeable force would be ashore and ready to juggernaut its way to Seoul. Because the Marines had to keep moving, they had no time to mop up the city itself and flush out the North Korean troops and partisans still hiding in its winding streets and rubble. This job fell to the newly organized Republic of South Korean Marines, and they were accepting it with enthusiasm.

Mild-mannered Major Koh, who had recruited his 1st Battalion from the farm boys and high-school students of Cheju-do, rode proudly ashore in one of the later waves, set up his command post near the right extremity of Red Beach, not far from the causeway, and then waited for his battalion. He waited hours and still they didn't appear. When he finally got word of them he learned that they hadn't understood the departure signals and were still in their landing craft, circling the control ship.[10]

But part of Major Koh's "Damned-Near-Lost Battalion" had made its way ashore, and among the units now moving inland in the wake of Murray's 5th Marines was the weapons platoon of the 4th Company, commanded by 2nd Lieutenant Eung Duk Lee. Lee was a native of Seoul and knew the area fairly well. He was short, stocky and tough; he much admired the cockiness of American Marines and tried to emulate it at all times. As his unit got ashore, they were grabbed by some American commander—Lee never did remember exactly which one—and told to follow on the heels of an American unit that had just taken the crest of Observatory Hill, relieve them there, and mop up along the way.

Lee was delighted with the assignment. He was sure his men would do well, even if most of them had been farm boys on Cheju-do only a few weeks before. Many of them, he noticed, now had modern M-1's instead of the old-fashioned bolt-action Springfields. How had this happened? Well, it seemed that many of the older U. S. Marines preferred the ancient Springfield—Lee couldn't imagine why—and had traded their M-1's to the Korean Marines to get the familiar weapons for themselves. They had a notion that the Springfields were simpler in construction and more reliable than the fast firing M-1's. It sounded crazy, but it was all right with Lee, and delighted most of the South Korean Marines who received the newer weapons.

As they moved up the hill, they drew some light sniper fire from windows and from behind fences or rubble. The farm boys returned the fire bravely but wildly, and the few who had Browning Automatic Rifles poured out long, inaccurate bursts that tended to ruin the barrels of their weapons. Much of their fire came too near to Lee, who was running in the lead, and he felt himself in as much danger from his own men as from the enemy.

Private Young Don Lee—no relation to the lieutenant—coming along behind, suddenly saw a North Korean pop out of a hole some thirty yards ahead of him and aim a rifle directly at him. Private Lee, stocky and husky, was one of the farm lads that had been more or less impressed into the battalion. The terrible noise of the bombardment that preceded the landing had frightened him more than anything else. Now, without thinking, he raised his new M-1 and shot without aiming at the North Korean. Much to his surprise, the man toppled. He rushed forward and looked at his victim. He had hit him full in the chest. The man hadn't shaved for some time and looked old—possibly in his fifties. He was dressed in civilian trousers and a North Korean blouse. Lee supposed he had been in the midst of changing to civilian clothes, for many North Korean soldiers still in the city were doing that in order to escape. But when he saw what an old man he had killed, he was saddened. Back on peaceful Cheju-do, he'd been taught to respect old people. The elation he had felt at first suddenly left him. He was disappointed in war. Then somebody shouted and beckoned and he had to move on.

Lieutenant Lee kept moving forward through the streets toward his assigned position. Civilians, seeing someone who could understand their language, rushed toward him and began to point out houses where North Korean soldiers were hiding. Lee entered several of the houses and flushed out the enemy soldiers who emerged with their hands up.

There were four men and a woman in one house. The men were in civilian clothes, but since the villagers kept screaming they were really North Korean soldiers, he took them prisoner and had them quickly searched. They had no weapons. He was about to move on when he noticed in the eyes of the woman—she was small, thin and about thirty—what he thought was a look of hate and defiance. He ordered her searched, too. The search, conducted by two of his sergeants, was rough and thorough, and within seconds they found a pistol secreted in her private parts where she thought it wouldn't be found.

Lieutenant Lee moved on. Rounding a corner he came upon an American Marine who had his bayoneted rifle thrust into the ground and seemed to be leaning upon it. Lieutenant Lee, searching for the outfit he was supposed to relieve, came up to the Marine, shook his arm, and said, in just about the only English he knew, "Hey, Joe! Hey, Joe!" The Marine toppled and Lee realized that he was dead.[11]

It was nearly midnight of D-Day. Within minutes it would be D-plus-1. The city of Inchon was quiet except for occasional shots or bursts of shots, dark except for the dancing red light of burning things here and there. The last of the casualty reports were coming in. They were incredibly light. Of the landing force, only 20 Marines had been killed in action, one had died of wounds, one was missing in action, and 174 had been wounded in action.

There was a lull in the battle like the slack moments of a tide.

General MacArthur retired to his cabin aboard the *Mt. McKinley*, giving strict orders to the Marine guard outside his door to be roused promptly at dawn. The generals and admirals of his staff pleasantly said good night to each other, but there was no jubilation or backslapping. The great gamble of the landing seemed to have been won. That was fine. But now it remained to be seen whether their luck would hold just as well along the eighteen miles and the big river crossing between here and the capital of Seoul.

NOTES   *Chapter 10*

1. Capt. Norman W. Sears, USN (who had supervised the briefing group in the big August 23rd conference), rode that morning on an LCVP that was evacuating some wounded Marines. He noticed one stretchered man who had lost his leg. When this Marine's bundle of clothing came aboard he glanced at it, saw his shoes among the clothes, and said, "Hey, that's not mine . . . I'm wearing my shoes." Karig *et al*, p. 222.
2. Craig memo.
3. Interview author—Jaskilka, and from James Bell's account in *Time*, 25 Sept 50.
4. Interview author—Maize.
5. Interview author—Byrnes.
6. Interview author—Murray.
7. Interview author—Puller.
8. *Ibid.*
9. Letter Van Sant to author, 4 May 67.
10. Interview author—Koh.
11. Interviews author—Col Eung Duk Lee and MSgt Young Don Lee, R. O. K. Marines.

"Take Kimpo Airfield as soon as you can."

At the first light on September 16, D-plus-1, the Marines, after several brief conferences for most of the battalion and company commanders, moved forward again to break out of the city of Inchon and its environs and get on the road to Seoul fast. On the right, Chesty Puller's 1st Marines were moving forward, eastward, with some units fanning out a bit to the south to clean up the rest of the larger peninsula upon which Inchon and its suburbs stood. The belligerent Puller moved with his troops, his command post, as many of his own Marines liked to say, "in his hat." He jeeped through the littered streets that still smelled of smoke and explosive, carrying a pistol at his side and two hand grenades affixed to the chest straps of his haversack.[1] He heard shots all around, and he stopped several times to determine whether there was still scattered resistance in the city. Through his interpreter he learned that, as he put it later, "a lot of debts were being settled." Inchon's citizens were taking care of those who had collaborated too enthusiastically with the North Koreans. Puller ordered his troops to fire warning shots when they came across incidents of this sort, and in general, try to stop the slaughter.

Lieutenant Colonel Ray Murray's 5th Regiment was pushing forward on the left flank. The boundary line between the two assault teams was the main highway from Seoul which wound through the heart of the city and formed a natural center line all the way inland to the capital. With very little trouble the advance squads and platoons of both Puller's 1st and Murray's 5th Regiment had reached the various objective lines, O-A, O-1, O-2 and O-3, each something less than a mile apart, and now they were headed for a line beyond the city, its furthest point seven miles in crow flight from Red Beach, known as the FBHL, or Force Beachhead Line.

From the first, the assault on Inchon had followed a pattern of two-pronged attacks, like the blows of a boxer's right and left fists. The landing itself was a hard left hook, followed immediately by a straight right punch at the enemy's distant midsection by General Walker in the Perimeter. The attack on the beaches had consisted of a blow on the left at Red Beach, and a swift-coordinated right cross at Blue Beach, some three miles away. The right and left prongs were to continue now, toward Seoul, taking various objectives along the way.

How they would be used in the next few days depended largely on the enemy's response. He didn't seem to be in the fight in force yet. But it was inevitable that he would be soon. The divisions guarding the area south of Seoul would be moving north even now to meet the attack. In Seoul itself an estimated garrison of perhaps 5,000 men was being mustered. From Communist-held territory just north of Seoul, first-class soldiers were being rushed down to help defend the city, preferably at points outside the city itself.

Meanwhile, behind the advancing Marines, troops and supplies were pouring into the newly taken port of Inchon. The wildly enthusiastic and amiably inept R. O. K. Marines were right on the heels of Murray's regiment, still mopping up, most of them now wearing white armbands so they wouldn't be mistaken for North Koreans by trigger-happy GI's as they returned with groups of prisoners. Along the waterfront Navy Seabees (from C. B. for "Construction Battalion") were putting docks and ramps back into shape and building their own pontoon causeways here and there to speed up the flow of supply. In the harbor, the ships with the first elements of General Barr's 7th Army Division were arriving, and the soldiers would be put ashore within a day or two to march inland and secure the area south of Seoul, far down the road that led to the Perimeter, thus blocking any Communist reinforcements that might come up from that direction. General Almond, who at this point hadn't officially started to maneuver his X-Corps of one Marine and one Army division, was looking far ahead and anxious to get this blocking force into place; he urged Admiral Doyle to put all haste into the unloading of the Army troops and Doyle cheerfully obliged.

Lieutenant Colonel Murray moved his command post from the shack where the causeway joined the mainland, jeeping

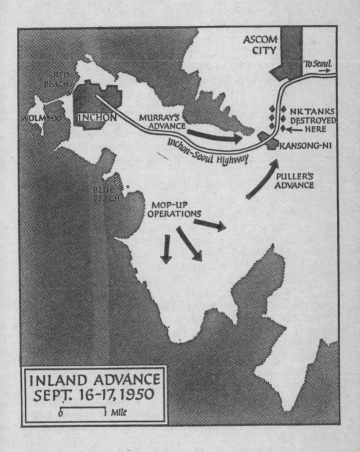

RED BEACH

WOLMI-DO

INCHON

MURRAY'S ADVANCE

ASCOM CITY

To Seoul

NK TANKS DESTROYED HERE

KANSONG-NI

Inchon-Seoul Highway

BLUE BEACH

PULLER'S ADVANCE

MOP-UP OPERATIONS

INLAND ADVANCE
SEPT. 16-17, 1950
0   1 Mile

through the city to its opposite outskirts. At about midnight, he and Puller had received General O. P. Smith's operational order from the *Mt. McKinley* to continue the attack immediately after dawn. With minimal resistance before them, it wasn't much of an attack, but it was still necessary to maneuver properly to bring the regiments abreast in their forward movement. As he reached the edge of the city, Murray found a printing shop beside the road that seemed a suitable site for his CP. Murray ordered his radio and field desk set up, and stood by to watch. Presently a truck came up the road from the city. It passed the printing shop and kept going toward the front. On it, Murray noticed the markings of the Combat Service Group—usually a rear-echelon supply unit. His pride was stung. No rear-echelon supply outfit was going to be forward of *his* command post. He turned to his executive officer, Lieutenant Colonel Lawrence C. Hays, Jr., and said, "All right, knock it down—we're going forward again!"[2]

Sam Jaskilka, moving E-Company out from the British Consulate to join the advance, found the city quiet as he moved along. Occasionally he saw frightened civilians peeping out from the windows or doors, but there was no sign of the enemy. Whatever troops had been in Inchon had evidently withdrawn in haste during the night.

At the break of dawn, eight Marine Corsairs took off from the aircraft carrier *Sicily* to fly cover over Inchon and the area for a few miles beyond it. Some minutes later, as the pilots glanced down at the Seoul highway perhaps three miles beyond the outskirts of Inchon, they were amazed to see six enemy T-34 tanks rumbling toward Inchon without infantry escort, in what could only be regarded as a quixotic and perhaps suicidal attack. From the air the tanks appeared to be buggish things sending up trails of dust that floated away and off to one side in the light morning breeze. It was such a surprising sight that it was moments before the pilots could actually convince themselves that these were indeed enemy tanks. The flight leader reported, and was ordered to strike at once.

At about that moment, Marines of Chesty Puller's 2nd Battalion had mounted a low hill two miles away and could clearly see both tanks and planes at a position just outside a tiny collection of houses that bore the village name of Kansong-ni. They cheered, as at a football game, as the Corsairs peeled off and swooped down on the tanks. On the first pass a tank was hit with flaming napalm. A rocket blew the tracks off a second. Five-hundred-pound bombs fell around the tanks, sending up great bouquets of gray smoke and yellow earth. A third tank, hit by bomb fragments, pulled off to the side, its crew leaping from it and abandoning it.

The remaining tanks were rushing for the cover of the village only a few hundred yards away. By now the bombs and napalm had blanketed the road with smoke, and this offered the vehicles some concealment. Then an F4U piloted by Captain William F. Simpson failed to pull out of its dive and plowed into the earth with a great explosion some distance beyond the tanks; he had apparently been hit by fire from one of them.[3] By this time the tanks had reached the cover of the village and the Corsairs continued to strike at them there, even though they were unseen, setting most of the houses aflame with napalm.

A second flight of planes came in to relieve the first. It was now apparent that there were some troops accompanying the tanks after all, and pilots of this second wave of planes discovered and struck at several well-camouflaged motor vehicles, including a jeep and weapons carrier. By this time the village was completely covered with smoke, and the pilots, assuming all six tanks had been destroyed, broke off their attack. But all six hadn't been destroyed; three tanks lay there, still waiting. An advance platoon of Murray's 5th Marines began to move toward them.

In order to capture Seoul several key points along the way would have to be seized. First there was a huge supply and maintenance complex northeast of Inchon and several miles beyond its city limits—only a mile and half north of the village where the Corsairs had caught the tanks, as a matter of fact. The Korean town originally in this spot was called Bupyang, but the American occupation troops previously in Korea had built a vast area of sheds, shops and warehouses that was now known as Ascom City, from Army Service Command. Ascom City lay directly north of the road inland and would have to be taken by Murray's 5th Regiment. If, within the next twenty-four hours or so, the enemy was able to mount any sort of counterattack, he would surely try to prevent the capture of this valuable supply center. After Ascom City, further along the road, was a little town called Sosa which might be valuable as a communications and staging point, and some miles beyond that, north of the road, was Kimpo Airfield, an objective that had to be secured before even the thought of an attack on Seoul was possible. Past Kimpo, directly south of and across the river from Seoul, was the satellite city of Yong Dong Po, another mandatory target since it controlled all road approaches to Seoul from the south.

Altogether, the two regimental prongs of the attacking Marines had perhaps sixteen or eighteen miles to march, depending on their route, to reach the outskirts of Seoul. Somewhere along the line the enemy would surely find a way to delay them.

Surprise had kept the North Koreans from moving enough troops to Inchon and striking back at the invasion force when it was most vulnerable. Until the day of the landing, everyone—with the possible exception of MacArthur—had been a little uneasy over the possibility of strong resistance showing up at the last minute. Even now most of the high-ranking officers were at a loss to explain why the Reds had been so completely surprised. Afterward, interrogation of prisoners and even of captured North Korean generals didn't do too much to clarify the matter. The failure of the People's Army to set up a defense at Inchon seems to have been the result of a number of factors. First, the North Korean high command in the aggregate was deceived. There were undoubtedly individuals among them who clearly saw Inchon as the place where the blow would fall, but there were others who frowned and worried and wondered if the feints at Wonsan on the opposite coast, at Chinnampo near the North Korean capital, and at Kunsan with its favorable landing beaches sixty miles below Inchon, didn't mean the landing would take place at one of these locations. Since they were unable to agree on a single course of action, no action was taken at all.

Second, the North Koreans, like the South Koreans and the Japanese, like most Orientals mistakenly thought to be "inscrutable" in the West, were at heart an emotional people, often given to following intuitive rather than cause-and-effect thought processes, often believing, as the Japanese did in World War II, that their own invincible spirit would ensure victory in the end—or, if it did not, sustaining a mad willingness to perish in the final *banzai* charges. They had started out to drive their enemy from the Perimeter and into the sea; they liked the poetic effect of a victory of this sort, and were unwilling to give up this near success even when common sense began to tell them that it couldn't be done without guarding their own flank a little more securely. There was thus, among the high command, a strange reluctance to pull troops from the Perimeter and deploy them elsewhere, especially when their attacks kept denting Walker's line and seemed always on the verge of success. These attacks did not succeed partly because of Walker's masterful and stubborn defense, the key to which was his rapid, fire-brigade shifting of elements back and forth along the line, and because somehow the North Koreans had not yet learned either to sustain an attack long enough or follow it with telling subsequent blows. They did not seem to plan the flow of their supplies properly; a North Korean division would advance, take key points, and then find itself forced to wait for more ammunition or matériel.

The third factor in the North Korean failure to meet the invasion at Inchon properly—which is to say, immediately and in force—was that, in a sense, they didn't have enough troops to spare. They were hammering so furiously at the Perimeter that they'd failed, strategically, to set up a proper reserve. They were expecting Chinese Communist help from the north, of course—the hordes of so-called volunteers who would pour down from the Manchurian border before ninety days were up and take over both North Korea and the war— but this assistance came too late to ward off the immediate threat.

Eighth Army intelligence overestimated enemy strength at the Perimeter as the Inchon landing took place. Their count showed over 100,000 men, broken down into thirteen infantry divisions, one armored division and two armored brigades attacking from all sides. But, as prisoner-of-war interrogation showed later, most North Korean units were down to about 50 per cent of their strength, and there were closer to 70,000 men hemming Walker in. They were badly equipped. The analysis of one enemy battalion dated September 14, showed 151 men with only 82 individual weapons and about one grenade for every two men. Their food was scarce; only about 30 per cent of the men were veterans, and the other 70 per cent consisted of recruits, many of them impressed, without much willingness to fight. In spite of this, there had been few desertions because the recruits had been made to believe the U. N. forces would kill them or treat them cruelly if they were captured.

Only about 2,000 troops had defended the island of Wolmi-do and the city of Inchon. Just before dawn on September 15, some units of the North Korean 22nd Regiment, which had been bivouacked near Seoul, had moved into Inchon to help with the defense, but as the terrifying bombardment began, they had retreated from the city. But by September 16, sizeable North Korean units were converging on the Seoul area. The fact of the landing at Inchon could no longer be ignored, not even by a committee, and since it takes a day or two to get regiments and divisions moving, it would seem that this hard truth hit the North Korean command just before the landing, perhaps on September 13, when the huge, final two-day air and sea bombardment on Inchon began. A whole regiment of the North Korean 9th Division was on its way up from the Perimeter, along with elements from their 18th Division. Because of the U. N. aerial cover they traveled at night, and their trains pulled into the concealment of tunnels in the daytime. Up from Suwon, the airfield only thirty miles below Seoul, moved the North Korean 70th Regiment. From the north a newly formed crack brigade was approaching, the 25th North Korean Brigade, made up of officers and NCO's who had fought with the Communist Chinese in their takeover of the mainland. There were about 2,500 men altogether commanded by 45-year-old Major General Wol Ki Chan, who had studied his military science in Russia and was considered brilliant. From the various garrison troops in and around Seoul, the 78th Independent Regiment was being formed.

The intelligence estimates of General Almond's X-Corps at about the time when the Marines were starting inland from Inchon accurately estimated that about 20,000 enemy troops were ready to defend Seoul. Within a week, however, this number doubled, making it over 40,000.

About 25,000 Marines were now ashore, or would be within the next few days. In addition, the 7th Army Division and the 7th Marine Regiment were still on their way. A total of around 70,000 troops was gathering for the Inchon-Seoul campaign with perhaps 50,000 of them taking part in actual combat assault and maneuver. This, in a rough way, evened the odds somewhat and made it about 50,000 U.N. troops attacking around 40,000 North Koreans, most of whom had the advantage of being dug in in defensive positions.

So it was that in the warm, clear noon of September 16, the Marine elements moved toward the Force Beachhead Line they had been ordered to seize by General O. P. Smith and thus conclude the assault phase of the amphibious operation.

The 2nd Battalion led the way for Murray's 5th Marines. Emerging from the outskirts of the city, it moved up the main road to Seoul which was now designated, in military parlance, the Main Supply Route (MSR). At the very point of the advance was approximately a squad of Marines—about twelve men—and two M-26 Pershing tanks. The day before, they had watched the planes attack the six North Korean tanks from high ground. Now they were on the road that wound between the slopes and hills and unable to see into the distance. Just before the village of Kansong-ni, where the fighter planes had driven the tanks into cover, they rounded a sharp bend and saw three enemy T-34 tanks still looking very much alive.

Alive they were, having somehow survived the aerial strafing the day before. When the men at the point of the advance saw them, they signaled and dove for cover, and within minutes a coordinated attack was arranged. The two Marine Pershing tanks turned off the road just before the bend, then crawled across a field perhaps a hundred yards to the top of a small rise; from here they could see the three enemy tanks, in single file, all about 300 yards beyond the bend, all with their hatches closed and their ungainly, long-barreled 85-mm. guns aimed at the bend of the road.

The Pershings fired and kept firing. Surprise was complete. They threw twenty armor-piercing 90-mm. shells at the enemy tanks and within minutes each of the monsters exploded and burned, their crews trapped inside.

The Marines moved on and the main column came along behind them. They passed the burning tanks and the others, in the village, that had been destroyed by the Corsairs the day before. Altogether, they found five ruined tanks and thus learned that in spite of the air attack, one of the T-34's must have escaped during the night.

As the day wore on, most of the units moving forward out of Inchon encountered no more than light sniping from the hills; the way to Seoul was still clear but the two prongs of the landing force had to be reformed and brought into line with each other, so that the advance troops waited while the elements of the main body were maneuvered into position. Puller's 1st Regiment Combat Team, which had landed just south of Inchon at Blue Beach, had the responsibility of mopping up their half of the peninsula before advancing—primarily to make certain that no major enemy forces were hidden there in positions from which they could make a flanking attack on the supply line to the interior.

During this mop-up operation there were occasional flurries of fighting—mostly in moving against sniper nests—and an estimated 120 of the enemy were killed. Thirty were taken prisoner. All day, all over the front, four Marines were killed and 21 wounded.

Admiral Struble, on his flagship, the *Rochester*, still anchored just off Inchon, was much interested in one of the many, continuing reports that came back from the shore that day. On one of the rail lines in the city the Marines had found a flat car loaded with ten of the heavy "ground mines" he'd feared might be planted in the channel. Somehow, the North Koreans hadn't gotten around to laying them before the morning of the invasion, and it seemed to Rip Struble another fantastic piece of luck that by all odds shouldn't have occurred.[4]

The beaches at Inchon were now the rear area. Marine General Smith prepared to go ashore on the evening of D-plus-1, set up his division headquarters, and command the advance from there. During the evening landing the day before, he had sent General Craig to establish an advance command post on the island of Wolmi-do. Craig found this location too crowded and out of touch with the forward units; he recommended that he prepare things at a spot on the southeastern outskirts of the city and Smith told him to do so. Smith did not yet make the complete move because he wanted to leave the beaches clear for the military build-up now taking place.

Two regimental combat teams were anywhere from five to seven miles inland. Behind them other battalions were pouring ashore. Within the next day or two, they would be outrunning their major base of operations, the fleet that had put them ashore. The supply problems were immense and complex: ammunition, equipment, transportation, medical care, communications, food and water had to be supplied in increasing quantities as increasing numbers of troops came ashore.

The water problem was one example. No individual would be able to carry his own water supply for several days of possible hard fighting, and the water they might find in villages or farmhouses would perhaps be in short supply or unsanitary. Thus, on D-plus-1, thirty-one heavy-distillation units were installed at Red Beach, to convert sea water into fresh water. They supplied 125,000 gallons in the next six days.

Just after lunch that day, Generals Almond and Shepherd went ashore on a quick inspection trip with a party of aides and several war correspondents. They saw the five big LST's grounded on the mud at Red Beach, supplies still pouring out of them. LST-898 was still a hospital, receiving patients as they were rushed back to the shore from the various points of the advance. Late that afternoon the party returned to the *Mt. McKinley*, and as they were about to come alongside the command ship, there was a startling, whining roar about a mile to the west. They saw a Navy Corsair that had evidently just been on a mission inland swooping down toward the water for a crash landing. Ned Almond immediately ordered the coxswain to rush the motorboat full of generals to the spot to see if they could be of assistance. The plane struck the surface of the sea with a great splash and came to a violent halt. Before the admiral's gig could reach it, a helicopter appeared and rescued the pilot.

At about the same time, General O. P. Smith was saying goodbye to General MacArthur on the bridge of the *Mt. McKinley* and preparing to go to the new 1st Marine Division command post that had been set up just beyond the city. "Good luck, General Smith," said MacArthur. "Take Kimpo Airfield as soon as you can."

Brigadier General Eddie Craig, jeeping toward the command post site to get it ready, looked up at the houses of Inchon, and to his astonishment saw dozens of signs here and there bearing such legends as "Welcome U. S. Marines," and "Welcome U. S. Forces." He couldn't imagine how they had been put up so quickly, for it was not yet twenty-four hours since the evening assault of D-Day, and he wondered if they had been put in place when the city was actually in Communist hands. At one point a white-bearded old peasant wearing the curious woven horsehair top hat of older Koreans approached Craig, held out his hand, and put something in the General's; Craig thought it a friendly gift. When he both felt and saw it, however, he was completely startled. It was a hand grenade. Then a quick second look told him that the pin had not been pulled and moments later, through an interpreter, Craig learned that the old man was simply returning something he'd seen an American Marine drop.

Craig was also impressed with the lack of looting and disorder in the city. The only thing close to it that he saw was a group of peasants carrying rice sacks away from a Communist storehouse. An officer in charge of the area was about to stop this activity, but Craig told him not to interfere.[5]

At 1800 hours, September 16, D-plus-1, just before dusk, Major General Oliver P. Smith arrived at the 1st Marine Division's command post ashore and sent the proper dispatch to Admiral Jimmy Doyle that he was taking over command of and responsibility for the landing and assault troops who, up to this point, were the Marines of his division. By this time all the units had set up their night defenses along a curved line cutting across the throat of the fat peninsula on which Inchon and its suburbs stood. In the morning they would go forward again. The amphibious assault phase of the campaign was finished and it had been, to everyone's still hesitant satisfaction, an absolute success.

It was time for a quick summing up before the push inland was resumed. Everything had been done in such haste that military statisticians would never know *exactly* how many troops had participated in the actual assault on those first two days, September 15 and 16, but the nearest estimates showed that both Murray's and Puller's Regimental Combat Teams had totaled 19,494 men—including certain support elements like the Marine aviators. There had been 2,786 men in the Korean Marine Corps regiment who came ashore on their heels. The U. S. Army enginer, signal and others units who accompanied them numbered 2,760. Thus, the grand total was 25,040 men, most of them ashore as dusk fell on D-plus-1.

Casualties were light for the landing force, heavy for the enemy. On D-Day, 21 Americans were killed, 174 wounded, 1 missing in action. On D-plus-1, 3 Americans died, 22 were wounded, and 1 was again missing in action. The total battle casualties on the American side for those two days numbered 222. The enemy suffered 1,350 casualties, both dead and wounded, and an estimated 300 of them were captured.

It was quiet at midnight of September 16. There were twenty-one tanks assigned to Company A, 1st Tank Battalion, five to a platoon, and the five tanks of the 1st Platoon, one of them commanded by Sergeant Patrick Byrnes, were deployed across the Inchon-Seoul highway at the furthest point of the advance. They were not so much parked as set up in an actual defensive position, a kind of curve across the road with the tanks on either extremity set slightly forward, what the Marines called a "deep mechanized defense," designed to stop any enemy armor that might appear. The platoon was on 100 per cent alert, which meant that no one could sleep, although the order was fudged just a little so that some members of the tank crews could doze in their seats while at least one man kept watch from the turret.

This spot on the road was a little less than two miles south of the big sprawling supply dump known as Ascom City. The highway, emerging from Inchon's outskirst, curved in a northerly direction for a mile or two after passing through the village of Kansong-ni. The 1st Platoon's defensive position was about a mile above that spot.

A truck with its lights out came grinding down the road from the north at low speed, and the sentries in the tanks flanking the highway blinked at it sleepily at first, supposing it was part of the big supply operation supporting the entire advance. It was only when the truck had rumbled about three hundred yards into the bivouac area that somebody realized it had come from the wrong direction. A tank on the road hastily leveled its 90-mm. gun at the truck. The vehicle halted. Lights were flashed on it. As armed Marines moved cautiously toward it, an amazed North Korean officer and four enlisted men stepped from it, their hands held high.

They were, of course, taken prisoner and sent to the rear for questioning. From them, as the next few hours passed, division headquarters interrogators learned that a hasty force of tanks and infantrymen had been put together just east of Ascom City, or at least was now in the process of being marshalled in these few hours before dawn. The tanks were of the 42nd North Korean Mechanized Regiment and the troops were from the 18th North Korean Division stationed in Seoul. They had been sent out to block any advance on the road to Seoul, but the remarkable thing was that the North Koreans apparently didn't know exactly where the U. S. Marines were. Evidently they had the idea that the assault troops were still in the city of Inchon.

As dawn broke, Lieutenant Hog Jaw Smith's D-Company stirred from its position on a high knoll just to the left of the highway. About 200 yards further on, the highway started to curve eastward again and at this point went between two hills. Smith, the night before, had sent his 2nd Platoon to man the smaller hill on the left, where they had machine guns and rocket launchers trained upon the road.

(The truck with the five Koreans in it must have passed this knoll the night before in order to reach the tanks about 800 yards further back; evidently it had not been noticed, or, what seems more likely, had been assumed to be friendly.)

The North Korean column was already on its way. There were six Russian T-34 tanks with infantrymen perched upon them. Other foot soldiers, about 200 altogether, were strung out in broken formation behind the tanks. As they approached the knoll the men of the 2nd Platoon, hugging the ground and watching quietly, were amazed to see those who were riding the tanks talking, laughing, gesturing and some even eating their breakfasts. The hatches were open on most of the tanks. The foot soldiers in the column seemed just as unaware that they were moving into a deadly ambush.

Second Lieutenant Lee R. Howard commanded this platoon atop the knoll. Just down the road, still on its left side on another, larger knoll, was Hog Jaw Smith's D-Company command post. Smith was small and slender, and at times seemed almost too slight to be a tough Marine. He was a taciturn Southerner who kept a wad of tobacco in his cheek in combat and always liked to move forward into the heat of the action—a laudable characteristic that was to bring about his death in later months when the Marines were fighting far north of Seoul.[6] He had set a powerful trap for the tank patrol. His own company—minus the platoon on the knoll ahead—had its entire firepower trained on the road 250 yards from them. The five tanks blocking the road had been joined by men with 3.5-inch rocket launchers and 75-mm. recoilless rifles. Right across the road was a company from Chesty Puller's regiment (F Company, 2nd Battalion) with more 75's and rocket launchers.

Howard, on the forward knoll, allowed the enemy tank column to go past him, as he'd been ordered. Then as the first tank rounded the bend of the road he called, "Let 'em have it!" and the men of his platoon began to pour rifle, machine gun and Browning Automatic Rifle fire into the North Koreans. It was a slaughter. The foot soldiers dropped immediately, dozens of them hit, and the soldiers who a moment Before had been chatting and eating on the tanks were knocked from their perches. Many of them were run over by the tanks that now quickly buttoned up and lumbered forward in surprise.

Corporal Okey J. Douglas of D-Company ran down the slope toward the road to meet the tanks. He carried the smaller, portable 2.36-inch rocket launcher that, according to reports from Army troops in the Perimeter, was inadequate as a weapon against the big Russian T-34 tanks. Chesty Puller had snorted at reports like this, and growled that if you had the guts to get near enough, you didn't need a big rocket to take out a tank. As a matter of fact the 2.36-inch launcher, or bazooka, would not penetrate T-34 armor in most spots but it could do damage at certain points, and most effectively destroy its treads and bring it to a halt. Corporal Douglas hit the first enemy tank at a range of about seventy-five yards in its front bogie, and the monster careened off the road, flaming. His second rocket struck the next tank at the base of the turret. Clouds of smoke poured from its ports and slits. From behind and around Douglas, who was just off the left-hand side of the road, the guns from other tanks, from 75-mm. recoilless rifles, and the missiles from the larger 3.5-inch rockets poured into the tank, utterly destroying it.

Corporal Douglas received a Bronze Star for that morning's action, and the citation said that he "performed these actions in spite of the intelligence that this type of tank could not be destroyed with his weapon."[7]

All six tanks were destroyed. The 90-mm. guns of the Marine tanks had struck them with forty-five rounds of armor-piercing shells within a space of five minutes. Countless 3.5-inch rockets and 75-mm. recoilless-rifle shells had been hurtled at them, all finding their marks at this short range. Their gasoline tanks had exploded and they were scattered now, so many hulks of smoking iron, around and across the road. Virtually all of the two hundred North Korean infantrymen lay dead or mortally wounded in the immediate area. The surprise was so complete that scarcely a shot had been fired in return, although there were a few scattered small-arms responses; only one Marine among the ambush force was wounded in the entire engagement.

As Lieutenant Hog Jaw Smith was setting his trap for the tanks on the outskirts of Seoul that morning, Admiral Struble was in the cabin of his flagship, the *Rochester,* shaving and preparing to go ashore with General MacArthur immediately after breakfast. He was drawing the safety razor in a long sweep across his chin, when he heard a tremendous boom outside and close behind.

Without looking through the port, he knew immediately

what it was. He had heard aerial bombs explode close to ships before. He rushed to the bridge—still only half-shaven —and discovered that the invasion fleet, lying off Inchon, was under attack by two obsolescent Russian propeller-driven Yak fighter planes. He was not surprised that they had slipped past the radar warning screen—he knew that one or two can always slip past—but he was disappointed that they hadn't been stopped by the air picket planes patrolling some distance north of the fleet. The first Yak, he saw, had dropped a stick of four bombs just astern of the *Rochester*, and was already curving off toward the north and west, anti-aircraft puffs following it but falling far behind. The second suicidal plane then came in from another direction; its bombs scored a near miss and water splashed over the deck of the cruiser. But one of its missiles—they were small 100-pound bombs— slammed into the *Rochester's* aircraft crane and by some miracle failed to explode and bounced back into the water. Rip Struble was beginning to think that miracles were a normal part of this entire landing operation.

Having dropped its bombs upon the *Rochester*—within sight of the *Mt. McKinley* where General MacArthur was getting ready to have breakfast—the second Yak curved northwestward toward the British cruiser, *Jamaica*, commanded by Captain J. S. C. Salter, D.S.O., O.B.E., Royal Navy, which had added its firepower to the shore bombardment the day before. It strafed the *Jamaica's* decks, killing one British seaman and wounding two. As it pulled up from its strafing run, the *Jamaica's* pompoms caught it and knocked it down, making it strike the water in a skidding ball of flame.[8]

Admiral Struble went back to his cabin, finished his shave, and then called for his barge to take him to MacArthur's ship. Just before 9:00 A.M. MacArthur went ashore with Struble, Ned Almond, Generals Wright, Fox and Whitney, plus several staff assistants and correspondents. He inspected Red Beach and the LST's still on the mud there, then jeeped on through the city to General O. P. Smith's 1st Marine Division headquarters near its outskirts. Here MacArthur conferred briefly with Smith, and then expressed a desire to see some of the forward positions; the members of his retinue traded quick, worried frowns but all of them knew how useless it would be to try to dissuade the Supreme Commander from going to the front.

When Douglas MacArthur went somewhere on a special occasion he had a way of attracting a retinue, and it was that way today. Down the Inchon-Seoul highway and toward the advance units of the Marine double spearhead went the Supreme Commander's now augmented parade of jeeps. In the lead was a jeep with three staff assistants, Colonels McCaffrey and Barsanti and a Captain Ladd. Next came MacArthur's jeep, Generals Almond, Smith and Admiral Struble crowded into it. Then three jeeps with Marine Pacific Commander General Shepherd, Almond's X-Corps chief of staff General Ruffner, Assistant 7th Division Commander General Hodes, the fascinated planner and observer General Wright, MacArthur's faithful aide since Philippine days General Whitney, the talented administrator General Fox, and to top it all off, a distinguished visitor from Washington, Major General Frank Lowe, a National Guard officer sent to Korea as President Truman's personal representative. General Lowe was sixty-six years old and the working generals feared that both his age and political status would pose problems; they were to be pleasantly surprised, however, at Lowe's physical spryness and at his consistent refusal to comment politically.

In the jeeps behind the generals were the correspondents and photographers, there to record the details of this procession for history. The procession first sought out Colonel Chesty Puller's 1st Marine command post, which was on a rise in the area to the right of the road. Puller was peering eastward through his binoculars when a runner came dashing up the hill to say that "MacArthur and a whole bunch of other generals" were on the way. "Let 'em come up here," grunted Chesty, and continued to look through the binoculars. MacArthur did come up the hill, leading the way and astonishing the younger generals around him at the vigor of his pace.[9]

At the hilltop, MacArthur, after being greeted by Puller, said that he would now award Chesty the Silver Star, along with Admiral Sohn Won Yil, Republic of Korea Chief of Naval Operations, the man who had had the foresight to purchase the patrol boats and who had aided materially in the landing operation. But when MacArthur, still smiling, reached into the pocket of his leather jacket he found he'd forgotten to bring the medals along, so he sighed and told General Whitney to make a note of it.

The party returned to the road where it headed in a northerly direction for a short distance and along the stretch where the North Korean tanks had been destroyed in the battles that morning and the day before. They passed the still smok-

ing wrecks of tanks in the village and on the road beyond. As
they approached one burning hulk nearer the road, Admiral
Struble peered ahead and saw several Marines crawling over
it, inspecting it. MacArthur ordered the jeep driver to stop
close to a deep culvert along the side of the road, not far
from the tank, and said to Struble, "I'm not getting out, but
if you want to look, go ahead."

Rip Struble stepped from the jeep, and with some others of
the party tagging along, went toward the tank. As he looked
more closely at the Marines moving around it, he thought,
"By God, one of them's got some really long blond hair."
A moment later he saw that it wasn't a Marine at all, but an
indefatigable woman correspondent, Maggie Higgins of the
New York *Herald Tribune*, whom he had met before at press
briefings. Maggie had talked her way aboard one of the transports at Pusan in spite of official objections that there were no
facilities for woman available. Before that she had been covering the action in the Perimeter, always as close as possible
to the shooting. And here she was at Inchon, slim, pretty and
eternally curious. Struble took her back to the jeep to speak
to MacArthur. MacArthur smiled, said a few pleasant words,
then pushed on to find Ray Murray's 5th Regiment command
post.[10]

General O. P. Smith watched from his perch in the rear of
a jeep, not liking any of this. The procession was almost in
enemy territory, and certainly within mortar range of any
North Korean units that might be lurking in the vicinity. One
round, aimed or accidental, could take out most of the top
command and the President's personal observer, and Smith,
who had just taken over area command, was responsible for
the safety of all these distinguished sightseers.

Minutes after they left the spot near the burning tank, a
platoon led by First Lieutenant George C. McNaughton came
along the highway in the usual loose combat formation. A
Marine on the flank thought he heard shuffling and scraping
sounds in the big culvert by the road, hand-signaled the others
to caution and then, with several mates, went forward to take
a look. They pointed their guns at the mouth of the culvert,
yelled for whoever was in there to come out, fired a few shots,
and a moment later seven North Korean soldiers, all armed,
came into the daylight with their hands raised. These were
the only survivors of the two hundred enemy infantrymen who
had been mowed down in the ambush that morning. They
had been crouching in the culvert, within hearing of Mac-

Arthur and the other generals, when the procession had stopped.

MacArthur's procession toured the front for about forty minutes, visited briefly at the stockade on Red Beach where over 600 prisoners were assembled, stopped at the island of Wolmi-do to look at some Russian artillery there, and finally returned to the *Mt. McKinley* at about 1:00 P.M.

Meanwhile, the Marines were pushing on. Their big objective was Kimpo Airfield, about two-thirds of the way to Seoul. Once it was taken, the big transports from Japan could land there and enormously simplify supply problems for the attack on the capital. But now that they had pushed inland, their front was widening, and they had to be concerned about their flanks, especially, at this time, the left or northern flank where many of their immediate minor objectives lay.

Ray Murray's 5th Regimental Combat Team still had this general area north of the Inchon-Seoul highway. The highway came out of Inchon, doglegged to the north for a little less than two miles, then headed abruptly east for the capital again. Directly north of this second bend was the big storage area known as Ascom City, an oblong a mile-and-a-half long and three-quarters of a mile wide.

Sam Jaskilka's E-Company had the point on this march into Ascom City, and his squads and platoons led the way cautiously. They received scattered fire from some of the houses, but mopped up without serious casualties as they moved forward. He moved up a road on the eastern edge of the city while F-Company pushed through the center—the characteristic two-pronged advance on a smaller scale.

By early afternoon, Lieutenant Colonel Murray had his ever-moving command post in Ascom City, and on his portable desk he spread out his maps to plan the advance to Kimpo Airfield whose runways were now scarcely seven miles to the northeast in a straight line. Roise's 2nd Battalion—with Sam Jaskilka's E-Company still in the lead—was to move more or less eastward on one of the roads that led to Kimpo eventually, taking two important hills south of Kimpo on the way. Company A's tanks would move along a parallel road on their left, protecting their flank. These roads, small, dusty and secondary, were all north of the main highway to Seoul, which ran eastward a good seven miles south of Kimpo Airfield.

Resistance seemed to be stiffening a bit here and there. Marines in the western part of Ascom City had stirred up two firefights, knocking out a machine-gun nest and flushing a strong enemy force from several buildings, killing eighteen and suffering three Marines wounded.

On the eastern fringe of the city, Lieutenant Colonel Hal Roise prepared to move his battalion forward, and suddenly discovered that where his map indicated a road to Kimpo, there was none. In the city, Murray fretted over this report. Murray wanted Kimpo by the end of the day—as did Generals Smith, Almond and MacArthur himself—and if his 2nd Battalion commander had to spent half the afternoon looking for a road, they'd never make it.

Suddenly word came in that Roise had found the road and was on his way. Minutes later several Marines appeared at Murray's field desk escorting a rather pretty Korean girl of about 21. "She found the road for Colonel Roise," said one of them. The girl had seen the puzzled officers poring over the map, walked right up to them and in good English asked if she might help. Murray questioned her briefly and learned that she had been the girl friend of some G.I. in Ascom City during the Occupation. Rather wistfully she was wondering if perhaps the Colonel knew where her boy friend was, back in the States somewhere. . . .[11]

That afternoon the two-pronged advance found the way to Kimpo relatively clear; by about 1600, Lieutenant Ed Deptula had taken his platoon to the crest of one of the hills 4,000 yards south of the airfield, had found dozens of empty trenches, but no defenders. Under the gathering clouds, the way to the airfield itself looked open. Sam Jaskilka's E-Company and Hog Jaw Smith's D-Company moved up toward the runways, meeting light sniper fire, and then Captain English's A-Company tanks came in from the other road, entering into a small skirmish about 1,000 yards south of the field, knocking out a small North Korean force grouped around a machine gun nest.

By 6:00 P.M. the two infantry companies and the tank detachment, the advance of Lieutenant Colonel Roise's 2nd Battalion, were at the southern tip of Kimpo Airfield and there they prepared to dig in for the night. On the other side of the airfield, a motley force of perhaps five hundred North Koreans from various units was being marshalled by a Chinese-trained 40-year-old Brigadier General named Wan Yong for a desperate attempt to drive them off. There was some scattered action while Lieutenant Colonel George R. Newton's 1st Battalion came up on the right. Actually there was more intense action back at the outskirts of Ascom City where Marines were still flushing out diehards within sight and sound of Murray's regimental command post. It was twenty minutes past eight and dark before Roise considered his objective at the airfield secured and finished digging in for what was hardly going to be a quiet night.

NOTES *Chapter 11*

1. Puller had worn hand grenades in combat ever since he had served in Haiti. Grenades became General Matthew Ridgway's trademark when he replaced MacArthur, and in later years Puller grumbled, "Ridgway got the idea from me." Interview author—Puller.
2. Interview author—Murray.
3. Ironically, Capt Simpson had just written an article, "Advice for the Replacement Pilot," which appeared posthumously in the February 1951 issue of the *Marine Corps Gazette,* in which he warned pilots to be wary of ground fire, saying that because of the smokeless enemy ammunition "you never realize that whole platoons are lined up firing at you every time you seem overhead." He was also flying Plane 17 from the aircraft carrier *U.S.S. Sicily Seventeen,* which turned out to be a jinx number, for that month planes marked "17" killed three other Marines. The number was barred for *Sicily* planes after the fourth death.
4. Interview author—Struble.
5. Craig memo.
6. Interview author—Jaskilka.
7. Montross, Lynn: "The Capture of Seoul," *Marine Corps Gazette,* Aug '51.
8. This was the second aerial attack on U. N. naval ships in the Yellow Sea. On September 4, 1950, two Russian twin-engined bombers, apparently flying out of the Chinese mainland, approached the destroyer *Herbert J. Thomas,* on picket duty off the North Korean coast. One turned back but the second fired on a Navy carrier plane sent to warn it off. The Navy plane shot it down. Its pilot, whose body was recovered, turned out to be a Russian officer.
9. Interviews author—Fox, Puller.
10. Interview Struble; letter Wright to author.
11. Interview author—Murray.

12

"This is Easy Company! Knock it off!"

IT HAD BEGUN TO RAIN. IT WAS MODERATE, STEADY RAIN WITH-
out much wind, but its sound was monotonous, and Korean
Marine Private Kong Jin Beck thought it gave a man a sense
of isolation and also prevented him from hearing whatever
might be going on around him in the darkness. Beck was a
messenger at the headquarters of the 23rd Company, 1st Battalion, R. O. K. Marines. Although he was one of the farm
boys from Cheju-do who had virtually been impressed into
service, he physically resembled some young Manchurian war-
lord with his willowy, slender build and long, hooked nose.
He had the thoughtful, reserved manner that went along with
this appearance, and some of his fellow Marines kidded him
about it, telling him he'd be happier if he didn't think about
things so much.[1] Right now he was thinking that although his
company, bivouacked on a hill near Ascom City, was theoretically behind the front, there was still plenty of potential opposition in the little pockets of North Korean resistance all
around them, and in this rain and darkness only a fool would
start to relax before daybreak.

Units of R. O. K. Marines had come along either behind
or on the flank of Lieutenant Colonel Murray's general advance, and their task in the past two days was to flush out any
North Koreans they could find. They had carried out this job
with fierce enthusiasm. Private Beck was surprised, although
not particularly shocked, to see his fellow Marines, after over-
running an enemy position, wander among the moaning
wounded on the ground and deliver the *coupe de grâce* with
pistol or rifle bullets in the head to those who seemed mortally
injured. He commented upon it to an officer who shrugged
and explained that it was really "mercy killing"; the Korean

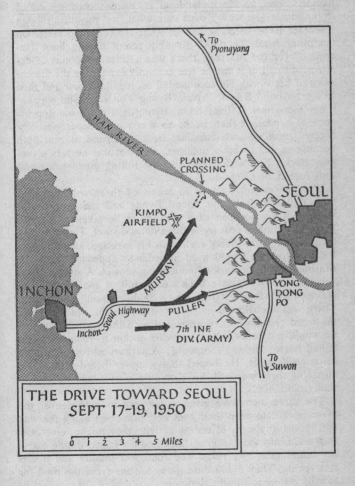

THE DRIVE TOWARD SEOUL
SEPT 17-19, 1950

0 1 2 3 4 5 Miles

Marines had no medics and the mortally wounded were going to die anyway. It was more efficient to put them out of their misery. If a man could speak, he usually wouldn't be shot.

Private Beck had no particular animosity toward North Koreans who, as he understood it, were something called Communists—he wasn't even sure what that meant, although it seemed to be different and for some reason undesirable. On the other hand, he didn't strongly resent having been "recruited" for the Marines; there was a certain amount of excitement to all of it and he was certainly expanding the dimensions of his world. He commented on it mildly now and then to his boyhood friend, Private Byong Yon Lee, who was another messenger in their team. Byong had more the appearance of a peasant than Beck; he was round-faced, generally happy, unruffled and outgoing. Beck was fond of him both because of his amiable qualities, and because he was somehow Beck's link with home and the rolling green fields and lush forests of Cheju-do.

The messengers traveled in teams of three and sometime after nightfall, Beck, his friend Byong and the team leader were each given copies of a message to be taken to a U. S. Marine command post some three miles distant. The company commander, after giving each man his message, also told him the password he would need in order to approach the U. S. Marine post in the dark without being shot at. A strange password it was, to Private Beck's ears, full of the clipped and chopped sounds of English, which he didn't at all understand. There was a challenge and a response, on the order of, say, the word "batting" to be answered with the word "average"; he would not recall it in later years except to remember that it had been somthing thoroughly American and to him quite incomprehensible. He hoped that whoever heard him repeat either of these words in his Korean accent would be able to understand him.

The three men were given orders not only to deliver the message, but to keep their eyes and ears open along the way and report any signs of enemy activity they might detect. Off they went into the darkness, Beck and his friend Byong carrying brand new M-1 rifles. The road was muddy and it was slow going. They didn't dare move too far from the road for fear of getting lost in the darkness.

Private Byong had the point, in the center of the road and a little forward. Beck and the team leader on the flanks, a little behind and in the right- and left-hand ditches of the road. They had progressed this way some ten or fifteen minutes, when Byong suddenly halted and held up his hand. They came alongside him, peered where he pointed, and in the dimness perhaps fifty yards ahead saw what seemed to be a number of soldiers lined up on either side of the road. They also heard an occasional low voice and the clanking and shuffling sounds of movement. Beck estimated about forty men were up there.

"Perhaps they are American Marines," said the team leader.

Beck had a feeling that they were not, but one of the things that had been drilled into him over and over again during his short Marine career was to obey orders without question, and so, when the team leader motioned them back into formation and said they would approach, Beck resumed his place on the left flank. They stepped forward cautiously, each man in a half-crouch and with his rifle ready, Beck turning the alien password over and over in his mind so he'd be sure to get it right.

They had taken a dozen steps when the figures ahead suddenly opened fire upon them.

Beck dropped into the ditch. They were getting rifle fire and he thought that fact in itself ominous, for the North Koreans, he'd been told, had few portable automatic weapons and used mostly Japanese pieces or what were called Russian "needle guns." He fired a shot in return; his second round missed fire. He began to wonder if the U. S. Marine who had traded weapons with him hadn't been right to prefer the older, simpler Springfield. He wasn't sure because the truth was he didn't know a great deal about weapons and, since being recruited on Cheju-do only weeks before, had fired scarcely a dozen rounds in practice. From across the road he heard the reports of what he supposed were the team leader's shots. He imagined his friend, Private Byong, must have gotten out of the middle of the road to join the team leader in the ditch on the right-hand side.

Suddenly the group of men ahead weren't firing at them any longer—the entire exchange of shots had taken something less than a minute—and now, as he strained his eyes to look through the darkness, he had the impression that a number of them were moving off, not forward but away from himself. It didn't make sense, but then Private Beck was learning that a great deal of what happens in combat doesn't seem to make sense, especially at lower levels. Perhaps, he thought, the North Korean detachment encountered had instructions to keep on the move and not be diverted, or perhaps they thought themselves under attack by a much larger unit than a three-man messenger team.

Everything became quiet again except for the soft hiss of the steady rain. Beck stayed where he was and kept peering. Minutes passed. He didn't dare risk calling across the road to his teammates, so finally, when he couldn't stand his isolation any longer, he bellied his way through the mud toward them and rolled into the ditch on the right.

There was no one near him. He called the team leader's name softly several times but heard no answer. Still crawling, he explored the ditch and some of the field around it. Nothing, no one. Private Beck's throat turned dry and he felt the acid of fear in his innards. Here he was out in the darkness without companions and carrying a rifle that didn't work. Your spittle doesn't flow when you're very, very scared, he discovered. He crawled forward, hoping to find his friends. When he had progressed about forty yards he saw the shadow of a vehicle ahead; it was a destroyed tank, but at the moment, Private Beck didn't know that. He turned back again and decided to return to his own command post. Then he heard someone groaning in the middle of the road.

If this was a wounded enemy soldier, reasoned Beck, he would be able to take his rifle and at least arm himself; he crawled toward the groaning sound and suddenly noticed a figure sprawled in the mud. It was wearing a helmet. The North Koreans didn't wear helmets. He went toward it and his hand fell upon a rifle. It was an M-1 and even the rain hadn't washed away the sticky blood with which it was covered. Beck crawled another few steps, came upon the body, and then saw that it was his friend, Private Byong.

Beck was saddened but also, suddenly, he was angered. He had had no intense feeling about the war before this; now he wanted to kill North Koreans, for they had slaughtered his friend. As a matter of fact, he even wanted to harm the team leader, whom he blamed for continuing the advance with Private Byong out in the middle of the road where he was so vulnerable. Beck picked up Byong's bloody M-1, and carrying both that piece and his own rifle, started back toward his company.

There was a line of poplar trees ahead of him. He thought he saw movement among them. He dropped to the side of the road again, crouched in the ditch, checked Byong's weapon and hastily manipulated his own until it was in working order again. Now, with two rifles, he thought, he could make some sort of stand if he were attacked.

A curious thing had happened to Private Beck. Although he still felt frightened, the dryness had left his mouth and his senses were clearer; everything now seemed less like a senseless nightmare. He didn't realize it, but he had become a veteran.

He lay there in the darkness and waited. He still thought he could see people among the poplar trees ahead, but it was hard to be certain. They might even, he thought, be the next team of messengers, for couriers were supposed to go back and forth at two-hour intervals. He kept waiting. He marked the passage of the hours by his cheap Japanese wrist watch, which was still ticking despite the mud and rain. Eleven, midnight, 1:00 A.M. Still no second team of messengers.

He heard the sound of motors or engines in the distance now and then. Each time he was encouraged and hoped it was a friendly vehicle approaching; the North Koreans had few trucks. But each time, he realized that it was an airplane engine or a distant tank. At any rate, no one came.

Shortly after 2:00 A.M. the rain abated, and the moonlight began to break through. He could now see the swaying poplars ahead more clearly and realized that it had been the movement of the trees and branches he'd mistaken for men. He was still reluctant to go forward and decided to wait either for dawn or someone's approach.

At about 3:30 A.M. three figures appeared, deployed like a messenger team, one man forward and in the middle of the road, two on each flank. He readied his rifle and wondered, if they were the enemy, if he'd be able to fire fast enough and aim well enough to kill all three before they killed him. When the man in the lead was no more than ten yards away, Beck thought he saw the shape of a helmet. He took a chance and called out the difficult American password.

Instead of giving the response, the answering voice called out in Korean: "Is that you, Beck?"

Beck grinned, rose, came forward to meet the messenger team, and to his surprise, noticed that his knees suddenly became wobbly. The four South Korean Marines now proceeded forward, and within another twenty minutes reached the U. S. Marine command post. Beck's team leader was there and Beck was furious with him both for ordering the advance and for not coming back to look for Beck and Byong afterward. The team leader protested that he had looked for Beck but failed to find him, and that after he'd arrived at the command post he had been ordered to stay there. Getting to the bottom of the matter would require a great deal of complicated conversation through the liaison officer who acted as translator, and Beck didn't think it worth it, so he found himself a spot in a tent and went to sleep for the rest of the morning.

While Private Beck was lying in the mud and peering at the poplar trees, Ned Almond, aboard the *Mt. McKinley* was conferring with Admiral Struble about some unorthodox artillery support that was planned for the 7th Army Division when it landed the next day. Its vanguard would be the 32nd Infantry Regiment, scheduled to take over the right flank of the advance south of the Inchon-Seoul highway, allowing the Marines to veer off toward Seoul itself in another two-pronged assault. All day the cruisers *Rochester* and *Toledo* had been firing occasional rounds inland in support of the Marines, sometimes at ranges up to 30,000 yards. For some reason the tactic hadn't been too successful; for one thing, the Marines encountered few targets they thought needed to be hit by the big guns, and for another, communications between their forward observers and the fire controllers on the ships were not too smooth, largely through lack of proper equipment.

Ned Almond wanted the big guns of the famed battleship *Missouri* to support the advance of the Army troops when they landed. The "Big Mo" was on its way from the opposite coast of Korea where it had been firing diversionary salvos to deceive the Communists into thinking the landing would be at Wonsan. Struble was ready to give it a try, but had his doubts about the idea's effectiveness. So, for that matter, did Almond. Nevertheless he felt that if any firepower was available it ought to be used, and the more the better.

General Almond was anxious to get his Army elements ashore so that his newly created X-Corps could begin to function in combat. The first phase of the invasion had been under Admiral Struble's command. The drive inland had been General Smith's show. Now the Army division would be fed in alongside the Marines for the storming of Seoul itself, and the entire force would be Almond's X-Corps.

The furiously energetic Almond, close to MacArthur, realized perhaps more intensely than anyone else the importance of capturing Seoul as quickly as possible. "Seoul," he wrote later, "was the key to the unlocking of the communications system throughout Central Korea . . . Seoul was the objective and the speed with which we could reach and capture it and restore the Rhee government was of paramount interest."[2]

When the plans for the Inchon landing began to jell firmly in early September, MacArthur had said to Almond, "I want to get into Seoul three days after the landing."

"Impossible, sir," Almond had replied.

The snapped answer startled MacArthur for a moment—his subordinates didn't usually tell him that his wishes were impossible, at least not so abruptly. But finally MacArthur smiled a little and said, "All right, Ned. How long, then?"

The truth was that Ned Almond at that point didn't have the wildest idea how long it would take him to fight his X-Corps into the heart of Seoul, but he knew MacArthur wanted some sort of answer, so he picked a figure out of the blue sky and said, "Two weeks."[3] Now he was stuck with his promise.

As of nightfall on September 17, it looked as though he'd be able to keep it. Murray's Marines were already at the edge of Kimpo Airfield; Chesty Puller's Marines had secured the highway and much of the territory south of the airfield. Still, the intelligence reports from aerial reconnaissance, from Korean agents, and from the interrogation of prisoners of war, showed without a doubt that the enemy was at last rushing troops from all directions toward Seoul, and Almond felt that a bitter, last-ditch defense was in the making. Pyongyang, the North Korean capital, had not yet broadcast any public announcement of the successful seaborne assault on Inchon. U. N. cargo planes—old workhorse C-47's, or Dakotas, as the British called them—had meanwhile been dropping leaflets, primarily along the Perimeter, telling of the landing in Korean and calling for enemy troops to surrender.

The leaflets, apparently, were not having much effect. The men of General Walker's Eighth Army were of course greatly heartened by the news of the Inchon landing, but it was possible that their opponents either didn't believe the propaganda leaflets, or did not receive them in great enough quantity. As a matter of fact, in many North Korean units a man would be punished severely and in some cases even shot for picking up or possessing a propaganda leaflet.[4] Whatever the reason, the news hadn't really spread among the fourteen enemy divisions still holding Walker in the Perimeter, and the pressure was still intense.

Walker tried to look at it optimistically. On the day of the landing, he had issued a statement to the press, saying. "Our days of purgatory have ended and we will pass to the offensive in the near future."[5] Walker, it will be remembered, had asked MacArthur for permission to delay his own counter-attack until one day after the landing, on the supposition that the North Koreans, hearing the news, would be demoralized. Unfortunately they either hadn't heard the news or didn"t quite believe it. In addition, General Walker had serious supply problems, partly brought about by the diversion of so much matérial to the Inchon-Seoul effort. For the attempted breakthrough, he had had to limit the ammunition issue to fifty rounds per day per man for primary attack, and twenty-five rounds for secondary attack. His combat-hardened Marines had been taken from him. Their air squadrons had been replaced by the 51st Fighter-Interceptor Wing of the U. S. Air Force, transferred from Okinawa to Itazuke in southern Japan with the 16th and 25th Fighter-Interceptor Squadrons. The Air Force pilots hadn't quite the experience or spirit of the Marines when it came to ground support. All of Walker's divisions except one were pinned down (or seemed to be) in their positions. Only immediately before the scheduled push was he able to move his one free division, the 24th, to the center of the line near Taegu where the breakout was meant to take place. On the Perimeter, in the first fifteen days of September, the Eighth Army had suffered higher casualties than in any other fifteen-day period since the beginning of the war.

What it all amounted to, strategically, was that the taking of Seoul was even more important than it had been. Mac-Arthur had envisioned the enemy crushed between his Inchon landing force and Walker's Eighth Army in a hammer-and-anvil effect. But now it looked as though the enemy would have to be weakened even further before any hammers could start swinging.

Not that the enemy himself was fresh or eager for battle. Walker's intelligence had actually overestimated his strength in the Perimeter, and his troops there were badly supplied, ill-fed and low in morale. But to know he was there and *think* he was strong meant attacking with at least some degree of prudence, and this kept Walker from breaking the cordon immediately.

Meanwhile, the enemy had troops to send to the Seoul area. They were, in effect, his reserve troops and this would ulti-mately mean that his safety factor was gone, but they were troops, and they were armed, and they would be operating from advantageous defensive positions. This meant that the attackers would be hurt even if they eventually took Seoul.

The third day after the landing was about to break, Ned Almond, poring over his maps until late at night aboard the *Mt. McKinley,* remembered MacArthur's previous wish that Seoul be taken in three days. He saw the intelligence reports which showed enemy units converging upon Seoul from both the north and the south. He shook his head. Considering the immense problems of supplying his X-Corps through the narrow bottleneck of the Inchon port (whose twice-daily low tides complicated things even further), he'd be lucky if he fulfilled his own ad-libbed promise of two weeks.

In the darkness of the morning of September 18, about one hour or so past midnight, Captain Sam Jaskilka (he was promoted on the way to Kimpo), commanding officer of Company E, 2nd Battalion, 5th Marines, crouched in a bomb hole on a low rise only about five hundred yards away from the main runway of Kimpo Airfield. In a way, he was waiting for the rain to stop so he could remove the poncho that was keeping him too warm and not really keeping out all of the rain. So, from a standpoint of comfort, he thought it would be nice if the rain would stop. But from another viewpoint he realized that a Communist counterattack on the airfield might come as soon as the weather cleared.

Sam Jaskilka's E-Company was part of a perimeter that surrounded, roughly, the southern half of the airfield. As night came on September 17, the advance units had reached only the tip of the airfield, but in the rain and darkness they had moved forward a little more to set up this perimeter in spite of the handicap of lowered visibility. Actually the battalion's defensive position was not so much a ring of men around the area as the positioning of three rifle companies on three strong points that surrounded the runways. The main runway of Kimpo Airfield ran for two thousand yards in a slanting line from the northwest to the southeast. A shorter runway crossed it in its upper part. The lower part, up to this intersection, was to be held by the Marines that night. E-Company was in its own oval perimeter, a long blob over a thousand yards long, off to the right of the runway. On the left, Hog Jaw Smith's D-Company formed a similar separate defense. At the lower end of the runway, in a blob shaped something like a fat boomerang, was Captain Uel D. Peters' F-Company. In the center of the triangle formed by these three long oval shapes, and on the runway itself, was the battalion command post, Lieutenant Ed Deptula's platoon had been sent as a picket element north along a road leading away from the air-field to an outpost a good thousand yards away from Jaskilka's bomb hole.

At his open air command post on the runway, which amounted to a few jeeps and some stacked portable equipment, Lieutenant Colonel Hal Roise knew that a North Korean force held the northern half of the airfield, or at least occupied territory that commanded it. He also knew that this force was made up of fragments from various regiments, battalions and companies that had somehow gathered at Kimpo Airfield in the past day or two, joining some of the technical and administrative troops already there.[6] He knew from experience that North Koreans liked to attack at night, and he therefore expected some kind of action before dawn. The men of Deptula's 2nd Platoon, dug in on both sides of the road, had heard an enemy column approaching—it later turned out to be about company size. In quick whispers and by a series of hand signals Deptula gave the orders to let the enemy column come forward and actually penetrate their position before opening fire. When the North Koreans were in the trap, Deptula gave the signal and a Marine sergeant nearby took it upon himself to jump to his feet and bellow at the enemy: "United States Marines!" With that, the entire platoon poured rifle and quick-stuttering rifle fire into the enemy, cutting down nearly twenty of them in one volley. The rest scrambled back into the darkness in disorder.

There were a few minutes of quiet, and then the Communists came again. Their second attack was thrown back, and their third and fourth. Suddenly, on the fifth attack, a big T-34 tank snarled down on Deptula's men. He had no anti-tank weapons, and signaled a quick withdrawal. In the engagement he had lost one man killed and another wounded; now, to his surprise, as he pulled back toward the airfield, the Communists and their tank did not press the attack.

By this time dawn was breaking, and Sam Jaskilka heard some firing from the left, across the runway, and imagined that Hog Jaw Smith's D-Company had spotted his own outfit and supposed it to be the enemy. He jumped from the bomb hole and on to the mound of dirt around it, and through cupped hands and at the top of his voice yelled, "Hey, you guys! This is Easy Company! Knock it off!"

Blam! Blam! Blam! said several small arms, and bullets rico-

cheted near where Sam stood. A second or so later, he realized
that D-Company *wasn't* in its position across the runway—it
had moved forward some eight hundred yards during the
night—and that the fire was coming from a couple of squads
of North Koreans. Sam hit the dirt fast.

At about that moment a larger enemy force—possibly the
same column that had attacked Deptula's outpost—started to
fire from the east, and Sam found himself engaged on two
fronts. Fortunately, his oval perimeter had been set up skill-
fully. Part of his defense force was a platoon equipped with
75-mm. recoilless rifles, and this artillery was turned on the
main enemy attack from the east. Riflemen of the 2nd Platoon
quickly fought off the two attacking squads on the west,
largely, Sam thought, because the enemy soldiers simply
seemed to lack the will to press their attack.[7]

The biggest attack in that hour or so of dawn came south
of the airfield and started toward the outer curve of the
boomerang-shaped perimeter held by F-Company. The North
Koreans ran into sheets of fire and into a rocket attack from
an Assault and an Engineer Platoon stationed just outside the
boomerang to hold an overpass across the road. To make the
rout complete, just as the enemy column scattered and was
withdrawing in a number of directions, a company from the
1st Battalion came along from the south and hit them hard
on the flanks.

For the next several hours Marine detachments pursued the
scattered groups of enemy soldiers for short distances and
cleared most of the area around the airfield. The march from
Ascom City to Kimpo and the night on the southern half of
the airfield cost the 2nd Battalion four men killed and nineteen
wounded. More than a hundred of the enemy were killed,
and ten prisoners were taken.

To make the airfield secure, the Marines now needed only
the high ground north of it between the runways and the
banks of the Han River. Their artillery hadn't caught up with
them yet, so Lieutenant Colonel Roise called for naval gunfire. From their positions off Inchon, below the horizon and
out of sight, the cruisers *Rochester* and *Toledo* laid down a
barrage and then Roise sent Hog Jaw Smith and Company
D forward to take the hill.

It was 11:45 A.M., September 18, 1950. Marines held the
best airfield in Korea.

Lieutenant Colonel Ray Murray loped onto the airfield

about midmorning to establish his regimental command post in a bullet-pocked administration building. At 10:00 A.M., General Shepherd and Colonel Victor H. Krulak, his G-3 for the Fleet Marine Force, Pacific, arrived at Kimpo by helicopter. Almost simultaneously Brigadier General Eddie Craig arrived in a jeep. As the day wore on, other high-ranking officers and swarms of news correspondents converged on Kimpo from all sides.

Murray knew he would not be staying at the airfield for long. Seoul was next, and there was a river to cross—at several places—and a number of hills and ridges that surrounded the capital like battlements to be stormed before the city could be taken.

At about two o'clock that afternoon Corporal Joe Maize, some distance from the headquarters building, was standing in the back of his jeep giving out mail to another unit. At heart a morale builder, Joe enjoyed the chore of distributing mail and he had once been most pleased when a fellow Marine had cocked an eye at him and said, "Joe, you're the happiest damn Indian I ever *did* see."

Suddenly the ground all around them, for a radius of about a hundred yards, began to erupt with the explosions of mortar shells. Some Marines hit the dirt and others ran for a nearby small brick building to avoid the shrapnel. The mortar fire was coming from semi-distant hills; no one could see the source of it. Another shell burst, nearer the jeep, and Joe fell to the ground, his right trouser leg ripped and peppered by shrapnel. There was some blood, but the wound hadn't started to hurt yet. To one side was a man who had been reaching out for mail when the explosion came; he was flat on his back now, badly hit in the chest. Joe realized that if he had been standing on the ground instead of up in the jeep, he too would have been hit in the chest.

Corpsmen appeared with a stretcher and picked up the seriously wounded man. Joe made it to his feet, then limped in the wake of the corpsmen toward the dispensary tent. By the time he arrived, the Marine with the chest wound was already on a makeshift operating table receiving quick emergency treatment. Presently a corpsman came, picked the metal fragments from Joe's leg with tweezers, bandaged it, and marked him fit for duty. Joe limped back to the jeep to see if he could put the pieces of scattered mail together again.[8]

The mortar rounds that fell on Joe Maize at mail call were

part of a stream of increasing signs that the enemy effort to defend Seoul vigorously was getting under way. Murray's 5th Regiment, the left-hand prong, had marched on their side of the Inchon-Seoul highway, veering away from it at Ascom City to head at an oblique angle for Kimpo Airfield. Chesty Puller's 1st Regiment, meanwhile, was pushing along the highway itself, and some elements were south of the highway moving forward on a broad front. On September 17, while Murray's men were cleaning out Ascom City and trying to find the road to Kimpo, Puller's units only a mile or so to the south were running into bothersome resistance both on the road and in the hills and ridges below it. They were using tanks and artillery to make a somewhat slower advance than they had anticipated to the next village of any size, a town called Sosa only a mile and a half beyond the dogleg in the road where the tanks had been destroyed. There were dozens of small clashes on the way and by nightfall of the 17th, the line was only halfway to Sosa and the Marines had lost a man killed and over thirty wounded. They had killed or wounded some 250 of the enemy, taken 70 prisoners, and destroyed another T-34 tank.

In the early morning of the 18th the Marines on the road to Sosa called for naval artillery support, and out at sea the H.M.S. *Kenya,* commanded by Captain P. W. Brock, RN, gave it to them with more than 300 six-inch shells. Other units of the regiment were strung out on high ground to the left, and in the morning they too would push forward on a mile-long front. The opposition was light and the scattered enemy units encountered the day before seemed to have withdrawn. Sosa was taken by noon of the 18th.

This morning the first elements of General Barr's 7th Army Division were coming ashore in Inchon to move up and join the fight. The 2nd Battalion of the 32nd Infantry landed before noon, and the rest of the regiment followed later in the day. This regiment numbered over 5,100 men: about 3,200 Americans and almost 1,900 R. O. K.'s.

At Lieutenant Colonel Murray's regimental headquarters on Kimpo Airfield, Navy Lieutenant Horace Underwood was busy interrogating dozens of Koreans congregated upon the command post with reports. Some were captured prisoners, some South Koreans brought in on general principles, some volunteers who thought they had information the Americans might find useful. Their testimony helped form the picture of the enemy rallying for his defense.

North of Inchon was a big land mass extending to the Han River that had not been properly explored. A number of reports, all matching each other in detail, described enemy concentrations in this area. It seemed obvious that they were gathering for a strike at Kimpo, and during the day, four Navy Skyraiders hit one column from the air, killing an estimated fifty soldiers, but reported afterward that there was still much activity in the vicinity.

Across the Han River, directly north of the airfield and almost three miles from its edges, was a large commanding hill where Marine pilots were noticing a build-up of enemy troops.

Two captured enemy officers revealed that a North Korean regiment had moved into the city of Yong Dong Po, just across the river from Seoul on the south bank of the Han; this industrial suburb six miles beyond Sosa would be Puller's next objective. His Marines were already beginning to discover that the road was well planted with land mines of the cheap but effective wooden-box variety manufactured by the North Koreans, and these were damaging tanks and vehicles and in general delaying the advance.

The Corsairs were still hunting tanks from the air. They found six that day near the road some miles ahead of Puller's advance and took out two of them with napalm.

Busy General Ned Almond had the basic strategy for taking Seoul quite clear in his mind by now, but he was in a peculiar position as far as setting up the assault. Strictly speaking, Marine General Oliver Smith was running the show on shore, and Almond had even given him the newly arrived 32nd Army Regiment to handle on his right flank. But within the next two days, all of the Army division would land, and X-Corps would be ready to command. Almond wanted to be sure that X-Corp's main elements—the 1st Marine Division and the 7th Army Division—were in place for the attack on Seoul as he envisioned it. Therefore he was hopping from command post to command post explaining his strategy to make sure that it was understood by everyone. This was to be his pattern in days to come; Ned Almond would always be on the move and regimental and even battalion commanders got to the point where they were ready to see him drop in at any time. If this habit disturbed Oliver Smith, he said nothing about it. The entire business was to come to a head in about a week's time.

Almond dropped in on Ray Murray at his headquarters in the basement of the Operations Building at Kimpo. There would be, basically, a pincers movement upon Seoul, he explained. Once they had taken Yong Dong Po, Puller's 1st Marines would swing left and up into the city; by that time some of Dave Barr's Army units would be alongside them and a little farther east. Murray, meanwhile, was to go directly north to the Han River, cross, and then advance down the north bank to hit Seoul from the west. Murray set the date for the river crossing on the 20th, and called for the waddling amphibious tractors that had landed at Blue Beach to effect it. The night before the crossing, he decided, he would send a small team across to establish observation posts from which they could give warning of any enemy approach or build-up.

The next day—September 19—Almond tightened the command reins of X-Corps. By now two regiments of the 7th Division were ashore, the 31st and 32nd, and he assigned them to the area south of the Inchon-Seoul highway, allowing Oliver Smith's 1st Marine Division to concentrate on the left flank and give more support to Murray's projected river crossing. To protect the right flank of the advance, he would start some elements of the 32nd Infantry across country in a wide swing south, so that eventually they would come to the main highway that led south from Seoul and be able to block any enemy forces marching from that direction.

All of this, of course, was based on the assumption that the advance would continue. On the 19th of September it suddenly came to a halt in the western approaches to Yong Dong Po. Not that this surprised anyone. Yong Dong Po was a city containing all manner of cover, and the area for three miles west of it was covered with scattered hills. It called for a pause, a deep breath, and then an assault, and while this assault would undoubtedly cost lives, the planners felt that the Communists, in the long run, would be foolish to waste artillery and armor in the defense of Yong Dong Po, cut off as it was from Seoul by a broad river and thus impossible to keep supplied.

On the morning of the 19th, Murray's 1st Battalion, commanded by Lieutenant Colonel Geoge R. Newton, moved forward far on the left flank, practically on the banks of the Han River, and after a brisk fight took a big hill overlooking Yong Dong Po, securing it by about 11·00 A.M. A little further south, the 2nd and 3rd Battalions of Puller's 1st Marines also pushed on, the 3rd Battalion swinging left off the road to storm an eminence called Lookout Hill, which also commanded the city. On the road itself, the tanks and vehicles of the 2nd Battalion began to encounter the mines that blew off tracks and knocked out vehicles.

By the end of the day the three battalions—one from Murray's regiment, two from Puller's—were spread out over a rather wide front with no precise contact between them and with squads and platoons of North Koreans sallying out from the city and roaming through the hills and draws in their midst. The lines were adjusted a bit just after nightfall and on the far left a company was withdrawn from two hills that were considered too far forward.

Just after midnight, five T-34 tanks clattered out of the city on the Inchon-Seoul highway, followed by a battalion of infantry and a dozen or so supply trucks. There was one truck grinding along in front of the tanks and, incredibly, this vulnerably placed vehicle was filled with ammunition. There was no explanation for this gaffe, and no one ever learned whether it was the result of inexperience or gross dim-wittedness. At any rate, there was the caravan, blacked out to be sure, but heading into a Marine ambush just as the tanks on the outskirts of Inchon had done.

Companies E, D and F of Lieltenant Colonel Alan Sutter's 2nd Battalion (of Puller's 1st Marines) were straddled across that road a shade over two miles from the edge of Yong Dong Po. Luck—which had been with the American forces all the way from the first concept of the Inchon-Seoul campaign—had now accumulated in such large amounts that it seemed to be earning interest, and a series of events during the day had caused Sutter to set up an almost perfect ambush position without knowing he'd be able to put it to good use. The Marines, it will be remembered, had been given the area north of the highway. During the day, the Army men of the 32nd Infantry were to make the advance south of the highway. But through a foul-up in communications, the Army units hadn't yet come quite that far, and at nightfall, Sutter, in order to protect his right flank, took the liberty of stringing Companies D and F forward on the high ground on the Army's side of the road, so that they paralleled and commanded the road for a good five hundred yards.

Into this trap came the North Korean column. The Marines on the heights heard the snarling of the tank engines —surprisingly like airplane engines—and the clanking of the treads as the vehicles approached. They let them pass down the 500-yard stretch, with the men of Companies D and F quietly watching them and holding their fire. E-Company was on the north side of the road and a little to the rear.

When the tanks came abreast of E-Company's position, a Marine private manning a machine-gun outpost rose and challenged the ammunition truck in the lead. The ambush had been hastily arranged—a matter of minutes, really—and it is possible that the young machine gunner was not aware of all the details. His challenge was answered by machine-gun fire and he was killed. Immediately the Marines began to pour fire into the enemy column, and their tanks and infantrymen began to return it.

It was a wild battle, and the North Koreans milled about on the road in panic as they were slaughtered. Minutes after its onset, the ammunition truck in the lead blew up with an immense burst of flame that became a huge orange ball with black smoke peeling from its surface like charred rind, with streamers shooting up and out from it like rockets in a fireworks display.

The tanks, buttoned up, were scuttling back and forth, seeking escape. In the heat of things, a Pfc. from F-Company ran down the hill while his comrades covered him with their fire, and coolly aimed his rocket launcher at the lead tank at short range. His projectile wrecked it. With bullets cutting the air all about him, he calmly swung the 3.5 inch bazooka at a second tank and destroyed it. He was aiming at a third tank when he was killed by machine-gun fire.

The fight lasted until dawn. Two tanks were destroyed, and a third was captured with its crew. All the trucks were burned. Three hundred enemy soldiers were killed and their bodies littered the road at daybreak.

NOTES   *Chapter 12*

1. Private Beck's name in some systems of writing Korean sounds in English is spelled "Paek"; he prefers "Beck" under the system generally used by the Republic of Korea Marine Corps. Interview author—MSgt Kong Jin Beck, R. O. K. Marines.
2. Letter Almond to author, 10 Apr 67.
3. Interview author—Almond.
4. Interview author—Jae Duk Hahn.

5. UP Dispatch, *Pacific Stars and Stripes*, 15 Sept 50.
6. Later intelligence reports gave the exact composition of the Kimpo defending force, revealing its motley character: One air division Hq unit; two engineering companies; one gunnery platoon; the 2nd Battalion of the 1st Regiment; a company of the 1st Battalion, 1st Regiment; one finance company; one supply company; the administrative 877th Air Force Unit and a few troops from both the 226th and 107th Regiment. Even as Big. Gen. Wan Yong tried to muster these troops for a counterattack, scores of them were slipping away and changing to civilian clothes. *1st Marine Division Special Action Reports,* Intelligence Annex, Hq USMC G-3 Historical Section.
7. Interview author—Jaskilka.
8. Joe Maize, in later action in North Korea, received and recovered from an even more serious wound. Shrapnel went through his helmet, making a virtual sieve of it. After a series of delicate brain operations Joe was returned to limited active duty. A photo of his shattered helmet on a stake illustrates a widely distributed Marine and Army training poster that says, "The man who wore this helmet lived—wear yours." Interview author—Maize.

13

"I'll give you that permission . . . .
Just take that town."

IN THE CROWDED BASEMENT OF THE OPERATIONS BUILDING at Kimp Airfield, Navy Lieutenant Hedge Underwood sat on an ammunition box in a far corner and tried to listen carefully as Lieutenant Colonel Ray Murray, pointing to a rather small and inadequate map on the wall, conducted a briefing for the advance party that was to cross the Han River as soon as it became dark on the evening of September 19. Underwood was one of the fourteen men in this scouting force and, as an interpreter, he was considered a valuable addition, for Murray hoped that prisoners or the people of the small village across the river might provide more information about the disposition of enemy forces on the north bank.

Information so far was sketchy. Marine General Eddie Craig had made a personal reconnaissance by helicopter of the area north of the river, had seen no troops, and had not been fired upon. But this was not necessarily a meaningful report; his reconnaissance had been incomplete, and he knew, as did everyone else, how adept the North Koreans could be at camouflage.

Murray did not anticipate serious trouble in crossing the river, but he was taking certain normal precautions in sending out an advance party under the cover of darkness. He was being pressed to get across the Han as quickly as possible, and there was no time to set up the usual alternate plan in case something went awry with this one; he therefore decided to put the fourteen men across first and let them establish observation posts that could give warning if any large numbers of the enemy approached while the main party was following in their amphibious tractors.

Now that Kimpo was taken—and the first planes from
Japan were already landing and taking off there—Murray's
command post had become a converging point for the press,
and there were times when the Marines thought they saw
more correspondents than infantrymen. Murray didn't see the
river crossing as an especially noteworthy operation, but the
drama of fourteen men swimming across in advance appealed
to the reporters, and most of them not only wanted stories
on it, but tried to get permission to go along. It was, of
course, too dangerous a mission to send untrained men along,
even though some of the correspondents were ex-Marines.
So it was agreed that a Navy public information officer, Ensign Judah Siegel, would accompany the team with a portable
tape recorder and try to get some material for the press.

Ex-missionary Underwood wasn't sure that this nighttime
sortie across the river would be as routine as the colonel believed. Earlier that day he had jeeped out from the airport
to a hamlet at the south bank where some people recognized
him from his missionary days. They reported no enemy soldiers in the vicinity of their own village, but said that there
were about two hundred North Koreans at a place called
Neung Gok on the other side of the river only a few miles
from the crossing point. Underwood wished Colonel Murray
would cross right away, but that, of course, was impossible;
the advance party had to be chosen and formed and the
Amtracs had to be brought up to cary the main force in after
them. Besides, Murray wanted to make a night crossing, which
would have the added advantage of surprising the enemy in
the morning.

Hedge Underwood had a certain romantic interest in this
crossing of the Han, which he didn't bother to mention to the
busy regimental commander. At almost this same spot, in
June of 1952, Japanese forces under the great general Hide-
yoshi had effected a crossing that resulted in the fall of Seoul.
On that occasion the Japanese had seen waterfowl peacefully
swimming on the north bank, judged from this that no hostile
forces were about, and had made the trip successfully. There
was another special meaning for Underwood in this operation. Once they traversed the river and swung east, toward
Seoul, they would be only miles from Underwood's lovely
colonial brick home in the hills west of the city.

The swimming team was chosen, and Captain Kenneth J.
Houghton, who commanded the 5th Regiment's Reconnaissance Company, was put in charge of it. His second in com-

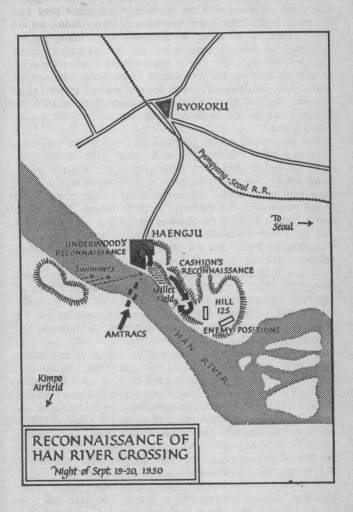

RECONNAISSANCE OF
HAN RIVER CROSSING
Night of Sept. 19-20, 1950

mand would be Second Lieutenant Dana M. Cashion, who had already taken part in night raids on the coast and was rapidly becoming enough of a veteran to impress various crusty old sergeants with his worth and prowess. There was one such NCO among the ten enlisted men, Gunnery Sergeant Ernest L. De Fazio, a tough Marine whose prime interest was in doing a combat job without asking too many questions or worrying about the whys and wherefores of strategy or politics. He was willing to go along with second lieutenants—you couldn't break down the whole system, after all—but Cashion was "in all due respects," as he said, "a young, green second lieutenant who was awed by the events taking place."[1]

The plan called for the fourteen men to wait for darkness, bring two small rubber boats to the river bank for carrying arms and other gear, then swim across, pushing the boats. They would also take with them a portable SCR-300 backpack field radio, and if all seemed clear on the north bank, would radio back for the main force to follow. There were two principal areas to be checked on the the other side; one was the rather formidable Hill 125 which lay to the left of their landing point, and the other the village of Haengju on whose waterfront they would come ashore.

Major General Frank Lowe, President Truman's representative, was much intrigued with the plan. Since his arrival at Murray's headquarters at Kimpo Airfield he had generally kept out of everyone's hair, giving the impression of being a quiet, pleasant and sensible man. But now, as darkness approached, an ember of adventurousness apparently flared in the sixty-six-year old gentleman, and he walked up to Captain Houghton and said he'd like to swim the river, too. Houghton reacted with surprise, then fixed his eyes upon the major general's and said flatly, "No!" Lowe began to argue—he was perfectly fit; he'd had combat experience—but Houghton answered that only a direct order from Major General Oliver Smith would persuade him to take Lowe along. Lowe sighed and went back to headquarters to find General Smith. Houghton smiled to himself; he was sure the old man wouldn't be able to contact the division commander in time.[2]

At 7:55 P.M. the fourteen swimmers trudged down to the Han and inflated the two rubber boats. The river was four hundred yards wide here and had a rather swift current. Houghton picked a starting point that would allow them to drift toward the desired stretch of shore, which was just a little to the right of the village. It was moonless and quite dark. Not a sound came from across the river. Behind them, back near the airfield, howitzers stood in place, ready to shell the village and the shore area around it.

At 8:00 P.M., the Marines slipped into the water and started swimming stripped to their underwear, two wearing the only foot fins that had been found, but finding them of little use since they had to adjust their pace to the slow and silent breaststrokes of the others. Ensign Siegel glanced anxiously from time to time at the plastic boat that held his portable tape recorder. Hedge Underwood peered at the shore ahead and worried a little, wondering if the North Koreans hadn't had time to move some troops into the village since that morning, or even worse, into positions on the long 400-foot hill on the right. Second Lieutenant Cashion swam along, quietly aware that this was not his first combat action and pleased to feel competent and in control of himself. Gunnery Sergeant De Fazio breaststroked his way with no particular thoughts other than to carry out his orders and hope that the second lieutenants and junior Navy officers would not cause any undue complications. Captain Houghton, in a mild way, was enjoying the drama of the thing. Although only fourteen men[3] and two inflatable boats were involved, to him it was another Marine landing in the tradition of Tripoli and all the rest.

The Marine artillery behind them began to send shells into the village. In a moment houses and shacks were burning, and they could see occasional moving figures silhouetted against the red light, but could not determine whether they were soldiers or civilians. Captain Houghton was fairly sure they were not troops, for late that afternoon he and Lieutenant Colonel Lawrence C. Hays, Jr., the regimental executive officer, had peered for two hours at the village and at Hill 125 without detecting the slightest indication of enemy activity. Hedge Underwood still worried a bit, but kept telling himself that the Marines probably knew what they were doing.

Kimpo Airfield was about three miles south of the river at the crossing point. Just before slipping into the water, Houghton radioed back to the executive officer of the Recon Company, 1st Lieutenant Ralph V. Crossman, that his party was on the way. Crossman then signaled for the Amtracs to start toward the river with the main advance group—three recon platoons and one of engineers—who would mine roadblocks once the beachhead was established. Crossman also had a few reservations in his mind about the operation. It was another of these hasty things, and he had received only the briefest of explanations and oral orders, at the Kimpo command post, with no overlay for his maps to show the precise routes desired. His force was crossing a river in darkness from an embarkation point they had never seen, and once on the other side, would seize three hills that hadn't been properly reconnoitered and whose features were known only by the indications on relatively small and possibly inaccurate maps.

Forty minutes after entering the water, the small party reached the other side. They scrambled ashore cautiously and several men dragged the plastic boats onto the beach. From these the raiders quickly took their weapons and some sketchy clothes to slip over their underwear. Parts of the village were burning rather brightly, but the shore dropped sharply about fifty feet from the water's edge, making an embankment one or two feet high, and this ground, with weeds and rough foliage upon it, offered concealement.

Captain Houghton immediately sent Lieutenant Cashion and three enlisted men inland and to the right to scout Hill 125. Ensign Siegel crouched at the embankment with his tape recorder, and in low tones, began to give a running account of what was going on. Houghton told Underwood to take a few men and make his way—cautiously, of course—into the village where he might find natives who would give him information as to the whereabouts of the enemy.

Just as Underwood was ready to proceed forward at a crouch, someone touched Houghton's arm and pointed to the figures of two men coming up the road a few yards inland from the direction of Seoul, their figures visible in the flickering light of the fires. Houghton signaled Sergeant De Fazio and a corporal named Anderson forward to the ditch along the road. They huddled there for a moment, and as the Korean men drew abreast, jumped out and pinned their arms down.

One prisoner, rather understandably, began to struggle and De Fazio started to punch him. The Koreans wore civilian clothes and looked harmless to Hedge Underwood, who jumped forward and somewhat sharply told the sergeant to stop. He questioned them in Korean as they were herded down toward the riverbank. They were nondescript, apparently uneducated men perhaps in their middle forties, and they told Underwood that they were fleeing Seoul. In the capital, they said, there was much apprehension, and everybody realized that before long there might be bitter fighting in its streets. They further said they knew nothing about the village of Haengju, toward which they'd been heading, and were fleeing more or less blindly with the major intention of getting as far away from Seoul as possible.[4] Their stories rang true to Underwood, but Houghton could not afford to believe them or assume that they were harmless civilians, and he ordered them held there at the beach until the reconnaissance was completed and they could be questioned more thoroughly.

Underwood took his men and went off toward the village. Houghton remained at the beach where De Fazio and several other men kept guard over the prisoners.

As they approached the village, Underwood and his men thought they heard some low whistling and what sounded like rustling in the bushes off to the side of the houses at an indeterminate distance. The sound was faint and hard to identify, and they were not even sure they had actually heard it at all. They decided it must have been normal night sounds and moved on until they reached the village, and began moving carefully through its streets. There were no people about, but Underwood hadn't expected any after the bombardment. Yet all along he had the strange, unexplicable feeling that they were not alone in the village, and that the enemy was somewhere nearby. Underwood returned to the riverbank.

At the beach it was still quiet. Captain Houghton watched as several men scouted the immediate area, finding nothing. It seemed to him that everything was clear and that it was time to bring the rest of the Recon Company over in the Amtracs. He sent a message back from the portable radio: "The Marines have landed and the situation is well in hand" —the classic words of a Marine amphibious success. On the road with his crawling Amtracs, Lieutenant Crossman received the message, but was still an hour away from the riverbank and sent a reply to this effect.

When the nine Amtracs reached the opposite shore almost an hour later, young Lieutenant Cashion was atop Hill 125. It was a long hill and he had not yet explored the entire crest. Suddenly, as though with a great single crash, enemy rifle, machine-gun and mortar fire erupted all around him from concealed positions. He was in the midst of an enemy force no one had known was there. The enemy was firing across the river at the Amtracs, and Marine artillery further back began to lob 4.2-inch shells in return. Their fire should have been directed by forward observers with the Amtrac party, but at this moment communications became fouled up. It was afterward thought that the Amtrac radios somehow interfered with the portable SCR-300's. The artillery fire began to fall wild, some of it exploding dangerously near Houghton and his men on the beach.

Cashion and three men ran back down the hill, passing a couple of blazing huts on the way and realizing that they were probably outlined against them. They came upon a small depression and dove into it for a momentary respite and a chance to sum up their situation. Cashion looked about and realized that one of his men, Pfc. Alphonse O. Ledet, Jr., was missing. A sergeant told Cashion Ledet had fallen near the blazing huts and he was sure he was dead. In Cashion's opinion there was no way humanly possible to cross the lighted area and look for Ledet's body, so he ordered that they continue the withdrawal, avoiding the river bank where the shells were falling and proceeding through a grain field back to Houghton's small command post.[5]

Houghton, Underwood, De Fazio and the other men at the riverbank were ducking fire both from the enemy and their own artillery across the river. In all the din, Underwood didn't hear the shots that killed their two Korean prisoners. Afterward, nobody could seem to establish exactly who had killed them. Two men were guarding them, one of them Sergeant De Fazio. According to his testimony, ". . . when our mortars started to land they tried to get away and one lunged at Captain Houghton and they both were killed."[6] Minutes later Hedge Underwood worked his way back to the spot and heard one of the several Marines there—he never remembered which one—say, "Well, I fixed those bastards." He still believed they were innocent civilians.[7]

Looking back across the river, Captain Houghton could see that the Amtracs were not exactly navigating with precision and that four had drifted too far to the right and were aground on the mud, their engines snarling and their treads spinning. They were, of course, sitting ducks for enemy fire. Houghton decided to swim back and guide the Amtracs into the proper spot.

Moments later, Second Lieutenant Cashion and his three men gained the beach and learned that Houghton had gone, taking Corporal James Morgan with him. This seemed to put Cashion, as the next ranking Marine officer, in command. By now all the members of the swimming party, minus Ledet, the captain and the corporal with him, were assembled on the beach. They were receiving light but steady fire from a position about two hundreds yards to the right and a hundred yards inland, near one of the burning huts. Cashion could hear the bullets cutting through the stalks of the grain field he had just crossed. He got on the SCR-300 radio and called back to the artillery, requesting mortar fire on that spot and giving the burning hut as a reference.

The rounds began to fall short. Several exploded near the beach and some out in the river where Captain Houghton was swimming toward the grounded Amtracs. One of the bursts exploded so near him that he was dazed and his back sprained by the concussion. Corporal Morgan swam up to him and somehow dragged him to the grounded vehicle where they both clambered aboard to discover that the men in it had already abandoned it to swim and wade back to the south bank.

At the beachhead, Lieutenant Cashion directed a withdrawal, a sound order that nevertheless rubbed Gunnery Sergeant De Fazio the wrong way; he just didn't like to see Marines withdraw under any circumstances. He also ordered everyone to destroy their equipment and field-strip and sink their carbines in the river to keep them from falling into enemy hands. This was an especially disappointing order to Ensign Siegel who had been putting, as he thought, deathless sounds and description on his tape recorder; instead of de-destroying the machine he hid it in the bushes.

The eleven remaining men of the team swam back through the exploding bursts in the river. On the other side, eight men immediately started down the bank in search of Captain Houghton and finally found him lying in the Amtrac. Cashion went back to Kimpo to make his report to the intelligence officer. At the command post, Colonel Murray heard everyone's account, finding Ensign Siegel's excited report of his first combat action almost incoherent, and finally ordered that a full assault crossing be made in the morning. Both he and General Craig, who was also present, were a bit embarassed at the failure of the operation. It looked bad, they believed, for the Marines, after the impossible storming of Inchon, to be stopped cold by a mere four hundred yards of river.[8]

The regimental commander wasn't the only Marine who felt the sting of this small failure, and afterwards recriminations flew back and forth among the men who had taken part in the crossing. Houghton was criticized by some of the men under him for leaving the beach to swim to the

Amtracs, although it had taken courage enough to paddle out among all those bursting shells. De Fazio was so incensed by the order to withdraw that afterwards he refused to state who had given it, feeling he would be tattling to do so.[9] No one ever did discover who ordered the Amtracs to turn back, and the best that could be assumed was that it had been a spontaneous movement. Practically everyone in the Recon Company believed it had been unwise to plan the crossing when there were some indications—like Underwood's report—of an enemy build-up in the area. Murray himself felt he had been pushed into the venture by the higher command's impatience to get the attack on Seoul rolling.[10]

But the strange part about the whole affair was that its results were salubrious, for the attackers had discovered that approximately a battalion of North Koreans lay in wait on Hill 125, a force that would have badly mauled the 126 men of the Recon Company if they had carried out the landing. Now Murray could do the job properly in the morning.

Shortly before dawn, the Marine artillery again began to pound the area on the north bank of the Han. This time they were joined by naval gunfire from the *Rochester* and *Toledo*, whose guns, as Admiral Struble put it, were "up against the stops," but at this long range the naval shelling was inaccurate, and most of the missiles fell in sand bars northwest of the target.

The bothersome Hill 125 was thus not at all softened and when the first Amtracs, carrying troops of the 3rd Battalion in waves of two to six vehicles, began to cross, accurate fire slammed into them from the other side. The enemy was, of course, thoroughly alerted by now, and during the night had been able to bring up additional men and armament. In addition to the machine-gun and small-arms fire, they were potting at the Amtracs with 14.5-mm antitank projectiles. The troops huddled behind the armor plate of the amphibious vehicles. A few men were wounded but none killed on the way over. When the first wave landed at 0650, however, the crossfire from the hill began to take casualties.

From there on in it was a successful but not easy battle. The Amtracs, after taking the Marines across, remained on the beach and covered the advance with their .50-caliber machine guns. Four Corsairs strafed and bombed the enemy position on Hill 125. Two platoons of Item Company—which had just joined the battalion at Pusan and was full of men with no combat experience, made a two-pronged attack

on the hill, got halfway up, were stopped, drew back to re-
assemble, then gained the crest on their second try.

Ensign Siegel came along presently after most of the firing
had died down to retrieve his precious tape recorder. He
found it in bushes at the bank where he had left it and
eagerly listened to the playback. Something had gone wrong;
there was nothing but unintelligible noise. That, as far as Ensign Siegel was concerned, made the entire operation *really*
a total loss.

As the green I-Company of the 3rd Battalion assaulted Hill
125, Marine General Lem Shepherd and Admiral Struble
watched the action through binoculars from the south bank
of the Han.

Everybody in the world seemed to have descended upon
Lieutenant Colonel Murray's headquarters at Kimpo Airfield.
By now all manner of planes and helicopters were arriving
and departing and General MacArthur himself was around
somewhere with his retinue, getting ready for a final quick
tour of the front before his return by air to Tokyo.

Murray was busy with his complex plans to change the Han
crossing operation from an administrative to an assault landing, and the throng of visitors and correspondents in the
room didn't make things any easier. He was finally forced to
rap for everybody's attention and say, as diplomatically as
he could, "Gentlemen, I would appreciate it very much if
you would leave." Some press and historical reports depicted
this as an angry encounter, but it seemed to Murray that
everyone understood and did leave quietly, without fuss or
argument.[11]

General Almond was still hopping about, taking sharp,
personal looks wherever a battle was forming or taking place,
and after watching the assault crossing at the Han he jotted
in his personal notes: *"The Marines advanced aggressively
against the enemy but it was noted that they utilized neither
artillery nor mortar support."*

Almond had left the *Mt. McKinley* at 0300 that morning
to watch the dawn attack across the river; at about 0800 he
rushed back across Kimpo Airfield and eastward to Chesty
Puller's command post on a hill overlooking Yong Dong Po.
The town was well fortified by now and from its smoke-
covered concealment, North Korean tanks and artillery were
pouring steady, heavy fire at the Marine forces drawn up on
its outskirts. The previous night, it will be remembered, Ma-

rines had withdrawn from two hills on the left flank near the river, because they were too far forward of the main line. The Communists had reoccupied these hills and set up tough defensive positions. Puller's 1st Battalion moved out to attack them again. While this was taking place, Puller kept his 3rd Battalion firm on Lookout Hill in the center, and sent the 2nd Battalion forward as a right-hand prong, mainly to take two important bridges on the road in the southern part of the town. He thus spent the day maneuvering his regiment into a position rather like a tightly drawn slingshot aimed at Yong Dong Po.

Almond found Puller by a jeep in a field atop the hill, puffing his stubby pipe, consulting sketchy maps, some of which he kept stuffed in his pockets, and glaring belligerently toward the stubborn town. The sound of artillery and small-arms fire was all about, and while no shells or bullets were falling near the command post, it semed likely that they might at any time.

The Marines were returning the heavy fire from the city with everything they had or could call upon in the way of missiles. Planes and howitzers hammered at the town. A 4.5-inch rocket battery was brought up, but it lacked the proper fuses, could not make its test missiles explode, and finally withdrew. Marine tanks took the heights and acted as artillery to shell the city.

Puller, as Ned Almond stood beside him, took his pipe from his mouth and pointed to the city. "There's one way to flush 'em out, General. This town ought to be burned."

"Then why don't you go ahead and do it?" asked Almond.

"Need permission," Puller grunted. "Been tryin' to contact General Smith and get it."

"I'll give you that permission," said Almond. "You go ahead and do what you think it best. Just take that town."[12]

There were delicate overtones to the matter. Almond was, of course, the Commanding General of X-Corps, which had been set up to maneuver its main components, Smith's Marine division and Barr's Army division, and thus it was his right to call the shots anywhere on the entire front. But Almond's X-Corps command post was still aboard the *Mt. McKinley* and wouldn't be moved ashore to Inchon until the next day when, in an official ceremony, Admiral Struble would turn over to Almond the command of the inland phase of the invasion. General Smith might well feel that General Almond was interfering with his phase of the operation.

But Yong Dong Po had to be taken as soon as possible, and so Puller went ahead and called for napalm strikes by the planes.

General Oliver Smith, as a matter of fact, had bigger things on his mind at this moment. He was in a caravan of jeeps with General Shepherd, Admiral Struble, a host of reporters and General MacArthur himself, touring along the Yong Dong Po front. MacArthur wanted one final look at things before taking his plane from Kimpo Airfield back to Tokyo the next day. This was General Smith's zone, and he was responsible for the safety of the Supreme Commander. He watched with his emotions tightly controlled as MacArthur, at one point, stepped from his jeep and strolled along the tiny dike of a rice paddy within sight of a small unit of Marines flushing out snipers on a hill.

He was only partially relieved when MacArthur's caravan, moving south, got onto the Inchon-Seoul highway and thus passed from his area of responsibility into General Barr's territory. Barr was well ashore by now, after some grumbling delay back at Inchon during which he felt the Marines were taking all the small boats needed to land his Army regiments. The spare general, with his Spartan habits and somewhat rural air, still felt a bit left out of things, since MacArthur seemed to be devoting all his attention to the Marines, and he still could not forget how he had been called in at the last moment to take part in the campaign, as thought it had all been an afterthought. He, too, was wandering in the front line area that day, and he ran into MacArthur on the road, conferred briefly, but still felt hurt that the Supreme Commander seemed to be visiting every command post but his own.[13]

With his regiment drawn up just outside of Yong Dong Po, Colonel Chesty Puller was facing the first really stiff resistance the North Koreans had offered in the defense of Seoul, and to the north, across the Han River, Lieutenant Colonel Murray was about to run into a similar stand in the bastionlike hills that ringed the capital. From this moment on there would be no more swift advances, only bloody fights up hills, across rivers and into towns.

All day on the 20th of September, Puller directed his battalions in the attack on Yong Dong Po, and his battalion commanders maneuvered their companies in a series of strikes on hills, at bridges, and along various roads. Whenever a squad or platoon took a forward position, others had to move into the areas nearby to flush out snipers or capture strong points that had been bypassed. The front, like a slowly moving squall line, was not a neatly scored line of demarcation, but rather a turbulent area in which all manner of movements and skirmishes were going on simultaneously. The heaviest fire still came from the city itself, but increasing numbers of North Koreans were moving out to meet and engage the Marines in the jumbled hills and draws of the outskirts.

On the far left, near the river, it took troops of the 1st Battalion all day and a complicated series of attacks to regain the two strategic hills that had been abandoned the night before. Among those killed was Second Lieutenant John N. Guild, who led a platoon toward the crest of Hill 85, was struck by machine-gun fire, but miraculously stayed on his feet long enough to wave his detachment forward, tell the company commander how his squads were deployed, and urge that the attack be pressed.

Puller's front extended almost four miles from the river down to the Inchon-Seoul highway. Here, on the far right, the 2nd Battalion moved forward after ambushing the tanks and the ammunition truck just before dawn. Between Puller's line and the city ran the natural defensive moat of the Kalchon River. The 2nd Battalion moved through scattered resistance down the road to the banks of this river and found the long concrete bridge there damaged but apparently still strong enough to support the M-26 tanks which would come along the next day for the attack on the city itself.

Lieutenant Colonel Alan Sutter, the 2nd Battalion commander, dug in at the bridge to await the tanks. Ahead was 2,000 yards of road leading into the town, and at its edge, another bridge. Just south of this road ran a long, high ridge and both North Koreans and their positions could be seen through the binoculars along this eminence. He knew that when he started advancing along the road the next day, the enemy would be able to pour a murderous flanking fire into his column, so he decided the hill ought to be shelled. This hill, however, being south of the road, was in the zone of the Army's 32nd Infantry Regiment, the advance element of Barr's 7th Division, and Sutter needed the Army's permission before a barrage could be laid upon it. This was not a matter of bureaucratic prerogative; it might well happen that Army troops would run into the barrage if the whole business wasn't coordinated. Sutter had little trouble making radio contact with the Army battalion commander across the road, Lieutenant Colonel Charles M. Mount, and Mount was all for shelling the ridge, but the request had to go up to higher headquarters, move across from the Army to the Marines, and then filter down to Sutter again before the action could be carried out. Mount said fine at 1300. It was seven hours before the approval came back. By then it was too dark to do any effective shelling.

The 20th of September was a transition period in which a number of important actions took place, putting the American forces into position for what was to be the final assault on Seoul. Until this point, it had been primarily a Marine show. Things simmered down momentarily on all fronts during the night of the 20th.

Puller had cleared the territory before him for his jump into Yong Dong Po. Murray was across the river and flexing his force to storm the hills between himself and Seoul. The Army men of the 32nd Regiment had driven forward in two prongs far to the south of the Inchon-Seoul highway, and in a bloody battle for two heights known as Tongdok Mountain and Copper Mine Hill, lost three tanks to the cheap but effective wooden land mines of the North Koreans. They were now almost to the main highway that ran south from Seoul— the principal supply line to the enemy's Perimeter forces, and the same road down which Ambassador Muccio had fled at the outbreak of war a little over two months and two weeks ago.

The seven hours needed by Sutter's Marine battalion to call in a barrage illustrated the need for central direction of the campaign, and so, at 0900 on the morning of the 21st, General Almond moved his X-Corps command post from the *Mt. McKinley* into the city of Inchon. He at once visited General Barr's command post, heard a complaint about a shortage of motor transport, ordered that it be rectified, and then told Barr to send a raider group ahead into the southern sector and make a reconnaissance in force near Suwon.

In the early afternoon, Almond hopped over to General Smith's 1st Marine Division command post, heard that the regiment of R. O. K. Marines beyond Kimpo Airfield was being heavily attacked, and approved a request of Smith's for a raider group to reinforce them. Here he heard reports that along the Inchon-Seoul highway, Marine and Army troops were accidentally firing on each other across the boundary; he had a staff officer phone back to X-Corps immediately to straighten out the situation. He was in control now; the whole thing felt tighter and more responsive.

Minutes later, he was at Kimpo Airfield to watch General MacArthur leave for Tokyo. MacArthur at planeside looked young, erect, full of the tonic of victory. He pinned a silver star on General Smith, and said, "To the gallant commander of a gallant division!" As his plane, the new four-engined SCAP, lifted from the runway at 3:35 P.M., Almond was already rushing from the strip to return to his command post in Inchon.

There was a 5:00 P.M. ceremony awaiting Ned Almond in the schoolyard that was the nerve center of X-Corps. Admiral Struble had heartily agreed that a brief ceremony in which command of the landed forces would be formally turned over from himself to Almond would make relationships and responsibilities clear; a few officers and correspondents were present as orders were read and an American flag hoisted. Struble, who had done away with such refinements as sideboys in his flagship, felt that this was war and anything elaborate would be out of place.[14] He shook hands with Almond and went back to the *Rochester*. The Inchon-Seoul operation was now officially a land campaign.

As Ned Almond, back in Inchon, was formally taking over the campaign late that afternoon of September 21, Chesty Puller, greatly frustrated, was bogged down in front of the city of Yong Dong Po. Within the city the Communists had rallied sufficiently to meet both of his thrusts from the left, up near the river, and from the right, where the Inchon-Seoul highway led into the southern part of the town.

From his hilltop command post, Chesty could stare across the broken terrain and into the heart of the city. As he scowled at everything and dug into his can of Prince Albert for his continuous pipe refills, he was mentally groping for an unorthodox answer to the assault.

As night fell, then, on the evening of the 21st, none of Puller's Marines were much nearer Yong Dong Po than they had been that morning. The town was a natural fortress if you approached it from the west. For two or three miles the terrain around it was covered with broken hills, mounds and draws. Just outside the town a small river, the Kalchon, came down from the Han River and formed a moat that extended far below the city and into the territory where the

Army's 32nd Infantry Regiment was advancing in an attempt to cut the road south of Seoul and Yong Dong Po. The moat was formidable enough, but on the other side of it and for almost its entire length ran a dike anywhere from six to ten feet high. It was a marvelous defensive position, and in the northern part of the town, up against the Han River, the Reds dug in upon it in reinforced strength. All day long infantry and artillery hammered at this position, making some slow advances at a cost of heavy casualties, but not taking any significant portions of the town. On the far right, at the southern edges of the town, Lieutenant Colonel Alan Sutter's 2nd Battalion had run into the difficulty he'd foreseen the day before—the fire from the enemy troops on the heights along. the road. Because of the administrative delay, he was unable to call down artillery fire upon them. He didn't wait for permission this time. His men were getting wounded and killed and it was not a moment for jurisdictional niceties; he had his own 4.2-inch mortars shell the heights, and then he sent two companies forward to attack them. Resistance was stiff. Sutter called in both tanks and aircraft to lay a barrage on the heights. The assault continued throughout the day—a barrage, a cautious advance by a squad or platoon, a small gain perhaps, then another barrage and another advance.

In the late morning, F-Company found itself pinned down by fire coming from a group of houses just outside the city. The defenders were enveloped in thick smoke and they couldn't see their targets. F-Company radioed back for an air strike, and at the battalion command post the request was taken by Forward Air Controller, First Lieutenant Norman Vining. At the moment he had no armed planes handy, but a group of four Corsairs, their guns and bomb racks empty, were on their way back to the carrier from another strike. Vining knew that North Koreans ducked for cover when they saw planes, and he asked these to make runs over the enemy positions even if they couldn't bomb or fire. The Corsairs made their swooping dummy runs and the enemy fire immediately fell off 75 per cent as F-Company advanced; before the air passes they had had thirty-seven casualties; after the attack they suffered very few.[15]

By late afternoon the 2nd Battalion was across the first bridge over the Kalchon, but still a good thousand yards from the city where another line of dikes and a second bridge had to be taken. Colonel Puller relieved Sutter's tired, hard-fighting men with his reserve battalion, the 3rd, and these fresh troops made some slow and difficult progress, but not a great deal. By the time it was dark, they had reached the second bridge. Sutter's battalion, instead of going all the way to the rear, stayed hard behind them along the Inchon-Seoul highway, and everybody dug trenches and foxholes for the night.

It was all a bit frustrating to Chesty Puller, who preferred smashing forward attacks to the beseiging of towns, and that evening, at least, as his regiment hung stalled before Yong Dong Po, he was ready to blame the high command—which really meant General Almond, though he would not criticize him by name—for allowing the huge gap to open between his right flank and the Army's 32nd Regiment, which had been given the territory south of the main highway. Actually, that gap had not been planned; it was just that the natural course of events caused the Army regiment to veer southward as they attacked and to head, as they'd been told, toward the main supply route to the Perimeter which ran south out of Yong Dong Po. Afterward, Puller admitted that this was a strategically sound move. At the moment, however, all he knew was that his right flank was not secure, and the fire from that direction was keeping his troops from advancing into the city.[16]

The 21st continued the period of transition. Ned Almond hadn't really begun to wield his X-Corps as a solid unit, and indeed, some of his time was being taken up by such ceremonious affairs as seeing MacArthur off at Kimpo. The coordination and communications between the Marines north of the highway and the Army south of it were admittedly bad, and it would be a good twenty-four hours before they got any better.

Now, as it happened, Puller had sent no particular pressure against the center of the line where the widest part of the stream and the highest dikes beyond it faced broken terrain unimproved by roads. This area therefore seemed the strongest stretch of wall in the entire fortress. Perhaps the North Korean commander inside the city gambled on this, or perhaps he simply didn't have enough troops to go around. At any rate, he was committing most of his forces to either flank where Puller's heaviest attacks were falling.

Lieutenant Colonel Jack Hawkins was using two companies of his 1st Battalion to attack Yong Dong Po along the banks of the Han River on the far left. He had his hands full with this, of course, but anchoring his own right flank was Company A, under Captain Robert Barrow.

Colonel Puller knew Barrow by sight, as he did all the company commanders in his regiment, but outside of assuming that he was a competent officer, he had no reason so far to take any special notice of the young captain. Barrow was as quiet and self-effacing as Chesty Puller was flamboyant. Although six feet four inches tall, he was the sort of man who stays unnoticed in a crowded briefing room, and a man who handled administrative details so smoothly that his excellence in this respect, too, had a way of going unnoticed. Much later, when Barrow, after several heroic performances, was taken out of combat in the midst of the war and given important staff duty back in the States, Puller grumbled: "They made a damned mail clerk out of him."[17]

Barrow was on a hill a good mile from the river and the center ramparts of the city. Hawkins decided to order him forward. There were several good reasons for this maneuver. First, it was wise to keep a little pressure on the enemy line even when you weren't attacking a specific area in the hope of penetration. Second, his left flank had advanced a bit, and Hawkins wanted to bring the right wing forward in line with it. Third, it would be valuable to know just how much resistance the enemy was offering at the western edge of the town. To accomplish these objectives meant a certain risk: Barrow's company would have to advance across a mile of open rice paddies and would be vulnerable to fire from the city, but it seemed to Hawkins that if their attack surprised the enemy and forced him to weaken his flanks, the risk was well worth the gain.

Barrow's A-Company moved out from their hill position in mid-morning. Barrow himself moved in the center of his formation, stooping as much as he could to keep his tall frame partly concealed by the grain stalks in the rice paddies. He was also advancing in a two-prong deployment: a platoon thrust forward on each side. Following along on the left was his reserve platoon, and on the right, in the rear, was a detachment of mortars, heavy machine guns and an assault squad—two hundred men all told.

It was strangely quiet where Barrow's men moved forward. They could hear the thick spattering of small arms up near the Han River where the regimental left was storming a dike, and down by the Inchon-Seoul highway where Sutter's battalion was trying to advance. Each of these prongs was roughly two miles away from them. There was also the heavy booming of air attack and artillery all along the front.

No one fired upon them as they advanced at a tense walk. Their longest delay came as they neared the river, where the mud in the rice paddies became so thick that they had to crawl through it. Suddenly they were at the stream and could see the dike beyond it, but still met no fire. Barrow peered hard at the dikes for several moments, then took a deep breath and swept his arm forward, his platoon leaders repeating the gesture. The first few men on the point, their hearts big in their throats, waded into the stream, walked and half-swam across with their rifles raised over their heads, and emerged on the far bank unscathed. Barrow signaled the others forward.

On the far bank of the river Barrow and his men came, dripping, out of the water and paused there to realign their formation. Everything was directed in low voices or by hand signals, and the relative silence added to the feeling of uneasiness—most of the Marines simply couldn't believe that the enemy had posted no defense here in the very center of his line. The men on the point scrambled across the dike and still nothing happened. The rest of the company followed.

The first houses of the town were only a hundred yards away. At this point, the city's main east-west street, joined the dike. There was not a sound, not a sign of motion. Far to the right and left the bombardment was still going on.

Barrow looped his arm forward again. The Marines moved cautiously, quickly checking doorways, windows and cul-de-sacs. The place was deserted. Barrow, in order to keep the search thorough, moved quite slowly, clearing a section or portion of a block, then sending another advance party forward under cover of those in the rear. He penetrated about three hundred yards into the town, and apparently not a North Korean in the world knew he was there. He called his backpack radio man forward and contacted Lieutenant Colonel Hawkins at his command post back near Lookout Hill. "I'm in the town and we can't find anybody. Looks like they're all busy up on the right and the left."

"Can you keep going?"

"I don't see why not."

"Keep going then."

"Roger, and out."

Barrow signaled the advance again. Marines in small groups went forward, hugging the structures on either side of

the wide main street, kicking doors open, keeping hand grenades, rifles and submachine guns ready to blast the interior
of any place that seemed to show resistance. There was not
so much as a stray cat on hand.

Barrow frowned at the map he'd been given. He saw that
if he went another half mile, the main Inchon-Seoul highway, slanting in from the south, would meet this main crosstown street. Far to his right, a little to the rear, and of course
out of sight, he could hear the furious spattering and booming of the fight as Sutter's 2nd Battalion, still outside the
town, fought to advance along that highway. He could
scarcely believe the golden opportunity shining right before
his eyes—it was possible that he could come up on the rear
of the force blocking Sutter's advance!

It was possible, but it was hardly the safest move in the
world. He was deep in enemy territory, and for all he knew,
surrounded by hostile forces. If he attacked the enemy on
the Inchon-Seoul highway, he himself might be attacked in
overwhelming numbers from almost any direction. And he
was now completely isolated, a floating company with no
supply line or easy route connecting him to the main force.
At this point, Captain Robert H. Barrow would have been
beyond criticism had he decided to withdraw from the town,
take up a better defensive position on its outskirts, and wait
for reinforcements there. Instead, he ordered his 3rd Platoon,
under First Lieutenant William McClelland, to the right and
toward the converging Inchon-Seoul highway.

McClelland's men, strung out in a cautious advance,
reached the edge of the highway. The move was so well
timed, it might have been rehearsed. No sooner had they
reached the highway than a large enemy column came marching down the street on its way to reinforce the detachments
holding Sutter's men in check. To make it even more bizarre,
the North Koreans were stepping along in spirited fashion,
singing a gay marching song.

McClelland's platoon allowed the column to come abreast
of them, go a little further, and then poured an utterly surprising and completely murderous fire into it. Scores of men
dropped, and those who did not scattered in confusion to the
other side of the highway. The column was literally blown
apart and, without a single casualty to the American platoon,
ceased to exist as a military force. McClelland left a few men
on the spot to mop up, and moved his platoon back up the
highway to meet the rest of the company. He could hear

firing from their direction now, and knew that they, too, were in action.

The main body had run into some North Korean troops at about the same moment McClelland opened up on the enemy column. They were rear-area soldiers in small groups, and for the most part, they broke and ran when fired upon. In some cases North Koreans who could be seen in the distance up side streets simply didn't recognize the Marines as the enemy and made no attempt to run when they saw them.

Barrow's company now reached the end of the main crosstown street. They had passed completely through the town, a distance of about 3,000 yards, and now they were at a point where three major roads—theirs included—came together sharply and ran up against the dike that bordered this opposite face of the city. Barrow immediately put his 3rd Platoon under Second Lieutenant John J. Swords atop this dike.

The could see Seoul, which lay across a wide sand flat and then the river; it was only about 3,500 yards away. There was an air landing strip on this sand flat that would later become a main supply airport for the capital. As they watched, a platoon or so of enemy soldiers started to withdraw from the city and cross the sand flat; they opened up with light machine guns and scattered this force.

The rest of Company A came up to the vital road junction, which Barrow now saw as the key to Yong Dong Po. They were receiving scattered fire from a number of directions, and each Marine was attempting to move as much as possible under cover. Only a couple of hundred yards away and a little beyond the intersection, was a mound about thirty feet high that seemed to be a huge coal pile. Some North Koreans were behind its crest, shooting. Barrow sent a squad foward to clear them out. The Marines advanced, crouching, covering each other and leapfrogging forward in the usual way and then one man threw a hand grenade.

Suddenly it seemed as though the entire city began to explode. From the mound came a series of violent explosions sending streamers and great clouds of black smoke into the air. It took Barrow only seconds to realize that this tiny hill was the camouflaged main ammunition dump for the defense of Yong Dong Po.

Back at the battalion command post, Lieutenant Colonel Hawkins had been worried about the location of his A-Company; the radios hadn't worked too well as they moved down that main street through the heart of the town, and as the afternoon drew to a close, he was hoping Barrow and his men weren't lost. He heard the big explosion as the ammunition dump was touched off and saw the black smoke billowing into the air. Then Barrow was on the radio. Did Hawkins see the smoke? He did. Well, that was where the company was now, holding the heart of Yong Dong Po and digging in for the night.

As darkness fell, the counterattack came. Barrow's company was strung all along the dike for about a hundred yards, deeply entrenched. Five T-34 tanks with snarling engines came along and cruised like a line of battleships along a parallel road only thirty yards from the dike, lobbing shells broadside into the Marine positions. Calmly the Marines aimed 3.5-inch rocket launchers from their holes, and on the first pass, blew one tank apart. The tanks made their parade five times altogether, two more were damaged, and then they withdrew. Their 85-mm. armor-piercing shells had exploded in the sand of the dike and the only casualty was one Marine knocked out by severe concussion.

In the darkness there was a two-hour rest as the dug-in Marines kept a careful watch on the city on one side, the big sand flat on the other. A little after 9:00 P.M., a large enemy infantry force came down from the north and struck at that end of the dike. Lieutenant Sword's platoon, holding the perimeter there, threw them back five times with relative ease.

There was only scattered firing on the isolated position throughout the rest of the night. Two hundred seventy-five dead Koreans were found scattered around the dike in the morning. By 8:00 A.M., September 22, the left and right prongs of Chesty Puller's 1st Marine Regiment entered the city of Yong Dong Po against virtually no resistance—for the enemy, his ranks decimated and his supplies destroyed, had fled during the night.

Now there would be another pause for everyone to catch his breath, for units to properly align again, and then the main assault on Seoul would be launched, with Ray Murray's 5th Regiment, already across the river, hitting it from the west, and Puller's 1st Regiment striking from the south.

But Puller's flank—which became his rear as he turned toward the capital—was still not completely secure. The main highway to the south, and eventually to the Perimeter, ran out of Yong Dong Po and toward Suwon and all those other points where the first tiny units thrown into the Korean War had originally tried so bravely and hopelessly to stem the enemy advance.

NOTES *Chapter 13*

1. Letter 1st Lt E. L. De Fazio to Canzona; Monograph and Comment File, Vol II, *Marine Operations in Korea,* Hq USMC Historical Section.
2. Interview Canzona—Maj K. J. Houghton. *Ibid.*
3. *Ibid.* Houghton gives the count as 13 men; most other sources say 14.
4. Interview author—Underwood.
5. Letter Cashion to author, 16 Nov 66. Sergeant De Fazio never was convinced that Lt. Cashion had made a proper reconnaissance and wrote later: "It was inconceivable to me that five men could roam the hill being infected with gooks without being seen. From my memory it seemed like that he was gone about 30 minutes the longest." Letter 1st Lt E. L. De Fazio to Canzona; Monograph and Comment File, Vol II, *Marine Operations in Korea,* Hq USMC Historical Section. (Pfc. Ledet was not dead but had stumbled and fallen during the flight. Rather than catch up with his companions, which meant running across the lighted terrain alone, he hid in a nearby shack that was not burning, where he was found the next morning.)
6. Letter 1st Lt E. L. De Fazio to Canzona; Monograph and Comment File, Vol II, *Marine Operations in Korea,* Hq USMC Historical Section.
7. Interview author—Underwood.
8. Interview author—Murray.
9. Letter 1st Lt E. L. De Fazio to Canzona; Monograph and Comment File, Vol II, *Marine Operations in Korea,* Hq USMC Historical Section.
10. Interview author—Murray.
11. *Ibid.*
12. The dialogue is approximate and reconstructed from interviews author—Almond, Puller.
13. Interview author—Barr.
14. Interview author—Struble.
15. Guisti, Ernest H., "Marine Air over Inchon-Seoul," *Marine Corps Gazette,* June 52.
16. Interview author—Puller.
17. *Ibid.*

"Go to hell, sir."

SECOND LIEUTENANT JESSE VAN SANT WAS WITH THE POINT of the Army division advancing across country four or five miles south of the fighting around the city of Yong Dong Po. He was proud to be in a forward position instead of following behind to hold areas others had already taken. He was aware, as all intelligent professional soldiers must be, of the paradoxes and dichotomies a man invites when he accepts combat and decides he actually likes the military life. He did not *really* enjoy killing or maiming other human beings but of course he would do it quickly enough, as an automatic reaction, when the time came. He did not *really* enjoy having the missiles of pain and death come close to his own person, but when it happened he would somehow endure them calmly and not permit his own effectiveness to be destroyed. The moments of absolute crisis in which you killed or got killed were only a small part of the time spent in a war, and if you got through them without flinching there was a great deal of satisfaction to be gained from the rest of it. The comradeship, the art and science of tactics, the opportunity to hold power over great machines such as tanks, all had a very masculine appeal, a little-boy appeal, you had to admit, and the deep thinkers might damn you for it, but when a threat to the country came, they were as anxious as anyone else to be protected by your skills.

Van Sant led the column through the quiet countryside. A fair-complexioned young man who looked not particularly formidable nor frightening even in his tanker's helmet, he was quietly secure in the knowledge that he was not new to combat and would be able to meet any trouble without panic. He felt, indeed, that he had more experience along this

line than some of the higher-ranking officers with the column.
He was a little uneasy about this and hoped they'd have the
good sense to call upon him for at least an educated opinion
or two if it became necessary.

This forward, inland movement far to the south of Seoul
was being carried out by only one regiment of General Barr's
7th Division, the 32nd Infantry Regiment, for his other regiment was still in the process of landing at Inchon. In General Almond's mind it was vitally important to secure the
southern approach to Seoul as quickly as possible, and there
wasn't time to wait for all the regiments to be neatly aligned
according to the book. So the 32nd was making a two-
pronged advance across the rough terrain on a broad front,
with the 2nd Battalion on the left, the 1st Battalion on the
right, and the 3rd Battalion coming along in reserve.

As we have noted before, there was some enemy resistance
on the 1st Battalion's line of march at two steep hills just
before they reached the highway running south out of Yong
Dong Po and Seoul. The column kept going, leaving enough
troops on the heights to hold them, and at about midday,
Jesse Van Sant and his platoon of five tanks were proceeding forward some distance behind the point, on a narrow
dirt road that wasn't even marked on most of the maps. With
Van Sant was another platoon of tanks taken from C-Company. Ahead of them were all the tanks of A-Company, 73rd
Tank Battalion, advancing in a road march, but with some
tanks thrown out on either flank and lumbering slowly across
the fields.

The column suddenly came to a halt. There were mines
up ahead, strung in a wide line across the direction of the
advance—the cheap, fifteen-pound wooden box mines the
North Koreans used so effectively, burying them only a few
inches in the dirt so that a person could walk across them
but the weight of a vehicle would set them off. Enemy troops
retreating from the fight at Copper Mountain a mile or so
back had perhaps sown these mines, or maybe they had been
there for several days as the result of some North Korean
commander's foresight. At any rate, they were thick across
the line of advance, and all of Company A's tanks, strung
abreast across the road, stopped short after two hit mines
and broke their tracks; everyone waited as enginers came
forward to find them and clear them out.

Perhaps fifty yards back, Lieutenant Van Sant stopped
his own tanks and stepped from the turret to stretch his

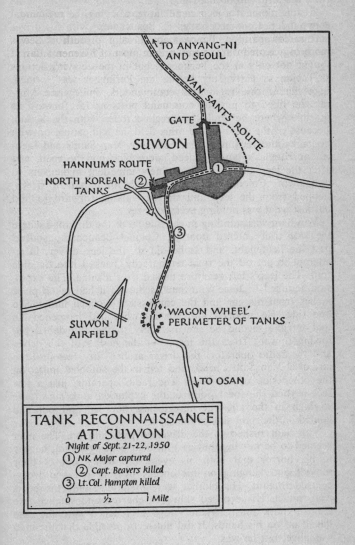

TO ANYANG-NI
AND SEOUL

VAN SANT'S ROUTE

GATE

SUWON

HANNUM'S ROUTE

NORTH KOREAN
TANKS

① ② ③

SUWON
AIRFIELD

'WAGON WHEEL'
PERIMETER OF TANKS

TO OSAN

**TANK RECONNAISSANCE
AT SUWON**
Night of Sept. 21-22, 1950
① NK Major captured
② Capt. Beavers killed
③ Lt.Col. Hampton killed

0   ½   1 Mile

legs. At this point there was a small side trail leading off from the dirt road on the right.

At this moment a jeep came along, carrying the regimental commander, Colonel Charles E. Beauchamp, with his driver and radio operator. Beauchamp, a calm professional, was more of a Korean War veteran than most of his men and had fought not only at the Perimeter, but in the delaying actions at Taejon in early July before the Perimeter was formed. Like the Marine regimental commanders, Puller and Murray, he liked to put his command posts as far forward as possible where he could be in close touch with the action. Because of the delay at the mine field, he had caught up with his tanks and reconnaissance company. Van Sant's and Lieutenant Hughes's tanks, indeed, were blocking the road, and after the jeep driver essayed a few impatient maneuvers to pass them, Colonel Beauchamp, with an impatient frown, stepped from the jeep and started walking forward to find out just what was holding everybody up.

Van Sant was standing in the middle of the dirt road where the side trail entered upon it. Colonel Beauchamp stalked past the lieutenant, and as he did so, the jeep driver, in an attempt to get off the road temporarily, backed into the side trail. The jeep's left rear tire passed over a mine. The explosion sounded to Jesse Van Sant as though it had taken place inches from his ear and the concussion knocked him far to one side. He realized immediately what had happened. In that terrible second he saw not only smoke and debris billowing upward from the jeep, but the bodies of the driver and the radio operator; the driver arched fifty feet into the air, over Van Sant's head, and fell in the stubbled millet on the other side of the road. The radio operator, just a few feet beyond the focal point of the explosion, didn't go quite so high in the air, but nevertheless flew up and out and landed on the right side of the road.

Van Sant rushed to the driver to pick him up. The man seemed to be moving, but as Van Sant bent over him, he saw to his horror that both his eyes were blown out of their sockets and hanging on his cheeks by tiny red and ivory-colored threads. His clothes were in tatters; only his boots were intact. His exposed skin was charred and smelled like a burnt pork roast. When Van Sant touched him, the skin flaked off on his hands. It did not seem possible that the man was alive, but he was.

"Shoot me," he said. "For God's sake, shoot me."

Van Sant muttered something he knew was inane: "You're okay. You're gonna be okay—" something like that.

"Just kill me. I can't stand it," said the burnt thing on the ground. "Look, tell my mother I'm okay, will you? Tell her I'm okay."

With help, Van Sant managed to carry the man to a litter jeep that arrived; he was still conscious and begging to be put out of his misery as he was loaded aboard, but within a few minutes he sank into a coma and Van Sant heard that he died shortly afterward. The radio operator, who had been thrown in another direction, had not been burned, but both his legs had been shattered below the knees and Van Sant also learned later that they were amputated.

It was not the first combat injury Jesse Van Sant had seen, but it was closer and more fearsome than most, and gave him a particular sense of anguish. He realized now that a professional soldier must not only be brave as far as his own safety was concerned, but learned to harden himself against shocking tableaux of the kind he'd just witnessed. Of the two requirements, he reflected, the second was the most difficult.

"All right . . . let's go . . . saddle up . . . move on. . . ."

The mine fields were cleared and there was war up ahead somewhere; the column had to push forward and find it. By late afternoon the first elements came upon the Seoul-Suwon highway. A tank platoon from Company A was in the lead and Van Sant and his tanks drew up on a small hill a little behind and on the flank just as this forward platoon ran into a small North Korean blocking position. With Van Sant was Captain Jack Dougherty, the Company A commander, and the two of them stood on the hill watching the engagement below as though from grandstand seats.

It seemed that the platoon leader on the narrow road below, Lieutenant John G. Hayes, had brought his tank right into the midst of about three dozen North Koreans who had set up entrenchments and breastworks at this part of the road. The North Koreans were swarming over the tank, evidently in an attempt to fire inside—North Koreans were nearly always short of grenades—and as they did so the platoon sergeant's tank pulled up a short distance behind and began to pick them off, its own bullets bouncing from Hayes's tank. It was a brief skirmish, and in a short time the enemy blocking force was completely routed and most of them slain.

Van Sant and Dougherty came forward to help, if they

could, and suddenly found Lieutenant Hayes wandering around his tank, staggering a bit, and yelling in hysterical fashion, "I'm hit! I'm hit!" From his expression he seemed to be in great pain, although the two other junior officers could see no wounds. Van Sant tried to ask him where he was hit, but evidently he was partly out of his mind with pain and couldn't answer the question..

They half led, half dragged Hayes to a medical tent, got him down on a folding cot and examined him closely, Van Sant paying particular attention to his head, as though he were looking for lice. He knew that serious head wounds sometimes went unnoticed. Meanwhile, they stripped his clothes and examined his entire body for injury.

"I don't see anything," said Dougherty. "Do you?"

"Hell, no," said Van Sant. "I think he's cracked up." Then he looked down and saw that the lieutenant's boots were still on. Just to be thorough he hastily unlaced and removed them. The wound was in his instep, with the bullet still lodged in the ball of his foot. Injuries were like the engagements in battles, thought Van Sant; no matter how much you'd seen of them, you could always come across the unpredictable reaction, and often the bizarre and unbelievable.[1]

It was September 21 when the Seoul-Suwon highway was reached; a few elements were even thrown across it to continue the advance. The prongs of the 1st and 2nd Battalions came together and made contact; there was, in effect, a line of advance along the highway. But this front was only between two and three miles wide and still some distance north of Suwon Airfield. The further it advanced eastward, the greater the danger that its right flank could be hit by North Korean units coming up from the south.

General Barr decided to do something about that situation. He had set up a command post in a tiny village some eight or ten miles to the northwest, and now, seeing how his elements were deployed, he ordered a reconnaissance party accompanied by tanks to go south toward Suwon and find out if the airfield could be taken. Information about the terrain and enemy order of battle in the area was so important that Barr also sent along the Division's assistant intelligence officer, Major Irwin A. Edwards, to make an estimate and to set up a forward intelligence post, if by some chance the airfield could be taken right away.

When the order came to go south, just before dark, the 7th

Division's Reconnaissance Company, commanded by First Lieutenant Miller, had occupied the small village of Angyangni, nearly ten miles north of Suwon and on the vital highway. Jesse Van Sant and his five tanks were also there, along with another tank platoon led by Lieutenant Billy D. Hughes. Van Sant had led the force into the town, a mess detachment had come along and prepared what struck him as a particularly fine lunch of steak, french fries, hot biscuits and peaches; he had fanned out his tanks into a defensive position, and new he was sitting pretty and enjoying the respite.

At about 4:00 P.M., Major Edwards, who had been talking to division headquarters over the radio, approached Van Sant and said, "Jesse, what do you think about going on to Suwon Airfield?"

Van Sant looked at his map and then at the sun. "It'll be dark in two hours, Major," he said. "If we expect to make it, we both better move out now. I want it to be still daylight when we get there."

Edwards smiled. "All right, if you've got the guts to go, I'll get the okay."

"I've got the guts," said Van Sant, "if we move now and get there before dark."

The major returned in fifteen minutes and said, "Let's go." Van Sant swept his arm in signal and the tanks began to clank forward, their engines snarling, the sharp odor of their exhaust fumes surrounding them.

All seemed quiet at first as the column moved rapidly down the road. The tanks were not buttoned up, but their crews were alert in their turrets as the foot soldiers fanned out on the flanks to guard against surprise. Not quite an hour later, Van Sant's lead tank rounded a bend in the road and in the first second or two all he saw ahead was a woman milking a cow in a field off to one side. In the next instant he saw hunched figures over several machine guns about twenty yards ahead and close to the road on either side. Van Sant gave arm signals to deploy, and called out quick directions by radio to the other tanks. The vehicles deployed into line in a heavy, clanking ballet movement and then everyone began to fire at the roadblock ahead, the 90-mm. guns and the .50- and .30-caliber machine guns making an unholy racket and throwing hundreds of pounds of hot metal at the North Korean position. A squad of engineers who were on Van Sant's tank took what individual cover they could find in the fields and directed small-arms fire on the roadblock.

As most of the engineers, led by a Master Sergeant Diaz, began to chase fleeing North Koreans, Van Sant suddenly noticed that one frightened young GI had taken refuge behind his tank's turret. Van Sant leaned out of the turret, grabbed the kid by the seat of the pants, eased him off the tank, and said, "Go get 'em!" The youngster was still wide-eyed, but at this he went forward and followed the others.

Van Sant was out of his turret by now. He happened to glance to his right. Fifteen or twenty feet away a North Korean in dirty khaki popped up from the stubbled plants along the side of the road and aimed a rifle at Van Sant. The lieutenant drew his .45 pistol from his shoulder holster and fired wildly with that essentially inaccurate weapon, sending seven rounds in quick succession at the enemy soldier. None of the pistol bullets found its mark—Van Sant hadn't really expected them to—but the fusillade evidently unnerved the North Korean, who dropped his rifle, threw his hands up in surrender, and then came down from the bank of the road and fell into place behind the tank.

It was no contest. The dozen or so enemy soldiers broke and ran from their machine guns and the tanks pushed forward again. Several dead North Koreans were sprawled in the field beside the road. Even further to one side, the Korean woman who had been milking was wringing her hands and wailing over her dead cow, which had somehow caught a bullet in the fight.

The column pushed on. By radio, Lieutenant Miller kept the command post back at Angyang-ni advised of its progress. Communications, he noticed, were becoming difficult the further south they moved from the village. Everything seemed clear after the roadblock. One of Van Sant's tank commanders radioed that his engine warning light was on red which meant it was heating up, and Van Sant radioed back, "Just keep going till it turns blue"—which of course it wouldn't.

Suddenly the ancient gray wall and the shapes of the buildings in the small city of Suwon were visible ahead. The column radioed back to Angyang-ni that it had almost reached its objective.

In a small commandeered schoolhouse in Angyang-ni, Lieutenant Colonel Henry Hampton was following the column's progress with much excitement as the radio reports came back. Hampton was General Barr's Division G-3, Plans and Operations, and was thus greatly concerned with overall strategy in the division's area. From the beginning he had regarded the taking of Suwon Airfield as one of the most important goals in the 7th Division's forward sweep south of Seoul, and when the advance troops reached the Seoul-Suwon highway, he had hurried down to that area to be in close touch with the action on the right flank.

Hampton was in his early forties and had struck Lieutenant Van Sant as "a kindly, graying, medium-height man . . . slightly over-weight, but not fat or obese," who gave him a feeling of "fatherly interest."[2] Hampton's immediate superior, General Dave Barr, saw him as "enthusiastic and excitable,"[3] so it was probable that Colonel Hampton showed two slightly different personalities in these two different relationships. He certainly seemed excitable as he radioed back to division headquarters. He was supposed to have returned there before nightfall, but now he didn't want to go back. The vital objective of Suwon was about to be taken far ahead of schedule by the Recon Company and the tanks, he reported, and he wanted to be on hand. Dave Barr frowned when he received Hampton's request and was going to deny it. Then he reflected upon Hampton's enthusiasm and his proven willingness to work hard, and finally he decided that the Colonel deserved to see the capture of the airfield after planning for it so vigorously and competently. Before long Dave Barr was to regret granting Hampton's request, and although no one ever censured him, he would ever afterward blame himself for what happened.[4] Hampton gathered together a platoon of B-Company, 18th Combat Engineers, and sallied out of the village to go south and join the force at the gates of Suwon.

Lieutenant Van Sant and his tanks moved cautiously toward the north gate of Suwon, the Recon Company close behind. The town and the surrounding area seemed quiet enough. It was not yet quite dark. Suwon was an old-fashioned oriental city with high, gray walls topped by gabled tiles, and its gateways were elaborate, archlike affairs flanked by small guard towers. That same day naval gunfire from the coastal waters, a good fifteen miles to the east, had lobbed shells into the area to soften it for the attack. Near the north gate, a wooden structure atop the wall had been demolished by some of this fire and had fallen, the debris completely blocking the entrance.

Van Sant surveyed the situation briefly, then pointed to his left along the road that partly circled the city, and led the tanks along the wall while he looked for another opening. At about this time, Lieutenant Colonel Hampton and his platoon of engineers arrived. Further along the wall, Van Sant found a hole and led the tanks into it. He noticed that both Colonel Hampton and Major Edwards—division staff officers—kept quite near the front of the column. He didn't like this too much, but as a mere second lieutenant, he didn't think it his place to comment.

The lead tank nosed into the city and down a secondary street. Van Sant had no street map but assumed that if he went forward and then swung back toward the center of town he'd soon reach the main street. He turned right at the next likely avenue, proceeded several blocks, and then, as he'd anticipated, saw the main street just ahead. At that moment he happened to glance to his right and into a side street. A few yards away, and staring back at Van Sant in equal astonishment, was a North Korean major in a bright blue dress uniform, sitting high in an American jeep with his driver and radio operator.

Van Sant stopped his tank. The engineer squad that had been riding the back of it, jumped off and ran toward the jeep. Master Sergeant Diaz, the squad leader, dragged the North Korean major from the vehicle and slammed him against a wall. Someone shot his radio operator, killing him, and in the confusion that followed, the driver, who had not tried to flee, was also killed. With sudden horror, Van Sant saw that Master Sergeant Diaz had pushed the major's chin up with his left hand and was reaching for his bayonet, evidently intending to cut his throat. "I Christian! I Christian!" the major kept shouting.

Van Sant jumped from his tank and ran up to Diaz. Throat-cutting wouldn't do—besides, he wanted that major alive. He shouted for Diaz to let the man go and when the sergeant didn't seem to hear, he punched him in the back several times to make him desist. Diaz moved off to one side looking sheepish, and Van Sant called for the R. O. K. soldier who accompanied the force as interpreter. Through him he asked the frightened North Korean officer where the airfield was and saw relief wash over his face as he realized he would not be harmed. He was only too eager to direct them to the airfield.

"Tell him to get on my tank and lead us there," Van Sant said to the interpreter.

He needed no translation to get the meaning of the major's

next outburst. The man frantically gestured at his hat and brightly colored blouse—he would be a vivid target on top of a moving tank. He wanted to take them off first. Van Sant shrugged and said, "Okay, take 'em off, then." When they had been removed, the major, in a dirty white shirt and dark trousers, looked to Van Sant like any Korean farmer. He climbed in front of the turrent and led the column on to the main street, where it turned to the left and headed south again.

He went forward slowly for about two blocks. Suddenly, about 200 yards ahead, he saw the running figures of several North Korean soldiers and the unmistakable silhouettes of two T-34 tanks lurking behind some rubbled buildings. Van Sant fired a quick round of high explosive down the street. It bounced and exploded about fifteen feet in the air. The enemy soldiers disappeared immediately.

Van Sant knew he had to get out before the North Koreans could react. He moved through the rest of the city as quickly as possible, passing the lurking enemy tanks. He came suddenly to a fork in the road, and the Korean major pointed to the left-hand fork, presumably to indicate the direction of the airfield. Van Sant veered left. Moments later he passed through another gate and was out of the town.

It was getting dark, and Van Sant was becoming uncomfortable. Recalling that day's events later, he wrote, "[it] was my exact intent since I first took the mission . . . to get to or man the airfield . . . before dark and set up a defense since we were well within North Korean territory, and intelligence indicated at least one N. K. division in Suwon. . . ."

He was perhaps a mile south of town now, virtually in open country, and in the gloom to his right he saw what looked like three U. S. Air Force planes parked in a great open space that paralleled the road and which was no doubt the airfield he sought.[5] But this was no time to go exploring airfields that were probably held in force by the enemy. Van Sant signaled for what he called an "old-fashioned wagon-wheel defense" right there astride the road. His own platoon formed a semicircle on the west side of the road, by the airfield. Lieutenant Hughes and his five tanks took the other side. The engineers and men of the Recon Company, plus their vehicles, filled the gaps between the tanks themselves.

Van Sant had the tanks turned so that each would cover a likely avenue of approach, and as darkness hastened upon them, he had "range cards" made, just as he had done at that memorable night ambush in the Bowling Alley almost exactly one month before. The terrain was open and flat, and Van Sant was thankful for that. An enemy force, he believed, would have one hell of a time getting to them.

Lieutenant Colonel Henry Hampton was observing all of this direct combat preparation with great interest—you didn't get this sort of excitement every day up at division headquarters. Until the last minute of daylight, Van Sant noticed, the visiting staff officer was enthusiastically photographing everything, including the capture of the North Korean major, with a home movie camera, as though he were a tourist in the midst of some tribal war. Van Sant was concerned for his safety, but realized that it was primarily the responsibility of the company commander and made no comment. He was in a rather odd position, anyway; although the lowest-ranking officer in the party, by some tacit agreement among the others he seemed to be calling most of the shots, largely because they knew of his combat experience.

Back at division headquarters, General Barr was getting worried about the fate of the Recon Company sent on to Suwon, to say nothing of his valuable staff officers, Lieutenant Colonel Hampton, the G-3, and Major Edwards, the assistant G-2. As the column had approached Suwon its radio communications with Angyang-ni, ten miles further back, had begun to go out and now it was completely incommunicado. The last report he had of its whereabouts was from the L-16 liaison plane, piloted by Captain Howard Lukens, which had seen it nearing the gate of Suwon and then had been forced to return to its own strip on account of darkness. Barr was beginning to cuss himself—aloud, as a matter of fact, and for the benefit of nearby members of his staff—for letting Colonel Hampton get carried away and go forward to join the advance party.[6]

A full moon was up. From his hilltop command post, Dave Barr stared to the southeast and scratched his lean cheek. The Recon Company was down there somewhere— ten miles or more away—and maybe in the midst of a whole North Korean division. Pressed by General Almond to move fast, and with the example of the hard-pushing Marines to the north of him, he had perhaps moved a little too fast and it might have been just as well to wait another day and take Suwon more surely.

He made a sudden decision. It was now 9:00 P.M. and he radioed immediately to Angyang-ni to Lieutenant Colonel

Calvin S. Hannum, commanding officer of the 73rd Tank Battalion. Hannum, he said, should form an immediate strong task force and go south in search of the lost Recon Company and the two tank platoons. Hannum was on his way in twenty-five minutes. In this incredibly short time, he mounted out his own B-Company of tanks, the 32nd Infantry's K-Company, the 48th Field Artillery Battalion's C-Battery and a small medical detachment, and headed south at the greatest possible speed with the foot soldiers riding the vehicles. But General Barr was still having trouble with overeager staff officers. This time it was Lieutenant Colonel John W. Paddock, 7th Division G-2 and Major Edwards's boss, who decided to go along.

On the point of Hannum's task force as it approached Suwon was another tanker, Captain Harold R. Beavers, who had been a close friend of Van Sant's since they both were called to war from Fort Benning, Georgia. It was sometime between 11:00 P.M. and midnight when the would-be rescue force reached the outskirts of the city. Beavers, as he approached, tried to raise Van Sant on the radio at intervals. "Amazing Able, this is Hardtack Charley, over. Amazing Able, this is Hardtack Charley, over." Suddenly Van Sant was there. "Hardtack Charley, this is Amazing Able; where the hell are you?"

"Look, Jess," said Beavers, forgetting the code in his astonishment, *"I'm* supposed to be asking that question."

The two men exchanged positions—in checkpoint code this time in case the enemy was listening. (As later events proved, undoubtedly he was.) Beavers said he was coming through the town to find Van Sant and the Recon Company. Transmission broke off for a few minutes and then Beavers's voice sounded again: "Goddamnit, Amazing Able, how do I get out of this burg?" Van Sant laughed; Beavers, as tough a tanker as ever came clanking down a dirt road, was noted for his rich profanity throughout the battalion. He told Beavers to take the left fork. "Goddamnit," came Beavers' reply, "It's too dark and I can't see the f—g left fork!"

"Okay, Hal," said Van Sant, "just follow the tank tracks."

That, as it developed, was unfortunate advice. Van Sant, in passing down the main street of Suwon, had dimly seen two North Korean T-34 tanks before they disappeared. Unknown to him, these enemy tanks had also fled down the main street, and upon coming to the work, had taken the right-hand turn. It was their tracks, instead of Van Sant's that Beavers followed.

At the wagon-wheel defense a mile or so south of town, Van Sant and the higher-ranking officers with him strained their ears suddenly to catch certain harsh, purring sounds that seemed to come out of the eerie, moonlit night. "That's Captain Beavers and the tanks," said Lieutenant Colonel Hampton, who still had about him, somehow, the air of a middle-aged tourist enjoying an exotic outing. Although it was too dark for pictures, he was still carrying the home-movie camera in a loop on his wrist. Major Edwards and Lieutenant Miller, the Recon Company commander, nodded and began to designate a welcoming party to go forward and lead Beavers' tanks in.

"I don't think they're our tanks," said Van Sant, who had been listening as the sounds grew louder. "They sound to me like T-34's." He knew the sound of a T-34 from the Bowling Alley. He had heard it at closer range than most people. Its engine has a heavier, more hollow sound, unmistakable to anyone with an ear for engines.

Colonel Hampton shook his head. "No, we know they're ours. We'll go lead them in."

Van Sant sighed to himself. He was quite conscious of his lowly second lieutenant's rank and his military aptitude and training had given him a conditioned reflex that made him reluctant to argue too firmly with lieutenant colonels, majors, and even first lieutenants like Miller. He didn't realize it yet, but the orders for his promotion to first lieutenant had come out on September 12, almost ten days before; they hadn't caught up with him yet. Later, he had an ironic thought. It occurred to him that if he had known he was a first lieutenant, he might have opposed the idea of a greeting party more vigorously, and perhaps even talked them out of leaving the wagon-wheel perimeter.

As Lieutenant Colonel Hampton, Major Edwards and First Lieutenant Miller took off in four jeeps with some enlisted men, Van Sant went back to his tank radio and suddenly heard Beavers' voice again. "Goddamnit, Amazing Able, will you quit shooting at me?"

"I'm not shooting at you, Hardtack Charley."

"Well somebody surer'n hell is!"

Somebody was indeed, back there in the town. Captain Beavers had finally caught up with the T-34 whose tracks he had been mistakenly following. He had suddenly come within range of the monster, which was hidden in the shadows of a building. As he broke off transmission with Van Sant, the T-34's turret gun suddenly blasted at his tank, knocking it out and killing him.

The other American tanks opened fire immediately and within minutes destroyed the T-34. In the moonlight and light from the gun flashes, they saw a second North Korean tank escaping to the south.

At the wagon-wheel perimeter, Van Sant, still monitoring the radio for further word from Captain Beavers, suddenly heard the boom of a tank gun up the road about two thousand yards away as he judged it. This was the shot that destroyed Beavers' tank.

The party in the four jeeps, proceeding slowly and without headlights, had spotted four tank silhouettes on the road, coming toward them. Major Edwards, in the lead jeep, flicked his headlights as a recognition signal. The tank stopped— and then suddenly its machine guns opened up on them, sending bright tracers slamming through the night.

Everyone hit the dirt.

Everyone except Lieutenant Colonel Hampton, who began to walk toward the vehicle, waving his arms and calling out, "Don't shoot! We're Americans!"

The 7.62-mm. bow machine gun of the tank pointed itself at Colonel Hampton and a flickering blast appeared at its muzzle. Colonel Hampton's body was cut in two at the waist. His home movie camera dropped to the ground.

The others in the party scrambled into the fields beside the road and those who could began to make their way in the shadows back to the oval of friendly tanks toward the south.

As soon as Lieutenant Van Sant heard the shooting up the road he ordered all tanks guns turned in that direction and said to the others, "When I fire, you fire, too!"

There was a round of high explosive in Van Sant's tank gun. He would have preferred armor piercing, which was better against tanks. But as he stared into the gloom, he saw the first of the enemy tanks coming around the bend toward him. This same tank had run over Colonel Hampton's body and crunched into the lead jeep, knocking it aside. Van Sant waited until the T-34 was only thirty or forty feet away before he fired. The high-explosive round stopped the tank and set it on fire. Now the other tanks in the wagon wheel were firing upon the second T-34, which was about a hundred feet behind the first. Within seconds this enemy tank, too, was halted and on fire. A number of North Korean infantrymen who were riding on the T-34's were cut down.

The remaining two North Korean tanks withdrew. Van Sant sat atop his own tank watching the two T-34's burn not far away, holding a fire extinguisher in case his own vehicle started to burn. Minutes later he thought he detected a small fire down by the treads and slid from the top of the tank to take a look. At that instant the 85-mm. gun of the burning T-34 cooked off with a huge explosion, and the projectile slammed through the spot where Van Sant had been sitting.

Abruptly he heard Colonel Hannum's voice on the radio, calling from the would-be rescue party somewhere up in the town, and learned that Beavers had been killed. Van Sant sadly reported that Hampton, Edwards and Miller were gone and strongly advised Hannum and his party not to try to reach them.

It was quiet for the rest of the night. In the gray dawn Major Edwards, Lieutenant Miller and their enlisted men stumbled into the wagon wheel, wet and cold. They were given dry fatigues and then Lieutenants Van Sant and Hughes moved their tanks westward to take Suwon Airfield. Within an hour a Navy four-engine plane had landed there, the first of many to use the newly taken strip.

Later in the day Colonel Hannum's task force and troops of the 31st Infantry arrived to secure the airfield. They dug foxholes and organized a command post among the buildings. Jesse Van Sant was lying under his tank, resting. As he put it, "I had been awake for five days and nights and my mind came and went."

Major Walter O. Wode, the battalion S-3, came up to Van Sant and said, "Jess, there's a couple of tank platoons trying to get down here through Suwon. How about going up there and leading them in?"

Second Lieutenant Van Sant was no longer awed by rank. He looked up at the major with dull eyes, said, "Go to hell, sir," and promptly curled up and went to sleep.[7]

NOTES *Chapter 14*

1. Details of incidents during this advance are from letters and map-sketches, Van Sant to author, 1 Apr & 4 May 67, plus Appleman, pp. 520–22.
2. Letter Van Sant to author, 1 Apr 67.
3. Interview author—Barr.
4. *Ibid.*
5. Major Edwards says the position was three miles south of Suwon and that they had unwittingly passed the airfield. (Appleman, p. 521.) Van Sant's map-sketch, prepared for the author, shows the tank perimeter adjacent to the airfield, which would make it between one and two miles south of the city limits.
6. Interview author—Barr.
7. Letter Van Sant to author, 4 May 67.

15

"You put sixteen men in each Amtrac, and we'll get them across."

IN A KOREAN HOUSE ABOUT FIVE MILES NORTHWEST OF SEOUL, Lieutenant Colonel Raymond Murray, regimental commander of the 5th Marines, was enjoying his first few hours of uninterrupted sleep in several days. It was just past 4:00 A.M. on the morning of September 22. A difficult phase of the approach to Seoul was completed; his regiment had finally crossed the Han River after the swimming team's near fiasco, and his battalions were moving on Seoul's western approaches on the north bank of the river along a front that extended perhaps two miles inland. From this direction a number of roads and a main railroad line led into Seoul. But between the regiment and the city were a number of jumbled hills and ridges where the reinforced enemy had his defenses.

The North Korean 78th Independent Regiment of about 2,000 men had reached Seoul, accompanied by a mortar and a 76-mm. gun company. About 5,000 men of the 25th Brigade, commanded by a Russian-trained major general, had joined them, bringing along mortar and artillery battalions and four heavy-weapons companies. The greatest strength of the defending troops, however, was a prevailing determination to throw back the invaders or die in the attempt. These were no garrison troops of recruits and older men such as had been encountered at Inchon and to a degree at Kimpo Airfield, but hard-core regular North Korean People's Army soldiers, well led and inspired to fanaticism by their commanders.

All day and into the night of the 21st, Murray's battalions, having crossed the Han, wheeled to the right and then pushed toward the city. General Almond's and General O. P. Smith's

288

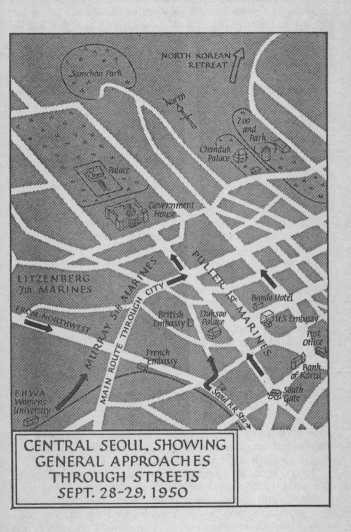

CENTRAL SEOUL, SHOWING
GENERAL APPROACHES
THROUGH STREETS
SEPT. 28–29, 1950

original plan had been for this force to penetrate into the southern part of Seoul and clear the waterfront there for a crossing by Chesty Puller's 1st Regimental Combat Team. But by the end of the day it was apparent that the plan needed revision, for Puller was blocked at Yong Dong Po just across the river from Seoul, and Murray's units were meeting stiffening resistance in the hills west of the city. They were now halted for the night in front of a long, high, irregular ridge designated Hill 104. All over this hill, and on surrounding eminences, the North Koreans had dug a huge complex of trenches and foxholes, it was about as formidable a defense position as could be made anywhere, with the river on one side and rugged inland mountains on the other protecting its flanks.

Ray Murray was awakened that night by a great crash. As he opened his eyes he saw a sheet of flame bursting in the room where he and his staff officers were sleeping. Something tickled the tip of his prominent nose—he scarcely noticed it at the moment. Staggering to his feet and moving through the eye-smarting fumes of burnt explosives, he saw that his executive officer, Lieutenant Colonel Lawrence C. Hays, Jr., was badly wounded by shrapnel, the major wound deep in his leg where it had severed a nerve. Several other staff members in the next room were wounded. A guard just outside the door lay upon the ground with the bottom half of his face blown away, and Murray thought he was surely dead, but he discovered later that surgeons miraculously saved his life and restored his face, although he was permanently blinded.[1]

In the confused minutes that followed, Murray tried to find out who was wounded and how much of his CP was gone; fortunately there was not enough damage to prevent continued operation. The round that had fallen through the roof and exploded in the house came from a North Korean antitank gun somewhere up on the heights, and it was to Murray a kind of warning shot, as though the enemy had chosen this way to tell him that they were strongly entrenched and well dug in up there in the hills.

Navy Lieutenant Horace Underwood and three members of the press, who were sleeping in another house about one hundred yards away, were also jolted awake by the explosion. The evening before they had moved into the hamlet along with Murray's command post, been invited to stay in the larger house with Murray and his staff, but had decided upon the smaller shack some distance away. The correspondents were Frank Gibney of *Time,* Keyes Beach of the Chicago *Daily News,* and Maggie Higgins of the New York *Herald Tribune.* These three had flown into Kimpo Airfield in June, when the Communists first moved down upon Seoul, and they had been covering the war in their various ways ever since. Underwood felt that their decision to sleep in the smaller house probably saved their lives that night.[2]

Awake now, Ray Murray pitched into the task of pushing on toward Seoul. As he began issuing orders to his battalion commanders he discovered their hastily issued maps were not only on too small a scale and occasionally inaccurate, but that they even disagreed as to the naming and spelling of various towns and villages. A trivial matter, on the face of it, but it actually caused delay in the maneuvering of units and, by leading some head on into stiff opposition they might have avoided, probably cost some lives.

George Newton's 1st Battalion went forward on the right flank, along the bank of the river. Bob Taplett's 3rd Battalion took the left flank, about three miles inland, and headed for a big hill designated Hill 216. The 1st Battalion of the Korean Marine Corps—Major Koh's "Damned-Near-Lost" Battalion—was in the center this time, attacking along the railroad toward Hill 104.

As the day wore on there were dozens of confused, desperate fights, spurs and eminences taken, lost and retaken, all along the line. Artillery slammed into hill positions and the Marine Corsairs flew innumerable strikes, strafing at times as little as thirty yards ahead of advancing troops. The smoke of battle, the din of explosive, the screams of wounded men hung along this jumbled natural wall to the west of Seoul. Progress was slow; every small squad and platoon advance was bitter, and usually uphill.

Cheerful, snub-nosed Lieutenant Underwood, moving along with Murray's command post, felt a sense of excitement now that he was scarcely a mile or so away from his family home west of Seoul. That morning the regimental headquarters went forward to another hamlet called Susaek, and in the central town building Underwood, still accompanied by the correspondents, found a working telephone exchange. On an impulse he called the central exchange in Seoul. Much to his surprise the connection was made, and he found himself conversing with an operator in the city. She was apparently no Communist sympathizer. Things were terrible in the city, she said, with food in short supply and prices inflated, and with

North Korean troops and Communist political officers restricting everyone's movements and virtually dictating the lives of individuals. Everyone in the city could see the pall of smoke to the west and hear the sounds of the battle. She was frightened. She wondered how many times the tide of war would roll across the city of Seoul again.

From this village Underwood could see the mass of Hill 104, where his home stood. He asked Murray's permission to go forward in the attack on this hill, and Murray, with some reluctance, assigned him to a battery of artillery. With his intimate knowledge of the terrain where he had played as a child, Hedge Underwood was able to direct the artillery fire most accurately, although he realized sadly that some of it would fall quite near and possibly even directly upon his home.[3]

During the day some probing units of the 3rd Battalion took Hill 104 in the center of the line, and the Korean Marine battalion moved up to secure it. By this time the enemy had thrown more troops into the hill's defenses and the Korean Marines bogged down. At first Ray Murray and most of his staff officers thought their South Korean allies somewhat lacking in push, but when they sent American units in to help them they found the defenses formidable indeed and realized that Major Koh's "Damned-Near-Lost" Battalion was fighting magnificently. Second Lieutenant Eung Duk Lee, who had flushed out the woman with the pistol concealed in her private parts back in Inchon, led his weapons platoon of the 4th Company up the hill, and there found foxholes filled with enemy dead like so many mass graves; there were two or three corpses in each hole, and strung along the ridges were so many of these open graves that he was unable to count them.

So the South Korean Marine Battalion took the hill that morning, were driven back, and then replaced by units from Lieutenant Colonel Roise's 2nd Battalion. Among these units were Captain Sam Jaskilka's E-Company, on the right of a two-pronged attack, with Hog Jaw Smith, tobacco quid in his cheek, bringing D-Company forward on the left. The eminence they were shooting for—a sharp hump that was part of the larger hill—had been dubbed "Nellie's Tit" by the men of the company, and this was how they referred to it even in their tactical messages over the radio.

Nellie's Tit was heavily defended, and Sam didn't want to move on it haphazardly; to be successful, the attack would have to be closely coordinated so that each company could advance alternately and support the other with its fire. Many of the squads and platoons would be hidden from each other by the rugged terrain, and thus clear radio communication was of the utmost importance. Sam also wanted plenty of support—artillery, 81-mm. mortars and air strikes. He called for this support and for extra radios from the reserve company and then stood there at his hillside company command post and waited.

The field phone rang. It was Colonel Murray. What the hell was the delay? Hadn't Sam received the orders to move on that hill? Sam, like everyone else, had been fighting almost continuously for several days; he was unshaven, tired, irritated, and he stank, and the normally reasonably query rubbed him the wrong way. "I'll go when I'm goddamn good and ready," he said, and not in a gentle tone of voice. He worried about it later when he had cooled off a bit, but Murray understood the tension that prompted the disrespectful retort, and even managed to smile a bit as he forced himself to be patient.[4]

The radios arrived, then the artillery barrage and the air strikes, and before the afternoon was over Nellie's Tit, and indeed the rest of Hill 104, was taken. When enemy prisoners were interviewed later, they attested to the effectiveness of the air strikes fifty yards or less before the advancing troops, and said they hadn't believed the foot soldiers would be that close behind the aerial strafing; most of them had been completely surprised in their foxholes.

Roise's 2nd Battalion, securing the hill, found one South Korean Marine platoon with only nineteen survivors. Roise sent the platoon leader back to Murray's command post to make his intelligence report. Murray said," Why didn't you fall back?" The young Korean lieutenant straightened his shoulders and said, "Sir, I never received any orders to fall back." Murray estimate of his R. O. K. Marine allies, he said, rose sharply.[5]

Past Hill 104 to the southwest were three hills of the same size strung in a curved line about five hundred yards apart; these were designated 105-N (north), 105-C (central), and 105-S (south). The assault continued on these eminences, and the fact that each was a Hill 105 added to some of the confusion in communications.

On the left, Taplett's 3rd Battalion at first seemed to move forward with ease, but before the day was out, bogged down in front of Hill 296. Murray's 5th Marines were strung along a front a little more than four miles wide, which ran in a relatively straight line northwest to southwest across the jumbled hills that formed Seoul's western wall. But all the units were not in contact along the line, and this front was also a turbulent area. In places, the men were unsure whether the enemy was on their flanks or behind them. Reserve units, coming along to hold ground already taken, might be just as likely to run into a fight as the men moving forward in points. The casualties mounted all day on the 22nd. They were higher than at any time since the Inchon landing, and they would continue to be heavy for the next several days. Since the Marines had come to Korea and fought in Walker's Perimeter further south, the entire brigade had lost seventeen of its eighteen original platoon leaders and five of its six company commanders.

As Murray and his 5th Regimental Combat Team were assaulting Seoul from the west and Puller and his 1st were pushing into Yong Dong Po, a third regiment—the 7th Marines—was landing at Inchon and preparing to come forward on the far left flank to attack Seoul near its northern extremities. Heading this 7th Regiment was able, studious, Colonel Homer L. Litzenberg, regarded as something of an intellectual and a scholar throughout the Corps.

The morning of the 23rd dawned, and the Korean Marines were directed forward from Hill 104 to the next ridge. Again they bogged down, again the men of the 2nd Battalion were sent forward, and once more they discovered that the Koreans had been halted by immensely strong defenses. Indeed, the entire attack was now reaching the heart of the North Korean defense line among the hills, and the few gains made were measured in feet instead of yards. There was plenty of smoke over the battlefield to make air attack and artillery spotting difficult; now the enemy added to the pall with a number of smoke pots.

In the center of the line, the 2nd Battalion somehow managed to gain most of the next ridge by nightfall. They sat there, units somewhat scattered, ranks thinned, and for the moment in short supply. Battalion and regimental officers agreed later that if the enemy had counterattacked that night, they could have wounded the battalion grievously and certainly driven it back. But there was no counterattack and the

Marines that night rested briefly while artillery flashes to the rear brightened the night sky till morning.

By morning of the 23rd, Yong Dong Po was taken, thanks to Captain Barrow's company-size penetration at the center of the town, and Puller's 1st Marines were poised on the south bank of the Han, facing Seoul.

Generals Almond and O. P. Smith met at Yong Dong Po in a small square near the center of the town where there was a park and a fountain. By now Almond had told Smith several times that he wanted Seoul taken by the 25th of the month; the fact that he repeated this desire seemed to irritate the rather correct and somewhat cold Marine general, although he was careful to show no reaction. "The 25th," Almond said again. "That will give us Seoul back three months to the day after the Communists took it." Like MacArthur, Ned Almond was thinking of the dramatic effect the recapture on that date would have throughout Asia. He then outlined his plan for the quick capture of the city. It would be another flanking movement, with Murray's force pushing in from the west and Puller's Marines crossing the river and entering the city several miles away from the southeast. For in the southeastern quarter of Seoul was the 900-foot mound of Namsan Peak— South Mountain—the dominant feature that could be seen from all parts of the city; a Korean saying had it that if you tossed a stone from the peak of South Mountain, it would land on the head of a Kim, a Lee, or a Pak, the three most common surnames of Korea. Take South Mountain, Almond felt, and the whole city was as good as occupied.

Smith demurred at this plan. He pointed out that Murray had already run into much stiffer resistance than anyone had anticipated and added that no matter what flanking maneuvers were taken, the last-stand defenders would fight bitterly in the streets and Seoul wouldn't really be taken until they were cleared out. Besides, he felt that to move Puller's 1st Marines so far to the right would be to split his division and reduce its effectiveness. Murray was having plenty of trouble where he was, assaulting that line of hills; he would be better served if the 1st Marines would land near him, hitting the enemy flank. Then both regiments could enter the city, and the newly arrived regiment, Litzenberg's 7th, could be brought around from the northwest to hit the retreating North Koreans almost in their rear.

The two generals discussed their difference of opinion tightly for several minutes, each trying to be reasonably polite to the other. At one point Almond called his old VMI classmate, General Shepherd, into the conference, to see if he could bring Smith over to his point of view. General Smith stuck to his guns. To send Puller around to the far right would disperse his division.

Almond agreed that Murray was having his difficulties at the hills west of Seoul, but somehow when Almond mentioned it Smith seemed to take it as criticism, and the discussion became tighter and warmer as it went on. Almond, as was his habit, had been hopping by helicopter among the Marine command posts for the past two days, keeping in close and personal touch with the progress of the battles on all fronts. He had visited Ray Murray near Hill 104 and for the second time had found fault with Murray's placement of his artillery; the guns, with a range of 8,800 yards, were placed so that they couldn't reach the flanks, and Almond had pointed out to Murray that this contradicted tactical doctrine.

Somehow this visit and some of Almond's other trips got into the conversation, and O. P. Smith reminded the corps commander that he preferred to handle his own regiments. "I'm not handling your regiments," said Almond, "I'm just seeing how they do after you handle them. It's my idea that Seoul can be captured by crossing the Han, southeast of the city. I'm going to visit your regiments tomorrow, and if no advances have been made I propose to narrow your sector so that South Mountain will be within the area of General Barr's 7th Division. I'll be here tomorrow at 2:00 P.M. and General Barr will meet me here when I make this decision."[6] For the moment, Ned Almond left it at that.

The next day, September 24, he was at the fountain in Yong Dong Po again. On hand at this conference were General Smith, General Barr, Brigadier General Hodes (Barr's assistant division commander), Marine Colonel Edward Forney, the X-Corps deputy chief of staff, and Almond's G-3, Lieutenant Colonel John H. Chiles. A number of correspondents were standing about, their ears perked up; by now the press, and much of the rank and file of X-Corps, sensed that there was disagreement between Smith and Almond. Both generals took great care to keep their differences from being noticed, but they couldn't quite conceal it from everyone, and when Almond mentioned that he'd been to the command posts of the 1st and 5th Marine regiments, Smith replied to the effect that he wished Almond would let him command his own regiments—or at least that was what it sounded like to Almond. Perhaps each remark was not as strong as it sounded to the other man; things had simply reached the point where the two generals rubbed each other the wrong way no matter what they said. The conversation just before the conference appeared to Almond to be within the hearing of the nearby correspondents, and this added to his sense of agitation.

As General Barr later recalled it, the conference proceeded with a modicum of calm, and he himself did not notice any particular sparks flying between the two commanders, only the military difference of opinion which each man stated in his own fashion.[7] It may have been that most of the conflict existed in the minds of these two able men who simply did not get along with each other.

Now, as Almond laid it out, General Smith was to keep his original plan of crossing the river at Yong Dong Po and keeping Puller's 1st Marines virtually alongside Murray's 5th Regimental Combat Team. The assault across the river from the southeast—the far right flank, in other words—would be handled by Colonel Beauchamp's 32nd Infantry Division of Army troops which had just swung up toward the river after the capture of Suwon, sixteen miles to the south.

Almond summed up his tactical thinking for these maneuvers in his *Personal Notes,* jotted down shortly afterward, and these best explain the reasons for his method of attack. The entry for 24 September, 1950, logs the conference and those attending, then goes on to say, "Gen. Smith, from the outset of the presentation, disagreed with the utilization of a regiment from the 7th Inf Div for the capture of Seoul. Gen. Almond stated that the purpose of this plan was for the most expeditious capture of Seoul; that he planned the utilization of a regiment from the 7th Inf Div to cross the Han River and, utilizing the maneuver space available, take the enemy resistance then confronting the 1st Mar Div in reverse and by maneuver from the south and southeast capture the dominant terrain feature of South Mountain, thus relieving the pressure against the 5th and 1st Marines, particularly the latter. It was further emphasized by the Corps commander that the 7th Inf Div, having advanced south of the Han and to a north and south line on its front, which was abreast of the eastern exit of Seoul, provided an excellent maneuver space for the enveloping operation which should be taken full advantage of. Although this maneuver involved the crossing of the Han River just prior to striking the key point, South Mountain, the Naval and Marine air and the 7th Inf Div and X Corps artillery available fully justified such an operation since the supporting fires, ground and air, were most adequate. . . ."

And that was the way it would be done; Almond would not only see that his plan was carried out but, as a commander, would take full responsibility for any untoward consequences. The courteous, deceptively mild warrior was showing his stubborn mettle. He now turned to General Smith and said, "Where are your Amtracs?" (He meant the same LVT's that had brought Puller's men ashore at Blue Beach.)

"They're up near Kimpo," said General Smith.

"Well, I'd like to have some to make a crossing with the 32nd."

Smith frowned. Puller's regiment would also need vehicles to take them across the river. He reminded Almond that the amphibious tractors had been assigned to the 1st Marine Division.

"That doesn't concern me a particle," said Almond. "They are necessary to this operation. How long will it be before I can get them?"

Standing beside them was the Marine major in charge of the Amtracs. "They can be here before dark," he said.

The 32nd Infantry commander, Colonel Beauchamp, now stepped forward and said to Almond, "Just a moment, sir. My men have never used Amtracs before. They wouldn't know how to run them."

"No sweat," said the Marine major. "You put sixteen men in each Amtrac, and we'll get them across."[8]

The conference ended, and Ned Almond immediately gathered General Barr and Colonel Beauchamp together, along with some of his staff officers, and sped by jeep out of the city, eastward along the south bank of the Han to the spot where the 32nd Infantry was to cross. There they halted and gazed at Seoul; it was exactly the spot from which MacArthur had viewed the city just after the Communist breakthrough in June and declined the use of Colonel Sterling Wright's binoculars. It was also, as the officers tried to remind Almond, beyond existing friendly lines at the moment. Almond pointed out some of the terrain features across the river, then said to General Barr, "Dave, you take your regiment across tomorrow as close to daylight as you can. You haven't much time—so get going."

"Sure, Ned," said gangling General Barr, who always had the unruffled air of a backwoodsman. It seemed to him that since the conference at the fountain General Almond was snapping his orders—on the point of giving everyone hell. Maybe, he figured, Ned Almond had just gotten up on the wrong side of the bed this morning.[9]

All that Saturday of September 24th the fighting was furious in Lieutenant Colonel Murray's sector to the west of Seoul. The Marines pushed forward doggedly, taking hills and ridges thickly pocked with bunkers and foxholes, many of which were strewn with hundreds of dead North Koreans. Every two hours five Corsairs took off from nearby Kimpo to fly in support of the Marine attacks, mounting a record total of forty-six sorties that day.

Murray saw that, slow as it was, he was definitely making progress. He was greatly pleased with his improved communications, for which he gave full credit to his communications officer, Major Kenneth Boyd, who improvised ingenious methods to keep the units in touch with each other. Down along the railroad, for example, he managed to hook into a commercial wire and save the Marines the trouble of laying their own.[10]

As the 5th Regiment kept up its assault on the hills, Chesty Puller started across the river near Yong Dong Po. Mines along the shore delayed the first units of the 1st Regiment for a while, and when they reached the far bank they ran into enemy fire, but with the flamboyant Puller pushing them, they kept going. At one point heavy fire came from a hill supposedly secured by the 5th Marines, and this demonstrated quite vividly the enemy's ability to hide out behind the lines and make trouble.

By afternoon Puller's men made contact with Murray's. By the time Almond took Barr and the others to the river to view the crossing site, far to the east, Puller's 1st Battalion was on a hill overlooking the railroad marshaling yards in the southwest corner of Seoul. Murray's bitter fighting had secured most of the hills west of the city. Litzenberg and the 7th Regiment was approaching the northwestern corner of the city. The three regiments were close enough to each other to be virtually in contact, and in the morning the fight would be carried into the streets of Seoul itself.

Ned Almond was up at 3:00 A.M. on the morning of the 25th. He had moved his X-Corps command post to Kimpo Airfield, where he gathered some of his staff officers and aides, and Admiral Struble, whose Seventh Fleet ships were still contributing fire support from the sea, and who thus had a vested interest in the campaign. To augment the fire from the cruisers *Rochester* and *Toledo*, the *Missouri* had been brought up just off Inchon, and although naval gunfire at this distance did not prove too effective, it was in a way an historic occasion—the last combat action by an American battleship in any war. The carrier was queen now; the cruiser was the principal fire-support ship, and within a few years would be armed with ballistic missiles as its principal weapon instead of guns.[11]

Almond left his command post at 4:00 A.M. and took his party to the site overlooking the river at Seoul. Early-morning haze covered the water and the beaches on the other side. The men of the 32nd Infantry Regiment were moving up to the river to prepare for the crossing. At 6:00 A.M., on schedule, a heavy and deafening artillery barrage began.

At 6:30 the artillery barrage ceased. In the sudden silence four Amtracs started across with advance troops of Lieutenant Colonel Charles M. Mount's 2nd Battalion, partly under cover of the mist. The crossing took ten minutes, and by that time the haze had risen enough for Almond to see that the men had landed without opposition. Successive waves of Amtracs followed in their wake and the rest of the battalion began to go ashore.

At 7:40 there was a tremendous explosion as an enemy mortar round landed only a hundred yards away from Almond's observation post. The entire group moved back a bit.

The air attack on the far shore had already begun, and Almond watched its effectiveness with some satisfaction. At 9:00, accompanied by Admiral Struble, he motored down to the river's edge, stepped into one of the Amtracs, and told its startled skipper to take him across. On the far shore Lieutenant Colonel Donald Faith, commander of the 1st Battalion, informed him that the numerous trenches and gun emplacements on the high ground inland were only lightly manned and that opposition seemed negligible. Almond himself then proceeded a short distance inland and presently came upon Lieutenant Colonel Mount who had halted his battalion at a railroad track. "Why are you just sitting here?" asked Almond. Mount said he wasn't sure where he was or how he was supposed to link up with the other battalions. Almond took him to a rise and pointed out some of the prominent landmarks of Seoul, and then told him to get going.

At about 12:15 P.M., Almond headed back for the south shore in an Amtrac. Halfway across the river he saw General Barr coming across in another amphibious vehicle. Almond laughed and said, "Good morning. How's the attack going?"

"Pretty good," said Barr.

Almond couldn't resist teasing a little. "Where've you been all morning, Dave?"

It was an innocent remark between two men who had by now become moderately friendly, and Dave Barr—"Pappy" Barr, some of his troops called him—was not about to let it destroy their friendship, but he took the words as mild criticism and came up with an immediate defensive answer, although he, too, smiled as he spoke. He pointed back to the high bluff on the south side of the river where he had put his 7th Division command post, and from where he had decided to cross only when he could see the first of his troops atop South Mountain. "I stayed up there," said Barr, "where I could fight my whole division, and not just those two battalions across the river." Both men laughed, and that was that, for the time being.[12]

Almond reached the south bank again and paused for a while to observe the progress of some engineers who were assembling a pontoon ferry. Presently he returned to his command post at Kimpo. By 3:30 P.M. he was off again, this time in a liaison plane flying south to Suwon where the 31st Infantry Regiment, commanded by Colonel Richard P. Ovenshine, was holding the area south of Seoul. Here Almond learned that Ovenshine had sent a battalion down toward Osan, the next major town ten miles down the road, and that the battalion, upon receiving enemy fire, had stopped halfway to its objective. It now wished to withdraw and Colonel Ovenshine was apparently about to let it do so. Almond promptly and firmly began to lecture the colonel on the need for aggressive action.

It was always a little surprising when the normally courteous Almond hardened his light blue eyes and began to speak in no uncertain terms. Ironically, Ovenshine, a taller man with a rugged, battered face, who wore his fatigues with a dashing air and carried a swagger stick, looked more like a swashbuckling soldier than Almond, whose field clothes always seemed a little too large for him and who, in his in-

stinctive neatness, always kept his boots highly polished and
his buttons neatly buttoned even in the midst of battle.
Almond stood Ovenshine tall there, as the military saying
goes, and Ovenshine, still convinced he was only fighting with
proper caution, but like a good commander standing behind the decision of his battalion leader, stood there quietly
and took it with his cheeks burning.

Presently General Barr came along and, hearing all about
it, seemed to Almond to add his agreement to the X-Corps
commander's contentions. The whole matter was discussed,
and between them, the two generals made it plain that no
patrols were to return simply because the enemy happened
to be between them and their objective; if they received
fire and couldn't handle it, they were to hold their ground
and call for assistance.

Almond's view that commanders ought to be aggressive
was incontrovertible, and as philosophy, Barr went along
with it. He was disturbed in spite of himself, however, and
knew he would have preferred to make the correction himself, without the corps commander's participation. As a
matter of fact, Dave Barr was still blaming Almond somewhat for the ragtag and bobtail division he'd been given in
Japan and—as it always seemed to him—for being left out
of high councils and hearing of decisions at the last moment. It was no open break; Barr was too good a soldier
for that, and Almond was satisfied with his fighting qualities.
It was just that Barr found Almond's presence something
less than completely amiable. Almond would not have been
concerned with that, had he realized it. He had a campaign
on his hands, and a deadline to meet, and he was going to
do it aggressively and as a perfectionist, let the chips fall
where they may.[13]

Although the two Army battalions had crossed the river
in the southeastern part of Seoul and had taken most of
South Mountain without bitter fighting, there were a number of pure slugging matches taking place to the west where
Puller had crossed into the city's outskirts and where Murray was coming down from the hills and into the heavily
defended streets. The North Koreans had filled these streets
with barricades. At intervals of about five hundred yards on
most of the major avenues, they had built eight-foot-high
breastworks of woven fiber sandbags extending from one
house wall to the other. At each of these barricades antitank

and machine guns were placed, along with infantry troops. At other points, the big T-34 tanks were stationed to act as defensive artillery, and at the approach to each barricade mines were thickly sown.

Puller's 1st Marines moved up and into the city, fighting house to house. Each attack was a frontal assault, and because of the streets lined with houses, there were few chances for flanking movements. Puller had learned about street fighting many years before in Haiti (which the United States occupied for nineteen years after 1915 because of political unrest), and drawing upon this knowledge, he directed his men to advance where possible through the houses themselves, breaking down the walls between each house as they went forward, and thus avoiding exposure to sniper fire. The technique had been used in Vera Cruz, Mexico, by a former commander of Puller's, and he recalled it now; he felt afterward that using it saved his regiment a thousand casualties.[14]

The battle in the western part of Seoul raged into the night of the 25th without let-up, the Marines pressing slowly but methodically forward, some still fighting among hills and draws beyond the edge of the city, others definitely in urban surroundings. Artillery and air kept pounding the objectives ahead of them. In some streets the heat from burning buildings was so intense that the Marines had to cover their faces with their helmets as they advanced. Even so, they were unable to bear it for more than a few seconds. They would run forward to escape it, bunch up in the street, and then snipers would shoot at them, dispersing them once more. All through the streets, added to the sounds of explosions, were the screams and cries of wounded and there were so many shouts of "Corpsman! Corpsman!" that it seemed to one participant like a chant.[15]

At his command post, General Almond received a report just before nightfall that enemy columns were leaving the city from the north. He called for immediate air attack on these columns by Marine night fighters and, to enable them to see the targets, called in planes from the Far East Air Forces, the arm that had been excluded from the Inchon-Seoul campaign by Pinky Wright's swinging compass. FEAF responded with a B-29 to drop flares and in the light of these, the Marine planes attacked the columns for two hours.

Almond had been right about the importance of South Mountain as the key to Seoul. As prisoner interrogation later revealed, the North Korean commander of the city's defense, seeing South Mountain taken, decided that the city was doomed and began to evacuate the 18th Division, nevertheless leaving behind strong units to defend and delay. With such a retreat already underway, it seemed to Almond a superb opportunity to smash forward even harder and exploit the enemy's withdrawal. He sent a message to O. P. Smith's 1st Marine Division headquarters shortly after 8:00 P.M.: "enemy fleeing city of Seoul on road north . . . you will push attack now to the limit of your objective in order to insure maximum destruction of enemy forces."[16]

The message was sent so urgently that it was not even encoded. At Smith's headquarters, the division operations officer, Colonel Alpha C. Bowser, was surprised to see it. He had been following the slow advances of Murray's and Puller's regiments quite carefully, and the present battle situation seemed to indicate that the enemy was far from fleeing the city. He telephoned back to X-Corps, questioned the order, and was told that it was no mistake—the Marine division was to attack *now*, just as the order said. Bowser brought the order to General O. P. Smith, who immediately telephoned Almond's chief of staff, General Ruffner, and objected to the order. Ruffner said Almond had issued it personally and it was to be followed without delay.

Smith was not a man to show his emotions, and above all, he had the iner need to be always correct; whatever his private opinion of Almond's judgment, he passed the order along to Murray, Puller, and to Litzenberg's 7th Regiment in the northwest corner of the city, ordering all three regiments to keep in close touch with each other and to concentrate their advances along streets that could be easily identified at night.[17]

Ray Murray, whose regiment now in effect formed the center of an L-shaped line, with Litzenberg above him and Puller the shorter base of the L, was surprised as General Smith personally gave him the order by telephone. At the moment his 3rd Battalion was actually staving off a counterattack. He said to Smith, "General, I can't very well launch a pursuit on anybody when I'm busy fighting off a counterattack!" Smith emotionlessly repeated that the order would be obeyed. Murray sighed and called Taplett, his 3rd Battalion commander. Tapplett said, "I can't pursue anything!"[18]

Puller's spearhead also ran head-on into a North Korean counterattack and fought it off in the middle of the main street with mortars, tanks and automatic fire. This battle, too, took the rest of the night, as the Marines drove off seven hundred troops, twelve tanks, and stormed two self-propelled guns.

On the morning of the 26th, the Marine lines were still about where they had been at dusk on the previous day.

There was an echo of Manila that night of the 25th. Correspondents who had covered the Pacific fighting in World War II recalled how MacArthur had announced the fall of Manila before it was really taken.

Just before midnight on the 25th, General Almond, at his command post, broke the news of the fleeing North Korean columns, of the success at South Mountain, and of the general penetration and foothold in the city to the correspondents at his Kimpo headquarters. He did mention that this significant gain had been accomplished on September 25th, three months to the day after Seoul had been captured by the Communists. It was perhaps a matter of semantics; at any rate it seemed to the correspondents present that he was declaring Seoul recaptured on this date.[19] Almond's recollections and his *Personal Notes*, compiled each day during the campaign, support his contention that he did not mean that Seoul was fully under the control of his forces. The notes for September 26 say: "Generally speaking, the Marine Division was steadily advancing through the city and it was becoming apparent that the enemy was withdrawing, leaving small pockets of enemy resistance behind."

Unfortunately the report of the day's gains came out of MacArthur's Tokyo headquarters the next day in slightly exaggerated fashion, and there United Nations Communique #9 declared, in part, that "Seoul, the capital of the Republic of Korea, is again in friendly hands. United Nations forces, including the 17th Regiment of the R.O.K. Army elements of the U. S. 7th and 1st Marine Divisions, have completed the envelopment and seizure of the city."

Puller's and Murray's Marines, still fighting forward against stiff and bitter opposition as dawn broke, could not exactly agree with that appraisal.

Ray Murray had set up his regimental command post at Ewha Women's University in the western part of Seoul where he had found a suitable building, new and empty. As an added touch of luxury, some of his men had managed to borrow from the University's woman president a small mimeograph machine that was perfect for reproducing orders.

General Almond, still command-post-hopping, dropped in on Murray. The matter of the previous night's orders to push forward and pursue—when all the time Murray was under counterattack—came up in the conversation. Without thinking, and forgetting momentarily that it had been Almond's order, Murray said, "Last night reminded me of the story of the lion and the rabbit. There's always some sonofabitch who doesn't get the word."

Murray had meant it had been the North Koreans who hadn't gotten the word, but immediately after he spoke he realized that it sounded as though he had meant Almond himself. He was much chagrined and thought of himself: *What do you turn in when you haven't got a sword?* But Almond apparently didn't notice, and the words were forgotten.

Almond continued his tour of the front, concerned not only with the advance into Seoul but with the movements far south of the city where the 31st Regiment would, hopefully, soon link up with the first of Walker's troops, which were finally breaking out of the Perimeter.

On the way he encountered Marine General Shepherd, recalled how he had more or less commandeered the Amtracs for the Army's river crossing, and took pains to explain to the Pacific Marine commander all the reasons for it. Shepherd said, "Yes, I know. Ollie Smith explained everything. But, you know, Ned, we took a chance letting them go—those are the only Amtracs in the entire Marine Corps!"

Navy Lieutenant Horace Underwood stood on a ridge west of Seoul and looked down at the fighting in the city's streets. It was a clear day, but the smoke from scores of fires kept him from seeing the details of the various street battles taking place. He noted that Severance Hospital, a missionary institution, was burning.

Behind him was a brick colonial house badly burned and gutted, its roof gone, its windows empty and staring like the eyes of the dead. He did not wish to turn and look at it. It was the house in which he had grown up.

NOTES   *Chapter 15*

1. Interview author—Murray.
2. Interviews author—Underwood, Gibney.
3. Underwood's Korean friends later liked to tell the dramatic story of how he called the shots on his own home. Actually, he merely directed fire upon landmarks in the area. Interview author—Underwood.
4. Interviews author—Jaskilka, Murray.
5. Interview author—Murray.
6. General Almond's recollection is that the conference was scheduled for 2:00 P.M. He apparently arrived at Yong Dong Po at 12:30 P.M. Interview author—Almond; *Personal Notes,* Almond.
7. General Barr recalls that as the meeting dispersed General Smith turned to him and said, "This is purely political." At the time Barr did not understand what Smith was talking about. Interview author—Barr.
8. Interview author—Almond.
9. Interview author—Barr.
10. Interview author—Murray.
11. At this writing there are newspaper reports saying that a battleship will be recommissioned for use in the Vietnam War.
12. Interviews author—Almond, Barr.
13. General Almond relieved Ovenshine of his regimental command on 5 Oct 50; General Barr says it was done without consulting him. Barr did not make an issue of the matter, however, because he was given a favorite officer who had formerly worked for him to replace Ovenshine. Interview author—Barr; *Personal Notes,* Almond, 12 Oct 50.
14. Interview author—Puller.
15. Tallent, Robert, "Street Fight in Seoul," *Marine Corps Gazette,* Jan 51.
16. 1st Marine Div Special Action Reports, 25 Sept 50; Hq USMC Historical Section.
17. The controversy over the actual need for this attack still rages whenever higher ranking veterans of the Inchon-Seoul operation gather. General O. P. Smith, in his way of commenting by citing facts, writes: "For the period of September 25th [when the enemy was supposed to be fleeing from Seoul] to September 28th [when Seoul was considered secured] the 1st Marine Division suffered 708 battle casualties. The battle casualties of the 7th Infantry Division for the entire Inchon-Seoul Operation totalled 572." Manuscript review comments for author by Smith, 2 Jul 67.
18. Interview author—Murray.
19. Interview author—Frank Gibney.

16

"By the grace of a merciful Providence ..."

IN A STREET SOMEWHERE IN SEOUL, CAPTAIN SAM JASKILKA trotted along with his radio operator and a combined rifle-man and runner in order to bring his E-Company command post forward. Only a block or so away he could hear the nearly constant firing where his lead platoon was making a slow, steady advance, much like all the other lead platoons all over the city, along a kind of half-moon that curved down from the northwestern part to the south-central section on the waterfront. Sam's company was about in the middle of this arc. On this morning of September 26, the attack that had been unfeasible the night before was reordered and both Murray's and Puller's regiments, now in closer contact, continued the assault, Puller up a main road that led to the central crossroads hub of Seoul, and Murray down from the hills and toward that hub from the west. There were innumerable actions as barricade after barricade was taken, as tanks, machine-gun nests and snipers were rooted out of positions behind houses, fences and walls.

Jaskilka's troops were busy only a few hundred yards ahead of him. He was looking for a suitable place to set up his CP so that he could direct his platoons through the streets in a coordinated attack rather than an aimless push. There was nothing on his mind but the battle now; he had even forgotten to worry about the University of Connecti-cut's football schedule. The streets were hot with fires; the smell of smoke and burnt explosive was thick in the air and made breathing unpleasant. For Sam Jaskilka and the other company commanders moving forward all along the

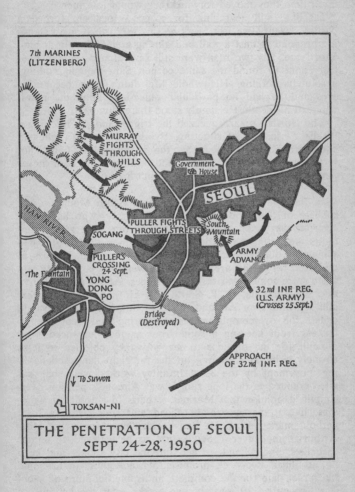

7th MARINES
(LITZENBERG)

MURRAY
FIGHTS
THROUGH
HILLS

Government
House

SEOUL

HAN RIVER

PULLER FIGHTS
THROUGH STREETS

SOGANG

South
Mountain

ARMY
ADVANCE

PULLER'S
CROSSING
24 Sept.

The Fountain

YONG
DONG
PO

32nd INF. REG.
(U.S. ARMY)
(Crosses 25 Sept.)

Bridge
(Destroyed)

APPROACH
OF 32nd INF. REG.

↓ To Suwon

TOKSAN-NI

THE PENETRATION OF SEOUL
SEPT 24-28, 1950

line, it was a day of taking one objective after another with their advances marked in yards, their objectives often in sight, and with little time to rest or regroup between them. Each time they moved forward they would lose men.

Jaskilka, still searching for a good location, turned a corner. Twenty-five feet away he saw a North Korean standing propped against a wall and aiming a rifle directly at him. Sam froze. His two men were still several steps behind him, just about to round the same corner. Sam thought nothing, absolutely nothing. His whole life didn't flash before his eyes and he had no particular reflections upon the imminence of his death. He simply stood there, dumb.

The North Korean squeezed the trigger and the rifle merely clicked instead of shooting. By that time Sam's rifleman came around the corner, saw the enemy soldier, and shot him several times, dropping and killing him. Sam never paused to find out why his piece hadn't fired.[1]

In the eastern part of the city near South Mountain, the soldiers of the 32nd Infantry, U. S. Army, who had made such an easy river crossing the day before, were at last running into bitter opposition, although they were fighting a somewhat different battle of maneuver than the Marines to the west, for in this area the houses were less jampacked and there were some open fields and ridges. At 1st Marine Division headquarters, O. P. Smith and his staff members were still scowling over Almond's plan of attack which, they felt, called for overcomplicated maneuvering and kept the attackers from keeping a solid front as they advanced. It is difficult for the outsider to see why they objected to it so strongly. Almond's landing on the far right flank and flanking movement by the 32nd Infantry worked well; that was what counted in the long run. It was Almond's perhaps oversimplified opinion that Marines, experts in amphibious landings, like to barge straight ahead and smash into a front without maneuvering. He had decided on a somewhat Mac-Arthurian maneuver at Seoul, first, as he believed, to reduce casualties, and second, to get into the city sooner and keep his ad-libbed two-week promise to MacArthur. In his mind the target date for the complete undisputed capture of Seoul was September 29, exactly two weeks after the landing on September 15. As the fighting raged in the streets on September 26, a less confident man might have worried about meeting that deadline. Almond, still choppering over the battlefield and hopping from command post to command post by helicopter, never had the slightest doubt.

Ned Almond was, in fact, so certain he'd have Seoul by the 29th that about a month before, in Tokyo, he had told X-Corps's engineer officer, Colonel Edward L. Rowney, "When we get to Seoul, General MacArthur, Syngman Rhee and a large staff are going to hold a big ceremony there to mark the retaking of the capital. Start figuring right now for every nut. bolt and screw so you can build a pontoon bridge. I want General MacArthur and Syngman Rhee to ride across in a sedan.²

He even accorded to Rowney the responsibility of feeding the big party that would gather for the ceremony at the ornate Government House in the north-central quarter of Seoul. Rowney and his staff had made all the plans. But on the way to Inchon the backlash of Typhoon Kezia had blown some of Rowney's bridge matériel from the deck of the LST transporting it. Shortly after the landing at Inchon, Rowney reported this loss and told Almond that to replace it he'd need an air shipment into Kimpo of about eighty tons. Almond had feared that this might interfere with the air supply of ammunition that was to come into Kimpo, but his chief of staff, General Ruffner, finally gave assurance that it would not, and as X-Corps was fighting its way into the streets of Seoul, Rowney was bringing up his matériel to put a pontoon bridge across the river.

One of the objectives along the northwestern edge of Seoul was Sodaemun Prison, a commanding compound of walls and concrete buildings manned by a North Korean garrison. On the morning of the 26th, a company of Colonel Litzenberg's newly committed 7th Marine Regiment came down the main highway from the northwest to take the prison and make contact with Murray's 5th Marines who were pushing in from the west. The first units to approach received machine-gun fire from a 400-foot tower in the prison compound. As they hit the sides of the road, additional fire began from the hills on their flanks. The company had probed a little too far forward. Before they could be reinforced, fire came from the rear, and they realized that they were surrounded. The commander of this D-Company formed a perimeter and braced himself for an all-night stand. By late afternoon planes passed overhead and dropped supplies for them.

Within the prison itself, ex-journalist Chul Hoe Koo, a slight, bespectacled man of about forty, listened to the firing outside and to the sounds of planes passing overhead with his heart beating wildly. He was crouched in a space over the ceiling rafters of a cell bloc where he had been hiding for two nights. He had escaped from his cell but found it impossible to scale the walls to the outside.

Chul had been in this prison—which the Communists called the "West Gate Culture House"—since early August. He was one of 8,000 South Korean political prisoners. He supposed it was because he'd worked for a newspaper that had occasionally been critical of the North Korean regime. He was not a man who thought much about politics; he was not physically formidable, knew nothing of military matters, and certainly did not consider himself daring or even physically courageous. But now, heart in mouth, he had escaped immediate captivity and was hoping fervently that the rescuers outside, whoever they might be, would soon make their way into the compound.

Six days before he had heard the rumble of gunfire in the distance. The rumor that the Americans had landed at Inchon and were driving upon Seoul had already swept through the prison. He had then been one of four inmates in cell No. 10, second floor, house No. 1. His closest friend was a Protestant minister, Pastor Yun-Sil Kim, a rather frail man with a temperament as mild as Chul's. The day they heard the gunfire, they had looked from their cell window and seen North Korean soldiers climbing into positions on a mountain near the prison. They had also seen a large crowd of prisoners—the criminal convicts in blue and the political prisoners in white—file into the yard where they were all shot down by machine-gun fire.

Ever since he had been in the prison Chul had dreamed of escape, not so much to avoid the torture and interrogation he was forced to endure, as to find out what was happening to his wife and two children and get to them secretly, somehow, help them perhaps, or at the very least assure them that he was alive.

Four days before, as the sound of bombardment drew nearer to Seoul, their prison guards—whom the Communists called "instructors"—had directed everyone in the cell bloc to gather outside at the Detention House. The order sounded suspicious to Chul, who had seen the mass of prisoners slaughtered in the courtyard.

There was apparently much confusion among the guards and soldiers in the compound as the attacking force approached the city, and in all the coming and going they seemed unable to keep track of all the prisoners as closely as they had previously. Instead of reporting to the Detention House, Chul and three companions climbed into a hole in the ceiling they had previously discovered and hid among the rafters through the next night. They listened to the explosions come closer. By now shells were falling or perhaps aerial bombs were exploding on nearby Inwang Mountain.

The next morning Pastor Kim left the ceiling hideout, made his way to the kitchen, and finding no "instructors" there, accepted some rice and dried fish from the kitchen workers. On the way back, in the hall, he met an instructor who asked what was in his bag; he told him it was food for sick inmates and hurried on. When he finally returned to the space above the ceiling, he, Chul and the others ate greedily.

Later that day the four men could stand their cramped quarters no longer, crawled out, made their way to a room with seven or eight bedridden patients, and crawled into blankets there as though they, too, were ill. That night the bombardment became heavier and plaster fell from the ceiling and walls.

In the morning an officer, dressed in the fancy blue dress tunic of the North Korean Army, came into the room. "Comrades, you are sick, and we are going to take you to the Army hospital in the rear. The ambulance will be ready in about an hour." He ordered an instructor to tie them in pairs by the arms.

Chul dared to speak. "Why incur extra expense for the state? Let us go to our homes."

The officer shook his head. "We are taking you to the Army hospital to protect you. If we left you here you might be massacred when the Americans and the remnants of the National Army arrive."

It was late that night before the officer returned with four soldiers and two armed instructors. The four prisoners —all white and trembling—were led outside. They were taken to the front of an air-raid shelter next to the prison doctor's office and told to stand in line there.

It was as Chul had feared. As soon as the prisoners formed the line, the officer, the soldiers and instructors aimed their guns at them. All this time Chul had been working at the rope that held his wrist. By some queer coincidence it came free at almost the moment the guns were pointed, and, simultaneously, and in surprise, Chul staggered backward. He fell into the slit trench in front of the air-raid shelter just as the guns were fired.

Pastor Kim and the other two prisoners also fell backward into the trench, shot. Kim and the man he was bound to lay still; Chul heard the fourth man still groaning. Chul rounded a corner of the slit trench and flattened against the wall. Beams from the Communists' flashlights came into the trench, darting back and forth. He heard someone say, "One of the scoundrels isn't there." The soldiers and guards fired into the trench again, a number of times. Chul saw the muzzle flashes in the darkness and pressed hard to the wall. Seconds later the firing stopped. He came forward, crouched, put his hand on one of the prisoners lying there and felt warm, sticky blood. Suddenly, overhead, the shooting started again. The beam of a flashlight touched his knee. He held himself still.

One of the guards said, "Let's put the rest in and cover them up." With that, the guards appeared to go away.

Chul rose cautiously and looked about the yard. It was apparently empty, though it was difficult to tell for sure in the darkness. He climbed from the trench and then into the open window of the doctor's office. He heard the sound of shots from the infirmary nearby and knew the sick who couldn't walk were being slaughtered.

All the doors in the doctor's office were locked; he couldn't get out by another route. He tried to squeeze himself into an empty oil drum in the corner of the room, but it was not large enough for an effective hiding place. Men were moving about outside. Flashlights were sending beams along the ground and over the walls. Someone said, "Have you seen a man going in this direction?"

When it seemed clear, Chul climbed from the open window again, moved flat along the building wall and saw another building on his right that had a low parapet along its roof. The parapet, he believed, would hide him and, with much agonizing effort, he managed to climb to the roof and duck behind it.

It was a long night there on the roof, with fear eating away at his insides. When dawn came he could see the mountain behind the prison and the branches of an apricot tree that came over his head. He stayed in this hiding place all day, hearing shouts and commotion below, but not daring to show himself. The sound of bombardment came closer all day and all through the next night. The next morning, unable to hear his thirst any longer, he cupped his hands, caught some of his own urine, and drank it. It was bitter, but gave him some relief.

Then he heard machine-gun fire on the mountain. Peering in that direction he saw soldiers in steel helmets and uniforms that were different from those of the Communists. Suddenly rocket shells began to explode within the prison compound. Chul closed his eyes and prayed to God to save his life.

The compound seemed empty now. He climbed down from the roof and went to a nearby gate in the wall. It was shut and locked. In the upper stories of some of the buildings across the compound, he saw and heard North Korean soldiers firing at their attackers outside.

Suddenly a fighter plane came roaring across and little spurts of bullets ran across the courtyard, barely missing him. He saw a woodpile next to a flower garden, ran to it, made himself a kind of hole, and crawled into it. Four more planes came by on strafing runs.

Then the Communists in the upper windows began to fire upon his woodpile. He heard the bullets strike and dislodge sticks and logs, some only inches from his person. Suddenly he smelled smoke. The woodpile had caught fire. At about this time the Communists seemed to find other targets, and he emerged from the woodpile and ran toward a cell house. Its walls were battered, its interior a shambles. After he was inside he glanced from a window and saw a North Korean soldier carrying a bayonet enter the main door. He spotted a room marked "DARKROOM, NO ADMITTANCE," and ducked into it. For the next several minutes he heard the soldier poking about outside, but his hiding place was not discovered. When Chul finally came out of the darkroom, he saw flames and realized the soldier had set the building on fire.

Chul felt in that moment that he might die of pure discouragement. Every life force seemed drained out of him and he had scarcely the strength to stand. How many more obstacles? How much longer could it go on?

He left the burning building and ran toward the infirmary. On the way he stumbled on a broken pipe with water gushing from it. He stopped and slaked his thirst.

He continued, entered another building, and returned to the hole in the ceiling that had been his original hiding place. He stayed there for the next two nights, sneaking out occasionally to break into the infirmary stores and break the vials of vitamin C there for nourishment. The firing continued outside the prison somewhere.

It was not until the morning of the 27th that he heard children's voices and learned that Seoul's gamins had broken into the now deserted compound to steal expensive drugs they could sell on the black market. He was overwhelmed with joy to see them and made no attempt to halt their pilfering.[3]

Although units all along the great curved line slowly closing upon Seoul like a drawn net were running into vicious fights, and some were even losing ground, Company D of the 7th Marines, which had found itself surrounded when darkness fell on the 26th of September, spent a quiet night with no attacks directed on them. The North Koreans were either busy elsewhere or failed to realize that they had Company D in a trap. In the morning a tank-infantry team moved down from the northwest to rescue them and everyone marched out without being fired upon.

Slightly to the south, Murray's 5th Marines were well into the city and headed northward toward the tactically and symbolically important objective of Government House. Puller's 1st Marines, slugging their way through the center of the city, were now on Murray's right, and despite the bitter fighting going on, members of both regiments had time to think about the flag-raising at the capital and race each other toward it. As a matter of fact, division headquarters had supplied each regiment with flags specifically intended for raising above the capital when it should be secured.

The men of Hog Jaw Smith's D-Company, 2nd Battalion, 5th Marine Regiment, pushed forward all day on the left, meeting barriers, tanks, mines and snipers, taking objective after slow objective. On their right were units of the 1st Marine Regiment's 2nd Battalion now close enough for contact, and in fact, various elements of both regiments were now converging upon the great hub crossroads that was the heart of Seoul and upon the Government House further north.

It was not all forward motion. As soon as a stretch of street was taken, parties had to fan out into the side streets to clear out mines, snipers and sometimes lurking tanks.

There was scarcely a building passed that the Marines did not fire into or blast with a precautionary grenade. The heat, smoke and noise of firing was still all over the city.

By midafternoon advanced troops of Taplett's 3rd Battalion ran into the grounds of Government House, and several Marines—ignoring shouted warnings about mines—rushed to the flagpole and began to haul down the North Korean flag, fouling the halyards in their haste so that they had to climb each other's shoulders and stand three high to free them. Presently the Stars and Stripes flew from the mast, and moments later another American flag was at the top of the capitol building's cupola, with the yellow and black insignia of Taplett's 3rd Battalion beneath it.

Just outside the walls of the Government House park, small arms, artillery and machine guns were still sounding as the fight continued. At an adjacent hillside Corsairs were strafing and dropping napalm. But above this sound the cheers of the Marines at the flagpole could be heard.[4] It was just past 3:00 P.M., September 27, 1950.

About a half hour later men of the 2nd Battalion in Chesty Puller's 1st Marine Regiment raised a flag over the United States Consulate (as flags had already been raised over the French and Russian Consulates) and for some reason it was this flag-raising that was most widely reported in the press, much to the disgust of the members of the 5th Regiment.

In the northern part of the city the advance and the opposition were lessening somewhat, but still bitter. Back at X-Corps a number of Ned Almond's busy assistants turned their attention to plans for the liberation ceremony, hopefully on the morning of the 29th. It was hopeful, indeed, at this point. The North Koreans were marshalling their units for several counterattacks in the northern part of the city. And Colonel Rowney's pontoon bridge across the Han wasn't even built yet.

Late in the afternoon of the 27th, seventeen-year-old Thomas Cha stood on the side of a steep hill near the cottage where he lived in the northern part of Seoul and watched a column of North Koreans move slowly along the road out of the city in the valley below him. Tom lived on this hillside with his mother, young brother and two young sisters. The Chas were Roman Catholics, but they had taken care not to call attention to this fact in the past three months

of Communist occupation of their city. Tom's father, originally from Pyongyang, had fled the Communist regime there
to come to Seoul in 1947. He was a police lieutenant in one
of Seoul's precincts, and when the Communists descended
upon the city in late June, he fled south to Pusan to join in
the resistance. Somehow the family managed to conceal most
of this from the Reds, and so far they had not been seriously molested.

Tom was filled with excitement as he watched the North
Korean column in retreat. He was a medium-sized but strong
youth, with his father's long-nosed Manchurian features; he
had studied English for about nine years in missionary
school and his family had always had great hopes for his
future, perhaps in foreign trade or some equally profitable
field.

If Seoul was at last really retaken, it would mean the re-
uniting of his family and perhaps an end to the terrible
hardship they had known in the past ninety days. In family
conference they had all practically forced Tom's father to
flee, knowing that the Communists would undoubtedly im-
prison and probably kill him. But after he had gone they had
no source of money. His father had left behind a good collection of men's suits—rare in those days—and Tom had
sold them off one by one in order to feed the family. Sometimes he carried a suit twenty-five miles into the country to
sell it for a sack of grain weighing perhaps forty or fifty
pounds which he would carry back by foot, using a hiking
rucksack. As a city boy, he envied the farmer lads who knew
how to use the traditional Korean A-frames for carrying
heavy loads.

Now, for the last three days, from his vantage point on
the hill to the north, he had watched the city burn. At night
the sky was blood red, and both the light and the sound of
explosions kept the children awake. On the 25th he wandered around the city, seeing bodies lying everywhere,
many of them bloated, and holding a handkerchief to his
nose to keep from choking at the stink. A man had warned
him that it was dangerous; the retreating North Korean
soldiers had the habit of shooting anyone on sight.

Late on the afternoon of the 27th, Tom was startled to
see a North Korean soldier running down the hill toward
him. He was about to flee when the soldier called to him.
As the man approached, he saw that he carried a sniper's
rifle with telescopic sights. The soldier asked Tom if the

columns in the valley were Americans. Tom said they were not and the sniper ran to join them.

That night Tom, his mother, two sisters and one brother again tried to sleep as the shelling and bombing continued all around them. Just before 6:00 A.M., shells began to fall near their house. In the back yard was a tiny reinforced dugout they had built as a bomb shelter—it would hold only two persons. The mother rushed Tom and his young brother into it. Tom protested and she insisted; it was her belief that the males of the family ought to be preserved so that they could carry on the blood line.

In the tiny bomb shelter, Tom and his brother, whose name was Tong Moon, listened to the forbidden radio that was hidden there, picking up the Korean language broadcast of the U. N. command and learning about the advances of the liberation troops into Seoul.

Suddenly they heard a great explosion nearer than any of the others and felt the ground in their bomb shelter shake from its concussion. They rushed back into the house. The inside was filled with smoke. The mother and the ten-year-old sister were wailing over the prone form of little Moon Suk, age 7, who had been struck by shrapnel in the back, a jagged piece of it penetrating her heart. She was dead.

The shelling stopped about ten minutes later. Tom, half dazed, wandered out of the house. Some time later he saw a squad of U. S. Marines wandering toward the house. They looked at him warily at first, rifles ready, and then he spoke English to them. This made them grin.

One of the Marines said, "Hey, kid, where can we get some beer around here?"

"Down in the city," said Tom, pointing.

"You know where? Can you get it for us? Here—maybe you can pay for it with this." The Marine handed him three boxes of K-rations.

Tom scrambled down the hill, found a shop with beer, paid with the food, and returned with twelve bottles. The Marines were delighted and sat down to drink it, shucking the haversacks and rifles. They tipped Tom with one box of C-rations—a generous day's supply of food for one man. Tom brought it into the house where he and the rest of the family wolfed their first adequate meal in months.

After that they went outside and buried the body of seven-year-old Moon Suk in the back yard.[5]

The pontoon bridge over the Han River was completed. The last bolt was put into place by one of Colonel Rowney's engineers at a few minutes before 7:00 A.M. on the morning of September 29. MacArthur and Syngman Rhee were due to cross it and ride triumphantly into the capital at 9:00 o'clock, two hours hence.

A headquarters had been set up at Yonsei University in the southwestern quarter of Seoul. Here Captain Morrel called in Corporal Joe Maize and said, "There's a generator back across the river we need badly. They've got a bridge now. Take a jeep and a driver and go get it."

Joe and a pfc. drove off on the routine errand. They crossed the new bridge without difficulty, although Joe noticed that traffic was increasing on it. Now that it was built every unit in the area, it seemed, wanted to use it to get into Seoul. They found the generator, hitched it to the jeep, and began to drive back. By the time they reached the bridge again, convoys were streaming across it. It looked at though it would be another hour before his turn to cross would come along.

Joe looked at his driver, grinned, and said, "I'm an Indian and I don't know if I can do it, but I'll try."

The driver said, "Huh?"

Joe pointed to a big Army master sergeant directing traffic at the bridge. "I'm going up to talk to him. Give me one minute, then you come up, salute me, and say, 'We're all ready, sir.'"

"Huh?" said the driver.

"Just do what I say," said Joe.

He walked up to the master sergeant. He said things sure looked pretty busy and the master sergeant scowled down at him and kept directing traffic. The driver walked up, saluted and said, "We're ready, sir!"

The master sergeant frowned dubiously at Joe for a moment, then finally said, "Okay, sir, if you want to get that generator across, you can slip in right now."

Joe proudly brought his prize across the river. The Marine Corps was a good life for a man, he decided. You got shot at now and then, but you always had a lot of laughs. He was glad he'd come back in. It was a good feeling to know he'd helped take Seoul. He wondered where they'd be sent next. It would be somewhere, that was for sure. In the Marine Corps you were always going somewhere.

Although the sound of the fighting just beyond the northern outskirts of Seoul was quite audible in the center of the city, in mid-morning, high-ranking officers and civilian dignitaries converged on the Government House. Marine guards lined the main approach.

All unit commanders down to regimental level had been invited to the ceremony. Colonels Murray and Litzenberg, still busy with the enemy, were unable to make it. Colonel Puller, whose command post was nearer the Government House, came along in a jeep, and on the way met Marine Generals Smith and Craig driving from their new 1st Division command post in Seoul. General Almond, his own moment of triumph at hand, arrived with the senior members of his hard-working X-Corps staff. Ambassador John Muccio came with the aging but doughty President Syngman Rhee and MacArthur himself, wearing his old, braided Philippine field marshal's hat. Admirals Struble and Joy had come ashore to attend. A vast corps of correspondents, including the ubiquitous Maggie Higgins, was there.

The main room of the Government House was topped by a huge glass dome. About the platform and stairs of the big auditorium stood MacArthur's honor guard of military policemen in brightly shining helmets, and more than one Marine officer turned to another as he entered to ask who took the city, anyway—the Marines or the Army?

General Walker arrived, strutting in like the tough bulldog he was. His Eighth Army had broken out of the Perimeter and was in contact with units of Dave Barr's 7th Division far to the south of Seoul. The North Korean Army was broken and in retreat; it was total victory.

Smoke lay in the big room. Parts of the building were still smoldering.

At noon, MacArthur and Rhee stepped to the platform.

"By the grace of a merciful Providence," intoned MacArthur, "our forces fighting under the standard of that greatest hope and inspiration of mankind, the United Nations, have liberated this ancient capital city of Korea. . . ."

The rumble of artillery continued outside, in the near distance.

Navy Lieutenant Horace Underwood stood beside a junior Marine officer in dirty fatigues. The Marine looked at the startched and polished staff officers at the head of the room. He whispered to Underwood: "*They* didn't take the city. What are *they* doing, giving it back?"

"I now ask that you join me in the Lord's Prayer. . . ."

As the assemblage began to repeat the words, large fragments of glass began to fall from the dome overhead. A number of people ducked. Admiral Struble looked up as a large pane fell and shattered about two feet from him. He said in a low voice to Admiral Joy, who was beside him, "Maybe those helmets aren't such a bad idea."

MacArthur continued, imperturbable, as though nothing were falling . . . as though his very presence meant no accident would dare to happen.

". . . and the power . . . and the glory . . . forever and ever . . . Amen."

Outside the wind blew. Some of the parts of the building that had been smoldering burst into open flame. Everyone waited until MacArthur had departed, then hurried outside. The fires of war were still burning.

NOTES   *Chapter 16*

1. Interview author—Jaskilka.
2. Interview author—Almond.
3. Chul Hoe Koo in Riley, John W. Jr., and Shramm, Wilbur, *The Reds Take a City,* New Brunswick, N.J., Rutgers University Press, 1951.
4. Tallent, Robert, "Street Fight in Seoul," *Marine Corps Gazette,* Jan 51.
5. Interview author—Thomas Cha.

Bibliography

Books and Periodicals

Appleman, Roy E. *South to the Naktong, North of the Yalu; The United States Army in the Korean War*. Washington, D.C., Department of the Army, 1961.

Banks, C. L., "Inchon to Seoul." *Marine Corps Gazette*, May, 1951. *Battle Reports of the ROK Marine Corps*. Seoul, ROK Marine Corps, 1962.

Bell, James, Correspondent's report. *Time*, September 25, 1950.

Cagle, Malcolm and Mansin, Frank A., *The Sea War in Korea*. Annapolis, U. S. Naval Institute, 1957.

Caldwell, Joseph C., *The Korea Story*. Chicago, Henry Regnery Company, 1952.

Canzona, Nicholas, "Reflections on Korea." *Marine Corps Gazette*, November, 1951.

Davis, Burke, *Marine: The Life of Chesty Puller*. Boston, Little, Brown and Company, 1962.

Field, James A., *History of United States Naval Operations in Korea*. Washington, D. C., U. S. Government Printing Office, 1962.

Geer, Andrew, *The New Breed*. New York, Harper and Row, 1952.

Gibney, Frank, Correspondent's report. *Time*, September 25, 1950.

Griffin, William J. K., "Typhoon at Kobe." *Marine Corps Gazette*, September, 1951.

Gugeler, Russell A., *Combat Actions in Korea*. Washington, D. C., Combat Forces Press, 1954.

Guisti, Ernest H., "Marine Air Over Inchon-Seoul." *Marine Corps Gazette*, June, 1952.

Hahn, Jae Duk, *Memoir of Life Under North Korean Labor Party Rule*. Seoul, 1965. (In Korean.)

Holly. David C., "The ROK Navy." *Proceedings of the Naval Institute*, November, 1952.

Karig, Walter, Cagle, Malcolm, and Manson, Frank A., *Battle Report, Vol VI, The War in Korea*. New York, Holt, Rinehart and Winston, Inc., 1952.

Leckie, Robert, *Conflict, the History of the Korean War*. New York, G. P. Putnam's Sons, 1962.

Montross, Lynn and Canzona, Nicholas, *The Inchon-Seoul*

Operation, Vol II, *U. S. Marine Operations in Korea*. Wash-
  ington, D. C., G-3 Historical Branch, U. S. Marine Corps,
  1955.
Mydans, Carl, Correspondent's report. *Time*, September 25,
  1950.
Riley, John W., Jr., and Schramm, Wilbur, *The Reds Take a
  City*. New Brunswick, N.J., Rutgers University Press, 1951.
Sawyer, Robert K., *Military Advisors in Korea, KMAG in
  Peace and War*. Washington, D. C., Department of the Army,
  1955.
Schnabel, J. F., "The Inchon Landing." *Army*, May, 1959.
Schott, Joseph L., *Above and Beyond*. New York, G. P. Put-
  nam's Sons, 1963.
Simpson, W. F., "Advice for the Replacement Pilot." *Marine
  Corps Gazette*, February, 1951.
Smith, P. M., "The Tong Yong Operation." *Marine Corps Ga-
  zette*, September, 1960.
Stanford, N. R., "Road Junction." *Marine Corps Gazette*, Sep-
  tember, 1951.
Tallent, Robert W., "Street Fight in Seoul." *Marine Corps Ga-
  zette*, January, 1951.
U. S. Army Chief of Military History, *Korea, 1950*. Washing-
  ton, D. C., Department of the Army, 1952.
Worden, William L., "The Trick That Won Seoul." *Saturday
  Evening Post*, November 11, 1950.

Documents

*Hq X-Corps Operation Chromite War Diary Summary, August
  15–September 30, 1950.*
*Personal Notes of General E. M. Almond Covering Military
  Operations in Korea, September 1950–July 1951.*
Monograph and Comment File, Vol II. *Marine Operations in
  Korea,* Historical Section, G-3, Hq USMC.
Personal Notes, Jae Duk Hahn, Chief, Republic of Korea Re-
  search Center. (In Korean.)
Untitled Manuscript for Korean War History, Brig Gen (Ret)
  Hui Sok Mun, Korean War Compilation Committee, Re-
  public of Korea Ministry of National Defense. (In Korean.)
1st Marine Division Special Action Reports, FMF, for the In-
  chon-Seoul Operation, Vol I. Historical Section, G-3, Hq
  USMC.
*Chronicle of the Operations of the 1st Marine Division During
  the First Nine Months of the Korean War, 1950–1951,* Maj
  Gen Oliver P. Smith, USMC.
*Far East Command GHQ Support and Participation in the
  Korean War,* notes and manuscript by Lt Col J. F. Schnabel.

Index

Index

The never-before-told story of the most deadly chess game in history—with spies as the chessmasters and nations as the pawns

THE WAR IN THE SHADOWS

Charles Whiting

World War II

While nations clashed openly, a select group of men and women deliberated moves and counter-moves behind the scenes. These were the spies—whose activities have up until now been only partially chronicled and who have been romanticized to a credulous public.

Now, Charles Whiting has ripped the veil of illusion from the tortured face of spying and reveals the true story and how the players—whether British, American, Czech, French, Dutch, Russian or German—lost.

$1.50

OUTSTANDING
BALLANTINE
WAR BOOKS

Gehlen, Charles Whiting	$1.25
Nazi Olympics, Richard D. Mandell	$1.50
The War in the Air, Gavin Lyall	$1.65
Guerrilla Submarines, Edward Dissette and H. C. Adamson	$1.25
The Day the Red Baron Died, Dale Titler	$1.50
THE OSS in World War II, Edward Hymoff	$1.65
The Hunt for Martin Bormann, Charles Whiting	$1.25
Fork-Tailed Devil: The P-38, Martin Caidin	$1.65
The Blond Knight of Germany, Trevor Constable and Raymond Toliver	$1.65
War Fish, George Grider and Lydel Sims	$1.50
Hitler's Last Offensive, Peter Elstob	$1.65
Reach for the Sky, Paul Brickhill	$1.25